# PEACEFUL MEASURES:

Canada's Way Out of the 'War on Drugs'

# PEACEFUL MEASURES

Canada's Way Out of the 'War on Drugs'

BRUCE K. ALEXANDER

UNIVERSITY OF TORONTO PRESS

Toronto Buffalo London

© University of Toronto Press 1990
Toronto Buffalo London
Printed in Canada

ISBN 0-8020-2722-9 (cloth)
ISBN 0-8020-6753-0 (paper)

Printed on acid-free paper

---

**Canadian Cataloguing in Publication Data**

Alexander, Bruce K.
  Peaceful measures: Canada's way out of the 'War on drugs'

  Includes bibliographical references.
  ISBN 0-8020-2722-9 (bound). – ISBN 0-8020-6753-0 (pbk.)

  1. Drug abuse – Canada. I. Title.

HV5840.C3A73 1990      362.29'15'0971      C90-093681-9

# Contents

This book is dedicated to my mother and father,

ELSA AND HENRY ALEXANDER.

# Acknowledgments

This book owes much to colleagues at Simon Fraser University who have conducted research with me, listened to my ranting, read my manuscripts, and volunteered crucial ideas and references. Many of these colleagues were students who, I hope, learned from me as I learned from them. Generous colleagues at other universities in Canada, the United States, Europe, and Australia have fulfilled the same functions from very long distances with letters, phone calls, and occasional meetings.

As well, this book owes much to the members of a grass-roots organization called the Concerned Citizens Drug Study and Education Society, of Burnaby, BC. Some of these concerned citizens are doctors, lawyers, academics, and other members of mainstream society. Some are long-time heroin and methadone addicts. This has allowed for a unique collaboration, combining information from professional circles with observations from some of the darker streets and alleys of Vancouver.

A number of policemen have also made essential contributions to this book. Some of these have been students at the university, and others have visited my classes year after year to tell their stories publicly and discuss them with me privately. The policemen who have visited my classes have put up with some abuse, because I have told the students that much in law is wrong and some of what the police have done is unconscionable. The students did not hesitate to pass these views on to the police, with a bit of their own emphasis. The police could have shunned these encounters, but instead they patiently explained their side of the story, corrected errors, and admitted some mistakes (although the latter was mostly done outside the class-room and this material is used in the book only in guarded ways). These policemen have given me the confidence that this book should be published, even if they might deny some parts of it.

In publicly acknowledging some of the people who have contributed to the book, I hope also to convey my gratitude to others who, for various reasons, have not been named. Thanks to Paul Alexander, Murray Allen, Alice Arce, Frank Archer, Kim Bartholomew, Barry Beyerstein, Judith Blackwell, Mark Brunke, Greg Chesher, Robert Coambs, Peter Cohen, Charles Crawford, John Damron, Glen Davies, Gary Dawes, Steve Dawydiak, Patricia Erickson, Susan Evans, R.L. Foster, Richard Freeman, Howard Gabert, Patricia Hadaway, Ted Harrison, Patricia Holborn, Dion Horvat, Shelley Horvat, Ivan Illich, Jenny Jones, Colby Lewis, Wendi Chui Fun Lewis, Ken Low, Teresa MacInnes, Mary McInnes, John Morgan, Stanton Peele, Bruce Petrie, Guy Richmond, Alex and Michael Roy, John Russell, Brenda and Pete Schneider, Tony Schweighofer, Michael Scott, Stefa Shaler, Shepard Siegel, Julian Somers, Benjamin Staat, Wendy Staat, Don Todd, Malcolm Toms, Arnold Trebach, Wayne Tressel, Gail Weisbeck, Govert van de Wijngaart, Patricia Wilensky, and the late Norman Zinberg. A special thank-you to Linda S. Wong for a summer of seven-day work weeks that got the manuscript to the publisher on time and to Patricia Holborn whose contributions to this project cannot be counted.

Finally, much of what I value in this book belongs to those cherished friends and relatives whose thoughts have turned me and it in new, unexpected directions and whose affection has sustained me throughout.

# Introduction

Along with much of the world, Canada has been swept into a 'War on Drugs' that clouds its values, brutalizes its actions, and, in the end, exacerbates the problems it was intended to solve. The War on Drugs is a cruel and costly failure. Moreover, there are good alternatives to it. By adopting 'peaceful measures' in place of war measures, drug-related problems can be approached with both greater humanity and better prospects for success.

This book addresses five major issues. The first is whether a War on Drugs really exists. The phrase itself suggests a bizarre comedy – weary soldiers confronting battalions of capsules, pills, and syringes. Some people may take this strange phrase for mere bureaucratese or political bluster. Others may see it as describing a genuine conflagration carried on in New York, Miami, London, Turkey, Colombia, and Bolivia, but not in Canada.

However, chapter 1 will show that the War on Drugs is a real war in many ways, and that Canada has been involved since the battles began in the nineteenth century. The extent of Canada's involvement cannot be assessed simply by counting bodies, although there has been violence enough, but is best measured in terms of other wartime tactics: propaganda, spying, abrogation of normal peace-time rights, centralized authority, outrageously uncontrolled spending, and so forth. Chapter 1 will show that many otherwise inexplicable aspects of drug policy are best understood as war measures.

I do not want to overstate the case. Exercising normal social and legal control in support of community standards on drug use is not part of the

War on Drugs. However, attempts to create a 'drug-free' nation or world, to exercise 'zero tolerance,' and to achieve desired standards of behaviour through violent repression domestically and in the Third World are more like war measures than normal social control.

The second issue in this book is whether the War on Drugs has successfully achieved its objectives. Chapter 2 will show that it has failed to control the social problem that instigated it, failed to deter drug use, and created serious new problems in the process. My point is not that the War on Drugs has been conducted incompetently, but that it is fundamentally misconceived and therefore *cannot* succeed.

The book's third issue is the validity of the familiar justifications for the War on Drugs. Because they seem to be based on science, critical analysis of these justifications requires digging into research findings from pharmacology, psychology, and sociology, clinical reports from medicine and psychiatry, and the philosophy of science itself. These labours are undertaken in chapters 3–8. Many articles of conventional wisdom will be challenged in these chapters, including the familiar claims that all use of illicit drugs constitutes drug abuse or addiction, that there is an epidemic of addiction, that prohibited drugs are more addictive and physically harmful than legal drugs, and that addiction is a kind of disease caused by genetic predispositions and by exposure to certain 'addictive' drugs. The last of these claims will receive great attention, for it is currently the central justification for the drug war.

It may seem uncivil to challenge the wisdom of polite society. Society is founded on shared beliefs whose validity comes more from their utility than from strict correspondence with research findings. However, it is because this conventional wisdom has become harmful, not merely because it is scientifically weak, that I attempt to discredit it here.

The fourth issue concerns possible alternatives to the present warlike drug policies. Defenders of the War on Drugs often take the position that the drug war is better than nothing at all – that there is no other way to confront drug-related problems. There is, however, a rich pool of peaceful measures to draw from once the compulsion to use war measures has passed. These alternatives will be discussed in chapter 9. At this point two major differences may become evident between this book and some other approaches to drug-policy reform. First, although present drug-prohibition laws are unworkable, I do not claim that the solution lies in simply 'legalizing' drugs; our is a regulated society in which laissez-faire is only an ideology, not a practical possibility. The alternative to the present bad policy is not no policy at all, but good policy.

Secondly, I do not think that the correct replacement for drug prohibition is 'education,' 'prevention,' or 'treatment,' at least not in the sense that these words are currently used. The outrageously exaggerated scare stories about drugs that fill the electronic media are often called 'education' or 'prevention.' The word 'treatment' often refers to coercive or ineffective techniques bureaucratically applied to drug users. These measures are part of the War on Drugs, not alternatives to it. I believe that truly practical alternatives relate more to 'domestication' of current illicit drugs, a concept elaborated by the late Edward Brecher. Domestication involves learning to treat drugs with the same pragmatism that society applies to other familiar and sometimes dangerous household articles – collectively learning when and how they can be used advantageously and when they should be avoided. Of course, normalizing drug policy is a complex and difficult process.

The fifth and final issue will be discussed in chapter 10. It is this: if the War on Drugs has failed and if more promising alternative policies are at hand, why has the war not ended and these alternative policies been adopted? I believe that a psychological analysis of the active participants on both sides of the drug war reveals the answer. The War on Drugs is more a symbolic crusade (Gusfield 1963) than a pragmatic attempt to control drug use or drug-related problems. It serves some of the deepest fears and conflicts of participants on both sides, specifically those involving guilt and power. Only when these motives are laid bare, I believe, does it become possible to comprehend the passion behind the War on Drugs and, therefore, to realistically discuss ending it. In the process, the War on Drugs comes to provide a window onto other perennial conflicts in human society.

Decrying the current War on Drugs is not just my private whim. Many serious North American scholars have worked at exposing its cruelty and futility. These include Marie-Andrée Bertrand and a number of other workers with the Le Dain Commission; Barry Beyerstein and Neil Boyd at Simon Fraser University; Judith Blackwell, formerly of the Addiction Research Foundation of Ontario and now of Brock University; the late Edward M. Brecher, author of the classic *Licit and Illicit Drugs*; the late Isidor Chein and his colleagues in New York City; R.A. Draper, former director-general of Canada's Health Protection Directorate; Patricia

Erickson and her colleagues at the Addiction Research Foundation; William Ghent, surgeon and former chairman of the Canadian Medical Association's Council on Health Care; Lester Grinspoon and James Bakalar of Harvard Medical School; Chet Mitchell of the law school at Carleton University; Ethan Nadelmann at Princeton; Stanton Peele of Morristown, New Jersey; Robert Soloman at the University of Western Ontario Law School; Thomas Szasz of the State University of New York; Arnold Trebach, founder of the Drug Policy Foundation in Washington, DC; Andrew Weil of the University of Arizona; Steven Wisotsky of Nova University in Florida; and the late Norman Zinberg at Harvard Medical School. The work of these scholars and their colleagues is cited throughout this book.

In Europe there is a great deal of vocal opposition to the War on Drugs, which is seen by many as an unwelcome imposition of American ideology. Unfortunately, much of the European writing on the drug war is not yet available in English. However, the critical writings of European philosophers like Michel Foucault, Louk Hulsman, and Ivan Illich are available in English and these help to put the drug war in perspective as part of larger movements in Western civilization.

On the other side of the issue, there are eminent authorities and scholars who defend existing drug policy. These include Robert L. DuPont, Mark Gold, James Inciardi, Hardin and Helen Jones, John Kaplan, and the majority of the Royal Commission on the Non-Medical Use of Drugs. These scholars too are cited extensively in this book.

Curiously, the media and most of the Canadian public seem still unaware that there is a serious controversy on this topic, and the logic of a perpetual War on Drugs still goes largely unquestioned outside of scholarly circles. Many issues smoulder for years in academia before they become matters of public attention, but there are many signs that the War on Drugs controversy may soon ignite.

When the War on Drugs does become a matter of public debate, I hope *Peaceful Measures* may help to show Canadians what our part in it has been. I hope this book will also provide a creative synthesis of the alternatives – the 'peaceful measures' – that have been devised by many admirable scholars and practitioners and are ready to apply in Canada. I hope it may also show Canadian readers the connection between drug issues and the problem of cultural sovereignty. Canada began to attack drugs on its own initiative in the last century, but in the 1980s most of the initiative in the War on Drugs comes from the United States, to our detriment. To turn from this war, now that it has failed, would be to function with the wisdom and confidence of an autonomous nation.

I hope this book will also be of service to Canadians whose families suffer because of drug-related problems. The hopelessness that such people feel is unnecessary. There are bases for renewed hope outside the harsh doctrines of the War on Drugs.

For readers outside North America, I hope to provide a look at the misfortunes of a country that enlisted in the War on Drugs at the very beginning, in the hopes that their countries might see the need to reject it sooner than Canada has.

For readers in the United States I hope this book might help to document the immense cultural power of their country. In this case, American media imagery and economic leverage are major forces in maintaining the War on Drugs long after it should have been abandoned. American cultural power over other countries is difficult to imagine unless one is directly exposed to it. But like nuclear energy, this force must be constantly scrutinized, checked, and restrained. In the end, Americans can gain only a tormented solitude – the fate of emperors – by making the world over with their own images and destroying its cultural diversity.

My investigation of drug issues began in 1971 when I was assigned, as the newest member of a department of psychology, to teach a course called 'Social Issues.' As a comparative psychologist whose previous work had all been done in laboratories, I had no academic training that related to any pressing social issues, so I chose drugs as a topic because it dominated the headlines of that Trudeau/Nixon era. My understanding of this topic emerged slowly as I investigated the puzzles that I encountered.

Along the way, I have learned that to question current drug policy is to be accused of bias and irresponsibility. Such charges are painful and simplistic. They divide the world too sharply into allies and enemies. Once that division is made, further discussion is impossible; swords must be drawn. My hope is to avoid this kind of conflict by neither condemning those who disagree with me nor taking their condemnations too seriously.

However, I feel the need to defend myself against the charge of 'bias' that is sometimes laid against me. As a matter of fact, my personal feelings about illicit drugs are not particularly intense. I have no history of drug addiction and I do not make a living either by treating or punishing those who use drugs. I have no motivation to ignore facts that disagree with my conclusions and have changed my mind several times in the course of writing this book.

I do plead guilty to the charge that this book is one-sided. It does not dwell on the horrors of illicit drug addiction or the violence of drug traffickers, although it does not deny that they exist. There is no need to reiterate information that is broadcast by the popular media every day. This book focuses on more normal patterns of using illicit drugs and on the seldom-documented violence of drug warriors. It is intended to show a different side of the War on Drugs.

This book has provided several frustrations. One is that I had hoped to write a comprehensively Canadian book, but soon realized that Canada is too big for me. Too much of the Canadian information presented here is from Ontario, which collects the best statistics on drug use among the provinces, and from British Columbia, where I live. I have had neither the time nor the reach to write a more geographically balanced book.

I have suffered a similar frustration with the vast scholarly literature on drugs, addiction, and related problems. I have found that the scientific literature, while essential, is not sufficient to analyse the drug war. Therefore I have delved more deeply than I could have ever imagined into clinical reports, history, sociology, classical philosophy, and literature. I could not read it all. I believe I have read as much as can be expected of a normal human being in nineteen years, and, more important, that I have read it fairly. I have searched out material that disagrees with my view. I have always asked the people who disagree with me for their sources and have traced these as far as possible. I don't think any major ideas have escaped me, but a great deal of detail certainly has. I hope readers will bring my attention to important omissions.

Finally, I am troubled by a lingering fear that this book might seem disrespectful towards Canada because it criticizes currently held beliefs and policy. However, my aim is not to disparage my country or my compatriots, but instead to urge greater exercise of some of the virtues that make Canada unique: non-belligerence, level-headedness, and appreciation of human diversity.

# PEACEFUL MEASURES:

Canada's Way Out of the 'War on Drugs'

# 1    Is there a 'War on Drugs'?

For most Canadians, the War on Drugs is a dim half-reality. The phrase is familiar, but is there really such a war? If there is, does Canada really participate? Is not military terminology imprecisely applied to many contemporary problems? Unfortunately, the phrase is all too accurate. For over a century, drug-control policy around the world and in Canada has been growing increasingly warlike. The costs of this drug war, in both money and human suffering, have been steadily increasing, although its objectives have not been met.

The single most conspicuous feature of wars is violence. Although a relatively small number of people have been killed in Canada itself, a great deal of sub-lethal violence has occurred in the Canadian drug war. Moreover, Canada gives tacit support to wholesale brutality and killing carried out by allies in the War on Drugs. Beyond violence, wars entail propaganda, suspension of normal civil rights, secrecy, spying, seizure of property, increased centralization of authority, and uncontrolled consumption of resources (see Dyer 1985; Fussell 1989). Some of these activities are identified as rights of government during wartime in the War Measures Act (*Revised Statutes of Canada* 1970), and all are part of the current war on drugs. Beyond these visible manifestations, wars also entail a special way of thinking. War mentality cleaves the world into noble allies and despicable enemies; justifies any measures necessary to prevail, including violence to innocent bystanders; and disdains accommodation, compromise, or any questioning of authority until total victory is achieved. In essence, war mentality suspends normal human compassion and intelligence. This mentality pervades current Canadian drug-control efforts.

Not all efforts to control drug use are part of the War on Drugs. For example, parents who caution their children not to use certain drugs and punish them if they do are simply exercising normal parental functions. Likewise, communities, provinces, and national governments that use the law and communications media to discourage use of socially unacceptable drugs cannot be accused of war measures. The War on Drugs goes beyond normal social control measures into extraordinary methods intended to eradicate the enemy. In the drug-war jargon of 1989 this means achieving a 'drug-free' nation by the exercise of 'zero tolerance.'

This chapter documents the fact that many of society's efforts to control drugs are more like war measures than ordinary forms of social control. Because the United States defines most of the methods, goals, and symbols of the War on Drugs, its drug war is described first. Next, the War on Drugs as it exists in the Third World and in Europe is briefly described. Having set the stage, the chapter then describes the Canadian War on Drugs. Whereas this first chapter is only meant to show that a War on Drugs actually exists, the remainder of the book will undertake the larger task of showing that it should and can be ended.

In this book, the word 'drug' includes all the chemicals, regardless of their legal status, that are taken to affect the way people think and feel. Thus, alcohol and ASA are here considered drugs, although sometimes in ordinary conversation they are not. The term 'psycho-active drugs' will sometimes be used to make it clear that the book is not about purely medical drug use. Where this chapter and the next contradict popular misconceptions, the text will be in **bold face** type and bibliographic sources that support the contradiction will be cited. In addition to external sources, bold-face sections will refer to later chapters in this book (abbreviated *PM*, for *Peaceful Measures*) where the evidence for the contradiction will be discussed. This format enables some major theses to be laid out in two chapters at the beginning while deferring the more lengthy examination of evidence until later chapters.

## The American War on Drugs

George Bush declared war against drugs in his first major televised speech to the United States after becoming president (5 September 1989). He promised billions of dollars, more troops and military technology, and inflexible resolve. He claimed that this was the first time that an entire national effort against drugs had been co-ordinated. He failed to mention that this was the latest in a long series of declarations of war against drugs and that co-ordinated national efforts had often been part of these declarations. For example, Ronald Reagan declared in 1986: 'My generation will remember how America swung into action when we were attacked in World War II. The war was not just fought by the fellows flying the planes or driving the tanks. It was fought at home by a mobilized nation – men and women alike – Well, now we're in another war for our freedom, and it's time for all of us to pull together again. So, for example, if your friend or neighbor or family member has a drug or alcohol problem, don't turn the other way' (Office of the Press Secretary, 1986). President Nixon told a 1971 meeting of media executives that 'drug traffic is public enemy number one domestically in the United States today and we must wage a total offensive, world-wide, nation wide, government wide, and if I may say so, media wide' (cited by Epstein 1977, 178).

## ORIGINS OF THE AMERICAN WAR ON DRUGS

Perpetual re-declarations of war obscure the fact that the American War on Drugs is not a new undertaking, but one that began early in the nineteenth century and has changed little since then (King 1972; Musto 1973; Epstein 1977; Bellis 1981; Trebach 1987).

### The Temperance Movement

The origins of the American War on Drugs can be traced to the Temperance movement, which popularized the idea that American social problems can be controlled by attacking a particular drug, namely alcohol. There was nothing resembling a 'war' on alcohol until the early nineteenth century, when the temperance movement appeared (Levine 1978, 1984). The movement quickly evolved from urging moderation on 'inebriates' to militantly demanding universal prohibition of alcohol (Levine 1984).

As well as pressing for prohibition, the temperance movement promoted physical coercion and propaganda, which were represented as 'treatment' and 'education.' Benjamin Rush, arguably the father of

American temperance doctrine, recommended 'fright, bleeding, whipping, and aversive therapy with emetics' as treatments for alcohol addiction (Aaron and Musto 1981, 139), although in those days treatment for more conventional diseases was often as horrendous. The Women's Christian Temperance Union had a 'department of scientific temperance instruction' which clearly equated education with propaganda: 'Under its aegis, an elaborate curriculum was developed that school systems all across the country soon made mandatory … [It taught that] the majority of drinkers die of dropsy … When alcohol passes down the throat it burns off the skin leaving it bare and burning … Alcohol clogs the brain and turns the liver quickly from yellow to green to black' (Aaron and Musto 1981, 147).

By the turn of the century the American temperance movement was dominated by the militant Anti-Saloon League, which specialized in warlike rhetoric and heavy-handed political pressure tactics. In this context, the famous prohibitionist Carry Nation and her supporters made a ritual of physically destroying saloons. For these felonious acts, Mrs Nation became the hero of much of the nation and an object of idolatry in the American press (Taylor 1966).

National alcohol prohibition (1920–33) intensified the violence (Kobler 1973; Cashman 1981). Killings by prohibition-era gangsters like Al Capone are well remembered, but the violence of the enforcement agents was as great. For example: 'In Aurora Illinois, on March 29, 1929, six state enforcement agents invaded the home of Peter De King, a suspected bootlegger. One of them clubbed him over the head with the butt of a shotgun. As he dropped senseless, his wife Lillian sprang to his side. A blast from the shotgun killed her. When told of the atrocity, Ella Boole of the WCTU remarked, "Well, she was evading the law wasn't she?"' (Kobler 1973, 291).

It has been estimated that at least one thousand Americans were killed by prohibition enforcement agents between 1920 and 1930, along with about seventy-five enforcement agents (Kobler 1973). Many more people were beaten, wounded, or intimidated and large amounts of property was destroyed during illegal police raids. Enforcement agents and prohibitionist volunteers were sometimes charged with murder, but federal intervention frequently prevented convictions in spite of damning evidence (Kobler 1973).

*The Anti-opium Movement*

Opium and its derivative, morphine, were abundant in nineteenth-century America. For example, in 1885 Iowa had a population of three million people and three thousand stores openly and legally sold opium products. Some popular brand names were Mrs Winslow's Soothing Syrup, Godfrey's Cordial, Dover's Powder, McMunn's Elixer of Opium, and Ayer's Cherry Pectoral (Brecher 1972).

Iowa was not unusual in its appetite for opium. Opium products were sold throughout the world. In the United States, as elsewhere, opium and morphine preparations were regarded as medicine. There were no sanctions against using them. It was known that much of the population used them medicinally and that some people used them for non-medical purposes. Dependence and addiction were understood and were generally regarded as undesirable or even tragic. However, people who were dependent on opium or morphine were not jailed, ostracized, divorced, or fired from their jobs because of it. Opiates were cheap and dependent people often retained a normal position in their community. Until the anti-opium movement began to spread late in the nineteenth century, there was no thought that users should be legally punished (Brecher 1972; Morgan 1981).

Dependence and addiction to opium and morphine became more common after morphine was first made available in pure pharmaceutical form and after the hypodermic syringe was invented in the 1840s. However, by the end of the nineteenth century, it was widely recognized that injected morphine had to be used with care and dependence declined. Even at the peak around 1890, the frequency of dependence and addiction probably never reached 1 per cent of the population, and probably only comprised a small fraction of that, although no certain figures are available (Brecher 1972; Morgan 1981; Courtwright 1982).

A militant anti-opium movement emerged in nineteenth-century America, although it did not become as large or as active as the temperance movement until the twentieth century (King 1972). The anti-opium movement quickly went beyond warning the public of the real dangers associated with opium use to urging universal prohibition and lobbying for its enactment.

The first federal attempt to prohibit the use of opium by force was an

aftermath of the Spanish-American War and of the emergence of the
United States as a colonial power controlling the Philippines. Opium use
was heavy in the Philippines, and Congress reacted with a series of laws.
By 1908 all non-medical use of opium in the Philippines was banned and
the colonial authorities were authorized to suppress it. The result was that
'the entire traffic quickly went underground, and Americans soon had
their first taste of big-scale clandestine drug operations' (King 1972, 12–
13).

*War on 'Narcotics'*

In the twentieth century American fears shifted from alcohol and opium to
a class of drugs identified as 'narcotics.' The word 'narcotics' had earlier
referred to drugs that induce drowsiness or 'narcosis,' but late in the
nineteenth century it came to refer to all drugs that were stringently
prohibited, including opium, morphine, heroin, cocaine, and later
marijuana. Many of these 'narcotics,' notably cocaine and marijuana,
were not narcotic in the original sense of the term.

The law that opened the war against domestic American narcotic use
was the Harrison Narcotic Act, passed in 1914. Although ostensibly
designed to tax medical use of opiate drugs and cocaine and to
systematize their distribution, the act was seen by many as a way to
prohibit the use of narcotics completely, using tax law to circumvent
constitutional restrictions on federal control of individual behaviour
(Musto 1973). Many doctors who had been providing narcotics to
dependent users opposed this prohibition. The narcotic prohibitionists
were foiled at first. Treasury agents were able to jail merchants who sold
narcotics in violation of the law, but when they prosecuted doctors who
prescribed narcotics in good faith to dependent patients, the Supreme
Court overturned their convictions. The Court interpreted the law
literally, as a tax act that could not prevent doctors from prescribing
according to their interpretations of their patients' needs, provided that
they paid the tax.

In this case, as in many others, the escalation of narcotics control to the
level of war measures was closely related to outbreaks of fear concerning
America's foreign enemies. Wartime propaganda had fused fears of illicit
drugs with fears of Germany. For example, the *New York Times* of April
1918 reported that German agents were actively smuggling drugs on a

large scale into American army training centres. The Treasury Department announced officially that new addicts were found in large numbers among young soldiers. Illicit drugs were undermining the nation's defence (King 1972, 26)! The *New York Times* of December 1919 revealed the following story of a fiendish German plan: 'Into well-known German brands of toothpaste and patent medicines – naturally for export only – habit forming drugs were to be introduced, at first a little, then more, as the habit grew its non-German victim and his system craved ever-greater quantities ... in a few years Germany would have fallen on a world which cried for its German toothpaste and soothing syrup – a world of "cokeys" [cocaine addicts] and "hop-fiends" [opium addicts] which would have been absolutely helpless when a German embargo shut off the supply of its pet poison' (cited by King 1972, 261).

Public acceptance of such stories helped to justify almost any measures taken against the Germans. However, **the plan is totally impossible. Both cocaine and opium are offensively bitter in quantities large enough to have any effect. More important, no known drug can produce mass enslavement as a result of simple exposure** (Alexander and Hadaway 1982; *PM*, chaps 4, 5).

Another set of fears about narcotics was mobilized by a 1919 federal report, *Traffic in Narcotic Drugs*. This inflammatory document pandered to the post-war fears of domestic dissidents. These fears were later characterized as the 'Red Scare of 1919.' *Traffic in Narcotic Drugs* claimed that a million drug addicts, through their crime and immorality, threatened the safety of the entire country. The report was 'received by a nation in the grasp of a panic reaction to Bolshevik bombings directed at institutions and national leaders, violent and widespread labor strikes, IWW agitation, and anarchist plots. Once again the Treasury agents went into action [enforcing the Harrison Narcotics Act] but without the legal resistance of 1915' (Musto 1973, 139). Under these conditions, the Harrison Narcotic Act was reinterpreted by the Supreme Court to justify broad national narcotic prohibition, including prevention of the prescription of narcotics to addicts.

Reports indicate that about twenty-five thousand American physicians were reported to legal authorities and five thousand were convicted of violations of the Harrison act between 1915 and 1938. 'For most physicians, the fear of being charged was sufficient to scare them away from ever talking to an addict, much less treating one' (Trebach 1982, 125).

Along with the prosecution of physicians, the War on Drugs brought the large-scale imposition of unwanted treatment on addicts. Treatment was not a sideline of the War on Drugs, but a major part of the effort, strongly endorsed by Harry Anslinger, the archetypical American drug warrior and predecessor to the current 'drug czar' (Courtwright, Joseph, and DesJarlais 1989). For example, large narcotics farms were set up in Lexington (1935) and Fort Worth (1938) in which addicts were incarcerated and 'rehabilitated.' For most addicts who were incarcerated there, these institutions were simply another form of prison, although some went voluntarily to escape street life for a while (Courtwright, Joseph, and DesJarlais 1989, chap. 13). Although serious efforts at treatment were conducted at the narcotics farms, there is good evidence that they were totally ineffective in curing people of drug addiction (Brecher 1972).

Following the Second World War, further strengthening of American narcotics legislation to include harsh mandatory minimum sentences and death penalties was again closely linked to war-related fears: 'Congress decreed mandatory minimum sentences for narcotic offenders in an emotional atmosphere similar to the years of the first Red Scare. Hale Bogg's bill, which contained the mandatory sentences, was passed in 1951 at the beginning of the McCarthy era and fears of the Communists, and suspicion of domestic groups and persons who seemed to threaten overthrow of the government. Narcotics were later associated directly with the Communist conspiracy: the Federal Bureau of Narcotics linked Red China's attempts to get hard cash, as well as to destroy Western society, to the clandestine sale of large amounts of heroin to drug pushers in the United States' (Musto 1973, 230–1).

When the Nixon administration took up the battle in 1968 at the height of the Vietnam crisis, new war measures against domestic drug use were introduced and warlike rhetoric was further escalated. The media of those days were as full of the menace of marijuana and LSD as today's are of the menace of cocaine and 'crack.' During the Nixon administration, plans to curtail drug use were given military code names, like 'Operation Intercept.' Special 'task forces' were assembled with extraordinary funding and quasi-military power, which included the power to seize the bank accounts of suspected traffickers, to manipulate commercial television broadcasting, and, according to one authority, to arrange assassinations of overseas traffickers (Epstein 1977). These operations were carried out on a massive scale and, except for the last, with intense publicity. They formed a part of accepted everyday reality of the 1960s in the United States, along with the Vietnam War.

Perhaps the most successful drug warrior of the Nixon era was Nelson Rockefeller, first as governor of New York and later as vice-president. Rockefeller gained political power, in part, by skillful use of antidrug propaganda. He grossly overstated the drug problem and associated himself with a series of Draconian laws adopted by the New York State legislature. Epstein has summarized Rockefeller's campaign against drugs as follows: 'Rockefeller's crusade against addicts reached its zenith in 1973, when the governor declared that a reign of terror existed with "whole neighborhoods ... as effectively destroyed by addicts as by an invading army" ... addicts had taken the place of medieval vampires – infecting innocent children with their disease, murdering citizens at large, causing all crime and disorder' (Epstein 1977, 43).

Rockefeller used his propaganda campaign to gain support for laws that provided a mandatory life sentence for anyone over fifteen convicted of possessing more than a fraction of an ounce of heroin, amphetamines, or LSD. The manadatory life sentence was also applied to anyone convicted of taking a 'hard' drug within twenty-four hours of committing several crimes including criminal mischief, sodomy, burglary, assault, and arson (Epstein 1977). This meant, for example, that the law required a life sentence for anyone convicted of homosexual intercourse within twenty-four hours of snorting cocaine or heroin. Rockefeller later justified the severity of these laws by explaining that about 135,000 addicts were committing crimes 'day in and day out' to support their habits. Epstein pointed out that

> though this depiction of a huge army of addicts carrying out daily mayhem against the citizens of New York no doubt further excited popular fears, it hardly fit the police statistics at Rockefeller's disposal. If 135,000 addicts maintained their 'day-in, day-out' schedule, they would have had to commit something on the order of 49,275,000 robberies, muggings, and murders a year, which would mean that the residents of New York would be robbed, mugged, and murdered approximately seven times a year. In fact, there were only about 110,000 such crimes reported in New York in 1973, or only 1/445th the number of crimes that Rockefeller claimed were being committed solely by addicts. Even here, as Rockefeller was well

aware, virtually all analyses showed that the addicts were responsible for
only a minute fraction of the violent crimes he attributed to them in his
constant rhetoric. Most murders and manslaughters were the result of intra-
family disputes, not addiction. Most muggings were the work of juveniles, not hardened addicts ... Only 4.4 per cent of those arrested in the city
for felonies against persons – which include murders, muggings, and
robberies – were confirmed drug users (and only a small percentage of these
could possibly be classified as addicts). (Epstein 1977, 43–5)

Nixon ordered an unparalleled expansion in the international component of American drug-enforcement efforts. For the first time, U.S.
embassies around the world were instructed to give the drug issue top
priority; cabinet-level officials travelled abroad to exhort foreign leaders
to adopt U.S. goals, methods, and doctrine; millions of dollars were paid
out to support crop substitution; successful efforts were made abroad to
inflame public opinion against drugs; and foreign-aid cutoffs and vetos on
international bank loans became vehicles for controlling drug policy in
foreign countries (Nadelmann 1987, 208–17).

The assault on drugs escalated during the presidency of Ronald Reagan
(Trebach 1987). The 1878 Posse Comatatus Act had long been regarded
as an essential American protection against militarism, because it
prohibited the use of federal soldiers to enforce civilian law. However, it
was amended in 1982 to provide for the use of American armed forces in
the enforcement of drug laws (Inciardi 1986, 208). The Reagan administration drug strategy was executed in part by military personnel and
military intelligence units along with the Coast Guard, police, Drug
Enforcement Administration, FBI, customs officials, and other armed
agents (Williamson 1983; McConnell 1985). Of nearly $4 billion spent
by the federal government on the War on Drugs in 1987, $389 million was
spent by the Department of Defence (Marshall 1988, 1988a). In 1987
over one-third of all federal-prison inmates were drug offenders (New
York Times, 25 September 1987, cited by Ostrowski 1989, 20), as were
10 per cent of all state-prison inmates (Nadelmann 1989).

Carlton Turner, President Reagan's drug-policy adviser until January
1987, explicity affirmed the connection between the War on Drugs and
American efforts to combat communism. He alleged that a goal of the
supposedly communistic drug dealers in Latin America is to destroy
American democracy (Trebach 1987). In 1983 and 1984 congressional

hearings specifically attempted to link the governments of Cuba, Nicaragua, and Bulgaria to the drug trade. However, blatant involvement in drug trafficking by governments ideologically allied to the United States, such as Panama, was overlooked in these hearings (Nadelmann 1987, 201). Moreover, the 'Irangate' inquiry has linked drug profits with the *pro-American* side on the Nicaraguan war and with 'former CIA men [and] officials with high-level connections inside the Reagan administration' (White and Tran 1987).

The full extent of violence perpetrated by American drug-enforcement officers in the United States and abroad under Reagan was not a topic of official communication. Unofficial reports, however, indicate that the measures employed against U.S. citizens were harsh and those employed abroad were ruthless and deadly. Residents of northern California, for example, were subjected to paramilitary harassment by 'posses' of drug-enforcement officials dressed in camouflage uniforms and armed with automatic and semi-automatic rifles. The same areas of California (labelled the 'emerald triangle' by enforcement officials) were subjected to aerial surveillance (including overflights by U-2 spy planes). Helicopters were used for surveillance and also for intimidation. For example, some local residents were driven from their homes and followed down roads by closely hovering helicopters – a tactic especially terrifying to children. The purpose of these raids was to destroy marijuana grown by many of the small farmers in the area (Trebach 1987). U.S. courts ruled that such raids were illegal and issued injunctions against some of the practices, including helicopter harassment, but the raids continued (Trebach 1987).

Beyond war measures of the sort carried out in northern California, suffering and indignity were routinely inflicted on many U.S. citizens whose behaviour was quite harmless by any normal standards. For example, by 1987 about five million Americans had been urine tested in the pursuit of drug users (Trebach 1987). Many thousands had their careers cut short by a positive urine test. About six hundred people were fired by Georgia Power & Light Company alone (Price 1986). American urine testing increased dramatically, even though it was repeatedly shown that large-scale urine tests produce a substantial percentage of 'false positive' results (Morgan 1984; Altman 1986), so that some of those fired were almost certainly innocent of any illicit drug use whatsoever. **An even larger number were certain to be harmless**

**recreational users, for this is by far the largest category of users of any drug, with the possible exception of nicotine** (Erickson, Adlaf, Murray, and Smart 1987; *PM*, chaps 3, 4, 5).

The extent of the internal War on Drugs under Reagan was further revealed by new laws and judicial decisions that dramatically reduced the ability of people accused of drug offences to defend themselves. According to a 1986 article in the prestigious *National Law Journal*, 'In the past few years the government has changed radically the rules in drug cases so that the traditional concepts of American justice no longer apply' (Zeese 1986, 13). Some of the new American practices make it difficult for a person accused of drug crimes to obtain a legal defence. The court was empowered to seize all of a charged person's assets, making it impossible for him or her to pay for a legal defence. In some cases, the government could keep seized property even if the accused was acquitted. As well, it became a crime for a lawyer to accept legal fees that were proven to be the gains of drug trafficking (Zeese 1987). Twenty-four per cent of lawyers that specialized in drug cases reported having been subpoenaed to testify against their own clients. Forty-one per cent reported that they had encountered informants from the government. Zeese (1986) concluded, 'the dice have been so loaded that the results of drug cases are almost pre-ordained' (13).

The twentieth century has seen the emergence of a new variety of war called 'total war.' In total war, public information, manufacturing, agriculture, and personal life are subordinated to war to a degree that was previously inconceivable (Dyer 1985). The concept of total war appears to have been applied as well to the War on Drugs. The American *National Strategy for Prevention of Drug Abuse and Drug Trafficking*, published by President Reagan's highest drug-policy advisers, hammered at this point incessantly:'all individuals, all business, civic and social organizations; all levels of government; and all agencies, departments and activities within each level of government are called upon to lead, direct, sponsor and support efforts to eliminate drug abuse in families, businesses and communities' (Drug Abuse Policy Office 1984, 5). Perhaps the desired response was achieved in the summer of 1986 in California when a thirteen-year-old girl turned both her parents in to the police for possession of cocaine and paraphernalia. Whereas many Americans found this turn of events repellent (or ridiculous), others applauded it, including Nancy Reagan, the u.s. Drug Enforcement

Agency, and the 'Parents for a Drug Free Youth.' A spokesman for the Maryland State Police eloquently summarized his nonchalance about family loyalty in the context of the drug war by commenting, 'Hey, we'll take information from anybody' (*Baltimore Sun* 1986, 1B, 8B).

The new Bush administration promises to escalate the Reagan administration's War on Drugs. President Bush served as head of the National Narcotics Interdiction System and chief of the South Florida Task Force during his vice-presidency. Under Bush's administration the Civil Air Patrol and the National Guard have been added to military and paramilitary participants in the War on Drugs (Isikoff 1889a). President Bush has appointed William Bennett as director of the new Office of National Drug Control Policy, a position universally referred to as 'drug czar,' with the task of co-ordinating fifty-eight federal agencies now involved in the drug war and a proposed $7.5 billion federal expenditure for 1989 (Barrett 1989; McCarthy 1989; Morganthau and Miller 1989; MacKenzie 1989).

Bennett has publicly stated about illicit drugs that 'This stuff is destroying the lives of millions of Americans, and it is virtually eliminating the possibility of upward mobility for an awful lot of people' (Morganthau and Miller, 1989, 21–2). This is the perennial claim of the American War on Drugs – the problems of the nation are caused by drugs, and all government forces must be drawn into action to elimate this scourge. Bennett has publicly identified the following as ideas that are under serious consideration by his office: placing first-time recreational drug users in 'boot camps' for paramilitary training and anti-drug therapy; confiscating the cars of people caught buying drugs for the first time; using U.S. soldiers as part of military units attacking drug laboratories and distribution points in Latin America; and prosecuting the parents of young drug abusers (Barrett 1989; Isikoff 1989b). Like other American drug warriors, Bennett favours treatment as well as prosecution, including civil commitment for addicts before conviction (MacKenzie 1989).

CAUSES OF THE AMERICAN WAR ON DRUGS

The public often has an unclear idea of the reasons for the wars it must endure. This is also true of the American War on Drugs. Most Americans believe that their drug war emerged as a reaction to an epidemic of drug or alcohol addiction. But this is untrue. **Per-capita alcohol consumption was higher in the United States during the eighteenth century than during the nineteenth and twentieth when temperance and prohibition movements became influential** (Levine, 1984). **Similarly, no epidemic of addiction to opium or cocaine existed at the time they became objects of the War on Drugs around the turn of the century** (Brecher 1972; Musto 1973; Courtwright 1982; *PM*, chaps 4, 5). **Likewise, addiction to marijuana constituted no substantial problem in the United States at the time it was prohibited in 1937** (Brecher 1972). **As well, the current 'epidemic' of cocaine addiction and reports of medical emergencies may be as vastly exaggerated as earlier reports concerning other drugs** (Reinarman and Levine, forthcoming; Erickson and Alexander, 1989; *PM*, chap. 5).

What, then, instigated the American War on Drugs? Scholars have provided many possible answers. Many historians believe that the war emerged primarily because drugs became a scapegoat for social problems. Nineteenth-century America experienced growing violence, lawlessness, and family breakdown in the frontier west and the overcrowded eastern cities. Whisky was cheap and many perpetrators of violence and other criminality were drunkards. The American public was gradually won over to the view that alcohol, and later other drugs, *caused* the burgeoning social problems with which they were often associated. Some proponents of this view were professional moralists, or, as they later came to be called, 'moral entrepreneurs.' Others were broader thinkers, such as Thomas Jefferson, who noted the relationship between bad conduct and alcohol consumption and thought it reasonable to blame one on the other (Aaron and Musto 1981, 138).

This view was energetically promoted by the temperance movement. An 1832 circular, delivered door-to-door by the New York State Temperance Society, stated unequivocally: 'That ardent spirit makes three-fourths of our criminals is the united testimony of judges and lawyers in this country and in England ... Almost all cases of assault and battery likewise. Those guilty of burglary, larceny, counterfeiting, riots, etc. are almost uniformly ascertained to have destroyed their moral sensibilities and emboldened themselves for the violation of their country's laws by the inebriating cup' (New York State Temperance Society, 1832, cited by Levine 1984, 109–10). Almost ninety years later, this view was being promoted on network radio, the newborn media giant. In 1919, on the eve of national prohibition of alcohol, preacher Billy Sunday told a national radio audience and a live audience of ten thousand: 'The reign of tears is over. The slums will soon be a memory. We will turn our prisons into factories, our jails into storehouses and corncribs. Men will walk upright now, women will smile and the children will laugh. Hell will be forever for rent' (cited by Levine 1984, 110).

The War on Drugs assumed its modern form as this same analysis was applied to numerous other drugs including opium, morphine, heroin, cocaine, marijuana, LSD, and currently continuing up to 'crack.' Why was there growing prostitution, thievery, violence, sickness, depravity, despair, weakness, corruption? Why did so many draftees prove unfit for military service? Why were so many parents unable to control their own children? Why were corrupt, despotic countries able to threaten the security of the United States? Why was upward mobility difficult for black Americans? Why did gun-toting Americans shoot each other? Why were so many babies unhealthy? For more and more Americans the answer to such questions became simple – drugs!

The following excerpt from a speech made on national radio by Richard Hobson, American congressman and prohibition propagandist, shows that claims about the harmfulness of drugs had become limitless by 1928: 'Most of the daylight robberies, daring holdups, cruel murders, and similar crimes of violence are now known to be committed chiefly by [heroin] addicts, who constitute the primary cause of our alarming crime wave. Drug addiction is more communicable and less curable than leprosy. Drug addicts are the principal carriers of vice diseases, and with their lowered resistance are incubators and carriers of the strepticoccus, pneumococcus, the germ of flu, of tuberculosis, and other diseases. Upon the issue hangs the perpetuation of civilization, the destiny of the world and the future of the human race' (cited by Musto 1973, 191).

The belief that drugs cause virtually all major social ills continues to serve the major justification for the War on Drugs. A 1988 public-opinion poll found that Americans regard 'the battle against international drug trafficking' as the most important goal for their national security (Cameron 1988). **However, this belief is unwarranted. There is no good evidence that drugs cause any substantial part of the social pathology that is attributed to them. On the contrary, there is good evidence that social pathology causes destructive forms of drug use** (*PM*, chap. 8).

Historians have shown that, in addition to providing a simple explanation and a scapegoat for social problems, the emerging War on Drugs has served a number of special interests in the United States. For example, the drug war served the doctors who wanted drunkenness and opiate dependence defined as diseases that they could treat. It served politicians who used the popular anti-drug movement to gain power (Levine 1978, 1984). It served the enforcement bureaucracies that wanted to expand their domain (*Newsweek* 1989, 24–6). It served New York socialites who competed ruthlessly to win status by promoting popular causes (King 1972). And it appeared to serve the interests of industrialists who hoped that prohibiting alchol and drugs would create a sober, reliable work-force content to spend their lives at stupefying factory labour for low pay.

Social scientists have argued that cultures generally label particular life-styles as deviant in order to define and dramatize standards of conduct that maintain the status quo (Ericson, Baranek, and Chan 1987, chaps. 1, 2). This analysis appears to help explain the War on Drugs, which created a new class of deviant life-styles and thereby popularized an image of how people should live (Gusfield 1963).

Beyond providing scapegoats, supporting special-interest groups, and dramatizing social norms, the American War on Drugs can be understood as manifesting a dramatically new way of thinking that appeared at the beginning of the nineteenth century (Foucault 1970). Part of this change was that the previously broad range of acceptable personal conduct was narrowed by a new concept of man as a member of industrial society. There was an accompanying movement towards establishing institutions of discipline, reform, penance, and treatment to enforce the new standards (Foucault 1979). Drug use, even when safe or beneficial, fell outside the newly restricted range. This change in nineteenth-century America has been described as follows: 'A new society was aborning ... emphasizing a set of standards for individual conduct that rested on sobriety, productivity, and order. It stressed the inherited ideal of individualism, but only within the confines of a system that rested on efficiency, practicality, and predictability ... The new industrial society would frown upon, ostracize, and then attempt to control deviations' (Morgan 1981, 8–9).

It is impossible to identify the exact combination of forces that instigated the American War on Drugs. However, the social reality of the twentieth century is that drugs have become one of the unquestioned scapegoats for all that is evil, and the War on Drugs has come to seem an essential remedy.

Notwithstanding its warlike attitudes towards drugs, the United States has a proud tradition of domestic civil rights that protects American citizens from the worst excesses of governmental zeal or popular passion. For example, the 'McCarthy Era,' although painfully repressive, did not involve physical torture and did not continue long. It was eventually denounced by the American media and civil-liberties groups. However, in other countries, and particularly in the Third World, the War on Drugs is conducted with less restraint.

## The War on Drugs in the Third World

Thirteen Third-World nations currently impose a death penalty for distributing or using drugs (Hanreich 1984; *Edmonton Journal* 1986; Trebach 1987, 111). Other Third World countries enforce drug laws without visible concern for the survival of suspects or prisoners, much less their civil rights. Traffickers and users are routinely flogged in Pakistan and other Third World countries (see picture in *Vancouver Sun* 5 June 1987, A5). The *Bulletin on Narcotics*, a United Nations periodical with authors from diverse countries, bristles with references to 'wars,' 'campaigns,' 'counter-attacks,' 'battles,' and so on. Narcotics police are hated and feared in many countries and, in the case of Colombia, have openly helped to suppress peasant uprisings (Amnesty International 1985, 137).

Indirect support for this violence comes from the ubiquitous American media with their incessant association of illicit drugs with the worst evils of mankind, and their fictional depictions of violent destruction of traffickers by U.S. film and television idols. Direct support for drug-war violence comes from U.S. funding, participation by U.S. government employees, and U.S. government pressure to maintain a 'vigorous' enforcement policy.

The American interventionist policy is stated explicitly in public documents, such as the 1984 *National Strategy for Prevention of Drug Abuse and Drug Trafficking*: 'The *Strategy* calls for U.S. decisions on foreign aid *and other matters*, such as refinancing of debt, to be tied to the willingness of the recipient country to execute vigorous enforcement programs against narcotic traffickers' (Drug Abuse Policy Office 1984,

11; italics added). The intrusive nature of American political pressure may be indicated by the vague reference to 'other matters' in the above policy document. There are indications that diplomatic pressure is exerted on Third World countries through American embassies, undercover agents, and international agencies controlled by the United States (Nadelmann 1987), and that the United States uses its massive drug-research establishment to press distorted information about drugs on representatives of foreign countries (Chesher 1987; Hendtlass 1987).

Although such behind-the-scenes manipulations are almost invisible, direct American involvement in violent drug-law enforcement in Third World countries is easier to see. In the past, these efforts have relied on massive military force: 'Much of this missionary activity occurred during World War II ... In the Far East for example ... the Bureau of Narcotics was able to move in behind Allied armies and demand the elimination of culturally ingrained patterns of narcotic use, such as opium smoking; these were replaced by strict abstinence supported by the criminal sanction. In many of these areas today – Hong Kong, Thailand, Borneo, and Singapore among others – opium smoking has been replaced by virtual epidemics of heroin smoking or injecting. Japan and Germany also adopted their own versions of the Harrison Narcotic Act and the strict enforcement ethic' (Trebach 1982, 167–8).

In the 1980s the United States acknowledges using its military forces and equipment to aid local drug enforcement around the world (for example, New York Times 1986). In Latin American countries, U.S. Drug Enforcement Agency workers have created local drug-enforcement units by handpicking their leaders and training, equipping, and paying the members. Such units sometimes function by arresting and illegally deporting citizens of the host countries to the United States for prosecution. Such actions have sometimes involved torture by police under American supervision or with American agents present (Nadelmann 1987, 338–9, 360–1). Cocaine cultivation throughout Central and South America is monitored by satellite (Wisotsky 1983, 1315).

Foreign aid and refinancing of debt, the lever of U.S. power specifically mentioned in the American strategy document cited above, sustain the economies of many Third World countries. It seems inescapable that the price of non-compliance with U.S. drug policy for some Third World nations will be death by starvation for some of their poorer citizens. For example, the United States suspended most foreign aid to Bolivia in 1980, when a government unfriendly to u.s. concerns about cocaine came to power (Wisotsky 1983, 1340). By 1986, Bolivia's position was reversed, and 'a United States Army detachment was sent to Bolivia on July 14 at the request of the La Paz Government. It has been used to ferry Bolivian police and civilian United States Drug Enforcement Administration agents into the interior to distant cocaine labs,' (*New York Times* 1986, B6).

In Peru, the United States provided $18 million between 1982 and 1986 to support attempts to curtail coca production (Morales 1987). The money was provided through the Agency for International Development (AID). In addition, the United States Bureau of International Narcotics Matters (INM) directly funded the Peruvian cocaine-eradication police force, UMOPAR. The AID money went into low-interest loans for farmers in the rain-forest regions who pledged not to grow cocaine on their land (although most of this money was used by opportunistic farmers to capitalize coca production). The INM money went to an 'eradication force' that included hundreds of 'pullers.' Under the protection of UMOPAR, pullers uprooted about fifty hectares of coca bushes per day. Police protection was necessary because of assaults on the pullers by farmers whose livelihood was being destroyed (Morales 1989). In the process of these confrontations many arrests were made (16,565 between 1978 and 1984) and people were sometimes killed (Morales 1987).

Peru continue to suffer many kinds of harm from the drug war. Peasants are imprisoned in large numbers and many die during long terms in primitive prisons. The narcotics police are at least as corrupt as the traffickers. It requires a large bribe to obtain a posting in the cocaine-producing region because of the opportunities for payoffs. Wealthy cocaine producers are almost invariably released after payment of bribes to officials, whereas peasants and poor workers often receive lengthy sentences. As well, the stripping of land by 'pullers' damages the soil so as to make it useless for the following decade (Morales 1989). Recent statements by American officials indicate that destruction of crops is a major priority in the War on Drugs. According to a high-ranking official, 'eradication of illicit crops is the most effective weapon and a key to the suppression of foreign drug trafficking' (Caffrey 1984, 60).

Such actions bespeak a lack of concern for innocent bystanders that is typical of the war mentality. Coca production is a good source of income for thousands of peasants in countries where starvation or malnutrition is often the alternative (Morales 1989). This is especially true in Bolivia, which is the poorest country in South America (Wisotsky 1983, 134). Moreover, chewing coca leaves is an ancient tradition among more than four million Indians and peasants in Peru and Bolivia. **Notwithstanding the current media image of cocaine, coca-leaf chewing provides a relatively harmless mild stimulant, like coffee or tea in Canada, for these people. It also serves as a hunger suppressant for often malnourished people, and the leaves add a few calories to the daily food intake** (Wisotsky 1983, 1341; *PM*, chap. 4).

## The War on Drugs in Europe

Like North Americans, Western Europeans are protected by a cherished tradition of civil rights. Nevertheless, anti-drug zeal and repressive drug-prohibition measures have flourished in the last few years. Throughout Europe, abhorrence of undercover police and *agents provocateurs* incited by the Second World War has been superseded by zeal for drug prosecutions (Nadelmann 1987, 282–9). In 1986 the parliament of the European Economic Community passed a report advocating strict drug laws and uniform enforcement throughout the European community. The wording of the report reveals a wholesale endorsement of the War on Drugs mentality, and has been interpreted as a repudiation of one EEC member-nation, the Netherlands, which has *successfully* introduced less punitive drug policy (Malyon 1986). There are also indications that a War on Drugs is also gathering strength in Eastern Europe. Recent developments in Britain and the USSR will be summarized here to illustrate these trends.

### Britain

By the early twentieth century Britons, like Americans, acquired the habit of blaming their social problems on drugs, although they seemed to have escaped the worst excesses of the War on Drugs, as witnessed by their relatively humane policy of allowing physicians to prescribe heroin and cocaine to addicts (Trebach 1982). However, British controls began to tighten in the early 1970s. Margaret Thatcher's Britain has abandoned the earlier liberal approach and moved to the forefront of the War on

Drugs. An all-party committee of the British parliament recently called for an 'all-out drug war.' Britain subsequently announced 'the most Draconian measures ever taken to curb drug smuggling' (Massam 1985, 1985a). A British author has pointed out: 'The ... Drug Trafficking Offences Act which received the royal assent on 8 July [1986] ... overturns a fundamental cornerstone of British justice, the presumption that a defendant is innocent until proven guilty. Anyone convicted in Crown Court of a drug trafficking offense, however small, is now liable to have all assets acquired during the last six years confiscated, unless they can prove the the assets were legally acquired. This assumption, that assets are illegal unless proven otherwise, is dryly described in the Law Society Gazette, not an organ prone to overstatement, as "most unusual in a criminal statute"' (Malyon 1986, 8).

Urine testing of British military personnel has been introduced and there are indications that mass testing in British industry is on the way (*Lancet* 1987). In foreign policy Britain has apparently followed the u.s. lead in providing money to Third World governments to help repress drugs (Home Office 1986; Malyon 1986, 8). It is not yet clear that British enforcement of its Draconian new laws will be entirely as harsh as similar measures in the United States and the Third World. It is possible that British traditions of moderation (Trebach 1982; Spurgeon and Black 1987) will prevail over the zeal of its drug warriors.

## The USSR

For years, the Soviet Union denied the existence of drug problems, beyond a celebrated national passion for vodka. The ussr maintained that other drug use was spawned by capitalist decadence. The official position has now changed. In a recent interview, the ussr minister of the interior has condemned drug addiction as a 'tremendous social threat' and promised to 'use every means to root out the vice that debilitates the body, corrupts the soul and kills.' Reponses to the problem in Russia include compulsory treatment for young adults, school check-ups to detect drug use in adolescents, and use of the militia to register all drug addicts and to 'properly guard crops and raw narcotics, destroy stubble and wild narcotic-bearing plants.' According to the minister, the defoliation of an entire valley in which marijuana plants grow profusely is under consideration (Vlasov 1987).

The new position of the USSR shows that it is simplistic to blame the War on Drugs entirely on the United States. European and Third World countries may well be strongly influenced by American policy, but this cannot be true of the Russians. The War on Drugs is a truly international movement.

## Canada's War on Drugs

Canada's prime minister has declared tough new measures directed at the 'epidemic' of drug abuse that is undermining 'our economic as well as social fabric' (Sears 1986). However, the 'new' National Drug Strategy of 1987 is not new in concept, but is built on assumptions and policies that go back to nineteenth-century Canada and had achieved their modern form by 1930.

Canada's War on Drugs began more or less independently of the American one (although many of the early temperance leaders were American). However, as decades passed, Canada has surrendered more and more of its initiative to American influence. Although drug use and drug arrests are still far less frequent in Canada than in the United States (Johnson 1988), the current government of Canada seems to be enlisting the nation for the duration of U.S.-style drug war, without pausing to consider alternatives.

### HISTORY OF CANADA'S DRUG WAR

Canadians did not always blame their problems on drugs. Prior to the nineteenth century, violence was abundant among settlers. Although many of the perpetrators used drugs that were available, chiefly alcohol and opium, drugs were usually not considered to be the cause of their violence. The history of the Hudson's Bay Company provides an early example.

Prodigious alcohol consumption by the seventeenth- and eighteenth-century fur traders and Indians is well documented because of the compulsive record-keeping of the Hudson's Bay Company, who imported the alcohol (Newman 1985). The situation at 'Moose Factory' on Hudson Bay in the mid-eighteenth century was described as follows: 'Many of the work accidents at Moose were alcohol-related. One man consumed so much "bumbo" – that fur-trade mixture of rum, water, sugar, and nutmeg – that he fell off the sloop and promptly drowned. With some regret and much haste, his mates lost no time in auctioning off the contents of his chest. The chief factors were always afraid that the men on watch, who were too often drunk, would spitefully or accidentally set fire to the buildings. The courage to commit suicide could also be found in the bottle. "Brandy-death" was common, and known in Rupert's Land as a Northwester's Death' (Pannekoek 1979, 5). Although drunkenness was common, 'addiction' and 'alcoholism' were not matters of concern, or even part of the vocabulary used to discuss drinking. A new factor was sent from London in 1741 to improve discipline at Moose Factory. He did not blame the serious problems that he found on alcohol. Rather, he identified the basic problem as the influence of the Masonic Order among the men at Moose Factory, who excluded him from the secrets of their society (Newman 1985, 164).

In the more densely settled areas of Upper and Lower Canada, eighteenth-century settlers probably consumed more alcohol than do modern Canadians. The abundant drinking establishments were often the centre of community life and there was little public outrage about alcohol and few attempts to control it except at a few localities where it got out of hand (Smart and Ogborne 1986)

*Alcohol Prohibition in Canada*

The Canadian temperance movement, similar in many ways to its American counterpart, emerged early in the nineteenth century. In its earliest days it tried to reduce drunkenness by persuasion, but its rhetoric soon intensified and 'temperance' came to mean enforced universal abstinence. The temperance movement became enormously popular throughout nineteenth-century Canada. For example, it was one of the few patches of common ground for English and French people in Quebec after the bloody rebellion of 1837 (Woods 1983). Temperance societies became centres of social life for the abstinent and were associated with most of the popular reform issues of the nineteenth century, including women's suffrage and observance of the Lord's Day (Smart and Ogborne 1986). Warlike rhetoric emerged early in the movement. By 1847 the official watchword of Montreal's Temperance Society had become 'War to the Death with the Demon of Intemperance' (Chiniquy 1847, 26). Songs in a Canadian temperance songbook included 'Sound the Battle Cry' and 'The Temperance Army' (Smart and Ogborne 1986). Voluminous early Canadian temperance literature left little doubt that drunkenness was the source of most of society's evils and that a single drink could convert a person into a drunkard (Hallowell 1972; Smart and Ogborne 1986).

Canada's first drug prohibition was introduced in a truly military context. In 1873 parliament created a new military unit called the North-West Mounted Rifles and eventually sent it west to supervise the settlers, contain hostile Indians, control American marauders, and enforce the total prohibition of alcohol ordered by the Northwest Territories Act of 1875 (*Revised Statutes of Canada* 1970). Alcohol was prohibited in a vast area of Canada by this act, since the Northwest Territories included present-day Saskatchewan, Alberta, Manitoba, the Yukon, and portions of northern Ontario and Quebec, as well as the present Northwest Territories.

The movement of a military unit into territory adjacent to the U.S. border set off serious protests in Washington, DC. Consequently, the North-West Mounted Rifles were diplomatically renamed the North-West Mounted Police. Other terminological changes complete the camouflage: for example, the lieutenant-colonel became a 'commissioner' and privates were re-classified as 'constables.' What remained was a 'military force in everything but name' (Gray 1972, 22). The powers of the NWMP in the early west were equivalent to martial law: 'The North West Mounted Police was not only an enforcer of the law, it was the law. The force could search and make arrests without warrant. A prisoner so arrested was brought before a senior officer who could try him at once or remand him in custody' (Gray 1972, 25).

The NWMP's taming of the wild west is legendary. It is now mostly forgotten, however, that 'overriding all else in the consumption of time and effort ... was the enforcement of Prohibition' (Gray 1972, 24). Whereas the NWMP succeeded in most of what it undertook, it lost face in its attempts at controlling liquor:

> The respect, the genuine regard the homesteaders had for the Mounties, in all respects save one, was universal. Their efforts to enforce the unenforceable liquor laws brought them into contempt ... When the Mounties were not chasing whisky smugglers across the prairies, arresting white men caught plying Indians with alcohol, or riding herd on disorderly drunks in the towns and villages, they were themselves getting roaring drunk in their

barracks. On one occasion in 1886, 'H' Troop in Lethbridge got its
back pay and went on a prolonged collective binge that terrorized the town.
There was another time at Fort Macleod when a couple of drunken
Mounties who had run out of money held up a visitor from Saskatoon on
the main street of the town. (Gray 1972, 24–5)

The temperance movement agitated for alcohol prohibition in eastern
Canada as well as on the frontier. The 1864 Dunkin Act and the 1878
Canada Temperance Act were attempts at compromise with the movement. Quite reasonably, they allowed cities and counties to enact local
alcohol prohibition if the majority voted for it, leading to local prohibition
in many parts of eastern Canada (Spence 1919, 124; Smart and Ogborne
1986). Unappeased, however, the temperance movement succeeded in
forcing a national plebiscite on alcohol prohibition in 1898. When the
ballots were counted, a small majority of voters had supported national
prohibition. The Liberal government of Sir Wilfrid Laurier did not enact
prohibition, however, on the basis that less than 50 per cent of eligible
voters had actually cast a ballot (Spence 1919, 252).

The prohibition movement achieved real popular support during the
First World War with the inspiration of wartime rhetoric such as the
following: 'Reverend J. F. Hughson of Winnipeg urged ... "use ballots
for bullets and shoot straight and strong in order that the demon of drink
might be banished from the haunts of men" ... the *Cypress River Western
Prairie* warned on the eve of the Manitoba balloting [on prohibition]
"anyone who will vote in favor of liquor might as well enlist under the
Kaiser as far as patriotism goes"' (Thompson 1972, 230, 233). Such
rhetoric drew many to the prohibitionists, especially recent immigrants
eager to prove their patriotism (Thompson 1972). The movement had
become irresistible. All the provinces plus Newfoundland and the Yukon
territory enacted alcohol prohibition during the First World War or
shortly before. Federal prohibition was enacted as well in 1918 as a
wartime economy, but it lasted for only one year (Hallowell 1985).

The notorious 'Spracklin Gang' of Ontario illustrates the extremes of
violence that were reached during Canadian prohibition. The Reverend
J.O.L. Spracklin was minister of the Sandwich (now part of Windsor),
Ontario, Methodist church from 1919 to 1921. An avid pulpit spokesman
for strict enforcement of prohibition, he was appointed head of a special
force of liquor licence inspectors by the Ontario attorney-general. At that

point, the word became flesh: 'In less than five months ... Reverend Spracklin polarized the extremes of prohibition. With guns strapped to his belt, he ... roamed the streets till the early hours of the morning, busting down doors with pistols blazing and a squad of men who were tougher than the surly rum-runners. And when not being chauffeured in his large touring car provided by Ontario's Attorney General William E. Raney, he was patrolling the Detroit River with the provincial speed boat, *Panther II*, zooming into remote docks and canals to spy upon and catch whisky dealers red-handed' (Gervais 1980, 119).

Spracklin and his men used their guns (there was at least one shooting death), beat people badly (at least one died), and carried blank search warrants that Reverend Spracklin filled out as needed. In short, they created a kind of martial law for the enforcement of alcohol prohibition. Spracklin maintained his post as liquor inspector in spite of being charged with killing the owner of a roadhouse. He pleaded self-defence and was acquitted in spite of eyewitness testimony against him, and retained the support of the prohibitionists. He was in fact commended by the WCTU and various Methodist organizations (Hallowell 1972, 126). Spracklin was investigated by the temperance committee of the Ontario legislature, whose chairman concluded: 'extreme measures must be taken where there are extreme conditions ... Mr. Spracklin went in as a matter of public service. I think the ends justify the means' (Gervais 1980, 124). The tide began to turn when Spracklin was charged and convicted of trespassing following the gunpoint search of a yacht whose wealthy passengers were not carrying liquor. His final downfall and departure from the Windsor area came after being charged in his own congregation of 'sexual propositions' to some female parishioners (Gervais 1980, 129).

Spracklin represented an aberrant extreme. The day-to-day stresses of prohibition in Canada had more to do with practices that the regular police felt it necessary to adopt in their vain attempts to abolish liquor. These police practices bear an obvious similarity to the techniques used by contemporary police to enforce narcotics laws (Schweighofer 1988). The following article, headlined 'Spy Evidence,' appeared in the *Victoria Colonist*, 20 October 1922.

Judge Lampman, in his court, has added a contribution to the tide of judicial obloquy which is rising against the despicable methods that have recently been employed in the Province, whereby hirelings have been induced to break the law from the distorted viewpoint that the end justifies the means. The employment of 'stool pigeons' is a stain on the operations of the Liquor Control Board. That the practice should be countenanced and connived at by the Attorney-General's Department is a stain on the methods of our law administration. In all common decency it is time the practice ceased.

Another point of even graver significance ... is the appeal which was taken by the Crown against an acquittal in the Police Court. The Crown sought, through this means, to put a man in jeopardy of his liberty for a second time for the same alleged offense. It was not only an 'unseemly thing' which the Crown attempted to do, but it was a step in violation of the fundamental principles of British Criminal Law. (4)

Official corruption became an everyday event during alcohol prohibition. One unnerving case directly involved the prohibition commissioner of British Columbia, W.C. Findlay. Mr. Findlay was a prominent member of the political movement to enact prohibition in the province. Within a few months after being appointed prohibition commissioner he was found to be involved in bootlegging. He was fined $1000 for refusing to answer questions in court and eventually spent two years in the penitentiary. Several other 'prominent citizens' were involved in the case and two of them left for the United States (Hiebert 1969, 114–15).

Restrained by a deep-rooted sense of 'British Justice,' Canadian alcohol prohibition was tame relative to its American counterpart. None the less, it became obvious to the majority of Canadians that costs were too high. Alcohol prohibition quickly passed from Canadian history in a series of provincial plebiscites in the early 1920s. It persisted until 1929 in Nova Scotia and until 1948 in Prince Edward Island (Smart and Ogborne 1986).

## Narcotics Prohibition in Canada

By contrast to alcohol prohibition, Canadian prohibition of opium, cocaine, and other illicit drugs has been as warlike as its American counterpart, and has not yet been discarded.

Canadian opposition to opium gathered force in western Canada during the end of the nineteenth century in the context of growing racial tension between white society and Chinese immigrants (Solomon and Green

1982; Boyd 1984). Many of the Chinese were single men who would work for lower wages than Caucasian workers could accept. The Chinese were therefore bitterly resented. Opium was resented because the hated Chinese consumed it and because some whites who used it mixed with the Chinese. However, smoking opium was not considered physically harmful (Solomon and Green 1982). In fact, such a judgment would have been absurd – the opuim-using Chinese worked harder and longer with less raucous misbehaviour than the whites who despised opium. In the aftermath of the violent 1907 'Anti-Asiatic Riot' in Vancouver's Chinatown, and in response to persistent pressure from the British Columbia government, the federal government enacted the Opium Act in 1908. For the first time in Canada, the sale, importation, and manufacture of opium was prohibited. This law provided penalties ranging from a $50 fine to a maximum of three years in prison. It allowed merchants six months to sell off existing stocks before enforcement began.

In eastern Canada, the main impetus towards opium prohibition came from the medical establishment, which feared competition from the purveyors of patent medicines, especially in view of the outrageous claims made in patent-medicine advertising (Murray 1988). In 1908, the same year as the Opium Act, parliament passed the Proprietary and Patent Medicine Act, which required that patent medicines containing heroin, morphine, opium, and other drugs must list their contents on the label and that medicines must not contain more alcohol than was necessary as a solvent. The use of cocaine in patent medicines was prohibited entirely. Infractions of these rules were punishable by fines of up to $100 and loss of registration for the medicine involved.

Both of these enactments were amazingly mild by modern standards. Obviously, parliament did not feel they were responding to a crisis, in spite of the plentiful, low-cost narcotics that were available to the public. However, sentiment changed quickly once the first prohibition laws had passed. Extravagantly moralistic testimony about drugs became common in parliament and in the popular press. Punitive legislation followed. The 1911 Opium and Drug Act banned cocaine entirely and created penalties for using opium or being present when it was being smoked. Tobacco was considered for addition to the act in parliament, but was excluded, the House apparently accepting Mackenzie King's argument that it was not a habit-forming drug (Boyd 1984).

By 1921 amendments to the Opium and Drug Act provided a maximum seven-year penalty for the importation, manufacture, and sale of opium or any other drug mentioned in the act. It shifted the burden of proof so that it was an offence to be in a building that also contained narcotics, unless the accused could prove 'the drugs were there without his authority, knowledge or consent' (Boyd 1984, 126). In 1922 whipping and deportation were added as penalties.

In 1922 both the full-fledged War on Drugs mentality and the American influence that inflamed it were spelled out in a highly influential book entitled *The Black Candle* (Murphy 1922). This book, and the series of *Maclean's* articles on which it was based, were written by a remarkable Canadian. Emily Murphy, an early feminist, Edmonton police magistrate, and juvenile-court judge, was reportedly the first woman jurist in the British empire. Her book is a thorough introduction to the War on Drugs mentality in its modern form. For example, in her chapter 'War on the Drug Ring' she declares total war:

> Any one who starts out to seriously enforce the law against the [drug] Ring finds he is combatting large financial interests and that these are in the hands of dangerous and unscrupulous persons. It means if you are getting anywhere with law enforcement, that your character is assailed and even your life threatened ...
>
> Resolutions, however well framed, mean nothing in this fight which is going to be a fight to the finish. Unless the forces of civilization strangle the Rings – choke them to death, the Rings are going to choke civilization.
>
> Does this sound hysterical or immoderate? Then listen to the words of Dr. Erwin C. Ruth, head of the Narcotic Division of the Internal Revenue Department of Boston who has during the present year made an amazing exposure of the illicit drug traffic which he says is costing the people of America many million dollars a year and wrecking hundreds of thousand of human lives ... [this is followed by a long recital of American statistics]. (Murphy 1922, 166–7)

Mrs Murphy did not soft-pedal the military and racist underpinnings of her convictions. For example:

> It is hardly credible that the average Chinese pedlar has any definite idea in his mind of bringing about the downfall of the white race, his swaying motive being probably that of greed, but in the hands of his superiors, he

may become a powerful instrument to this very end ...

Naturally, the aliens are silent on the subject, but an addict who died this year in British Columbia told how he was frequently jeered at as a 'white man accounted for.' This man belonged to a prominent family and, in 1917, was drawing a salary of six thousand dollars a year. He fell a victim to a drug 'booster' till, ultimately, he became a ragged wreck living in the noisome alleys of Chinatown, 'lost to use, and name and fame.'

This man used to relate how the Chinese pedlars taunted him with their superiority at being able to sell the dope without using it, and by telling him how the yellow race would rule the world. They were too wise, they urged, to attempt to win in battle but would win by wits; would strike at the white race through 'dope' and when the time was ripe would command the world ...

Some of the Negroes coming into Canada – and they are no fiddle-faddle fellows either – have similar ideas, and one of their greatest writers has boasted how ultimately they will control the white men. (Murphy 1922, 188–9)

The *Black Candle* aroused national sentiment to demand stringent penalties against drug users and traffickers, with many of Mrs Murphy's punitive recommendations eventually becoming law. The racist component was prominent in public debate. The increasingly punitive drug legislation of the 1920s was made acceptable to the public by assurances that it would be used against Chinese rather than white citizens (Cook 1969, 37–8). Out of 853 convictions in 1921–2, 634 were against Chinese. In 1929 this legislative escalation culminated in the Opium and Narcotic Drug Act, 'one of the country's most punitive pieces of criminal legislation' (Solomon and Green 1982, 98). In the process, 'the drug user's image had been changed from that of a morally weak, but otherwise benign individual to that of a fiendish criminal, obsessed with the need to addict others and motivated by lust and greed. Moral reformers, prominent citizens, the RCMP, the Narcotic Division, and legislators were all clamoring for stern action against these particularly loathsome dregs of humanity ... Public acceptance of the dope-fiend mythology permitted the virtually unchallenged passage of legislation that defined addiction as a law enforcement problem, extended the range of the criminal sanctions, increased the punitive consequences of conviction, and encroached on traditional civil liberties' (Solomon and Green 1982, 100).

## THE CURRENT CANADIAN WAR ON DRUGS

In the last few decades Canada's attempts to control drug use have become more and more like war policy.

### War Language

Those responsible for Canada's drug policy speak in the language of war. Canada's former solicitor-general, Robert Kaplan, spoke to a 1982 conference in Ottawa of 'the war against drug abuse' and the 'need for a coordinated assault' (Kaplan 1982). Stephen Lewis, Canada's current ambassador to the United Nations, may have introduced a new phrase, 'narco-terrorism,' into the War on Drugs vocabulary when he associated drug trafficking with international terrorism in a speech to the United Nations (*Vancouver Sun* 1985). The current revenue minister, Elmer MacKay, explained in a recent speech that the fight against illicit drugs 'is a war really ... It sounds like a cliché, but it's us against them' (Jones 1987).

Modern advocates of warlike drug policy raise health, moralistic, and economic concerns, rather than racial fears. **But later chapters will show that the modern justifications have no better basis than the earlier racial ones** (Brecher 1972; Le Dain 1973; *PM*, chaps 3, 4, 5, 7, 8). Moreover, the violence of the War on Drugs mentality shows through when the veneer of medical and social concern is scratched. Contemporary drug warriors are no 'fiddle-faddle fellows' either.

### Violent Imagery

Whereas current Canadian politicians do not explicitly condone anti-drug violence, some parts of society appear to. Current news and media entertainment seem to justify violence by their portrayals of drug users and traffickers as deranged or depraved. A popular Canadian novel about drug users and traffickers, *Needles*, is an example (Deverell 1979). In one episode, Laszlo Plizit, a known amphetamine addict whom the omniscient reader knows to have committed a murder, is in custody. Detective Harrison, one of the heroes of the novel, enters the cell and interrogates the prisoner. In the course of the interrogation he throws his coat over Plizit's head while he is asleep, slams Plizit into the wall, kicks him in the head ('above the hairline, where no mark would show'), kicks him in the

hand ('breaking a couple of fingers'), throws him into the wall, kicks him
in the stomach ('grasping, too much in pain to scream'), kicks him again
in the stomach ('I still got the best corner kick in the police league,' says
Harrison), and, it is implied, continues beating him as the author changes
the scene (Deverell 1979, 104–7).

Few Canadians condone brutalizing prisoners. In the case of the unfortunate Plizit, however, the brutality appears justified by the War on Drugs
context of the novel. Plizit is not brutalized because he is a drug addict,
but in order to solve a murder and prevent another one. Yet his brutaliza-
tion seems somehow just because he is a drug addict, and Detective
Harrison's actions seem somehow admirable. I can testify to this reaction
personally because I found the novel exciting and entertaining when I first
read it. Only later did I analyse why I was not repulsed by this depiction of
brutality. *Needles* is fictional, of course, but a novel that is accepted by
mainstream society must tell something about how the society thinks.
*Needles* was published by a serious Canadian publisher, McClelland and
Stewart, and won the $50,000 Seal First Novel Award in 1979. The
author, William Deverell, is a successful Vancouver lawyer and former
president of the British Columbia Civil Liberties Association. This
fictionalization of extravagant violence by police towards criminals in the
War on Drugs appears to bear the seal of approval of Canadian society.

## Legal Violence

Apart from fiction and rhetoric, the extent of actual violence used in
enforcing Canadian drug laws is hard to determine precisely, because
contradictory accounts are given by police and drug users. However, it is
clear that many Canadian citizens have been legally subjected to cruel and
unusual punishment in the prosecution of the War on Drugs. This is
possible partly because Canadian drug laws have bestowed enormous
power on the enforcement system. As Robert Solomon (1988) put it:
'Police have far broader enforcement powers in even a minor drug case
than they have in a murder, arson, rape or other serious criminal
investigation' (263).

Most Canadians might not think it overly severe that the Narcotics
Control Act specifies life imprisonment as the maximum penalty for
trafficking or 'possession for the purpose of trafficking' in narcotics.
However, most Canadians do not know that the act defines the word

'traffic' in a way that is much more inclusive than its everyday meaning. Under the act, 'traffic' means 'to manufacture, sell, give, administer, transport, send, deliver, or distribute, or ... to offer to do' any of these. Moreover, the list of 'narcotics' in which one may 'traffic' is 4½ pages long. Many of the listed drugs are commonly prescribed in medical practice, and many citizens have had them in their medicine cabinet from time to time. Marijuana is on the list of 'narcotics' (Solomon 1988, 1988a). Under the act, a person who offers a pill from their medicine cabinet to another person who may have run out is 'trafficking' if the pill happens to be included in the 4½ pages of 'narcotics' specified by the act. For one person to give (or offer to give) a marijuana cigarette to another, a common practice of youthful marijuana users, also constitutes 'trafficking.' Under the Narcotic Control Act, *both of these crimes are punishable by a life sentence.*

To my knowledge, convictions this ridiculous have not actually occurred. However, a Canadian court has ruled that purchasing marijuana for personal use and subsequently giving it to a friend for safe keeping constitutes 'possession for the purpose of trafficking,' a crime that potentially carries a life sentence. Similarly, the act of converting marijuana into cannabis resin for one's personal use has been ruled 'trafficking' because it constitutes 'manufacture' (*Canada Statute Citator* 1986; Solomon, Single, and Erickson 1988).

The Narcotics Control Act also includes a 'reverse onus' provision for the crime of 'possession for the purpose of trafficking,' meaning that a person convicted of possession of a narcotic must prove to the court that he or she was not in possession with the intention of trafficking. A look at the definition of trafficking above will reveal that such proof is virtually impossible: How could accused persons prove that they did not intend to share their drug with someone else? This reverse-onus provision was regularly applied for more than two decades from passage of the act in 1961 until the clause was successfully challenged in 1982 and 1983 under the Canadian Charter of Rights and Freedoms (*Canada Statute Citator* 1986, 128–1, 128–2).

Even though Canadian courts have rarely inflicted the life sentence for trafficking (Boyd 1983) and generally make rulings that are much more sensible than the wording of the law, the law confers enormous discretionary power on enforcement agencies to intimidate and control people who are involved with drugs in any way, even if their involvement does not do the slightest harm to themselves or others (Solomon 1988, 1988a; Fiffen and Lambert 1988, 360).

The strongest potential for legal violence in the Narcotic Control Act may be its provision for search and seizure in drug cases. Because the power to search has proved vulnerable to abuse throughout history, it is severely limited under common law and by the Canadian criminal code – except in the case of drug offences. The Narcotic Control Act gives the police almost unrestricted powers of search and seizure in drug cases, and these have been interpreted liberally by the courts (Solomon, Single, and Erickson 1988, 378). Under section 10 of the act:

(1) A peace officer may, at any time,
(a) without a warrant enter and search any place other than a dwelling-house, and under the authority of a writ of assistance issued under this section, enter and search any dwelling-house in which he reasonably believes there is a narcotic by means of or in respect of which an offense under this Act has been committed;
(b) search any person found in such place; and
(c) seize and take away any narcotic found in such a place, any thing in such place in which he reasonably suspects a narcotic is contained or concealed, or any other thing by means of or in respect of which he reasonably believes an offense under this Act has been committed or that may be evidence of the commission of such an offense ...
(3) A judge of the Exchequer Court of Canada shall, upon application by the Minister, issue a writ of assistance authorizing and empowering the person named therein, aided and assisted by such person as the person named therein may require, at any time, to enter any dwelling-house and search for narcotics.
(4) For the purpose of exercising his authority under this section, a peace officer may, with such assistance as he deems necessary, break open any door, window, lock, fastener, floor, wall, ceiling, compartment, plumbing fixture, box, container, or any other thing.

This law and a series of related court decisions have allowed the police to legally break into homes at night, without warnings, warrants, or explanations, to smash the furnishings, to manhandle and beat the occupants, and to punch and choke people who are suspected of trying to swallow drugs. Within five miles of the office where this is being written, a drug dealer was choked in the course of swallowing a packet of drugs (that is, was 'searched') and subsequently died in hospital. The coroner's jury ruled that the death was accidental in spite of the written statement of a Vancouver doctor that the police version of the event was impossible ('Inquest on the body of John Dennis Williams' 1980; personal communication, Dr R.G. Schulze, 1981). In Canadian drug enforcement, 'search' may have become a kind of summary punishment that the police can administer without a conviction. Although addicts say that this kind of police activity has become less common recently in Vancouver, it still occurs, and remains legal.

Whereas recent judgments in Canadian courts have led to the reduction of the use of writs of assistance in drug cases, and their eventual elimination in 1985, these legal instruments long constituted the most visible aspect of the extraordinary powers of search and seizure that prevailed in drug cases:

> The drug writs ... were introduced in 1929 in response to enforcement difficulties encountered by RCMP drug officers. To gain the necessary committee support for the writs, the government drug administrator promised that new writs would be issued and then only to officers he personally trusted. The administrator envisaged that there would be a maximum of 10 writs. However, when a moratorium on writ applications was imposed in 1977, the RCMP held over 240 writs under the NCA and a similar number under the FDA. The RCMP also held a large number of writs of assistance under the *Customs and Excise Acts* ... As the Law Reform Commission of Canada noted: 'This kind of sweeping discretion has been the focus of bitter conflicts in common law jurisdictions ... The general reaction of the English courts was to brand such warrants as 'oppressive,' 'nameless,' and 'worse than the Spanish Inquisition,' and invalidate them in the absence of express statutory authority. The great historical conflict over so-called 'general' warrants, however, occurred in pre-revolutionary America ... triggering a series of protests that were to lead to the struggle that became the American Revolution.' (Solomon 1988, 283)

While the federal government curtailed the writs of assistance, their function is now at least partly replaced by a new device called a 'telewarrant.' There are strong reasons to suspect that this quick system for issuing warrants by telephone cannot afford the protections that a judicial warrant is intended to provide under English common law (Solomon 1988), although the way they will be administered in practice remains to be seen.

Moreover, legislation that came into effect in 1989 extends the already vast police powers of search and seizure in new directions, by making it possible to seize the assets of suspects in organized-crime investigations, including suspected drug traffickers (Poirier 1986). Under this legislation, a charged person's assets may be seized if he or she is suspected of a 'designated drug crime' or an 'enterprise crime,' even if he or she has not been charged or convicted (*Canadian Legislative Index* 1987). People whose property has been confiscated may only have access to it for living expenses or legal expenses if they can convince a judge that the expenses are reasonable. In effect, the judge must approve the budget for the defence against the Crown.

## Illegal Police Violence

The actions against suspected drug users and traffickers that have been described up to this point are legal. However, the police do not always follow the law perfectly. Canadian police have frequently found it necessary to break even the loose constraints applied to them in drug cases. Violence has occurred at a level that Canadians would not normally condone, although in the context of the War on Drugs it has not provoked protest.

Police violence as brutal as the episode in *Needles* has been described to me by numerous Vancouver heroin addicts. One difference from the fictional account in *Needles* is that in some of the stories I have been told no interrogation was under way. The assaults were unexplained and appear to have been simple, illegal brutality. Of course, the people who told me these stories are all criminals, so it is impossible to accept their stories unquestioningly, especially since policemen publicly deny that such events take place.

However, I am convinced that this kind of violence has occurred. My own conviction comes partly from the sheer number of such stories told by addicts and partly from corroborating statements made in confidence by present and former RCMP officers who have witnessed and participated in such events. The most convincing evidence for me personally is the report of a 70-year-old woman whom I have known for many years and whom I consider a personal friend. Her son was a heroin addict and dealer in Vancouver. At one point he was living in a basement suite in her home and the police raided the house. Two aspects of the raid particularly baffled and terrified my friend, as they might most people, for they fall outside of normal Canadian experience in peace-time. One was that after the police broke through her front door without warning, one officer turned, *from inside the house*, and smashed the door with his axe. The second was that after knocking her son unconscious, an officer continued to beat him on the head with a flashlight as he lay on the floor and menaced her when she screamed at him to stop.

Beyond private evidence, two particularly revealing stories appeared in the same day's edition of the *Vancouver Sun* (1977). The two front-page stories appear as figure 1. In the story headlined 'City officers guilty of beating Mountie,' RCMP Constable Barry Milewski was reported to have testified that two Vancouver city police officers 'punched and kicked him to the ground and hit him with a flashlight' when, in his capacity as an undercover agent, he was 'walking to a drug-dealing contact in Gastown.' He did not identify himself as an RCMP officer when questioned by the city police, because of his undercover assignment.

The defence of the city police was that Constable Milewski, appearing to be merely a local resident, swore at them as he jaywalked across the street. City policeman Michael Carpenter, a former British amateur boxing champion, testified that he hit Milewski only once and that 'he had no idea how Milewski received a series of bruises to his back and side.' This kind of violence is not normally acceptable in peace-time Canada and both Vancouver policemen were convicted. Would they have been convicted if their victim was not another policeman? The answer is unequivocally 'no.' The drug police, in effect, stand above the law (except when they abuse another drug policeman) because of various buffers that protect them from prosecution.

A clear demonstration that ordinary citizens do not have normal protection against the drug police is illustrated by the other story in this same edition of the *Vancouver Sun*. A couple from Surrey, BC, who were established as having no connection with illicit drugs, were mistakenly identified by three plain-clothes RCMP officers and arrested. The husband described the incident to the newspaper reporter as follows: 'A man grabbed me with both hands around the neck ... and started to squeeze. Another grabbed a handful of my hair and yanked out a handful of it ... I

# City officers guilty of beating Mountie

Two Vancouver police constables were convicted today in provincial court of assaulting an undercover RCMP constable last April in Gastown.

Const. Mervin Douglas Morrison, 31, was convicted of assault causing bodily harm and of common assault against RCMP Const. Barry Milewski. Const. Michael Carpenter, 34, was convicted of assault against the RCMP con-

Carpenter said Milewski swore and struggled throughout the arrest for jaywalking, then lunged at Morrison.

"It was then that I delivered a right hook to the solar plexus," he testified.

That was the only blow delivered by the morotcycle policemen, they said.

Milewski testified during the trial that he was walking toward a drug-dealing contact in Gastown April 19 when he crossed in front of

# Innocent couple 'manhandled'

By MARTHA ROBINSON

A young Surrey couple say they were dragged from their car, manhandled, handcuffed and searched by three under-cover RCMP narcotics agents in Vancouver in what later proved to be a case of mistaken identity.

But for Gerald and Sharon Schuck, both 29, of 9414-132A St., Surrey, it was, in Sharon's words, "like a horror movie come to life."

And when it was all over, said the Schucks in an interview Wednesday, the only comment one of the RCMP trio made

was: "Well, we just can't be right all the time."

The Schucks' nightmare started when they left the Odeon Theatre on Granville about 9:45 p.m. Tuesday and started walking south toward Helmcken where their car was parked. They walked slowly, looking into shop windows and quietly enjoying themselves because, as Sharon said, "we don't come into Vancouver all that often - it was a night out for us."

Granville was crowded and they didn't realize that a man had brushed against Gerry outside a cafe in the 1000 block

making it appear that he had passed something over to him.

"We got in our car and drove over Granville Bridge and then as we both felt thirsty we headed for the A & W on Kingsway for a root beer." Gerry said.

"Our drinks had just been served on a tray when out of the blue the car door on Sharon's side was ripped open.

"I was trying to get out to help her when a man grabbed me with both hands around the neck - one hand at the back of the neck, on hand in front - and started to squeeze. Another grabbed my hair and yanked out a handful of it.

"They dragged me out of the car. I was yelling: 'What do you want? Do you want money?' I was struggling. I thought we

Figure 1

think I swore at them, and the fellow who had been choking me said, "Watch it, buddy, or it will get tougher. You haven't seen anything yet." '

After the incident, the husband attempted to instigate action against the police through the mayor of Vancouver, the RCMP, and a private lawyer. He described his conversation with a lawyer as follows: 'He told me I could personally lay an assault charge, or lay charges through him, but he cautioned me it would be expensive ... it could run into thousands of dollars ... I just don't have that kind of money' (*Vancouver Sun* 1977, 1–2).

## Spying

Although Canadian drug police are usually mute on the issue of illegal violence, they speak openly of the use of informers, undercover agents, electronic-surveillance techniques, and other warlike tactics. The following description is by an investigative reporter who accompanied members of the Vancouver Police drug squad on their duties and reported on their activities with approval:

> I had missed their spotter inside the hotel, although I looked right at him. He was an undercover member of their team, sitting at a table, apparently dead drunk, wired with an FM transmitter, and in a position to see everything that went on. Since most of the dealers were known, and most of the hypes were unmistakable, the spotter's job was to identify the actual moment when the 'shooter' passed a cap or two of heroin to a hype. When he was sure ... he called out to the teams waiting at various points around the surrounding blocks. All of the teams were in radio contact on a special tactical channel ... The spotter inside was a man they referred to as Finn. It's unlikely that Finn was his real name ... [A drug squad officer explains further:] 'When we walked you through the room, did you notice a table near the door? Three guys sitting at it? ... Each of those guys is a fink, an informer. We pay each of them fifty, a hundred, five hundred bucks for information about drug dealing in Vancouver. Each one of those guys is a hype ... The thing is, not one of those guys has any idea that the other two are finks. When I walked by, each of them was hiding his face from the other two and giving me a negative signal, no dealing yet.' (Stroud 1983, 149)

Spies are not only used as informers, but also as *agents provocateurs*, enticing or cajoling people into crimes for which they are then prosecuted. Obviously this is a distasteful procedure, one that most Canadians would not find acceptable except under the most extraordinary conditions. Canadian law permits the use of *agents provocateurs*, yet they are rarely used outside of drug enforcement (see Stober 1985). In a recent case Victor Amato, a Vancouver hairdresser, was convicted of trafficking in cocaine. Apparently the police were using pressure on Mr Amato to try to develop a case against a former girl-friend whom they believed to be a genuine trafficker. Prior to this case, Mr Amato had been neither a dealer nor a user of cocaine and it required three months of coaxing to get him to deliver cocaine to a police informer. Ultimately, he was told by an undercover police constable that 'drug dealers with guns would be coming down to see him if he failed to deliver $2\frac{1}{2}$ ounces of cocaine to the friend of a hairdressing client' (Boyd 1983, 1). He arranged a sale, for which he received no money or other compensation himself. Five months after the sale he was arrested and charged. Although the Amato case received widespread publicity, the conviction was eventually upheld by the Supreme Court of Canada in a split decision (Boyd 1983; *Amato v. R.* 1982).

The Supreme Court ruled that the existence of a police scheme to provoke a crime can only be used as a defence against conviction in Canada 'if the scheme so perpetrated is so shocking and outrageous as to bring the administration of justice into disrepute' (*Amato v. R.* 1982, 232). This decision explicity puts the identification of unacceptable police conduct in the lap of public opinion. Under normal conditions, this is probably good protection against overzealous policing. However, it is little protection where public opinion is inflamed, as in the case of the War on Drugs. Cases since 1982 suggest that the public considers almost nothing shocking and outrageous where the enforcement of drug law is concerned. The use of *agents provocateurs* has continued to be standard police practice and the 'entrapment defence' is seldom even attempted by defence lawyers, because the possibility of success seems so slight. The present latitude for *agents provocateurs* can be illustrated by a case in which the entrapment defence was rejected and the accused was convicted (*R. v. Coupal* 1987). The uncontested facts of the case, as given in the judge's written reasons for judgment at the pre-trial hearing, are that a Mrs Bloome was charged with possession of stolen goods and cocaine in late 1983. After charges were laid, 'she approached the police and asked if they would drop them if she were to help them obtain evidence against a drug dealer ... She contacted Sergeant Simpson ... He warned her of the risks involved and told her to contact him again if she could arrange a sale. Sergeant Simpson said he could give no guarantees concerning the charges that were outstanding, but if a successful sale were arranged he would advise the lawyer prosecuting the charges she faced' (Hutchinson 1985, 4).

In January 1984, Mrs Bloome contacted a Gary Coupal, formerly her daughter's boy-friend, and, according to the judge,

> told him she was ill with cancer and she needed to get some cocaine. She was running out of supplies. She asked him to find some for her and he refused. He said she called him frequently and left messages for him to call back when he was not in. These telephone calls increased in frequency. At first, the accused refused to help her, but then he agreed to keep an eye out for her. He said these telephone calls and attempts to contact him increased even further and in April she was calling several times a week. On the 16th of April she called him up, suggesting he help her, not by buying cocaine, but to stand as a bodyguard during a transaction ... He agreed in order, in his words, 'to get her off his back' ... At some stage in the discussions with Mrs Bloome, she said he would get $700 out of it. At first, he refused but then she pleaded that she was dying and needed money for doctors' bills, so finally he agreed.' (Hutchinson 1985, 2)

Two days later, following Mrs Bloome's instructions, Mr Coupal met a man at Pay-and-Save in Richmond, BC, picked up a package of cocaine, hid it, took a sample to Mrs Bloome, went to the River Inn with the cocaine, and was introduced to a supposed buyer of cocaine who was actually a police constable. On Mrs Bloome's instructions, Mr Coupal represented himself as a dealer, sold the cocaine, and was arrested. Mrs Bloome was not paid by the police, but the charges against her were stayed and the allegedly stolen property that had been taken from her home, worth $61,000, was returned to her (Hutchinson 1985).

At trial it was revealed that Mr Coupal had no criminal record. Moreover, he maintained, apparently without contradiction from the prosecution, that he was neither a dealer nor a user of cocaine prior to the incident for which he was accused. His defence was that he was a victim of entrapment and that he was denied a fair trial because Mrs Bloome did not appear in court. The police maintained that she had left the province because 'someone placed a bomb in her car.' The police claimed they did not have a forwarding address for her but they did have a telephone number at which she received messages. The police had asked her to come for the trial but she refused and they had not subpoenaed her, traced her phone number, or made any effort to locate her until one week before the trial (Hutchinson 1985).

There are many points at which the veracity of both the accused and the police witness be might challenged in this case. However, these facts, *as presented here*, were taken by Judge Hutchinson as indicating that the police were behaving within acceptable limits and that the matter could proceed to trial. At trial, Mr Coupal was convicted of trafficking and sentenced to six months in prison on 14 February 1985. Obviously, in the eyes of the trial judge, the conduct of this affair was not 'shocking and outrageous.' The BC Appeals Court that upheld the conviction did not seriously consider the issue of whether Mrs Bloome's behaviour was 'shocking and outrageous.' Instead, they dissociated her actions from the police, as follows: 'The police authorities were merely passive recipients of the offer of the informant to provide evidence of trafficking in cocaine. Throughout she was acting in her own interests and not at the behest of or under the control of the police' (*R. v. Coupal* 1987, 32).

Can Canadian police escape the responsibility for illegal actions undertaken by criminals acting as their agents? Can Canadian police use illegal actions to lure people into crimes and then prosecute them? Apparently so, when drugs are involved. It seems to me that such practices would not be tolerated in this country under any circumstances except as part of the War on Drugs.

A historic 1986 court decision stayed proceedings in a trafficking trial when the violations of normal reason seemed too extreme for the trial judge. This was the first successful use of the 'entrapment defence' in Canada (*Vancouver Sun* 1986a; Hogarth 1986). However, the success was short-lived. In this case, the trial judge heard evidence that Frederick Gudbrandson was pressured by police agents over a long period into eventually selling an ounce of cocaine. The pressure came from an *agent provocateur* named Walker with a lengthy criminal record. Walker, in the trial judge's words, used 'continuous telephoning day and night' and 'nefarious means of persuasion' on Gudbrandson. A lesser amount of pressure was applied by a policeman, posing as a 'biker,' who eventually bought the cocaine from Gudbrandson. Five witnesses, including Gudbrandson's wife, testified that they had known Gudbrandson for many years and knew him to be of good character and not a narcotics dealer. Gudbrandson testified that he was an employed commercial fish-buyer, financially solvent, married with two children. He claimed that he only agreed to deliver the cocaine from a seller that was pre-aranged by Walker to the policeman in order to get the policeman 'off his back' (Hogarth 1986). The Crown subsequently charged Gudbrandson with perjury, but later dropped the perjury charge.

The judge appeared to be particularly incensed because the police turned a blind eye to the fact that Walker was busily selling drugs to 'young children and adolescents who frequented an arcade in one of the Richmond shopping centres,' while using him to entrap a person with no criminal record who, in the judge's words, 'was not, nor was ... likely to be a person who trafficked in drugs' (Hogarth 1986, 28). Moreover, the judge found that the police falsely claimed not to be able to locate Walker at a time when he was still in their employ, even though he was an essential witness for Gudbrandson's defence. Indeed, it is very hard to see why the cause of justice would not have been better served simply by prosecuting Walker, rather than allowing him to proceed with his trafficking while paying him $50 per day and an additional $10,000 at the conclusion of the Gudbrandson affair.

Such puzzling actions are regarded as normal in drug cases, according to the Crown attorney. The Crown defended the police action on several grounds, including that the use of 'shabby people' to contact criminals is common in drug cases, that Walker engaged in 'scandalous behaviour' only when not under the control of the RCMP, and that his behaviour was therefore irrelevant to the Gudbrandson case (testimony given before the Court of Appeal, 18 June 1987). The court eventually accepted this argument and overturned the stay, endorsing the Crown's contention that the police conduct was *not* 'a clear case of unfair and highly questionable conduct that under the circumstances is oppressive and thus an abuse of process' (*R. v. Gudbrandson* 1987). Gudbrandson subsequently stood trial and was convicted.

Why would the police use obviously guilty people to entrap and convict people who might not otherwise commit a crime and who, in some cases, appear innocent of criminal intent? When narcotics officers are asked this question, they reply that the accused in these cases really are major criminals, but that there was no evidence to convict them without the use of entrapment. This seems a strange logic to me. The legal system is designed precisely to protect people from punishment when there is no evidence to prove them guilty of a crime. I believe that police entrapment could only seem logical within a war mentality, which, for example, justifies incarcerating suspected enemies, such as Japanese Canadians, on evidence that would be inadequate in peacetime.

CASUALTIES OF THE WAR ON DRUGS

*Recreational Drug Users*

The people who are most threatened by Canada's drug laws are not narcotic addicts, traffickers, or international criminals, but rather ordinary people who use illegal drugs recreationally. In 1987, 67 per cent of all drug offences were for simple possession. Possession comprised 45 per cent of all cocaine offences, 40 per cent of all heroin offences, and 72 per cent of all marijuana offences.

In spite of the long list of drugs banned under the Narcotics Control Act, the great majority of convictions have been for marijuana. Of the 329,000 convictions in Canada between 1977 and 1985, almost 93 per cent were for cannabis offences (Solomon 1988a, 119). By 1987, however, Statistics Canada (1988) reported that the size of the marijuana majority had shrunk to 69.9 per cent. Marijuana offenders often receive conditional or absolute discharges or suspended sentences, but in 1984, of 20,203 people convicted of simple possession of marijuana, 13,492 were fined and 1644 went to jail. Thirty-eight received jail sentences greater than one year, including five indefinite sentences and two life sentences (Bureau of Dangerous Drugs 1984, 138–40). Curiously, the government seems reluctant to publish criminal statistics on marijuana. A Bureau of Dangerous Drugs publication (1986, i) announced without explanation that 'convictions for cannabis are no longer maintained nor included in the 1986 publication of legal statistics.'

*Police as Casualties*

Along with recreational drug users, the police themselves are among the casualties of the War on Drugs (Trebach 1987). In their vain struggle to enforce futile laws, drug police, especially 'undercover' agents, are required to lie, deceive, and brutalize. These job requirements could hardly foster good character development. In fact, these conditions regularly lead to corruption (Skolnik 1984) and despair (Girodo 1984). Girodo has studied the effect of undercover work on Canadian police officers. Many officers suffer depression, alienation from friends and family, conflict of loyalty, and even conversion to the values of the drug users. In the most serious cases these problems have led to criminal misconduct, insanity, and self-mutilation.

Within the mentality of the War on Drugs, this harm to police officers appears to be one of the inevitable costs of a heroic struggle against evil. Drug police are portrayed in popular fiction as gloriously doomed heroes, much as were fighter pilots in the First World War (for instance, Fowler 1930). Wars are not conducted with the health of the combatants as a priority, and the drug police seem to be expendable in the War on Drugs.

*Medical Patients*

Many patients with cancer, glaucoma, and other serious diseases are drug-war casualties. These people have been denied relief from their cruel sufferings because drugs like heroin and marijuana have been banned from medical practice. These unfortunates reveal the loss of compassion that characterizes the war mentality. Only in war is it conceivable to let the innocent literally die in agony or go blind when relief is available. Yet heroin was kept from cancer patients and from all medical uses in Canada from 1955 to 1985 on the grounds that the ban would control illicit use (Appleby 1985; Ghent 1986). This ban persisted for thirty years in spite of substantial indications in the medical literature that some cancer patients can only be given relief from their excruciating pain by heroin (Trebach 1982; Ghent 1986). Of greater importance than banning heroin, Canadian medicine adopted the practice of meagrely rationing doses of morphine and other opiate drugs to cancer patients on the grounds of avoiding addiction. The resulting suffering was pointless because street use of opiates continued. Even recently, it has been estimated that 25 per cent of all cancer patients in Canada still die without adequate pain relief (Health and Welfare Canada 1984, 5).

I feel the following description captures the tragedy of this situation. Stuart Alsop wrote a weekly column in *Newsweek* until he died of cancer

in 1974. As he was dying he continued his column from the hospital.
From there, he sent the following description of his room-mate:

[Jack] had a melanoma in his belly, a malignant solid tumor that the doctors
guessed was about the size of a softball. The cancer had started a few
months before with a small tumor in his left shoulder, and there had been
several operations since. The doctors planned to remove the softball-sized
tumor, but they knew Jack would soon die. The cancer had metastasized – it
had spread beyond control. Jack was good-looking, about 28, and brave.
He was in constant pain, and his doctor had prescribed an intravenous shot of
a synthetic opiate – a pain-killer, or analgesic – every four hours. His wife
spent many of the daylight hours with him, and she would sit or lie on his
bed and pat him all over, as one pats a child, only more methodically, and
this seemed to help control the pain. But at night, when his pretty wife had
left (wives cannot stay overnight at the NIH clinic) and darkness fell, the
pain would attack without pity.

At the prescribed hour a nurse would give Jack a shot of the synthetic
analgesic, and this would control the pain for perhaps two hours or a bit
more. Then he would begin to moan, or whimper, very low, as though he
didn't want to wake me. Then he would begin to howl, like a dog. When
this happened, either he or I would ring for a nurse, and ask for a painkiller.
She would give him some codeine or the like by mouth, but it never did
any real good ... it affected him no more than half an aspirin might affect a
man who had just broken his arm. Always the nurse would explain as
encouragingly as she could that there was not long to go before the intravenous shot – 'Only about 50 more minutes now.' And always poor Jack's
whimpers and howls would become more loud and frequent until at last
blessed relief came. On the third night of this scenario the terrible thought
emerged: 'If Jack were a dog – what would be done with him?' The
answer was obvious: the pound, and chloroform. No human being with a
spark of pity could let a living thing suffer so, to no good end. (Alsop
1974)

Recent publicity may ameliorate this problem. Some current articles in
Canadian and American medical journals urge doctors to prescribe
adequate doses of opiate drugs to manage pain in cancer patients (Tuttle
1985; Hill 1987). However, recent newspaper reports suggest that many

doctors and hospitals are not even experimenting with heroin in the management of serious pain, even though it has been legal to do so since 1985 (Gifford-Jones 1987). Beyond the issue of heroin, I have personally met people in recent years whose doctors, out of fear or ignorance, will not prescribe the conventional pain relievers they need to manage severe, intractable pain. They speak bitterly of being suspected of addiction by their doctors and even their own families. A recent series of articles in the Canadian Medical Association *Journal* cautions doctors sternly against overprescribing, without mentioning the converse problem of becoming so rigid in their prescribing that they sentence people to needless agony (Goldman 1987, 1987a, 1987b).

*Children*

A final set of casualties in the War on Drugs is the young people whose serious problems are ignored by a society that simplistically blames drugs instead of real causes. A recent newspaper article illustrates the problem. It appeared under the headline 'Students Drop Out to Party' (McIntyre 1988):

> Students would rather get high than get to class. And that's why they're dropping out and flunking out in record numbers, according to B.C.'s top education expert.
>
> Lawyer Barry Sullivan, head of a royal commission on education, said high school drug abuse is to blame for the alarming numbers of dropouts.
>
> The Ministry of Education's annual report released last week shows nearly three out of every 10 students failed to graduate in 1986 – compared with two in 10 in 1980 ...
>
> 'All one has to look at is the alcohol and drug problem – that wasn't there seven or 10 years ago – that the secondary system has to cope with,' said Sullivan, who's held 16 public hearings since last October.

In the same article a teacher is described as protesting that the drop-out rate has more complex causes. However, those who listen to the province's 'top education expert' need not concern themselves with quibblers in the education system and the larger society, for the culprit is simply drugs. People are thereby encouraged by the highest authority to overlook the terribly difficult problems that confront students in a complex and sometimes inhospitable world, and children become another set of casualties in the War on Drugs.

## Conclusion

Much of what society currently does to control drug use can reasonably be described as a War on Drugs, carried out by governments with strong public approval. Warlike aspects of current drug-control policy and practice include the following: massive application of military and civil force; consistent use of war language by drug-policy officials; imposition of compulsory treatment on drug users who have not been convicted of crimes; promulgation of wildly exaggerated anti-drug propaganda; imposition of harsh criminal penalties, including death, that are normally reserved for murder and treason; abrogation of normal protection for civil rights (as under martial law); public and official support for people who inform on members of their own families; support for violence, including torture, in the Third World; use of economic levers against the Third World that will cause the starvation of large numbers of people; widespread use of spies and *agents provocateurs* by enforcement agencies; imposition of suffering not only on drug traffickers and users, but also on police and medical patients.

In addition to the use of war measures as means of enforcing drug policy, there is an interweaving of the drug war and international political conflict. There is a close relationship between escalations of anti-drug measures and outbreaks of public fear of political enemies. Moreover, governments appear to use public revulsion towards drugs as a way of inflaming antagonism towards international foes and justifying violent action.

Although the War on Drugs makes use of the methods, language, and mentality of regular, military wars, it differs in some obvious ways from the First and Second World war, the prototypical wars of this century. Instead, it fits the pattern of wars of persecution. Drug users and distributors are currently treated in much the same way as heretics during the Inquisition, the dispossessed English poor during the eighteenth century, and political dissidents in the unstable countries of the Third World. In each case, the miscreants seem to stand for real evils that threaten society, which allays its fears symbolically by organized persecution.

The object of this chapter has not been so much to claim that current drug policy is wrong, as to show that it is correctly labelled as a war. Wars, even wars of persecution, may sometimes be the only way to achieve essential ends. However, the remainder of this book is intended to show that this argument cannot be made for the War on Drugs. The next chapter will demonstrate that this war has curtailed neither drug use nor social problems associated with drugs. Subsequent chapters will show that the underlying justifications, which might make even a futile drug war seem necessary, are invalid. Chapter 9 will show that good policy alternatives to the drug war are available, and the final chapter will return to the question of why there is a War on Drugs at all.

# 2  The faces of failure: Three aspects of the War on Drugs

In spite of the War on Drugs, large numbers of people use prohibited drugs and social problems associated with drugs dominate the news. Family breakdown and physical abuse, the problems that have been most directly linked to drugs since the early temperance movement (Aaron and Musto 1981, 142–4), are the bane of life in current North American society. This chapter is intended to show that the War on Drugs has failed and, in the process, worsened the problems it was supposed to solve. Although the drug war has many aspects, summarized at the end of chapter 1, only three can be explored within the confines of this chapter. These are prohibition, propaganda, and treatment.

## Prohibition

### THE FAILURE OF DRUG PROHIBITION

Drug prohibition is the attempt to prevent drug use by force. This section of the chapter will provide examples of the failure of drug prohibition in Canada and elsewhere.

### Marijuana

Virtually the entire spread of marijauna use in Canada occurred *after* it was prohibited and its use subjected to the harshest penalties.

Canadians first became aware of marijuana through second-hand American propaganda. Emily Murphy made it clear in *The Black Candle* (1922) that most of her wisdom about marijuana was imported from the

United States. For example: 'Charles A. Jones, the Chief of Police for [Los Angeles] ... says ... "The [marijuana] addict loses all sense of moral responsibility. Addicts to this drug, while under its influence are immune to pain ... While in this condition they become raving maniacs and are liable to kill or indulge in any form of violence to other persons using the most savage methods of cruelty without ... any sense of moral responsibility"' (Murphy 1922, 332-3). At the time of these dire warnings, almost no marijuana was being used in Canada, and little was used for years afterwards. None the less, it was banned in 1923. Illicit use of marijuana was first officially discovered in Canada in 1931, *eight years after it had been prohibited* (Abel 1980, 233). In spite of vigorous enforcement of the anti-marijuana law, there were only twenty-five convictions in all of Canada between 1930 and 1946 (Green and Miller 1975).

In 1961, marijuana was included in the new Narcotic Control Act, making users and traffickers subject to the same severe penalties and harsh enforcement procedures as users of heroin. Although this act is among the harshest drug-prohibition laws in the Western world (Le Dain 1973, 89; Smart 1983, 158), marijuana use became commonplace in Canada after its enactment. An RCMP report stated that 'prior to 1962, isolated cases of cannabis use were encountered, but generally in connection with entertainers and visitors from the United States. Although marijuana arrests were effected sporadically in the middle 40s, its use on a more frequent basis appeared in Montreal only in 1962, in Toronto in 1963, and in Vancouver in 1965' (cited by Green and Miller 1975, 498-9). After reaching a peak early in the 1980s, cannabis use is now declining somewhat.

The best way to evaluate marijuana prohibition laws would be to repeal them experimentally to see if marijuana use increased. This experiment has not been tried in Canada, but marijuana 'decriminalization' has occurred in several American states and de facto legalization has occurred in the Netherlands, with no measurable increase in marijuana use (Kaplan 1983; Engelsman 1987; Ruter 1987; van de Wijngaart and Vendelbosch 1987; Zeese 1987). Kaplan sums up the American experience thus: 'In recent years eleven [U.S. states] have removed their criminalization of small scale possession and use. Several studies ... [have] concluded that repeal has no discernible effect on the number of users or on their frequency of use' (Kaplan 1983, 198).

The Dutch experience is that use of marijuana has declined steadily since its de facto legalization in much of the country in the 1970s and is now much lower than that of Canada, the United States, West Germany, and England, all of which have punitive marijuana laws (Holthuis 1987; Ruter 1987; Trebach 1987, 105; van de Wijngaart and Vendelbosch 1987; Cohen 1988). For example, in 1976, 10 per cent of Dutch youth reported having used marijuana at least once in their lives; in 1983, 6 per cent reported having done so. By contrast, in 1977, 25 per cent of Ontario students in grades 7–13 reported using cannabis at least once in the previous year; in 1983, 24 per cent reported having done so (Smart and Adlaf 1987, 12). Even in Amsterdam, where cannabis products are freely available and advertised by the coffee shops that sell them, most people do not use cannabis. A 1988 survey of the Amsterdam population over twelve years of age found that only 9.3 per cent of the respondents had used cannabis in the year of the interview and only 5.5 per cent has used it in the month of the interview (Sandwijk, Westerterp, and Musterd 1988, cited by Cohen 1988). By contrast, a survey in 1981 in Toronto found that 13.4 per cent of the adult population had used cannabis during the previous year (Smart 1983, 36). Although there are no precisely controlled international comparisons of marijuana use, the available data provide no evidence that marijauna prohibition reduces consumption.

I do not mean these data to imply that anti-marijuana laws increase marijauna use. It would seem, rather, that the spread of marijauna that began in the 1960s was part of a shift in attitudes and preferences throughout the Western world. Drug prohibition was impotent in preventing the spread of marijuana then, and has no measurable deterrent effect now. By contrast, the costs of marijuana law enforcement, in both money and the suffering that it causes, are large and easily assessed. In Canada these costs can be measured in the millions of dollars and thousands of people in jail.

## Amphetamines and Cocaine

The history of amphetamine prohibition in Canada illustrates another form of failure. Amphetamine prescribing was severely restricted under Canada's Food and Drug Act in 1973. Its importation dropped from 789 kg in 1971 and 1972 to 3 kg in 1973 and 1974 and the proportion of 'speed' users in Toronto schools was halved between 1970 and 1974, as approvingly reported by Smart (1983, 137–8). However, cocaine use quickly rose to fill the vacuum. **Although it is little known to the general public, cocaine and the amphetamines are virtually interchangeable drugs. Under some conditions, even experienced users cannot tell them apart** (Van Dyke and Byck 1982; *PM,* chap. 5). Cocaine convictions rose from 19 in 1971 to 237 in 1974 and the number of known cocaine users increased fifteenfold in the same period (Smart 1983, 84). Canada's compulsive amphetamine users had apparently switched to cocaine. Cocaine use increased steadily throughout the 1970s. Prohibition's success is spurious when it merely drives users from one prohibited drug to another.

*Opium*

The opium laws of the early twentieth century apparently curtailed the massive consumption of opium by Chinese immigrant workers in Canada (Smart 1983). However, I cannot see how, on balance, this constitutes a success for prohibition. Prior to the opium prohibition, the Chinese had been among the hardest workers and the best-behaved citizens of the raucous frontier. Their communities were generally law-abiding and they adopted the customs of their adopted country willingly (Morton 1974). The great majority of Chinese opium-smokers were not criminals or layabouts, but rather working men who used their drug to forget the cares of the day, in the same way that white workers used their whisky – except that whisky-drinking was closely associated with violence and opium-smoking was not. There is little justification for counting drug prohibition a success when the drug in question was not a problem and when the prohibition grew out of racial prejudice and increased the hardships of a powerless minority.

Although there were no clear benefits of opium prohibition, the harm it caused was easily visible. Legal supplies were replaced by a black market that soon shifted to distributing heroin, which is less bulky than opium and therefore easier to smuggle. The black market created a world of criminality surrounding opiate drugs that was unknown before opium prohibition. It is likely, although I have found no direct evidence, that cutting off the opium supply for Chinese immigrants turned many of them to Western drug habits, particularly alcohol and tobacco. **These legal drugs cause more physical harm and may well lead more predictably to addiction than does smoking opium** (Ostrowski 1989; *PM*, chap. 4).

*Drug Prohibition outside Canada*

It is easy to multiply examples of failed drug prohibitions outside of Canada. Prohibition of opium in many lands has led directly to the importation of heroin, corruption of officials, and destitution of users. This trend has been documented in the United States, the Netherlands, and Laos (Brecher 1972; Westermeyer 1982; Kooyman 1983). In past centuries, coffee was unsuccessfully prohibited in Islamic countries and punished by fines, beating, and other cruel corporal punishments (Brecher 1972). Tobacco use has been, in various places, punished by whipping, slitting the nostrils, imprisonment, and death, but it has never been eliminated in any country (Brecher 1972, 212–13). Opiate use has been punished in present-day Iran and Malaysia by all the weapons of state terror, including hundreds of executions, with no success (Trebach 1983, 1989).

American alcohol prohibition provides the most famous example of failure. The costs of alcohol prohibition clearly came to exceed the benefits for the American electorate that swept it in enthusiastically after the First World War, but rejected it with a similar enthusiasm thirteen years later.

During the period of alcohol prohibition, there was a measurable reduction of cirrhosis of the liver in the United States (u.s. Bureau of the Census 1975, 58) and relief from alcoholic problems in some families (Aaron and Musto 1981, 165). These changes are sometimes used to argue that prohibition was a success in spite of the judgment of the electorate, but this argument is too simple. Correlation does not prove causation: many factors other than prohibition can account for the changing patterns of American life after the First World War (Cashman 1981, 251–8). Moreover, prohibition coincided with many undesirable changes in addition to desirable ones. The American homicide rate jumped above pre-prohibition levels in 1921 and rose gradually during the remainder of prohibition. It peaked in 1933, the final year of prohibition, at 9.7 murders per 100,000 population, a rate it had not reached before in the twentieth century. It began a steady decline in 1934 and did not reach 9.7 again until another peak in the 1970s (U.S. Bureau of the Census 1975, 414). Even in the violent 1980s the rate is lower than the prohibition peak, 8.3 in 1985 (U.S. Bureau of the Census 1988, 77). Suicide showed a similar pattern, dropping in the first year of prohibition, but climbing steadily through the 1920s to a record high for the twentieth century in 1932, and falling off after prohibition (U.S. Bureau of the Census 1975, 414). Current levels are well below the prohibition high (U.S. Bureau of the Census 1988). Prohibition also coincided with the first major upswing in American marijuana use (Brecher 1972, 410–12).

All indications are that the current American prohibition of cocaine has also failed. The International Narcotics Control Board reports that coca production is increasing in Bolivia, steady in Peru, and appears to be spreading in other South American countries (Arnao 1988). American per-capita consumption in 1980 was about double that of 1906 when cocaine was cheap, fashionable, and legal in the United States (Wisotsky 1983, 1382). The wholesale price of cocaine dropped 80 per cent in the 1980s, while the concentration of the drug increased from about 12 per cent to about 60 per cent (Nadelmann 1989). Meanwhile, the cocaine wars have devastated the civility of American life.

In sum, there is no evidence that drug use is substantially deterred by drug prohibition inside or outside of Canada. Arnold Trebach puts the conclusion this way: 'A sober assessment of the history of drug abuse control would fail to find one instance where a western democratic country has achieved a major, long term reduction in illicit drug trafficking or use through direct, rationally planned government intervention. If there is one such instance, wherein the reduction lasted for any significant length of time, I have not been able to discover it after over a decade of assiduous search of the available historical record' (Trebach 1984, 126–7).

WHY DRUG PROHIBITION FAILS

There are several reasons why drug prohibition fails. One lies in the nature of the groups of people the laws are meant to control. At the bottom of the social ladder, homeless juveniles haunt the downtown cores of major cities in Canada. Many have grim histories of physical and sexual abuse. On the street, they know disdain, untreated illness, violence, and hunger. They support themselves through petty crime and degrading forms of prostitution. Their depression and self-hate runs very deep. Drugs that can blur this reality are precious to them (James and McConville 1986). When prohibition interdicts cocaine or heroin, street children use alcohol, glue, or other solvents to obscure their awareness. For similar reasons, drug prohibition cannot affect drug producers in the Third World. 'Narcodollars' are the only hope for millions of people to escape malnutrition and to taste the wealth they see in their dreams. Naturally, they ignore prohibition laws (Nadelmann 1987, 192–4). In the affluent middle class there are equally desperate people who rely on illegal drugs to keep going in the face of overwhelming depression, despair, and boredom.

The failure of drug prohibition is just as inevitable among people who are not desperate at all, the socially integrated, recreational users. **For many such people, using drugs is pleasant and, with reasonable precautions, a relatively safe recreation** (*PM*, chaps 3, 4, 5). They cannot respect laws that punish people severely for no identifiable purpose.

In between these extreme groups there is a large middle group that is not inclined to use drugs at all. If they do use drugs occasionally, they are not likely to use them in a harmful way. Therefore prohibition laws cannot prevent any large amount of dangerous drug use in this middle group either.

Present drug laws must also fail because they are increasingly formulated on an international rather than a local level. It is conceivable for a community to evolve and enforce drug laws that it finds reasonable, as when an Indian reserve decides to ban alcohol because of local problems, or when the Netherlands decides to prohibit the use of 'hard' drugs in clubs and coffee shops but allows cannabis to be sold. Such laws grow from shared needs and experiences and can be respected. But, international treaties like the United Nations conventions on psychotropic substances require world-wide prohibition of a large number of drugs. Many strongly traditional societies have used some of these drugs for centuries, including cannabis, opium, and coca leaves. Even when internationally generated prohibitions do not violate a specific local custom, they still do not grow from the needs of any particular locality. Therefore, they generate little support, except for that which can be created by incessant propaganda and economic pressure (Nadelmann 1987, 192–4).

Beyond lack of popular support, there are purely technical problems associated with drug laws. Drug crimes require minimal resources to commit, are easily concealable, and generally produce satisfied customers. They are therefore highly resistant to governments' repressive efforts (Packer 1968; Nadelmann 1987, 25). Drug-bearing crops have presented a relatively conspicuous target in the past, but new manufacturing techniques make it easy and cheap to produce synthetics if organic sources should ever be substantially reduced (Blackwell 1988).

There is also a political element that erodes support for prohibition on an international level. The prime mover in international drug prohibition is the United States, but it has been consistently unwilling to attack drug traffickers whose profits support anti-Communist activities. It has turned a blind eye to drug trafficking when the profits supported anti-Castro Cuban expatriates, anti-Communist tribesmen in Afghanistan, and anti-Sandinista groups in Nicaragua (Blackwell 1988).

DEFENCES OF DRUG PROHIBITION

In spite of its history of failure, drug prohibition has been defended by well-informed scholars (see Gray 1972, 1982; Jones and Jones 1977; Kaplan 1983; Smart 1983; DuPont 1984; Gold 1984; Inciardi 1986). However, their defences are unimpressive. Most important, defences of drug prohibition almost invariably make the assumption that 'legalization,' meaning unrestricted access to drugs, is the only alternative to prohibition. More realistic alternatives than wholesale 'legalization' will be discussed in chapter 9.

To hold this discussion within reasonable limits, I have summarized below the key arguments that have been used to defend the prohibition of heroin and other opiate drugs. If a valid argument could be made for legally prohibiting any drug, surely it would be heroin, which has been regarded as the premier pharmacological evil for most of the twentieth century. The classic arguments for continued prohibition of opiate drugs are as follows:

1. There would be more addiction and criminality if opiates were legal (for example Inciardi 1986, 85–6). This familiar argument overlooks two historical facts. First, opiates, including heroin, were legal throughout much of the world until the early twentieth century and there was no greater opiate problem at that time than there is now (Brecher 1972). As

chapter 1 showed, opiates were prohibited for complex political reasons, not for protection against a rising tide of addiction (Brecher 1972; Musto 1973, esp. 244; Berridge and Edwards 1981; Boyd 1984). Second, the centuries of legally available opiate drugs were accompanied by far less drug-related crime, violence, and corruption than is the era of the War on Drugs. The present spate of drug crime is largely caused by prohibition laws that create the irresistible prospect of huge, easy profits (Brecher 1972; Ostrowski 1989). **Defenders of prohibition persistently mistake the violent side-effects of prohibition for the effects of the drugs themselves** (Brecher 1972; Nadelmann 1987; Ostrowski 1989; *PM*, chap 4).

2. Although drug prohibition was not warranted at the time it was introduced, it has changed society so much that it cannot now be revoked. Prohibition has, for example, spawned an avaricious black market and a shift from the use of opium to injectable heroin (Kaplan 1983, 128–9). This argument is profoundly ironic – it claims society has become addicted to drug prohibition! Drug laws have indeed harmed society, but normal logic would dictate removing or altering the source of harm, as occurred when alcohol prohibition was recognized as a failure. Obviously present laws must be changed in a way that takes into account the existing black market and provides for a transition period.

3. Removal of prohibition would imply government approval of addiction. This argument fairly tramples on normal logic. The legality of a substance never implies government approval of using it destructively. For example, whereas the government allows automobiles and bleach, it obviously does not condone reckless driving, or using bleach as an eyewash. It is most logical to replace prohibition laws with regulations that control distribution and limit it to the safest forms of drugs, as is the case with other dangerous products. Cautious marketing of this sort should convey a clear impression that the products involved must be used with care.

4. Canada cannot relax its prohibition laws because the addicts of the world would flood into the country. This fear of a junkie invasion contradicts history. In the 1960s, heroin was prescribed legally and inexpensively to opiate addicts in London, and a Canadian passport conferred the right to settle in Great Britain. However, very few Canadian addicts actually emigrated. In fact, the total between 1959 and 1969 was ninety-one people (Spear and Glatt 1971; Zacune 1971), of whom thirty-

five left Great Britain and presumably returned to Canada when they discovered the stresses of life abroad. In Amsterdam, where laws against buying and selling heroin in small amounts are no longer being enforced (effectively de-criminalizing heroin), there has been no overwhelming influx of foreign junkies (van de Wijngaart 1985).

5. The most powerful argument for continuing opiate prohibition comes from a more personal testimony. Many people have told me that they have themselves been prevented from using a particular drug by the prohibition laws. Therefore they favour drug prohibition because they feel personally protected by it. I do not doubt the truth of such testimony, but it is perplexing in light of the strong objective evidence, reviewed above, that prohibition does not work. How can this contradiction be explained?

I believe the contradiction dissolves when War on Drugs propaganda is considered. This propaganda consistently depicts drug users as having access to forbidden fruit that is dangerous but irresistibly pleasurable. This theme is illustrated, for example, in the titles of books like *It's So Good Don't Even Try It Once* (Smith and Gay 1972) and *Sensual Drugs* (Jones and Jones 1977). Naturally, such exaggerations create an impulse to try illicit drugs, an expectation that addiction and degradation would inevitably follow, and a feeling of gratitude for laws that prevent this outcome.

Thus, the personal argument for prohibition seems to me a product of decades of exposure to propaganda. **But the propaganda message is false. People who were accurately informed about the effects of illicit drugs would feel no need to be protected against irresistible pleasure-seeking impulses by drug prohibition. In the case of heroin, for example, most people do not find its use even mildly enjoyable and the overwhelming majority of people who use it do not become addicted. The facts about heroin and cocaine will be considered at length in later chapters** (*PM*, chaps 4, 5).

Prohibiton is only one face of the War on Drugs. The next two sections consider the failure of propaganda and bureaucratized treatment.

## Propaganda

Wartime propaganda differs from the normal ways in which people inform each other. It is extraordinarily simple, repetitive, and violent. It is designed to control, not to inform. In modern warfare, massive propaganda campaigns are directed both at the enemy and at compatriots. Public information about drugs has all the attributes of wartime propaganda. However, unlike wartime propaganda, drug propaganda consistently fails to achieve its objectives.

## THE NATURE OF DRUG PROPAGANDA

The popular media pump out sensational images, both pictorial and verbal, concerning drugs: Colombian drug lords, fortified 'crack houses,' RCMP activity in Pakistan, street junkies and prostitutes in Vancouver, dozens of new arrests in Montreal, a baseball mitt full of cocaine on the cover of *Maclean's*, mutilated bodies in Miami, children reporting their parents to the police, public floggings of traffickers in Pakistan, beautiful young women puncturing themselves with needles, strangled informers on the road in Peru, and so on. This flood of images makes it almost impossible not to be drawn, at least sometimes, into the War on Drugs mentality.

In the nineteenth century the stories featured alcohol, opium, and cocaine. In the twentieth century, the stories concentrated on heroin, cocaine, amphetamines, barbiturates, marijuana, glue, 'quaaludes,' 'angel dust,' 'designer drugs,' and, most recently, 'crack.' The horror stories and the images change very little, although the target drug changes from time to time. The new target drug is always represented as worse than the previous one.

A startling collection of lurid images from the American press over several decades has been published as a book (Silver and Aldrich 1979). This collection shows that the images associated with drugs in the past differ little from the images associated with the enemy by the propaganda of both sides in conventional wars (see Keen 1986). Current propaganda concentrates on horror stories about cocaine in the form of 'freebase,' 'crack,' and 'coca paste.' The following excerpts from a recent article in the *New York Times* (1989) verbally apply the familiar images to the newest menace:

> Crack poses a much greater threat than other drugs. It is reaching out to
> destroy the quality of life, and life itself, at all levels of American
> society.

Crack may be to the 80's and 90's what the great depression was to the 30's or the Vietnam War was to the 60's and 70's ... [Relative to heroin] crack is distributed by younger, wilder, more heavily armed gangs. They arrogantly intimidate whole communities and make war on each other to control the lucrative business. In community after community, crack violence has overwhelmed law enforcement ...

Meanwhile, urban emergency rooms report a surge of injuries – crushed bones, blasted organs, floods of internal bleeding – once known only on the battlefield. They are the gory aftermath of shootouts among drug gangs armed for war ...

Babies born to crack addicts tend to suffer low birthweight, brain damage and malformation. A recent report in The Times described such a child: 'a mere patch of flesh with a tangerine-sized head and limbs like splinters.' Intensive hospital care for *each* crack baby costs about $90,000. That translates to $190 million a year in New York. For the nation, the figure is 2.5 billion ... The Administration acts as though the American people fear taxes and big government more than drug gangs that are seizing control of their communities ... The crack invasion ... requires a national mobilization as if for war, headed by a President – not merely a sub-Cabinet czar. (A20)

These claims are terrifying. Yet they scarcely differ in substance from those that have characterized the War on Drugs for over a century. They should be compared to the claims already presented: about alcohol as the cause of virtually all crime in 1832 by the New York State Temperance Society; about cocaine and heroin as a German weapon by the *New York Times* in 1918; about opium as a tool for conquering the world and marijuana as the source of murder by Emily Murphy in 1922; and about heroin users as an invading army by Nelson Rockefeller throughout the 1960s. If the extravagant claims about crack have become questionable by the time this book is published, it is safe to predict that there will be a new devil-drug that will provide a fresh source of terror to justify the War on Drugs.

Of course, the information and images that support the War on Drugs are not understood as propaganda by the teachers, ministers, policemen, and journalists who disseminate them. Rather, the disseminators are taught to view such information as 'prevention campaigns,' 'drug education,' 'drug awareness programs,' and 'educating our society, in particular our youth, to establish a lifesyle without abusing mind altering substances' (Hauschildt 1988).

Ericson, Baranek, and Chan (1987) have shown that media in Canada and elsewhere normally create images of deviance as a way of identifying and dramatizing the norms that maintain order in society. The images of the War on Drugs are surely an instance of this normal process, but they are so exaggerated, violent, and threatening that they bear less resemblance to peace-time public information than to wartime propaganda.

Society does not speak entirely with one voice on this issue. Occasional newspaper items, books, and speakers challenge the dogma of the War on Drugs. But the major North American media follow the War on Drugs line relentlessly. Democratic regimes do not forcibly eliminate contrary views. Rather, contrary views are generally restricted to obscure publications by the economic and political sensitivities of the mass media. Technically, freedom of speech is retained but propaganda becomes none the less overwhelming because opposing views in obscure publications cannot compete with the barrage of orthodox sentiment (Herman and Chomsky 1988).

Chapters 3–9 of this book will show that although some of the current drug propaganda is true, much is unfounded, much is distorted, and a surprising portion is simply false. The net effect of this mixture is 'disinformation,' rather than information. For example, it is now well documented that widely publicized official estimates of heroin-related theft in New York City have been three or more times higher than the total amount stolen in that city by all offenders! (See Epstein 1977, 43–5; Kaplan 1983, 51–8.)

Blackwell (1987) has provided another example of wilful disinformation in anti-drug propaganda. She has summarized the efforts by American and Canadian authorities to deny the well-established fact that it is possible to use most illicit drugs safely. **A large body of careful research shows that recreational use of illicit drugs, including marijuana, cocaine, and heroin, does not lead to addiction or other harm for the majority of users** (*PM*, chaps 4, 5). Those who wish to convince the public otherwise sometimes acknowledge that valid scientific research stands in their way, as in the following statement by a former director of the American National Institute on Drug Abuse: 'The power of the chemical to pre-empt the brain's normal reward systems, normal behaviour patterns is enormous ... And that process begins with drug experimentation. Neither the drug user nor his family can control that process once it begins. Until we can get that life-saving message across, we are going to have a hard time with our prevention efforts. We are also going to continue to have a hard time with the scientists and many of their studies' (Robert DuPont, cited by Blackwell 1987).

As in wartime, propagandistic disinformation concerning drugs is accepted as normal or desirable. This attitude has been expressed, for example, by Reginald Smart, a leading Canadian drug authority. In connection with amphetamines, Smart has written: 'Most of the harmful effects of speed would not limit the lives of users in any significant way. Nonetheless, misleading as the phrase 'speed kills' seems to be, it may have had a very positive effect in discouraging young people from trying amphetamines in any form' (Smart 1983, 69). In the same book, Smart urges 'a clear need for anti-drug programs which suggest that drug use is in no way normal, interesting, or exciting' (Smart 1983, 179). This statement seems to me a call to misinform the public – **drug use is 'interesting' and/or 'exciting' to millions of users and is not only normal but very nearly universal, unless alcohol, nicotine, and caffeine are somehow not recognized as drugs** (Blum and Associates 1969; Weil 1972; Le Dain 1973) **and unless the experiences of typical users of illicit drugs like marijuana and cocaine are discounted** (Le Dain 1973; *PM*, chaps 3, 4, 5).

Propaganda successfully misinforms the public. At the beginning of my psychology course, I sometimes poll the students on their attitudes towards drug issues. One year I asked them to estimate the percentage of their fellow students who 'use each of the following drugs every day or almost every day.' This question was followed by a list of familiar drugs. Later in the semester, I asked the same students to report how many days they used each drug themselves in the last thirty days. On both occasions, the students were reminded of the importance of a careful, honest response, were assured of confidentiality, and were asked to simply leave the form blank if they did not wish to answer. As table 1 shows, the students drastically overestimated the use of drugs, particularly those that are most publicized in War on Drugs propaganda. Few students used heroin or cocaine at all, much less daily, but many incorrectly believed that daily use was rampant in those around them (Alexander 1985).

THE FAILURE OF DRUG-WAR PROPAGANDA

Drug-war propaganda may well increase demand for the very drugs it

TABLE 1
Estimated and self-reported frequencies of daily drug
use by university students in British Columbia

|  | Estimated (%) | Self-reported (%) |
| --- | --- | --- |
| Caffeine | 83.3 | 46.5 |
| Tobacco | 54.7 | 18.1 |
| Alcohol | 51.4 | 0.7 |
| Cannabis | 28.7 | 2.1 |
| Heroin | 6.3 | 0.0 |
| Cocaine | 12.3 | 0.0 |
| Tranquillizers | 17.0 | 0.0 |

condemns. This possibility is illustrated in the strange history of the campaign against glue-sniffing in the United States beginning in the 1960s, as reported by E.M. Brecher in his famous book *Licit and Illicit Drugs* (1972).

## The Great Glue Epidemic

In 1959 a few children in Tuscon, Arizona, and Pueblo, Colorado, were found to be sniffing glue for its intoxicating effects. Chronic glue-sniffing had long been known to social workers as the habit of a very small number of deeply troubled youths. In this case, the children were arrested. Reporters in Denver investigated and wrote a feature story in the Sunday newspaper magazine. Following a scare headline 'SOME GLUES ARE DANGEROUS: Heavy Inhalation Can Cause Anemia or Brain Damage' and a description of glue intoxication reminiscent of drunkenness, the story gave an explicit description of how to sniff glue: 'Police in Pueblo, Colorado and several other cities in the West and Midwest report that juveniles seeking a quick bang and a mild jag spread liquid glue on the palms of their hands, then cup their hands over their mouth and nose and inhale deeply' (cited by Brecher 1972, 321).

Following this article, Denver, which had only a few cases of glue sniffing prior to this time, reported fifty cases worthy of police investigation by June 1960. The response to the increased usage was simple – more propaganda! A police spokesman stated: 'This practice is extremely dangerous and a kid can die from it if he gets too much' (cited by Brecher, 1972, 322). The Denver *Post* in 1962 reported that glue-sniffing can cause stimulation, depression, and convulsions, and can affect the 'respiratory tract, mucous membranes, skin, liver, kidneys, heart and blood – depending on what type of glue is used' (cited by Brecher 1972, 323). The incidence of glue-sniffing rose even more dramatically after this report.

These dire, apparently authoritative medical warnings were entirely propagandistic, since there was *no* medical research on the effects of recreational glue-sniffing at the time, although there were reports of adverse effects from *eating* substantial amounts of glue or from continuous daily exposure to high concentrations in factories where solvents were used (Brecher 1972, 325). The existing facts were in no way sufficient to justify the terrifying propaganda.

Later research has not confirmed the dramatic claims of the anti-glue propaganda either. Research on this topic is quite complex, because there are many different kinds of solvent, because potentially toxic solvents cannot be administered experimentally to human beings, and because people who use solvents in large quantities invariably take other potentially harmful chemicals as well, and live generally unhealthy lives. Therefore, it is difficult to know what causes any symptoms that solvent users display. However, current indications are that toluene-based glues – the main kind that children in the 1960s would have been likely to sniff – are not particularly toxic. Some other solvents, particularly those delivered by aerosol sprays, may be quite dangerous, however (Herzberg and Wolkind 1983).

The glue-sniffing fad spread rapidly from Denver on the wings of anti-glue propaganda. The *New York Times* published a story in 1961. This and similar stories increased glue-sniffing to the point of producing 778 arrests in New York City for glue-sniffing in the following five months, and about two thousand in 1963.

Next, the glue companies got involved:

The glue interests contributed notably to expanding the anti-glue-sniffing campaign from a local to a nationwide phenomenon ... 'To help inform communities about the sniffing problem,' the Wall Street Journal announced on its front page of December 7, 1962, 'the Hobby Industry Association has produced a 15-minute color film, The Scent of Danger, which it soon will release to local civic groups. The film describes the harm

done by glue sniffing and mentions other products, such as cleaning fluid
and nail polish, which also contain solvents that can cause intoxication. It
recommends that communities make it illegal to sniff any substance with an
intoxicating effect.' For this the hobby industry won rewards of two kinds
– public approval for its dedication to the anti-glue-sniffing campaign, and a
marked rise in glue sales during subsequent years. (Brecher, 1972, 328)

Nobody can know with certainty why the glue propaganda backfired,
although the reason seems obvious to me because of my own experience
as a glue sniffer. This is one of the few topics in this book on which I can
offer a first-hand testimonial. Prior to the glue hysteria of the 1960s,
countless North American children, including myself, spent long hours
hunched over balsawood 'flying models' of fighters and bombers,
endlessly gluing their innumerable joints and struts and covering them
with gluey tissue paper. There is no indication that any of these youthful
aircraft fabricators became addicted to glue or brain damaged. My
childhood friends and I neither enjoyed the effect of the glue fumes,
deliberately inhaled more than necessary, nor thought to sniff glue when
not making models. We did not discuss glue-sniffing, although genuine
illicit pleasures were major topics in our conversations. As I recall, the
glue smell was not unpleasant and made a person light-headed if the room
was stuffy. However, it didn't remotely compare with the 'high' of
building air-worthy models and imagining oneself flying into battle, with
(or as) John Wayne. We were products of our culture, and the
post-Second World War media were proclaiming that *airplanes*, not
glue, were exciting and dangerous. Probably the only way to attract
people to as barren a pleasure as sniffing glue would be a massive
campaign of scare images of the sort conducted in the 1960s. That is why
the propaganda backfired. Without the benefit of sensationalized promotion by anti-drug propaganda, glue-sniffing is a habit that would attract
very few people. The propaganda campaign could only serve to increase
this number.

*Lessons of the 'Great Glue Epidemic'*

I believe it is reasonable to conclude that propaganda directed against
other drugs will be as counter-productive as the propaganda campaign
directed against glue. However, Smart (1983, 179) and others have

proposed that the anti-glue propaganda increased glue-sniffing only because it introduced a previously unfamiliar intoxicant to the public and provided explicit directions for its use. If this explanation is correct, better-designed propaganda could reduce the use of drugs.

There is a good reason to suppose that propaganda will backfire with familiar drugs as well as new ones. Research has shown that heavy drug users score highly on a psychological trait called 'sensation-seeking' or 'risk-taking' (Zuckerman, Buchsbaum, and Murphy 1980; Adlaf and Smart 1983). Sensation seekers or risk takers, who are heavily represented among marginal young people, habitually seek out novel and dangerous activities, including drug use (Adlaf and Smart 1983). Propaganda that overdramatizes the effects and dangers of drugs only makes them appealing to such people. Astute observers have pointed out that, to a lesser extent, propaganda can backfire with 'normal' people for the same reason.

Although the fear-based messages in anti-drug propaganda have great emotional impact (Leventhal, Watts, and Pagano 1967), positive messages are more effective in changing people's behaviour. Where fear-based messages work at all, the less terrifying ones are generally more effective that the more terrifying ones (Leventhal, Singer, and Jones 1965; Leventhal, Jones, and Tremblay 1966; Leventhal and Watts 1966; McGuire 1980). Therefore, the simple facts about drugs and their actual costs and benefits are enough to inform normal people. The terrifying exaggerations that are the essence of anti-drug propaganda add nothing, while increasing the appeal of the drugs to sensation seekers.

## The 'Crack' Scare

The contemporary equivalent of glue may prove to be crack. It seems only reasonable to predict that the current outpouring of anti-crack propaganda will spread its use. What teenager has not learned from the massive anti-crack propaganda campaign of the 1980s that an incredibly stimulating drug, previously available only to the rich and famous, now exists in a form affordable to teenagers? How many marginal youths with barren lives and little concern for their own safety can resist the glamour of flirting with the 'most addictive drug on earth,' as the media have sometimes called crack? Moreover, alluring tales are told of incredible riches to be made peddling crack. Could anyone think of a better way to promote a new drug fad?

A recent program on British television enlisted the aid of a London advertising agency in evaluating media coverage on crack. The agency staff pointed out that, in addition to the wondrous claims for the euphoria produced by the drug, the claims of its danger were so blatantly exaggerated ('instant addiction') that they were self-discrediting. The conclusion was that the British media have, in fact, created a market for crack. One staff member said, 'If crack doesn't take off in the U.K., it won't be the fault of the publicity campaign run by the media' (Jones 1987).

The media have exaggerated the use of crack as much as they earlier exaggerated the use of glue. An American authority has stated: 'As the crack hysteria was mounting during the summer of 1986, a number of reseachers in the drug community were somewhat perplexed. While *Newsweek* claimed that crack was the biggest story since Vietnam and the fall of the Nixon presidency, and other media giants compared the spread of crack with the plagues of medieval Europe, reseachers were finding crack to be, not a national epidemic, but a phenomenon isolated to the inner cities of less than a dozen urban areas' (Inciardi 1987, 482).

Is the crack propaganda more truthful about the dangers of the drug than about its prevalence? It is too early to say on the basis of existing research, but at this time there are strong indications that it is not, as will be shown in chapter 5.

Nobody can know what the impact of anti-crack propaganda will be in the long run. However, if history is a guide, the best guess is that it will turn out to sustain the War on Drugs in two ways: by stimulating new, violent efforts by police and by stimulating a market for the new drug.

OTHER HARMFUL EFFECTS OF PROPAGANDA

Beyond its ineffectiveness and tendency to increase consumption of the drugs it condemns, anti-drug propaganda may be harmful in more general ways.

*Propaganda Prolongs Wars*

Propaganda, in general, makes it difficult to end wars once they have begun. This has been explained by Canadian war historian Gwyn Dyer, as follows: 'When the people's willingness to go on making sacrifices has been sustained … by hate propaganda that depicts the war as a moral crusade against fathomless evil – then the governments cannot just stop the fighting, sort out the petty and obscure Balkan quarrel that triggered it, swap around a few colonies and trade routes, and thank the surviving soldiers and send them home. Total war requires the goal of total victory, and so the propaganda lies becomes the truth; the future of the nation (or survival of the regime) really does depend on victory, no matter what the war's origins were' (Dyer 1985, 86).

In the case of the War on Drugs, the impact of decades of propaganda is such that it is impossible to discuss psycho-active substances like heroin, LSD, cocaine, and airplane glue as anything but 'fathomless evils.' A plan to treat them in a normal way, allowing a reasonable amount of use under reasonable conditions, and providing regulations to control dangerous use, would seem defeatist, or treasonous. **Yet, use of these substances is not more dangerous, unhealthy, or addictive than countless other practices that Canadians engage in such as driving motorcycles or automobiles, skiing, smoking cigarettes, white-water rafting, playing hockey, playing poker, or eating chocolate. In each of these cases, and in the case of the feared drugs, most people use these practices in a constructive way, but a few people use them in such extreme and hazardous ways that their health is affected. In the most extreme cases, some people lose their lives** (*PM*, chaps 3–7).

## Propaganda Creates Stupidity

The biggest cost of the drug-war propaganda may be the systematic reduction of people's ability to think intelligently about drugs. Society faces genuinely terrifying, immensely complex problems in the last decade of the twentieth century. The environment, educational institutions, value systems, health institutions, and economy all need urgent attention. But the obsessive concern with drug problems stirred up by incessant propaganda distracts us from these to the point of collective stupidity.

## Propaganda Creates Hopelessness

How can parents respond calmly and helpfully to their own troubled offspring if they have been convinced that a child's use of drugs has already damaged his or her brain as well as 'respiratory tract, mucous membranes, skin, liver, kidneys, heart and blood' (as in the 1962 Denver *Post* story)? Weil (1972, 63) has described a 15-year-old hospitalized for acute depression because he had been convinced that brain deterioration would result from his previous LSD use. His 'cure' required only truthful reassurance that LSD is not known to cause brain damage. Mahoney (1982) has shown that hope is essential to successful outcome in any psychotherapy. Scare propaganda erodes hope for people who have used drugs, a substantial proportion of the population.

## *Propaganda Erodes Authority*

Drug-war propaganda 'cries wolf,' over and over. The targets of the propaganda ultimately learn to distrust all authoritative information about drugs. For example, children who have learned they can disregard media reports on airplane glue may be injured if they disregard similar-sounding reports on inhaling aerosol sprays.

## Treatment

Treatment is not normally considered to be a war measure, of course. However, medical and psychological treatment given to drug users is a special case. The first part of this section describes some treatments in which the influence of the War on Drugs is clearly evident. This 'drug-war treatment,'as I will call it, is generally imposed by force or threat of force, is bureaucratically controlled, is usually ineffective, and is occasionally fatal. The latter part of this section deals with more conventional treatment for addiction. My intention is to show that this too is largely futile.

   Conscientious treatment workers might recoil at the inclusion of their efforts in a chapter on the War on Drugs. I regret this apparent affront. However, the impact of these workers depends less on their personal skill and dedication than on the system in which their efforts are embedded, and that system is a War on Drugs.

### DRUG-WAR 'TREATMENT'

Normal medical treatment entails private consultation between a practitioner and a person who feels sick, leading to diagnosis and a prescription or some other course of action. Most decisions ultimately rest with the patient, in consultation with the practitioner. Persons have the right to refuse treatment, even at the risk of causing their own death (as in the case if Jehovah's Witnesses). If one diagnosis, therapy, or practitioner does not succeed in due course, the patient will try others. There are legal regulations that control this process, but these regulations remain in the background.

By contrast, drug-war treatment is monitored and stringently controlled by government agencies and police. Patients whose decisions violate the regulations, for example by 'double doctoring,' can be jailed for long periods. Often patients cannot refuse treatment and cannot make crucial choices about the course of treatment for themselves. Like their patients, medical doctors whose therapeutic choices violate the narcotic regulations are vulnerable to strict punishments, including criminal prosecution. Life sentences are possible for doctors whose prescribing practices are interpreted as 'trafficking' under the Narcotics Control Act (Peachy and Franklin 1985, 293). Doctors in Vancouver have been visited by police informers wired for sound who have tried to tempt them into prescribing illegally and prosecuted them if they did (Beyerstein and Alexander 1985).

When physicians are charged with wrongly prescribing narcotics, the burden of proof is on them to show that the 'narcotic was required for the condition for which the patient received treatment' (Statute Revision Commission 1978, 8389). This requirement violates the normal presumption that doctors should be able to make decisions based on their experience and intuition in consultation with their patient, decisions that they might not be able to justify to a third party. By constant surveillance and threat, the flexibility is removed from the doctor-patient relationship. In effect, the important decisions are made by bureaucrats before physician and patient meet each other.

Increasingly, individual doctors are being replaced in drug-war treatment by even more rigidly controlled agencies. In such institutions, patients and doctors have even less voice – the agency determines the aims and nature of treatment. Canadian drug users can be required by law to accept such treatment for long periods against their will. In this case, the 'diagnosis' is made by the legal system. This kind of treatment resembles military indoctrination or the kind of psychiatric 'treatment' that has been imposed upon dissidents in the Soviet Union rather than therapeutic medicine.

The details of institutional drug-war treatment are not generally made available to the public. However, a few instances have been carefully studied by independent investigators. Examples given here are the treatment of teenagers by 'Straight, inc.' in the United States and of methadone users in British Columbia.

## Straight Treatment

Arnold Trebach (1987) has documented the case of an American university student, Fred Collins, who was treated by Straight, inc. (Straight is a private, residential treatment system based in Florida, with branches in other American states. It has been warmly endorsed by highly placed American drug experts and by Nancy Reagan). There was conflicting testimony in the eventual legal action, but this summary is based on the account accepted by the court in Washington DC, that finally ruled on the case, and on Trebach's lengthy interviews of Fred Collins, other principals in the case, and some of the jurors.

Fred Collins was a relatively normal American university student – good marks, well liked in his fraternity, a good relationship with his girl-friend. However, prior to attending university his relationship with his parents had been tense for several years. In 1982, on a holiday trip with his parents to Florida during a break from his university studies, he was pressured by his parents and the staff of Straight, inc. into signing an agreement to accept treatment. The main argument directed at him was that his brother was already in treatment for drug problems, and that siblings of drug abusers were expected to have the same problems. He was told that the treatment would not last long and that he would be allowed to drop out if it proved unsuitable. His parents were told that unless they pressured Fred into treatment, their other son would be denied treatment, would 'go down ten times as far,' and would probably die.

Fred Collins was forcibly confined for the next 135 days by Straight. He was subjected to coercive techniques including undernourishment (he lost twenty-five pounds), complete deprivation of contact with the outside world including his university friends and his girl-friend, 24-hour surveillance, chronic sleep deprivation, intimidation, and social harassment.

After he finally escaped (by jumping through a window and eluding his pursuers), Fred Collins went to a lawyer and took legal action. Straight was eventually convicted of false imprisonment in a Washington, DC, court and the jury awarded Fred Collins $220,000 in damages. Straight centred their legal defence on the claim that Fred Collins had become permanently chemically dependent and their stringent actions therefore constituted treatment. However, the jury was convinced by independent testimony that he was not a drug addict. There was, in fact, no evidence that he was addicted, other than the suspicions of his parents and his open admission of infrequent marijuana use.

Fred Collins won his case because he was not addicted to a drug. If he had been addicted, the jury then may well have seen Straight's cruel measures as justifiable. Subsequent to trial, leading American drug-policy experts stated that they continue to view Straight as providing essential treatment to drug addicts (Trebach, personal communication). Subsequent legal actions confirm that Straight has continued its practices essentially unchanged in spite of the Fred Collins case (Trebach 1987, chap. 2).

Straight officials have generously allowed me to witness some of their group sessions firsthand, feeling that I would come to doubt Trebach's account of the Fred Collins case if I did so. However, my belief that Trebach's account is correct was strengthened by what I saw and heard. I believe that Straight's treatment can be fairly compared with 'brain-washing' in prisoner-of-war camps as documented by Brown (1963, chap. 2). Thus, procedures that would be reprehensible in any context outside of a prisoner-of-war camp are considered acceptable 'treatment' in the case of drug addiction.

Even if Straight's actions cannot be considered treatment in the normal sense, they might still be justified if they were necessary and effective. In spite of Straight's claims, however, their evidence is very weak. Straight officials have provided me with reports purporting to show that their treatment is effective (Malcolm and Malcolm 1981; Friedman unpublished), but these provide no comparisons of Straight clients with untreated controls, and suffer from other serious methodological deficiencies. The reports are adequate, however, to show that some children have been satisfied with the treatment they received from Straight and that others were totally dissatisfied and felt they were harmed by it. Determining the ratio of one outcome to the other would require more precise research.

*Methadone 'Treatment' in British Columbia*

The recent history of methadone dispensing in British Columbia provides
an illustration of drug-war treatment for addiction in Canada. Methadone
maintenance was introduced to British Columbia in 1963. It entails
providing chronic heroin addicts with a legal, orally administered
heroin-substitute, methadone, to keep them out of jail, away from
needles, and make a normal life possible in spite of their intractable
addictions. Methadone-dispensing was regulated by Narcotic Control
Regulations from the outset (Giffen and Lambert 1988). These regulations were tightened in 1972, with a corresponding decrease in the
number of patients between 1972 and 1975 (Committee of the Health
Protection Branch 1977).

As the system had evolved by 1985, methadone in British Columbia
was provided both through private doctors (about 500 patients) and
through government clinics (about 175 patients). The clinics handled the
younger and less stable addicts, whereas older, more stable addicts
received prescriptions through the small number of doctors licensed by
the federal government to prescribe methadone (Alexander, Beyerstein,
and MacInnes 1987). Although the independent physicians were generally more flexible than the government clinics, both were regulated by
federal laws, regulations, and guidelines, and monitored by the police,
the Federal Bureau of Dangerous Drugs, and the BC Medical Association.
Although these controls restricted the number of addicts who could
receive methadone, many addicts used the system to escape the role of
criminals. The most successful addicts eventually came off methadone
treatment and returned to normal life. Others received both methadone
and social assistance for long periods.

Early in 1986, the BC government proposed major changes. The BC
Ministry of Health asked the federal Department of National Health and
Welfare to remove all physicians' licences to prescribe methadone in the
province, except those of doctors in provincial clinics. New clinics were
to be opened and all of British Columbia's heroin addicts who wished to
receive methadone were to attend them (Alexander, Beyerstein, and
MacInnes 1987). The treatment that was to be offered at the new clinics
differed dramatically from normal medical treatment, as can be shown by
reviewing the rules of the largest clinic, the Vancouver Methadone
Treatment Clinic. These rules were given to 'clients' under a cover letter

dated 9 April 1986 and signed by the clinic manager (MacDonald 1986). Addicts were to place a legally witnessed signature on a statement of these rules as a condition for receiving methadone. As well, clinic doctors were required to sign a contract requiring them to adhere strictly to the clinic rules (personal communication, BC Ministry of Health officials).

Although these rules were not released to the public, a disgruntled patient managed to slip a copy out of the clinic. My colleagues and I publicized them through the *Canadian Medical Association Journal* (Alexander, Beyerstein, and MacInnes 1987). Not all the rules are described here, but only those that most clearly show how the proposed treatment differed from normal medical practice. Under the rules:

1. Neither the 'client' nor the doctor determined the goal of a patient's treatment. The rules stipulated that the goal for all clients was complete withdrawal from methadone. This rule applied even if client and doctor felt that the client could not function without methadone.

2. 'Regular contact with counseling staff' was required, whether or not the client or the 'counseling staff' perceived a need for psychotherapy.

3. The rules required 'responsibility and a social stability away from drug related activities and associations' both on and off the clinic site.

4. Clients were not allowed to consume any psycho-active medication without approval of the clinic staff. This included tranquillizers, sleeping medications, and codeine, all of which can be used legally and which are sometimes needed by methadone patients as well as other people.

5. Clients were forbidden to congregate 'in the area of the clinic.'

6. Clients were not eligible to receive methadone unless they were either already receiving it from a physician or had been dependent on narcotics for five years. Prospective clients were required to provide documentation that they had unsuccessfully tried 'drug-free' treatment. In practice this meant that addicts could not receive treatment unless they had attended a 'detox centre' in the province.

7. Clients were required to provide urine samples at any time when requested by clinic staff and daily for the first three months of treatment.

8. If patients agreed to all these conditions (and more) in a signed and witnessed document, they were evaluated by an 'assessment team.' If they passed the assessment they were required to attend the Great Northern Way Detox Centre for three or more days prior to receiving a methadone prescription. (In practice, patients went to the centre for five days.) During this period patients were to be withdrawn from opiates,

unless withdrawal was not possible owing to the severity of the symptoms. Provincial regulations explicity did not exempt pregnant women from this detoxification (British Columbia Alcohol and Drug Programs 1986, 8).

9. After assessment and 'detox,' clients were provided with a maximum of 80 mg of methadone per day, even if their actual needs were greater. They were required to consume the entire amount every day, whether they needed it or not.

10. New clients were required to pick up their methadone at the clinic daily. Patients who had been in treatment for six months or longer could pick up their 'medication' no fewer than three times per week, with two times per week allowed to working patients during a brief transition period.

11. Any infractions of these rules could be used by the clinic as a basis to terminate treatment.

According to clinic patients, these written rules were enforced inflexibly, although some staff members have denied this assertion.

Even readers who might consider these rules appropriate for heroin addicts will agree that they are not normal medical treatment. These readers will never be 'treated' in this way by their own doctors.

## The Failure of Drug-War 'Treatment'

It is of course possible for treatment that differs from normal medical practice to be successful. Since the BC methadone program was terminated shortly after it began, no direct evaluation is available. However, there is sufficient research already in existence to show that the program could not have helped its clients or the larger society. This research is summarized below.

A study of earlier methadone treatment programs in British Columbia reported favourable outcomes of 'high dose methadone maintenance' for patients with severe drug-dependence problems and long criminal records (Williams, Moy, and Johnston 1970). The average dose under the 'high dose' program was 100 mg/day, that is, about half the patients received *more than* 100 mg/day. Yet 80 mg/day was the maximum dose allowed under the new plan.

A recent American study with 6–7 years of follow-up observations on the patients' behaviour shows that low-dose, rigidly administered programs of the sort proposed in British Columbia produced higher rates of crime, arrest, narcotic use, and drug dealing than did flexibly administered programs that allow higher doses for users who need them (McGlothlin and Anglin 1981). Studies from England show that increased rigidity in prescribing of methadone and other opiates after 1970 was followed by major increases in the extent of addiction (Trebach 1982; Stimson and Oppenheimer 1982).

The necessity for doses higher than those allowed in the BC plan is shown by a rigorous review of all available studies on the methadone dosages conducted for the American National Institue on Drug Abuse (usually called NIDA). This review found substantial evidence that doses as high as 160 mg/day produce the best effects in some addicts, and evidence that, for some addicts, the correct dose is crucial for treatment success. This review concluded: 'NIDA should encourage state agencies to adopt regulations that freely allow the use of dose levels up to at least 100 mg' (Hargreaves 1983, 52).

A critique by Goldstein and Judson (included in Hargreaves 1983) pointed out that intrusive governmental regulations are antithetical to good medical practice: 'We add our voice ... in asking that the treatment of addicts be returned to its proper place as a medical endeavor; that physicians and ancillary health personnel be allowed to treat addicts according to the state of the art and to their best medical judgment; and that intrusive and counter-productive regulatory interventions by Federal, State and local governmental agencies be terminated (Hargreaves 1983, 87).

When addicts spoke about the humiliation and oppressiveness of the BC regulations, they were most passionate in their reactions to the daily 'supervised' urine testing, a procedure that requires that a clinic staff member to actually observe the urine leaving the patient's body, to prevent deception. This practice is particularly repugnant to women during menstruation. Furthermore, recent studies indicate that even the most technically advanced urine tests give a substantial number of 'false positives' (Morgan 1984; Atman 1986; Beyerstein 1987). Thus, in addition to the indignity of 'supervised' tests, some patients would inevitably be charged falsely with infractions of the rules that could lead to termination of their methadone treatment.

The bulk of published studies suggest that compulsory counselling, another feature of the ministry's proposal for methadone 'treatment,' could not work. Controlled studies have shown that compulsory psychological treatment and psychological treatment during incarceration do not cure addiction (Le Dain 1973; Annis 1979). It is easy to understand why. Psychotherapy at its best is an intimate personal encounter. The most protected feelings are exposed and examined. The difference between voluntary and forced psychotherapy is the difference between making love and rape.

Moreover, clinical research indicates that opiate withdrawal during pregnancy, required by the BC methadone 'treatment' program, is likely to produce fetal harm or miscarriage (Wallach, Jerez, and Blinick 1975; Fraser 1976; Connaughton et al. 1977). Animal research has shown that withdrawing females from opiates during pregnancy produces more still births, smaller litters, and greater post-natal weight loss by offspring than allowing the females to use opiates uninterruptedly during pregnancy (Lichtblau and Sparber 1981).

Even after the criticisms discussed above were published in the *Canadian Medical Association Journal* (Alexander, Beyerstein, and MacInnes 1987), the BC Ministry of Health offered no convincing arguments that its methadone program could, like normal medical treatment, benefit its patients. Rather, the program has been consistently justified in terms of benefits to society and the goals of the War on Drugs. However, even these alleged societal benefits seem doubtful.

*Social Justifications for BC Methadone 'Treatment'*

The publicly stated reasons for forcing methadone patients into government clinics were that (1) methadone was being prescribed irresponsibly and excessively by private physicians, making access to methadone 'too free and easy'; as a result (2) there was a 'significant amount' of medical methadone being sold on the streets, possibly causing new addictions and deaths among the drug-using population (Shaw and Baldrey 1986 *Vancouver Sun* 1986); as well, (3) clinics could dispense methadone at lower cost than private doctors could (Joint Advisory Committee 1985). In addition to these three publicly stated justifications, some ministry officials privately expressed great concern that physicians who prescribed methadone were making inordinate profits at government expense.

My colleagues and I decided to check these justifications when the ministry officials with whom we met were unable to produce any data to support them. In our subsequent investigations (Russell 1986; Alexander, Beyerstein, and MacInnes 1987) we became convinced that all of them were unsupported by facts, and were instead manifestations of a War on Drugs mentality. We were unable to locate any evidence of BC doctors being charged or convicted for over-prescribing methadone in the past several years, in spite of the fact that about five hundred addicts were receiving methadone prescriptions from independent doctors in 1986. The latest summary of convictions under the Narcotic Control Act then available revealed a total of seven convictions in Canada for any offence whatsoever involving methadone in 1984. Of these seven convictions, three were in British Columbia. To our knowledge, none of the three BC methadone convictions involved doctors (Bureau of Dangerous Drugs 1985).

A few BC doctors have had their licences to prescribe methadone revoked by the federal government in recent years, but after interviewing doctors, patients, and ministry officials we concluded that, in most of these cases, the Bureau of Dangerous Drugs simply disagreed with the clinical judgments made in good faith by conscientious doctors in consultation with their patients. Some doctors were guilty of interpreting the strict federal guidelines flexibly, to better meet the needs of their patient; others were guilty of following them rigidly, which raised the cost of the service to prohibitive levels.

We could find no basis for the private allegations about profiteering by doctors who prescribe methadone. The median gross income for the group of about thirty doctors who were licensed to prescribe methadone to addicts in British Columbia was about $110,000 in 1985, whereas the corresponding median for all BC doctors was about $115,000 (based on a random sample drawn from statistics published by the Medical Services Commission of British Columbia, 1985). Moreover, most BC doctors who prescribed methadone to addicts had fewer than ten addict patients (Peachy and Franklin 1985), hardly enough to elevate their income substantially.

Even the ministry's claim about the greater cost of prescribing methadone by private physicians was misleading on two counts. First, some BC physicians had proposed meeting with ministry officials to discuss lowering the fee schedules for prescribing methadone, in view of the quick and routine nature of many of the office calls involved. The ministry did not accept this invitation, but instead unilaterally lowered the fee for writing a methadone prescription to $7.00 in 1986. The government estimates of the cost of private prescribing were, inexplicably, based on the old fee of $17.60 (Russell 1986).

There was no real support for the ministry's contention that much of the methadone prescribed by private physicians was being diverted into the black market, thereby increasing addiction and overdose deaths. Our interviews with Vancouver addicts indicate that, when methadone is diverted to the street market, it is used primarily by people who are already addicted. The same conclusion has been reported in American and Dutch research (Inciardi 1977; Johnson 1978; Van Santen 1987).

Sixty-three Vancouver addicts were given a questionnaire asking what they believe to be the most important source of illicit methadone. Five reported 'private doctors,' whereas sixteen reported 'government clinics,' and twelve 'drugstore break-ins.' Two mentioned 'double doctoring' (which could involve either private doctors or clinic doctors) and twelve mentioned other sources. If the addicts' perceptions are correct, 'government clinics,' with fewer patients and more stringent regulations than independent physicians, are the most important source of methadone for the illicit market! This conclusion seem unlikely on the surface, but it is believable because rigidly administered methadone clinics in British Columbia and elsewhere are rarely successful in carrying out their programs. They often evolve into demoralized institutions run by disenchanted workers who cannot make them effective, and eventually do not care. (This is not intended to be a universal condemnation; there have been many successful clinics, including some of the branch clinics in British Columbia. But there have been frequent failures as well.)

In 1986 and 1987, numerous reports appeared in Vancouver newspapers of deaths attributed to methadone use. The implications of these stories was that methadone prescribing, especially by private doctors, constituted a major danger to the drug-using community. However, our review of the actual coroners' reports, which was published in the *British Columbia Medical Journal,* told a different story. Although there have been several *methadone-related* deaths among BC drug users, most of these deaths were not *caused* by methadone. In fact, methadone probably produces a net *reduction* in mortality among BC drug users (Alexander, MacInnes, and Beyerstein 1988).

In the five-year period between 1982 and 1986 inclusive, official BC coroners' reports identified eighty-three deaths where methadone was detected in the body. Of these cases, three died of natural causes, one was murdered, five were unclassified as to cause of death, and the remaining seventy-four are classified as accidental deaths due to drug overdose. Of these seventy-four 'methadone-related' deaths, methadone was the only drug detected in the blood in nineteen, whereas in all the rest a combination of drugs was detected. Death was attributed solely to methadone overdose or complications due to methadone overdose in twenty-six cases, whereas in forty-seven death was attributed to a combination of drugs including methadone. One death was attributed to heroin overdose (Alexander, MacInnes, and Beyerstein 1988).

On the surface, these coroners' reports suggest that methadone is causing about five deaths per year by itself, plus eight per year in combination with other drugs. However, these figures by themselves are misleading. To put them in perspective it is necessary to ask (a) what was the actual cause of these deaths? and (b) what was the overall effect of methadone on the death rate among addicts?

(a) The cause of 'methadone-related' deaths. It is doubtful that many of the seventy-four 'methadone-related' deaths were actually caused by methadone. According to the coroners' reports, the average blood level of methadone among the decedents was 0.42 mg/L, with a range from 0.0 to 1.9 mg/L. The average blood level of the twenty-six deaths attributed solely to methadone was 0.49 mg/L, with a range of 0.0 to 0.98 mg/L. However, the lethal range given in Baselt's definitive *Disposition of Toxic Drugs and Chemicals in Man* (1982) is 0.4 to 1.8 mg/L. Thus, almost half of BC's methadone-related deaths fell below the usually accepted minimum lethal dose of methadone.

Healthy methadone users may reach blood levels of methadone *every day* that are higher than those reported in most of the BC 'methadone-related' deaths. After a regular daily dose of between 100 and 120 mg of methadone, average blood levels peak at 0.83 mg/L at four hours and decline to 0.46 mg/L twenty-four hours after administration (Inturrisi and Verebely 1972). Addicts can take even higher doses of methadone, up to 200 mg/day, without adverse effects (Garriott, Sturner, and Mason 1973). Addicts habituated to heroin should be able to tolerate high levels of methadone too, since there is strong cross-tolerance between opiates (Jaffe 1985, 537).

How can the low methadone levels in the BC cases cause death? It has been suggested that these low doses were fatal to addicts who had lost their tolerance during a spell of abstinence. It is also possible that non-opiate-addicted drug users failed to realize the strength of methadone, and consequently overdosed. However, these explanations seem dubious.

Regular illicit drug users are pharmacologically sophisticated, and it is hard to imagine that any appreciable number of experienced users could make either of these elementary errors.

We have sought a more credible explanation for the low-dose deaths by studying the coroners' reports and by asking members of Vancouver's illicit-drug-using community about the individuals who died. These investigations suggested that the real cause of death in most cases was not methadone, but prolonged general deterioration. Typical decedents had lived miserable and unhealthy lives for years, even by the low standards of the drug-using community. They were frequently described by other addicts as 'pillheads' and as 'always staggering around,' and were seen as depressive or suicidal or physically unhealthy. Therefore, methadone may have merely been present at the time of death of people whose systems finally gave out from years of unusually severe abuse.

Similar observations have been reported in a study of deaths among heroin users in France (Ingold 1986). According to Ingold, 'the largest group of deaths occurred among persons who had been long-term drug addicts, had often been involved in multiple drug abuse and had regularly consumed large quantities of alcohol and psychotropic substances. As a rule such persons had been mentally and physically exhausted. It was as though a lethal threshold had been crossed, with death coming as an end to a whole process of unfavourable development ... The possibility of suicide could not be entirely ruled out' (86). Ingold adds: 'It is likely that such acute intoxication is not the sole or principal cause of death in the cases examined, since the impaired general condition and lesions (for example those affecting the liver and lungs) play such an important role that they alone may be the cause of death' (87–8). Similar observations have been reported in England (Stimson and Oppenheimer 1982, 122–8).

(b) Relation of methadone-related deaths to total addict death rate. It makes little sense to examine the possible costs of prescribing a drug without also assessing the benefits. Many radical medical treatments carry some risk of fatality, but are utilized because of their greater likelihood of success in serious cases. There is no evidence that the availability of methadone increased the *overall* death rate of addicts in British Columbia, and there are several reasons to suppose that it lowers the death rate instead.

Opiate addiction is a potentially fatal condition during a War on Drugs. Methadone maintenance treatment can control some of its worst hazards by reducing addicts' involvement with crime, prison, and contaminated injectable drugs (Inciardi 1977; McGlothlin and Anglin 1981a; Dole and Nyswander 1983; Kaplan 1983, chap. 5). The medical literature on this topic is not consistent, but some studies indicate that methadone saves many more lives that it takes (MacInnes 1988). A New York State study of death rates in addicts between 1966 and 1976 found that death rates from all causes in addicts after leaving methadone treatment were twice as great as death rates for the same addicts while in methodone treatment. The drug-related death rates after treatment were four times larger than those during treatment; opiate-related death rates (including those due to methadone) were fifty-one times larger after than during treatment (Joseph, Appel, and Schmeidler 1981).

With the advent of AIDS, the potential of methadone to keep addicts away from needles can mean the difference between life and a lingering, hopeless death for large numbers of intravenous drug users (Novick, Khan, and Kreek 1986). Since AIDS is spread by sexual contact and many prostitutes are heroin addicts, methadone, like needle-exchange programs, may well inhibit the spread of AIDS in the general population.

As well, methadone may reduce the likelihood of suicide among addicts. There are several stories circulating among Vancouver addicts of people who have committed suicide as a direct result of being refused or removed from methadone treatment by the clinics. One woman who had previously expressed her fears to one of my colleagues about not being able to obtain methadone fatally shot herself on 16 May 1987. According to her addict friends she had been depressed for the last month because she had been placed on involuntary withdrawal by the clinic. My colleagues and I have endeavoured to check this story through the methadone clinics, but have not been given enough information to either confirm or disconfirm it.

The BC government's plan for methadone 'treatment' has not yet been implemented. The federal Department of National Health and Welfare did not accede to the province's request to remove the methadone licences of all of British Columbia's independent methadone-prescribing physicians. Instead, it compromised by removing the licence of the doctor with the largest number of addict patients, thereby forcing 130 addicts into the clinics. It also tried to remove another doctor's licence to prescribe methadone, but was blocked by the courts (*Vancouver Sun* 1986a).

The BC government responded to the failure to achieve its goals by announcing that it would close *all* its clinics. This created a panic among methadone patients, faced with a reduction of physician-supplied methadone by the federal government and elimination of clinic-supplied methadone by the provincial government. Where the situation will go from here is unclear, although the federal government is currently allowing a number of new doctors to prescribe methadone. None the less, no long-term commitments have been made, and the possibility remains that the BC Ministry of Health plan may be imposed. A study group appointed by the federal Department of Health and Welfare planned to release a report on the situation in the summer of 1989, but it was not yet available as this book went to press. In the meantime, British Columbia methadone patients are embittered and confused. They perceive that the 'treatment' that is offered them is not only harsh and ineffective, but also inconsistent, confused, and unpredictable.

*Why Does Drug-War 'Treatment' Exist?*

The two situations described above illustrate the failure of War on Drugs treatment. The harm that can be done to people by subjecting them to treatment from Straight or a BC methadone clinic is obvious. There is no offsetting evidence that these practices help those who are treated or society at large. (There is a literature purporting to show that compulsory treatment for addiction can be effective, recently summarized by Leukefeld and Tims [1988], but the evidence and logic are badly strained. There is not space to provide a detailed summary of the counter-evidence here, but this has been done elsewhere; see, for instance, Brecher 1972; Le Dain 1973, appendices I, L; Alexander 1978.)

The facts are perplexing as well as dismal. Leading American politicians condone and praise a form of treatment that subjects teenagers to harsh brainwashing techniques. The government of British Columbia proposes a methadone treatment program that cannot be effective and appears likely to have had deadly results for some of its clients while demoralizing and embittering the rest. It justifies this proposal by publicly distorting the facts. Why?

The most parsimonious explanation is that warlike treatment of the sort described here is not designed to promote health *at all*, but to symbolize the goals of the War on Drugs. Warlike treatment subjects drug users to repressive measures intended to enforce pharmacological conformity. It is of secondary concern if the treatment is harmful to patients or clients as long as it expresses the demands of society. Because of society's distaste for cruelty these punitive measures are labelled medical treatment. Fiffen and Lambert (1988) have stated that many of Canada's treatment programs are merely 'embellishments to the criminal justice system' (361).

The more thoughtful proponents of the War on Drugs recognize this reality. It has been acknowledged forthrightly by Kaplan (1983) as follows: 'Though of course, the reduction [in crime resulting from methadone maintenance] might be even greater were [the addict] imprisoned for the same length of time, the far lower cost of treatment may make it a better buy for society. This is especially the case so long as our overcrowded jails and prisons would not permit us to imprison the majority of heroin addicts for very long terms anyway ... Methadone maintenance may use the discomfort of withdrawal as a 'chemical prison' to compel the addict to remain in treatment and, hence, make efforts to restructure his life' (225-6).

Kaplan is a thoughtful scholar and analyst who openly advocates using methadone treatment as a 'chemical prison,' a sophisticated device for controlling the behaviour of people who cannot exist without drugs. Less thoughtful drug warriors, like fanatical zealots in time of war, are more devoted to raw force. This would appear to be the mentality behind Straight, inc. and the BC government's methadone program. Such treatment cannot help people. Rather, it seeks to make the use of drugs so humiliating and painful that people will be forced to stop. Those who cannot stop must bear the painful consequences indefinitely.

CONVENTIONAL PROFESSIONAL TREATMENT

The kinds of treatment to be considered next are more conventional than the drug-war treatment described in the previous section. Conventional professional treatment for drug addiction is generally voluntary. It includes individual and group psychotherapy, drug maintenance, careful withdrawal from drugs, family therapy, behaviour modification, aversive conditioning treatment, and professionally run therapeutic communities. Such treatment for drug addiction is more humane and rational than the harsh drug-war treatment discussed in the previous section. However, it must be viewed critically, for the recovery rate in most forms of conventional treatment is very little better, if better at all, than the recovery rate of untreated addicts. Moreover, conventional professional treatment is a component of the overall system of control that constitutes the War on Drugs, and its outcome must be affected by that. To limit the discussion, this section will use psychotherapy for opiate addicts and flexible forms of methadone maintenance to illustrate the range of success found in conventional professsional treatment.

### Psychotherapeutic Treatment for Opiate Addiction

The effectiveness of psychotherapy for opiate addiction is not a matter that all professionals agree upon, but the bulk of evidence points to a clear conclusion. Although treatment programs for people addicted to opiates can usually point to a few successes, they are not helpful for the great majority of addicts. Most heroin users, especially if they have been through it before, will not voluntarily accept psychotherapy. Of those who do, most drop out quickly. Of those who complete a treatment program, most recommence compulsive drug use either immediately or within a few months or years. People who receive no professional treatment are about as likely to abandon their heroin habits as people who are treated. These conclusions are not new. Musto (1973) examined narcotic treatment methods prior to 1920 and found extravagant claims of success, but no real evidence of it. Brecher (1972) reviewed the decades of treatment for heroin addiction prior to 1970 with the same conclusion.

More recently, some careful American research has claimed mildly successful outcomes of psychotherapy for heroin addiction, but the research loses its lustre on close examination, for it does not report a lasting superiority of treated addicts over untreated addicts on crucial measures like the elimination of destructive drug use, or establishment of job and family stability. Rather, the reported effects of treatment usually involve indirect measures, like the reduction of methadone dosage and self-report psychopathology scales. The general picture is of a relatively small superiority of treated addicts over controls assigned to placebo treatments in short-term follow-ups (Stanton, Todd, and Associates 1982; Woody et al. 1983; Bale et al. 1984; Woody et al. 1987). Moreover, even the best of this research suffers other serious methodological limitations, including the absence of untreated control groups, the fact that only a minority of addicts could be induced to accept the treatment, and the fact that the treatment was provided by institutes that were funded and staffed at a level far above the means of most Canadian and American treatment centres. The authors of these studies tend to be judiciously reserved in claiming that their research provides substantial evidence that psychotherapy can be successful on a large scale.

Some research has claimed more success than the above careful studies (see Nurco et al. 1985 for a review) but their methodology is so weak as to lose all credibility. For example, some use control groups that would not accept treatment or lack control groups entirely (Simpson and Sells 1982; Simpson 1986). Others utilize indefensibly loose methods of collecting data (Sells and Simpson 1980) or have relied heavily on apparent positive results gathered while patients are seeking release from confinement, rather than after release (McGlothlin, Anglin, and Wilson 1977), and some have compared heavily self-selected populations at short and inconstant intervals after the completion of treatment (Collins and Allison 1983; Rawson et al. 1986).

*Psychotherapy for Other Drug Addictions*

Although heroin addiction is the most thoroughly studied, professional psychotherapy for addiction to other kinds of drugs, including alcohol, appears to be equally ineffective. As with heroin-addiction treatment, recovery rates in well-controlled studies are generally no better than the rate of natural recovery without professional treatment (Hunt, Barnet, and Branch 1971; Leventhal and Cleary 1980; Schachter 1982; Vaillant 1983; 187,227; Waldorf 1983; Zinberg 1984; Brown 1984; Orford 1985; Fingarette 1988). Vaillant, for example, as part of an extensively documented research program, reported that improvement and remission rates of alcoholic patients at his own clinic were not better than those of untreated groups (Vaillant 1983, 284). Leventhal and Cleary (1980), in a review of almost three hundred studies of smoking behaviour, concluded: 'All methods have failed to produce substantial change; neither public health programs nor face-to-face therapies have proven effective in achieving long term reductions in smoking when compared with control cases or with the rates of spontaneous quitting' (371). Some more positive results have been reported in a study of continuous interventions over a six-year period (Multiple Risk Factor Trial Intervention Group 1982), but even in this case the diffence between treated and untreated groups had become small by the end of six years. To my knowledge no follow-up data were reported after the treatment ended.

There is a controversy among psychologists about whether psychotherapy can be shown to be effective in general, based on an attempt to integrate the vast literature on psychotherapy with a statistical technique called meta-analysis. But even those meta-analysts who claim that psychotherapy is effective generally do not extend their claims to include psychotherapy for addiction to drugs or alcohol (*Lancet* 1984; Cousineau and Chambers, in preparation). Some professionals and treatment institutions insist that treatment for addiction is at least slightly effective (Holden 1987, 1988). As well, there are some former addicts who claim that professional psychotherapy has worked for them. Neither professionals nor addicts, however, can provide properly controlled empirical data to support their claims. Rather, they rely on personal experience and uncontrolled observations. They often deny that therapy can be evaluated by scientific methods, because of its intrinsic complexity.

Although I am loath to reject first-hand observations on the basis of impersonal data, I think in this case that it is reasonable to resolve the controversy in favour of the scientific data, for several reasons. First, history shows that desperate people are often fooled by valueless treatments for all sorts of conditions, as with phrenology, mesmerism, and dozens of other now discredited treatments. Second, most professionals who administer treatment regard methods of treatment for addiction *other than their own* as valueless or counter-productive. In other words, the majority of treatment professionals believe that the majority of treatments do not work. As well, even if some psychotherapy is slightly effective, it is so expensive that it can never play any significant part in the amelioration of widespread addiction.

In my mind, the clinching argument comes from the unwillingness of addicts to participate in professional psychotherapy. Surely sick people would eagerly seek out treatment that could reduce their painful, socially abhorrent, and often fatal condition. Yet most addicts shun therapy, even when it has no financial cost to them. Woody et al. (1983) found that only 60 per cent of new methadone patients could be persuaded to participate in psychotherapy. A further 60 per cent of those willing to participate dropped out in less than three sessions and the remainder attended less than half of twenty-four scheduled sessions in spite of persistent reminders from the clinic staff. Only 85 per cent of the therapy sessions lasted thirty minutes or longer. Stanton, Todd, and Associates (1982) found it necessary to make part of the salary for their family-therapy staff contingent on the recruitment of families into treatment, 'since the family recruitment endeavor required so much effort on the part of the therapists' (401). Brown (1984) reached similar conclusions in a review of studies of treatment on non-opiate addictions.

Although treatment for drug addiction is generally unwanted and ineffective, its existence creates the illusion that effective specialized help for addiction is available. This misapprehension causes friends, doctors, and others who might help to shunt addicted persons to specialized agencies that probably have less to offer. It puts addicts themselves in a dilemma, for they are told they cannot solve their 'drug problem' without specialized treatment, but they find that the specialists have little to offer.

## Why Psychotherapy for Addiction Fails

How can psychotherapy that is humane, well-funded, and carried out by trained professionals not succeed? In part, it may fail because even conventional psychotherapy for addiction is part of a larger system based on the War on Drugs mentality (Henderson 1983; Drug Abuse Policy Office 1984). It is hard to develop confidence and rapport when a patient is 'diverted' into psychotherapy by a court and knows the therapist's notes may send the patient back to jail if he or she does not seem co-operative. Likewise, it is hard to gain a patient's confidence in a publicly supported program in which the goals are not the patient's well-being, but his or her conformity. Yet conformity is the traditional goal of psychotherapy for heroin addiction (Brown 1984, 292) and, to a lesser extent, of treatment for other forms of addiction as well.

There is a more fundamental reason why treatment fails as well. Although it may seem a shocking idea in the present social climate, treatment fails because **drug addiction is not a disease, but a way of adapting to desperately difficult situations. People cannot be 'cured' of adaptive strategies unless better alternatives are available to them. Addiction has only been considered a 'disease' for a relatively short period in history, and there is insufficient scientific evidence to back this view of it** (Peele 1985; Fingarette 1988; *PM*, chap. 8).

When treatment fails, the War on Drugs offers a simple explanation that strips off the moralistic veneer and reveals the underlying doctrine. If treatment fails in spite of the best efforts of trained experts, the patient must be deliberately sabotaging it – he or she must not want to be cured. At this point apparent therapeutic concern is replaced, at best, by abandonment of the patient to his or her fate, and at worst by condemnation, compulsory treatment, or jail.

## Methadone Treatment for Heroin Addiction

The most successful professional treatment for heroin addiction in North America is methadone maintenance. Thousands of addicts have reduced their reliance on illegal drugs, their participation in crime, their dependence on welfare payments, and their ill-health when provided with a reliable supply of methadone through their doctor or a methadone clinic (Dole 1980; Newman 1987). Although many of these addicts do not become fully functioning members of society, staying out of jail and hospitals marks a major improvement. However, methadone's success is a modest one. It does not cure addiction or dependence (Newman 1987, 1987a). Pharmacologically, there is little difference between methadone and the heroin that it replaces. Even well-run methadone programs cannot keep more than a minority of addicts in treatment in any locality (Dole 1980; Kaplan 1983, 222). Therefore, methadone maintenance is probably not so much a treatment in the ordinary sense of the term as a humane suspension of the strictures of the War on Drugs for a particular group of people who have proved they cannot be coerced into abstinence.

## Conclusion

The major components of the War on Drugs – prohibition, propaganda, and treatment – have failed and must continue to fail. Meanwhile, the costs of these ineffective components, in money and in human misery, have become huge. Within the War on Drugs mentality, the harm done in prosecuting the war is seen as inevitable – the unavoidable tolls of an epic stuggle against evil. But a former RCMP undercover officer once suggested a different perspective to me. He had resigned from undercover work (but remained in the RCMP) because he found himself, as an undercover policeman, befriending people, sharing experiences with them, later sharing their drugs in a warm and accepting atmosphere, and eventually gaining their trust to the point where they would sell him drugs – whereupon betrayed them to arrest and prison. In the end he could see no justification for his treachery. He told me of this self-reflection with tears in his eyes. He restored his self-respect by resigning from narcotics enforcement while retaining his loyalty to the values that had originally brought him to police work. I mean to suggest the necessity of a similar change at a national level, in the interests of national self-respect. It is not values that need to be sacrificed, but cruel and ineffective methods.

Why does the War on Drugs continue in spite of its failures? Part of the answer is that deeply rooted popular wisdom about drugs and drug addiction justifies its continuation. Chapters 3–8 will critically examine this wisdom and show that much of it is distorted or simply false. I am sure it will be difficult for most readers to believe at first how much of what they have learned about drugs and addiction is wrong or unsubstantiated, and therefore these chapters are heavily documented with medical, psychological, and historical research.

# 3 Drug use, dependence, and addiction in Canada

Failure is no reason to give up a great cause. In fact, many people argue that the drug war must be *expanded* because it has failed until now. Their arguments are compelling and terrifying: drug use is a raging epidemic that threatens to destroy a generation of youth; prohibited drugs cause addiction, disease and crime; drug use causes drastic economic devastation measured in billions of dollars; drug dealers have built a powerful political base that threatens democratic governments; the newest drugs, currently cocaine and 'crack,' are far worse than the earlier ones.

This chapter and the following five are intended to show that these powerful justifications for continuing the drug war are invalid. This is no small task, because there are many interlocking justifications and a mountain of scholarly and technical evidence pertaining to each. I have tried to translate this evidence into readable English and to condense it into a few chapters, although space limitations have required selecting some topics as examples and leaving out other important ones. As a professional researcher, I have followed the normal rules of my trade, namely, choosing examples that fairly represent the whole, putting the greatest weight on evidence that is objective and quantitative, and subjecting all conclusions to the scrutiny of sceptical colleagues.

The following five chapters will consider specific drugs and theories in detail, but this one is intended to introduce some general issues, and a standard terminology, under three broad headings. The first section examines the extent of legal and illegal drug use in Canada. It is intended to show that there is much less drug consumption in Canada than the level suggested by familiar phrases like 'epidemic of drug abuse' and 'drug crisis.' The second section focuses on the ways that drugs are used. Contrary to drug-war doctrine, it shows that most Canadians use legal and prohibited drugs in relatively harmless ways, rather than as a manifestation of addiction or a prelude to violence. The third section concerns the way people talk about drugs. This section focuses primarily on the word 'addiction,' but it is intended to show that many familiar words and phrases have been given special meanings that carry built-in justifications for the War on Drugs and that these special meanings do not accord well with reality. Besides 'addiction,' this drug-war vocabulary includes 'epidemic,' 'drug abuse,' 'substance abuse,' 'addictive drugs,' 'physical dependence,' 'psychological addiction,' 'drug-related,' 'narcotics,' 'euphoria,' 'self-control,' and 'denial.'

## The Extent of Drug Use in Canada

The extent of drug use in Canada is much less than conventional wisdom and drug-war propaganda would have it. The previous chapter and Table 1 showed the disparity between the beliefs of university students about a high frequency of daily drug use among their fellow students and the lower frequencies of use they actually report. This section will review further evidence that the actual amount of drug consumption in Canada is much less than most people believe. As a recent article in *Science* points out, the data on frequency of drug use are 'soft,' because of the impossibility of making direct observation (Barnes 1988) None the less, many respected scholars have spent years measuring the extent of drug use, and this evidence provides a reasonably consistent picture. The bulk of the evidence comes from three sources: large-scale survey research, small-scale survey research, and police statistics. All three are discussed below.

### LARGE-SCALE SURVEY RESEARCH

Surveys based on interviews or questionnaires are widely used to provide information about drug use as well as sexuality, marital satisfaction, political preferences, personal income, religious beliefs, and other private information. Since the famous 'Kinsey Reports' in the 1950s, it has been widely accepted that, when assured of confidentiality, people will reveal behaviours in such surveys that are normally kept secret.

Obviously, there is a risk that drug use will be under-reported in surveys. Nevertheless, a number of investigators, including both supporters and opponents of the War on Drugs, have found that people report their drug use with reasonable accuracy if the questionnaires or interviews are carefully planned (see Westermeyer 1982, 83; Vaillant 1983, 31–2; Smart and Ogborne 1986, 66; Rootman 1988, 220). Zinberg (1984, 64–8) has described the positive results of an elaborate cross-checking scheme on the self-reports of controlled heroin users. By contrast, Annis (1979a) has found less consistency in the self-descriptions of skid-row alcoholics. My own experience is that university students who are asked about their drug use under the proper circumstances are willing and even eager to be frank. Such interviews often provide an unusual opportunity – people often have nobody else to whom they may tell their secrets. As well, university students are used to being questioned about their personal concerns and know that they can trust the promise of confidentiality. As with all imperfect measures, of course, survey studies must be cross-checked with other types of information.

Proponents of the drug war often disseminate selected findings from large-scale survey research to support their cause. However, a balanced review of existing survey research provides little justification for their generalizations. Although there are few national polls of Canadian drug use, large-scale surveys provide considerable information about the prevalence of drug use in individual provinces and other large populations. There are many such surveys in Ontario, thanks in large part to the energetic scientists at the Addiction Research Foundation in Toronto. The results of much of this research is summarized in a valuable book entitled *Forbidden Highs* (Smart 1983).

Considered together, Canadian survey studies reveal that most Canadians do not currently use illegal drugs; of those who experiment with them, most do not continue; most of those who continue use moderate quantities; illegal drug use peaked in the late 1970s and has generally declined or remained stable since; marijuana is by far the most-used illegal drug in Canada; and cocaine and heroin are unpopular drugs among Canadians (Smart 1983). Survey studies further reveal that heavy use of illegal drugs is more frequent in Ontario and British Columbia than in the rest of Canada, more frequent in the United States than in

Canada, and heavily concentrated in young, socially marginal subpopulations. At all levels of use, males use more illegal drugs than females (Smart 1983).

## Cannabis

A recent study of cannabis use among Ontario students provides an example of large-scale survey research and of typical Canadian results. A sample of 4737 Ontario students in grades 7, 9, 11, and 13, carefully selected to represent the provincial school population, were asked how much cannabis (marijuana, hashish, or 'hash oil') they had consumed in the previous year. Slightly more than four-fifths of the students reported consuming none at all. Of those who had used cannabis that year, slightly more than one-quarter reported consuming enough to yield more than 1500 mg of THC in the year, the equivalent of 188 marijuana 'joints.' Thus, in round numbers, 1 in 20 Ontario students consumed more than the equivalent of one marijuana joint every other day or more in the previous year, 3 out of 20 consumed less cannabis than this, and 16 out of 20 consumed none at all. Cannabis consumption among Ontario students was slightly lower in 1983 than it had been in 1977 (Smart and Adlaf 1986).

Cannabis consumption among Ontario students dropped significantly over the last decade. Students who reported any use in the twelve months preceding the interview constituted 25 per cent of the population in 1977, 30 per cent in 1981, 21 per cent in 1985, 16 per cent in 1987, and 14 per cent in 1989 (Smart and Adlaf 1989). Cannabis use among adults in Ontario has remained approximately stable. Between 8 and 11 per cent of Ontario adults report using marijuana once or more during the year prior to their interview (Smart and Adlaf 1988). Higher figures for cannabis consumption can be obtained by asking people if they have ever consumed cannabis, rather than if they have consumed it in the previous year as in this study. Many people experiment with marijuana and choose not to continue, or don't use it often enough to be included in the group who use it during any particular year.

## Cocaine

Far less cocaine is consumed than marijuana. For example, in a door-to-door 'household survey,' the proportion of Ontarians who reported ever having used cocaine at any time in their life doubled, from 3.3 to 6.1 per cent between 1984 and 1987. The number that reported using cocaine at least once in the past year was 1.7 per cent in 1984 and 1.8 per cent in 1987. Of those who had ever used cocaine, 95 per cent reported using it less than once a month in 1987 (Smart and Adlaf 1988, 34). Again in round numbers, slightly more than one Ontarian in twenty has ever used cocaine. Of this minority who have used cocaine, 1 in 20 (or 1 in 400 of the total sample) has used it once a month or more in the past year. Because cocaine is centrally important in the current justifications for the War on Drugs, Canadian data on cocaine use, including the use of 'crack' will be examined in detail in chapter 5.

### Alcohol

Canadians in general are occasional drinkers. About 45 per cent report drinking once a week or more and about 15 per cent drink once a day or more. The rate of consumption has been essentially stable or declining since 1974 (Smart 1989). There is a small number of very heavy drinkers whose drinking may reach tragic proportions, and there are some areas of the country where drinking greatly exceeds the national average, namely the Yukon, Northwest Territories, and to a lesser degree, British Columbia. Drinking is generally well below the national average in the Atlantic provinces.

Among the European and North American countries, Canadians are about average in alcohol consumption. At the extremes, Norwegians drink about half as much as Canadians and French people about twice as much. There is little difference in alcohol consumption between Canada and the United States (Smart and Ogborne 1986, chap. 4).

SMALL-SCALE SURVEY RESEARCH

In light of these typical figures from authoritative large-scale Canadian surveys, how is it possible for anyone to perceive an epidemic of destructive drug use in Canada? I believe it is only possible to get such an impression by concentrating attention on certain subgroups of the general population. Studies of smaller populations reveal that the prevalence of drug use varies dramatically between them. Drug use is concentrated among the poor, the unemployed, school drop-outs, street children, native Indians, and people in drug-treatment programs. In some of these subpopulations the term 'epidemic' might be fairly applied, although destructive drug use is only one of many problems that such groups must face and these extreme subpopulations represent only a small fraction of the country as a whole.

*School Drop-outs*

A study of school drop-outs provides an example of small-scale survey research and typical results. A sample of 915 students from 'a small northern Ontario city' were given a drug-use questionnaire at the beginning of grade 9 and again 13 months later. In the meantime, eighty-eight students had dropped out of school; two-thirds of the drop-outs were found and were willing to retake the drug-use questionnaire.

On the first questionnaire, the student who were later to drop out used each of the legal and illegal drugs that were covered on the questionnaire more than the other students. The differences were substantial for the drugs that are the object of the War on Drugs. For example, 17 per cent of the future drop-outs had used glue, compared to 6 per cent of the non-drop-outs. Ten per cent of the future drop-outs had used 'speed' (that is, amphetamines, a major focus of the drug war in the 1970s) compared to 4 per cent of the non-drop-outs. For opiates the reported use was 6 per cent and 1 per cent respectively (Annis and Watson 1975).

The second questionnaire showed that the differences between the two groups persisted after one group had dropped out. In addition, a larger proportion of the drop-outs initiated the use of new drugs that they had not used during the earlier period. During this post-drop-out period, 15 per cent of the drop-outs first used LSD, compared to 6 per cent of the non-drop-outs (Annis and Watson 1975).

Clearly, there is a major difference in drug use between the majority of students and the minority that drop out in grade 9. However, it is difficult to be confident of measures of drug use in socially marginal groups. Even in the careful study described above, it was only possible to obtain interviews from two-thirds of the drop-outs, compared to 99 per cent of the student who had not dropped out. It is likely that the more alienated drop-outs would be less available for interviews and more likely to use illegal drugs, but this possibility could not be checked. Another limitation of this study is that only data on ever having used drugs at all were

TABLE 2
Percentage of male young offenders and male high-school
graduates in British Columbia who have used specific drugs
beyond the experimental level

|              | Young offenders (%) | High-school graduates (%) |
|--------------|---------------------|---------------------------|
| Alcohol      | 61                  | 97                        |
| Nicotine     | 92                  | 45                        |
| Cannabis     | 87                  | 79                        |
| Cocaine      | 45                  | 27                        |
| Hallucinogens| 55                  | 27                        |
| Amphetamines | 53                  | 33                        |
| Barbiturates | 21                  | 3                         |
| Solvents     | 3                   | 0                         |

reported. Many young people experiment with drugs and do not continue
to use them and therefore data on drug use beyond the experimental
stage might show a clearer difference between subgroups.

## Young Offenders and High-School Graduates

My colleagues and I have carried out a study that controlled some of these
problems with the inmates in British Columbia's Youth Detention Centre
(Alexander, Driscoll, and Gayton, in preparation). Table 2 compares the
percentage of young men and boys who have used a number of common
drugs beyond occasional experimentation at some time in their lives in a
group of young offenders and a group of high-school graduates living in
an area not far from the Youth Detention Centre. The frequencies of drug
use among the high-school graduates in this study are higher than those in
the studies cited above. One reason is that we asked these graduates if
they had used the drugs beyond the experimental level *at any time* during
their lives, rather than during the past twelve months. Many who had
were no longer doing so. A second reason is that these data come from
males only. The way in which the data were collected will be discussed in
detail in the next section of this chapter.

With the exception of alcohol, a drug that is generally socially
acceptable in British Columbia, drug use is clearly much greater among

young offenders than among high-school graduates, even though the young offenders are about eight years younger on average than the high-school graduates. About twice as many of the young offenders have used nicotine, cocaine, and the hallucinogens beyond the level of experimentation. In the case of the barbiturates the difference is about 7:1. It is possible to create a misleading impression of the frequency of drug use by concentrating attention on groups like school drop-outs and young offenders and neglecting the difference between their levels of consumption and those of the general population. This problem comes to the fore in the interpretation of police statistics.

## POLICE STATISTICS

Police statistics provide valuable information in this era of the War on Drugs. However, none of it provides a basis to determine the amount of drug use among Canadians in general. Arrest rates, for example, are must more affected by police priorities than by the amount of drug use that occurs (Stoddart 1982; Johnson 1988, 7). Police may enforce marijuana laws strictly in high schools, only loosely at universities, and not at all at rock concerts. The resulting arrest statistics tell nothing about the frequency of marijuana use in these different settings. Saskatchewan had the second highest drug offence rate in Canada in 1987, following British Columbia. Saskatchewan's rate was more than double Quebec's, and substantially higher than Ontario's (Johnson 1988), but this does not mean that the prevalence of drug use in Saskatchewan was double that of Quebec and higher than that of Ontario.

It is often assumed that police seizures constitute 5 or 10 per cent of the total importation of illicit drugs into Canada, thus providing a way of estimating the total importation. However, the 5 or 10 per cent figures could be totally wrong, in spite of their universal acceptance. Moreover, total importation provides no information about who uses the drug and how they use it, about how much of the drug is used in Canada and how much is shipped elsewhere, or about the dangers that arise from the use of a drug. Although police statistics add no useful information about the amount or distribution of drug use in the general population, police experience does provide invaluable observations about the use of drugs by criminals and other socially marginal groups.

*Heroin*

Although heroin was the object of great national concern before the current concern over cocaine, it was never used by more than a fraction of 1 per cent of the Canadian population, and the number of addicts never exceeded a few thousand. Little can be known about the consumption of heroin through survey research, since so few Canadians use it that survey data could not yield reliable estimates unless thousands of people were interviewed. However, police statistics provide valuable information on this drug, because police attention was focused on heroin users for decades. The Le Dain commission, Canada's royal commission on drug use, relied on police and medical statistics as accumulated by the Bureau of Dangerous Drugs to estimate the number of heroin addicts and users in Canada. The commission reported that in 1972, at the height of national concern about heroin addiction, there were 15,000 daily heroin and methadone users in Canada, about 60 per cent of whom lived in British Columbia (Le Dain 1973, 677–83).

## How Canadians Use Drugs

The amount that a drug is used tells little about the way that it is used. For example, most authorities on addiction recognize that some addicted persons do not use large amounts of their drug, although their compulsive need for the drug may be as great as that of people who use much more. Conversely, some very large consumers of drugs are not addicted (Westermeyer 1982, 91; Zinberg 1984, 84–5). Therefore, a basic understanding of drug use in Canada involves knowing the ways that Canadians use drugs in addition to the amounts.

Misleading presuppositions about the way people use drugs are built into contemporary language, which, for example, presupposes that most people who use 'addictive drugs' like heroin and cocaine are addicted, or will shortly become so. For this reason the term 'heroin user' is often used interchangeably with 'heroin addict.' But this presupposition is false. This section will show that all psycho-active drugs can be used in many ways, of which addiction is only one, and that the 'addictive drugs' do not necessarily carry a higher risk of addiction than the rest.

## PATTERNS OF INVOLVEMENT WITH DRUGS

A very large number of terms with overlapping, often imprecise definitions have been used to describe different ways or patterns of using drugs. For clarity, this book will stick to a single, carefully defined set of terms. The terms were introduced by Jerome Jaffe (1985), former research director of the American National Institute on Drug Abuse. Jaffe's terms and their definitions have appeared in several editions of Goodman and Gilman's authoritative pharmacology text, *The Pharmacological Basis of Therapeutics*. These terms are used by professionals in many fields, although not always consistently.

Several years ago, I began asking university students to categorize their own use of drugs with Jaffe's definitions. In the course of hundreds of these interviews, I subdivided two of Jaffe's terms to conform to distinctions that the students insisted were important. I also expanded and slightly modified Jaffe's wording to make it clearer to university students. The vocabulary that emerged from this process should be usable by both professionals and non-professionals. Following Jaffe's thinking, the terms introduced in this book arrange patterns of using drugs along a continuum of *involvement*, ranging from none to 'overwhelming involvement.' Involvement in this sense encompasses both the frequency of use and the way a person thinks about their use.

The patterns are listed below with a brief explanation of each:

*Abstinence.* Abstinence means no involvement with a drug at all. The term may be applied to people who have never used it and to people with a history of excessive use who have ceased all involvement with it.

*Experimental Use.* This term means 'use of a drug on one or a few occasions, because of curiosity about its effects, or in order to conform to the expectations of peer groups' (Jaffe 1985, 532). Experimental use is generally undertaken to satisfy the curiosity of the user, but the term can also be applied to formal experiments in which the user is a subject and the primary motivating curiosity is the experimenter's.

*Circumstantial Use.* This occurs when 'certain drug effects are sought because they are helpful in particular circumstances, as when students or truck drivers take amphetamines to alleviate fatigue.' (Jaffe 1985, 532). Circumstantial use can be initiated by the user alone, or it can involve a doctor, as when codeine is prescribed for muscle spasm, amphetamines are prescribed to combat acute depression, or valium is prescribed to relieve tension following a heart attack. In Jaffe's (1985) original definitions 'circumstantial use' was reserved for non-medical use of a drug.

*Casual Use.* Casual use is the infrequent use of modest amounts of a drug for their pleasurable effect.

*Regular Recreational Use.* This pattern of involvement is more frequent than casual use but is still undertaken for pleasurable effects. Jaffe's (1985) original definitions do not distinguish casual use from regular recreational use, but students that were interviewed insisted on such a distinction in describing their own use. I have found it useful not to give 'regular' a quantitative definition but simply to ask people to define it as they normally do.

*Dependence.* Dependence occurs when users show 'diminished flexibility' in their behaviour towards a particular drug. 'They continue to take it in the absence of medical indications, often despite adverse social and medical consequences, and they behave as if the effects of the drug are needed for continued well-being' (Jaffe 1985, 532). Many cigarette smokers and coffee drinkers fit this definition, as well as many users of illicit drugs.

Dependence, as defined here, is not necessarily a serious problem. As Jaffe explains: 'Dependence on a drug per se is not necessarily cause for concern. If the substance used has low toxicity and is relatively inexpensive (e.g., caffeine), a drug-using behaviour may meet the criteria for dependence but may not constitute a significant medical or social problem' (Jaffe 1985, 533). In everyday conversation people often refer to dependencies, particularly to nicotine, as 'addictions.' However, the kind of habit described above will be consistently referred to as 'dependence,' and addiction will be defined differently.

*Addiction.* Addiction is defined as 'a behavioral pattern of drug use, characterized by overwhelming involvement with the use of a drug ..., the securing of its supply, and a high tendency to relapse after withdrawal' (Jaffe 1985, 533). The phrase 'overwhelming involvement' in this definition marks off addiction from dependence. Dependence may remain in the background of a person's life, but addiction is necessarily central and supplants other important activities.

The word 'addiction' inevitably complicates any discussion because it has so many meanings in everyday language. Addiction is such a central issue in the War on Drugs that much of the final section of this chapter will be devoted to clarifying this term. At this point, however, some complications concerning the meaning of addiction will be mentioned briefly, so that the word can be used consistently.

One issue is an ambiguity of values. 'Overwhelming involvement' may be either a good or a bad thing. The harm that can be associated with 'overwhelming involvement' is obvious in the disastrous lives of street addicts, alcoholics, and compulsive gamblers. The term 'negative addiction' will be used in this book to refer to tragic addictions of this sort. By contrast to negative addiction, many people describe their 'overwhelming involvement' in positive terms. For example, a person may become overwhelmingly involved with another person, a computer, or a drug and drug-consuming group of friends for a period and feel, both then and afterwards, that he or she has benefited from the experience. Addictions of this sort will be termed 'positive addictions.'

A second complication surrounding the term 'addiction' is that many people view addiction not as a way of using drugs, but as an *effect* of using them. The causes of addiction will be the entire topic of chapter 8. For the moment, it should be remembered that the term 'addiction' is used descriptively in this book to refer to a pattern of overwhelming involvement with drugs and does not imply any conclusion about how this pattern is caused.

FREQUENCY OF DIFFERENT PATTERNS OF DRUG USE

*The Le Dain Commission's Research on Ways of Using Cannabis*

The Le Dain commission conducted extensive national surveys on cannabis use among high-school students, university students, and the 'household population' (that is, people contacted by door-to-door survey research). This research was concluded in 1970, at the end of a decade of enormous growth in the use of marijuana and of unprecedented exuberance about its effects among students and others (Le Dain 1972).

The commission found that most Canadians in 1970 had never used marijuana and, of those who had, most had been experimental, casual, or regular recreational users. (I am using the terminology introduced above, rather than the commission's. This translation into the standard language of this book will be done wherever, as in this case, it can be done without distortion.) The royal commission's data indicated that by 1970, 10 per cent of high-school students, 29 per cent of university students, and 3 per cent of the household population had used marijuana at any time during their lives. Of this minority of the population that had used marijuana, 28 per cent of the high-school students, 40 per cent of the university students, and 71 per cent of the household population had 'apparently terminated use' by 1970. Most of the remainder were casual or regular recreational users. The commission classified 7 per cent of the high-school students and 9 per cent of the university students as either dependent, addicted, or negatively addicted users (Le Dain 1972, chap. 4).

In addition to the survey populations, the commission estimated that there were 25,000 to 50,000 'street people,' a fraction of 1 per cent of Canada's population, almost all of whom used marijuana. The use of marijuana by street people was described as follows: 'It is within these scenes that individuals who are "high" most of their waking day are most likely to be found, although, even here, they represent only a very small proportion of the total population. Nevertheless, the daily smoking of marijuana or hashish is more the rule than the exception,' (Le Dain 1972, 201).

*How Young British Columbians Use Drugs: Research Methods*

My students and I have carried out several studies to estimate the frequency for different ways of using drugs (Alexander 1985; Alexander and Schweighofer 1988; Alexander, Driscoll, and Gayton, in preparation). Most of this research has been conducted on university students, although some data from other populations of young people will be included here as well. The data from this research are cited throughout this chapter and in later chapters as well.

Because people are sensitive about the way they use drugs, we took great care to maximize accuracy by gaining the interest and co-operation of the subjects. Some of the procedures used to maximize accuracy are

TABLE 3
Patterns-of-involvement definitions

1. Did not use at all. (Abstention)[1]
2. Used on no more than a few occasions out of curiosity, or to conform to a group. (Experimental Use)
3. Used only in specific circumstances when effects were helpful, e.g., unusual fatigue, illness, pain, etc. (Circumstantial Use)
4. Used infrequently for its pleasurable effects. (Casual Use)
5. Used regularly for pleasurable effects. (Regular Use)
6. Used regularly, without medical necessity; effects felt as needed for continued well-being; probably would continue use in spite of adverse medical or social effect. (Dependence)
7. Overwhelmingly involved with using and/or obtaining it; pervades total life activity and controls behavior in a wide range of circumstances; high tendency to resume use after stopping. (Addiction)
8. (This category scored if subject gave a negative response to two follow-up questions following choice of category 7: 'Did you like being that involved with _____?' 'Did you feel good about yourself when you were that involved with _____?').[2] (Negative Addiction)
9. Continued use is necessary to prevent a syndrome which could include headaches, nausea, diarrhea, chill, cramps, mental imbalance, etc. (At least one physical manifestation, i.e., other than 'mental imbalance,' must be mentioned.) (Withdrawal Symptoms)

1  Subjects were not shown the material in parentheses.
2  Category 8 was omitted completely from the copy of the definitions that was given to the interview subjects, and the two follow-up questions were posed orally if the subject chose category 7.

described below, and a fuller description is available in Alexander and Schweighofer (1988). All data were gathered in face-to-face interviews. The interviewer's instructions and the subject's responses were discussed until both felt confident that they understood each other. To maintain the subjects' interest, they were allowed to digress at length if they wished.

The subjects were given written definitions of the ways of using drugs that are presented in table 3. These definitions were shorter and more formal than the explanations given on p. 104, but were amplified in discussion with the subjects, so that all the points in the explanations on p. 104 were discussed.

The subjects were asked to choose one of these definitions to describe their own involvement with each drug and each activity on a comprehensive list. To avoid forcing the subjects into arbitrary choices among involvement categories, they were asked to give a verbal description of their involvement if none of the definitions applied to them. In spite of this escape valve, the students chose to classify over 95 per cent of their involvements according to the list of definitions.

The last category in table 3 is 'withdrawal symptoms.' This term does not refer to a level of involvement, but to a susceptibility to sickness when the use of a drug or an activity is terminated. Because this definition was not an involvement category, subjects who selected it were always asked to choose one of the involvement categories (1–8) as well. Conversely, subjects who indicated regular use of any drug or activity were always asked whether or not they would apply category 9 as well. The subjects has little difficulty understanding the need to treat category 9 independently. At the end of the interview the students were asked to list any drugs they were actively attempting to quit using, or which they had actively worked at quitting in the past.

The student interviewers who collected most of the data were taught to invite the subjects to participate collaboratively in translating their complex life experiences into the set of numbers that were recorded. This approach created a comfortable atmosphere in which subjects generally responded both carefully and openly. In fact, many spontaneously commented that they enjoyed the interview because it gave them the opportunity to evaluate themselves in terms they hadn't considered before.

The student subjects were first asked their current level of involvement with the first drug on the interviewers' list. Next they reported the number of days they had used it during the previous thirty days. They were then asked the category of their 'highest ever' involvement with each drug or activity, that is, the involvement category during the period when their involvement had been the greatest, if it was higher than their current involvement.

Since the involvement categories were originally taken from a pharmacology text, their wording is more suitable for drugs than for other activities. In particular, the verb 'use' in the definitions was awkward for many subjects when categorizing their involvement with non-drug activities: it is awkward to say that one 'uses' love or children. Subjects were therefore asked to substitute an appropriate verb on the non-drug activities mentally, but to otherwise apply the definitions literally, as they had with the drug items.

To avoid self-selection of subjects, a perennial problem in research of this sort, lists of subjects were created in advance and the interviewers' assignment included finding a way to persuade every individual on the list to participate. A similar procedure was originally described by Schachter (1982). This procedure worked reasonably well at the university and only sometimes off-campus. The data reported here only include samples where at least 95 per cent of the pre-selected subjects were actually interviewed. This procedure trades away the advantages of random sampling for the advantages of minimizing self-selection.

## How Young British Columbians Use Drugs: Results

The data discussed here come from 207 young people: 136 male and female students at Simon Fraser University, 33 recent male and female graduates of a senior secondary school in Cloverdale, BC, many of whom were attending community colleges or other schools, and 38 prisoners, mostly male, at British Columbia's Youth Detention Centre, an institution for young offenders. The university, the high school, and the detention centre were all within twenty miles of each other.

Figure 2 shows the frequency of the different patterns of drug use for some commonly used drugs. These data are based on the highest pattern of involvement that the subjects reported ever having experienced with each drug – current levels of involvement were much lower. These data show that the drugs represented here have been used in all of the patterns of involvement defined earlier with the exception that circumstantial use of cocaine and cannabis was not reported. Although the drugs had all been used in almost all the possible ways, their profiles differ considerably. Cocaine stands out from the other drugs because experimental and casual use was more common than any of the higher levels of involvement. Nicotine is conspicuous because the likelihood of dependence, addiction, and negative addiction among its users was higher than with most of the other drugs and the likelihood of casual or regular use was relatively low. For alcohol, cannabis, and caffeine, casual and regular use was most common, although dependence, addiction, and negative addiction had occurred for some subjects. These results indicate that users of some drugs normally labelled 'addictive,' specifically cocaine, are not more likely to have been addicted than users of drugs that are not labelled addictive. Some drugs that are normally considered not addictive, marijuana and caffeine, seem to have led to addiction relatively frequently. The drug for which dependent and addictive use afflicted the highest proportion of users was clearly nicotine.

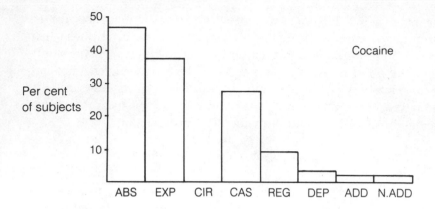

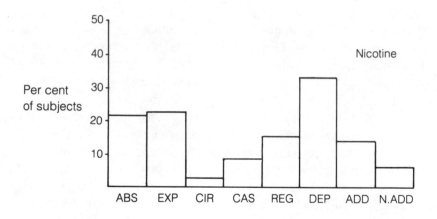

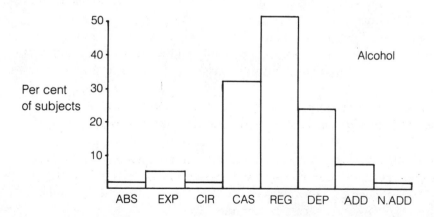

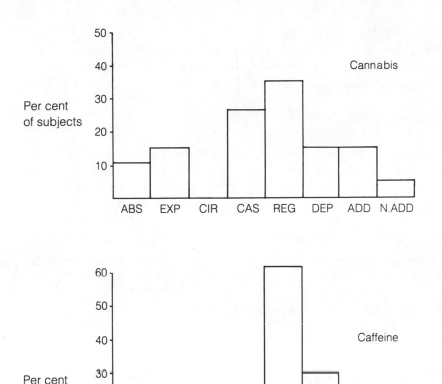

Figure 2
Distribution of lifetime highest drug involvements among young men and women in British Columbia. The involvement categories are abbreviated as follows:
ABS: abstinence, EXP: experimental use, CIR: circumstantial use, CAS: casual use, REG: regular recreational use, DEP: dependence use, ADD: addictive use, N.ADD: negative addictive use.

These findings clearly contradict some of the assumptions about 'addictive drugs' that justify the War on Drugs. In order to understand these contradictions fully it is necessary to reconsider the meaning of the confusing word 'addiction.' This task will be undertaken in the next section.

## How People Talk about Drugs

Justifications for the drug war are stated in familiar terms that have acquired special meanings. This section concentrates on the word 'addiction,' but will consider other terms briefly as well. It shows how these words have acquired special meanings that implicitly support the War on Drugs and how these special meanings often distort the reality of drug use. I have chosen addiction as the primary example here because the horrors of addiction have been a central image sustaining the War on Drugs from its start.

CHANGING MEANINGS OF 'ADDICTION'

*Traditional Definition*

The word 'addiction' comes from the Latin verb *addicere*, which means 'give over.' The Latin verb was used in both a positive and a negative sense. In Roman law, for example, an *addictus* was a person legally given over as a bond slave to his creditor, a very bad situation in ancient Rome. However, *addicere* could also be used to describe admirable devotion, as in the phrase *senatus, cui me semper addixi*, 'the senate to which I am always devoted,' and *agros omnes addixit deae*, 'he devoted the fields entirely to the goddess' (Lewis and Short 1879).

The traditional meaning of 'addiction' in English is close to the Latin. For example, addiction has been defined as: 'a formal giving over or delivery by sentence of court. Hence, a surrender or dedication of any one to a master ... The state of being (self-)addicted or given to a habit or pursuit; devotion.' (*Oxford English Dictionary* 1933, 104). A similar definition appears in Webster's original American dictionary (Webster 1828/1970). Uses of 'addiction' over several centuries, compiled in the *Oxford English Dictionary*, illustrate both its favourable sense ('His own proper Industry and Addiction to Books') and its unfavourable sense ('A man who causes grief to his family by his addiction to bad habits).

Traditional usage did not connect addiction with drugs. For example, drinking and drunkenness are as old as human history, but habitual drunkards were not generally labelled as addicts until the nineteenth century, although the phrase 'addicted to intemperance' was occasionally seen earlier (Levine 1978). Chronic opium users have also been known for centuries, but the word 'addiction' was rarely used to describe them prior to the nineteenth century (Parssinen and Kerner 1980). Opium was regarded as a medicine, not an addictive substance (Sonnedecker 1962, 1963).

## Drug-War Definition

A new definition of addiction emerged in the nineteenth century when the temperance and anti-opium movements began applying the term to habitual drunkenness and habitual opium use (Sonnedecker 1963; Levine 1978, 1984; Berridge and Edwards 1981). In this new usage, the meaning of addiction was narrowed in at least four ways. The new meaning (1) linked addiction to certain drugs, especially alcohol and opium; (2) gave addiction a necessarily unfavourable meaning as an illness or vice; (3) identified withdrawal symptoms and tolerance as criteria or operational definitions of addiction; and (4) attributed the cause of addiction to the drug itself – people were addicted by exposure to drugs, much as others might be possessed by a demon. Addicts were no longer in control of themselves, but were controlled by their drug. These changes in the meaning of addiction provided a major portion of the conceptual foundation for the War on Drugs.

The temperance movement used the narrowed definition of addiction as part of their campaign to arouse distaste and pity towards habitual drunkards and public support for alcohol prohibition (Levine 1978, 159). 'Addiction' was not the most common epithet used by the early temperance movement, which favoured terms like 'intemperance' or 'inebriety.' But 'addiction' survived the others, perhaps because it sounded more like a medical term and was used by the movement's most famous medical man, Benjamin Rush (Levine 1978). The status of the drug-war definition of addiction as a medical or scientific concept was, however, illusory. Though some doctors were active in the temperance and anti-opium movements, the drug-war definition of addiction was not an 'independent medical or scientific discovery, but ... part of a transformation in social thought grounded in fundamental changes in social life – in the stucture of society.' (Levine 1978, 165–6).

In England, a similar social transformation tied the term 'addiction' to opium use and made opium an 'addictive' drug. Underlying motives for applying the drug-war definition of addiction to habitual opium users included the wish of the health professionals to expand their territory by changing what had previously been considered weakness or folly into a disease called addiction (Parssinen and Kerner 1980). If regular opium use was a disease, then physicians could find employment treating it, and pharmacists could claim a monopoly on selling opium, rather than leaving it universally and cheaply available (Berridge and Edwards 1981). As well, the nineteenth-century English middle class needed a justification for condemning unruly segments of the lower class. Part of this justification was found in the lower classes' prodigious use of opium, which could be stigmatized as a disease or vice by the drug-war definition of addiction. The interplay of motives has been summarized this way: 'Addiction is now defined as an illness because doctors have categorized it thus ... It was a process which had its origins in the last quarter of the nineteenth century ... but such views were never, however, scientifically autonomous. Their putative objectivity disguised class and moral concerns which precluded an understanding of the social and cultural roots of opium use.' (Berridge and Edwards 1981, 150).

In the United States, the drug-war definition of addiction was used to equate opium use with horrifying (and greatly exaggerated) descriptions of the withdrawal symptoms of addicts (Musto 1973, chap. 4). Along with genuine public-health concerns, there was a clear commercial purpose behind these scare tactics. Resistance had emerged in China to U.S. trade, in reaction to the mistreatment of Chinese workers in nineteenth-century America. At the same time, the Chinese empress was mounting an anti-opium drive and President Theodore Roosevelt saw an opportunity to regain favour in the 'China Market' by supporting opium prohibition (Musto 1973, chap. 2).

## Confusion over Addiction in the Twentieth Century

Because the conflicting traditional and drug-war definitions of addiction have each survived into the twentieth century, the meaning of addiction has become confused and embattled. According to Berridge and Edwards

(1981), 'Images of addiction are in fact consistently and relentlessly marketed – in the nineteenth century to make opium the property of the medical profession. In the twentieth century to justify the position of enforcement agencies or the international control apparatus, or to win tomorrow's research budget. Images compete, and in the process the marketing becomes even more aggressive. The medical and scientific images feed and change the public, administrative and political view, and in return these perceptions give the doctors and scientists the needed support' (250).

Currently, the meaning of addiction is so confused that many authorities, including the World Health Organization (Edwards, Arif, and Hodgson 1982) and the American Psychiatric Association (1980), have urged abandoning it. In fact, treatises on compulsive drug use have been written without ever using it, a feat of considerable verbal agility. However, the word 'addiction' has refused to disappear. It is still used extensively in popular and scientific writing, both in the traditional sense and in the drug-war sense. Along the way, the word has also come to be used in everyday language, to describe regular recreational usage and dependence, like many people's use of coffee and cigarettes (see figure 2).

## Rescuing Addiction

In effect, the nineteenth-century anti-drug movements kidnapped a previously useful word to use as a public-relations tool in fomenting their War on Drugs. By representing 'addiction' as a drug-related medical-moral disease, the kidnappers created great confusion about what the word actually means. The confusion is best resolved, not by abandoning a perfectly good word, but by exposing the kidnappers. The kidnapping has distorted reality. Contemporary research shows that the traditional meaning of addiction better fits the way people actually behave.

### RESEARCH ON THE NATURE OF ADDICTION

In this section, modern addiction research will be used to evaluate three of the four key differences between the definitions. It will show that addiction is (1) not restricted to alcohol and illicit drugs, or to drugs at all, (2) not inevitably harmful, and (3) not necessarily linked to withdrawal symptoms or tolerance. The fourth difference between the two definitions concerns the cause of addiction. Because this is a difficult and centrally important topic, it will be deferred until more detailed information about drugs has been presented.

### Is Addiction Linked to Alcohol and Illicit Drugs?

Although drug-war rhetoric does not deny that people become addicted to other activities, it draws such a tight association between addiction, alcohol, and illicit drugs that the three have come to seem almost equivalent. In the War on Drugs doctrine, certain drugs are 'addictive' and other are not. However, the interview data on university students, high-school graduates, and young offenders suggest something quite different. As shown in figure 2 above, negative addiction seems as frequent among users of caffeine and cannabis as it is among users of the 'addictive' drugs alcohol and cocaine. Negative addiction to nicotine seems to be more probable than negative addiction to any other drug.

Genuine negative addiction to legal drugs, particularly to caffeine, seem improbable in the era of the War on Drugs. Surely addiction to coffee cannot be as serious as addiction to heroin. However, although our subjects were not overly concerned about regular use or dependence on caffeine and nicotine, they described negative addictions to these same drugs in grave terms. The few who reported negative addiction to nicotine or caffeine described vividly how their smoking or coffee-drinking had become an overwhelming involvement that adversely affected their eating and sleeping, choice of friends, relationships with family, work and school performance, and so forth, and stated that they disliked this involvement and disliked themselves because of it. The emotional tone of these descriptions was invariably depressed, no matter what drug or activity was involved. Of course, the majority of students were less involved with caffeine and nicotine than this, and the majority chose the definitions of dependence or addiction (not negative addiction) to describe these involvements.

Although caffeine is probably seen as one of the most innocuous drugs in modern culture, severe negative addiction to caffeine has been described unmistakably in the historical literature (Brecher 1972; Greden 1974; Troyer and Markle 1984). In modern medical literature, references to 'caffeinism' are increasing. These are case studies of people suffering from severe chronic anxiety, insomnia, headaches, dizziness, and restlessness whose symptoms were eliminated when their large daily caffeine intake was reduced (Greden 1974; Lutz 1978). Other studies document the resistance of some patients to giving up excessive consumption of caffeine (Sours 1983) and caffeine-analgesic preparations (Murray 1973; see also chapter 6) in the face of grave warnings from their doctors. James and Stirling (1983, 255) observed: 'It is doubtful whether the exhortations of health authorities will be any more effective in reducing the caffeine intake of heavy users than similar efforts have been in reducing the intake of other substances (e.g., nicotine, alcohol, heroin).' These authors have developed a multi-component treatment program to help heavy caffeine users moderate their intake.

Another perspective on caffeine addiction was suggested by the self-descriptions of university students who defined themselves as negatively addicted to it. Typically, they spent large amounts of their time drinking coffee, smoking (most were also negatively addicted to tobacco), and 'socializing,' and viewed this behaviour as excessive and wasteful. It may be that what is labelled negative addiction to caffeine in the context of this chapter would in other contexts be thought of as 'procrastination' which, in its extreme form, is fatal to the academic careers of many students (Daher 1984). Certainly, a group of students who habitually sat around smoking marijuana and snorting cocaine to the extent that they damaged their academic careers would automatically be defined as drug-addicted. Are not the same definitions appropriate if the drugs are nicotine and caffeine? The apparent link between caffeine addiction and extreme procrastination fits with Gilliland and Andress's report (1981) that students at an American university who consumed five or more cups of coffee per day suffered more anxiety and depression and received lower marks and more 'incompletes' than those who drank less. The thirty-nine students in Gilliland and Andress's highest caffeine-consuming group had a mean semester grade-point average of 1.83, a failing level.

Negative addiction to tobacco is currently more and more recognized, but it may be necessary to look at historical records to appreciate fully how serious it can be. Brecher (1972) has recounted how from tobacco's first introduction to Europe, fortunes were lost, lives destroyed, and health ruined in individuals who became overwhelmingly involved with it. Of course, their ruination was facilitated by the extremely high prices tobacco brought – at times in London it was exchanged in equal weights with gold. An example that reveals the severity of tobacco addiction when tobacco is difficult to obtain comes from an observation of life aboard the 'hulks' where British prisoners were kept in the eighteenth and nineteenth centuries before being transported to Australia: 'The great emblem of desire and repression in hulk life, more than sex or food or (in some cases) even freedom itself, was tobacco. Possession of tobacco was severely punished, but the nicotine addict would go through any degradation to get his "quid." Silverthorpe noted how this cycle of addiction and flogging broke prisoners down: "They grow different – they go on from bad to worse until they have shaken off all moral restraint"' (Hughes 1987, 141).

Even when tobacco is easily accessible, negative addiction to it is not uncommon. Anyone who has watched the slow strangulation of an unreformed smoker with emphysema or lung cancer knows the reality of nicotine addiction. I can find no reason to doubt that negative addiction to tobacco can be as tragic as negative addiction to heroin or cocaine, or to doubt the self-diagnosis of the students who defined themselves as negatively addicted to tobacco.

Just as our interview data show that addiction is not limited to alcohol and illicit drugs, they show that it is not limited to drugs at all. In fact, by almost any definition, addiction occurs more frequently to activities that do not involve drugs (Alexander and Schweighofer 1988). For example, of the negative addictions reported by 136 university students, only 19.3 per cent were addictions to drugs (mostly nicotine, caffeine, and cannabis, but a few illicit drugs as well). About 80 per cent of the students' negative addictions were to non-drug activities including love, food, and a variety of indiosyncratic habits. Likewise for positive addictions, dependence, and regular recreational use, non-drug activities constituted the majority of the habits that the students reported. Drug habits accounted for slightly more than half (55 per cent) of the habits for which the students reported physical withdrawal symptoms, but clearly even by this criterion addiction is not restricted to drug habits.

There is little difference between negative addictions to drugs and to other activities. This has been shown so often in recent research that there is hardly room to doubt it any more. For example, Peele and Brodsky in their famous book *Love and Addiction* (1975) showed that compulsive love relationships can be as intense, irrational, and ultimately self-destructive as severe heroin addiction. Apparent differences between the two kinds of negative addiction disappear once the distorted media view of heroin addiction is discounted and the two involvements are systematically compared on the same dimensions. Newspaper accounts of threats, shootings, and suicide by distraught lovers are common, although the term 'addiction' is not normally applied in journalistic accounts. Case studies of extreme love addicts, including women who remain devoted to men who batter them and their children, are as pathetic and grotesque as case studies of severe heroin addicts (Peele and Brodsky 1975; Orford 1985). This is not to say, of course, that everyone who loves is negatively addicted. Even when love fits the traditional definition of addiction (but not negative addiction), life is usually enhanced. Negative addiction is a very different event than positive addiction.

Negative addictive involvement to many activities other than love can be as compulsive and harmful as negative drug addictions. These activities include gambling (Orford 1985), exercise (Morgan 1979), pentecostal religion (Womack 1980), hoarding money (Slater 198), childish fantasizing (Alexander 1982), television-viewing (Winn 1977; Mingo 1983), working (Oates 1977), eating and dieting (Chase 1981), and numerous other activities (Hodgson and Miller 1982; Orford 1985; Peele 1985). Just as addictions to these activities can lead to the same kinds of problems as drug addictions, the same kind of remedies are employed. For example, the broken homes and destruction of self-respect that accompany negative addiction to Christian fundamentalism are strikingly similar to those associated with alcoholism, and the remedy is based directly on the techniques of Alcoholics Anonymous. A recently formed organization called 'Fundamentalists Anonymous' has 36,000 members world-wide and has just opened a chapter in Toronto (CBC Radio, 'Sunday Morning,' 1987).

I suspect that, for most people, the idea of negative addiction without drugs has only a tenuous half-reality, and I believe this can be attributed to the powerful impact of the drug-war definition of addiction and drug-war propaganda. The media tend to publicize disastrous cases of drug addiction and, conversely, to publicize rewarding experiences with love, exercise, and religion. This reporting bias clouds the fact that both benign involvements and severe negative addictions occur with each of these activities. Chapter 7 will be devoted to a fuller exploration of addiction without drugs.

*Is Addiction Always Harmful?*

Negative addiction can be terribly destructive or fatal, but positive
addiction, even to drugs, can be benign. The distinguished scientist
Edwin Land (1971), inventor of the Polaroid camera, has provided a
first-hand account of beneficial addiction in a *Science* magazine article
entitled 'Addiction as a Necessity and Opportunity.' Land describes his
own life as an alternation between two states, which he called
'multiple-man' on the one hand, and 'single-man' or 'addiction' on the
other. 'Multiple-man' is in touch with people and the environment.
'Single-man' is involuted and intensely focused. Land correctly recognized the 'single-man' condition as fitting the traditional definition of
addiction. He described it as a *temporary and beneficial* state. In his
words: 'You want to be undisturbed. You want to be free to think not for
an hour at a time, or three hours at a time, but for two days or two weeks,
if possible, without interruption. You don't want to drive the family car
or go to parties. You wish people would just go away and leave you alone
while you get something straight. Then, you get it straight and you
embody it, and during that period of embodiment you have a feeling of
almost divine guidance. Then it is done, and suddenly, you are alone, and
you have a need to go back to your friends and the world around you, and
to all history, to be refreshed, to feel alive and human once again' (Land
1971, 151–2).

Although it is easy to understand Land's argument, it may be harder to
acknowledge that addiction can be beneficial in less distinguished people
who are addicted to drugs rather than scientific achievement. However,
the evidence is just as clear. Interview subjects in our research described
some of their past drug addictions as negative, but some described positive addictions to drugs as well. Usually, the positive drug addictions
were time-limited ones. Several university students, for example,
described a summer in which they and their friends had been 'overwhelmingly involved' with marijuana, alcohol, or LSD and had enjoyed it
at the time, and looked back on it as a temporary and positive experience.

Of course, it may be claimed that these students' temporary periods of
drug addiction were harmful, regardless of how fondly they were remembered, but this is a risky argument. Adventurous or rebellious adolescents
often develop extravagant passions for dangerous sports, forbidden
loves, and so forth. Although such youthful involvements may offend the

larger society at the time, they may also serve important functions, as rites of passage or first tries at adult autonomy. They might also serve as experiments by which young people learn that they cannot long escape adult responsibilities with addictive pursuits. These hypothetical beneficial functions seem at least as plausible as the drug-war definition of addiction which insists that all drug addictions are harmful, whether the formerly addicted person thinks they were or not.

The possibility that some drug addictions can be positive as well as negative accords perfectly well with the traditional definition of addiction although it violates the drug-war definition. Because the drug-war mentality colours all perceptions of drug use in our culture, beneficial drug addiction may be better appreciated by looking abroad. Westermeyer (1982) has provided a valuable case study of a Chinese merchant and teacher in a remote Laotian village. As a young man, Wen Yu developed a chronic, severe lung disease. He was not relieved by the indigenous herbal medicines, so, on the suggestion of the villagers, he tried regular use of locally produced opium. He found that daily use of opium controlled his cough and restored his strength so that he could resume work.

At the time of his marriage, he successfully gave up opium, but eventually his debilitating cough returned. He returned to his habit, to the disappointment of his wife and himself. Eventually, however, his lungs deteriorated to the point that he could no longer endure long trading journeys, even with the support of opium, and the survival of his family was threatened. At his wife's suggestion, the family then moved to Vientiane, the capital, and started an opium den. The opium supplies supported Wen Yu's own needs and the family lived well on the surplus from the food they served their customers as they smoked. Wen Yu had become overwhelmingly involved with opium. Westermeyer concludes the case study as follows: 'When I knew him, Wen Yu was sorely wasted and could not walk from one room to another without panting. But his home, while small, was one of the sturdiest and cleanest in the district. All his children were literate, and most were still in school. His seventeen-year-old would be the man of the house soon. Wen Yu disdained opium and his addiction to it. But it had enabled him to persist in his labors even while ill in his younger years, and now its sale brought a good living to his family. "I owe my life to opium!" he told me' (Westermeyer 1982, 140–4).

It might at first seem that Wen Yu is a poor example, because he is not 'really' addicted in the way North American addicts are. However, this objection is too facile. Wen Yu claimed to genuinely need his opium, but so do many North American addicts – although it is somehow more difficult to believe them. But why is Wen Yu's claim easier to accept than that of a North American 'junkie'? I belive that the way Canadians view their countrymen and women is more controlled by the drug-war mentality.

So far, this chapter has not touched on the conditions under which addiction can have such dramatically different positive and negative impacts. Hundreds of interviews have led me to believe that the essential difference lies in the way an addiction is related to the other components in a person's life.

Some positive addictions integrate the vital components of the addicted person's life. Familiar examples would be people whose devotion to their religions, families, or communities organizes and enriches everything that they do. Their lives are not narrowed because they are overwhelmingly involved, but are enlarged. Wen Yu provides an example of such a case where the positive addiction is to a drug. Such positive addictions may be called 'centripetal' since they draw in the elements of a person's life around a central theme.

Negative addictions have the opposite effect. Whether people are negatively addicted to religion, family, community, opium, alcohol, heroin, or cocaine, their addiction creates a persistent barrier to essential parts of their personal and social potential. They can as well be described as obsessed or fanatic as addicted. Such addictions may be called 'centrifugal' since they drive potentially important aspects of life to the periphery.

However, it appears that centrifugal addictions may be positive *if they are temporary*. For example, Land described using his temporary centrifugal addictions to achieve mastery of scientific problems. His life was not impoverished by this practice because he interspersed his periods of centrifugal addiction with long non-addicted periods. Students who described summers given over to a drug and a drug-using circle of friends may have been describing another version of temporary centrifugal addiction, one that may occur only once or a few times in a lifetime.

Since both centripetal and short-term centrifugal addictions may be beneficial to the addicted person and to society, negative addictions may be best understood as those that are both prolonged and centrifugal.

Obviously, whether an addiction is positive or negative has little to do with the particular drug or activity that is the object of addiction.

## Are Withdrawal Symptoms and Tolerance Linked to Addiction?

There is a growing consensus among scientists that withdrawal symptoms and tolerance do not necessarily accompany addiction and that they are not a major part of its cause. This position was stated, for example, in a recent World Health Organization memorandum on drug concepts (Edwards, Arif, and Hodgson 1982) and in other authoritative sources (Jaffe 1985, 533). Withdrawal symptoms and tolerance are pharmacological effects of repeated exposure to heroin and numerous other drugs. However, these two pharmacological effects are not necessarily correlates of addiction.

Addiction to cocaine can be at least as profound as addiction to alcohol or heroin, although cocaine does not produce withdrawal symptoms that are nearly as severe. In fact, it is a matter of scholarly debate whether cocaine can be said to produce withdrawal symptoms at all (see chapter 5). As well, some drugs that do produce withdrawal symptoms are not used addictively, for example imipramine, a drug prescribed for depression (Jaffe, Peterson, and Hodgson 1980).

Many laboratories, including the methadone clinic at Toronto's Addiction Research Foundation, have found that a large proportion of street heroin addicts do not have withdrawal symptoms when their heroin supplies are interrupted or when they are pharmacologically deprived by a 'naloxone challenge' (Glaser 1974; O'Brien 1976; Peachy and Franklin 1985). Similar observations have been reported on alcoholics (Reich, Filstead, and Slaymaker 1984). Unfortunately, some methadone programs refuse treatment to patients who do not produce withdrawal symptoms, on the grounds that they are not 'really addicted.' This can be rationalized under the drug-war definition of addiction, but it leads to cruel paradoxes, such as refusing treatment for addiction to women who prostitute themselves to obtain heroin or to men who incur repeated jail sentences to obtain it.

Even some of the scholars who still define addiction in terms of withdrawal symptoms and tolerance implicitly acknowledge that the definition is inadequate. After defining addiction in terms of tolerance and withdrawal symptoms, Smart (1983) notes that 'frequently, street addicts

TABLE 4
Withdrawal symptoms accompanying dependence, addiction,
and negative addiction

|                    | Drugs | | Activities | |
| --- | --- | --- | --- | --- |
|                    | No | Yes | No | Yes |
| Dependence         | 93 | 9 | 377 | 2 |
| Addiction          | 11 | 6 | 346 | 15 |
| Negative addiction | 13 | 4 | 61 | 1 |

do not have the full-blown withdrawal reaction, for the street drugs they use are weak and adulterated' (47). If addictions are defined by the presence of tolerance and withdrawal symptoms, how can street addicts not show withdrawal?

The relationship between withdrawal symptoms and addiction was explored in the Simon Fraser research by determining the number of instances of dependence, addiction, and negative addiction that were accompanied by withdrawal symptoms. Whenever students applied one of these categories to themselves they were asked if they also had withdrawal symptoms. Table 4 presents these data. Contrary to the drug-war definition, this table shows that the majority of students who were dependent, addicted, or negatively addicted to drugs did not report withdrawal symptoms, even in the case of negative addiction. Table 4 also shows that, even though a clear somatic manifestation was required for withdrawal symptoms to be recorded, withdrawal symptoms followed the cessation of some non-drug habits, such as love and sports, as well as some drug habits. Therefore, withdrawal symptoms are not a purely pharmacological phenomenon, although they were more frequently reported with drug habits than with other activities.

It is becoming clear in recent research that tolerance is not linked to addiction either. People can become severely addicted to cocaine, but it is uncertain whether or not cocaine produces tolerance. Experimental reports indicate that repeated use of cocaine builds sensitivity, rather than tolerance, to some of its effects and that no tolerance develops to others (Fischman et al. 1976; Hinson and Poulos 1981; *PM*, chap. 5). As well, tolerance develops to the sedative effects of the phenothiazenes (chlor-promazine, etc.) and to other drugs that are not addicting (Rech and Moore 1971). Thus withdrawal symptoms and tolerance are not linked to addiction, except by the drug-war definition.

## ADDICTION AS JUSTIFICATION FOR THE WAR ON DRUGS

The drug-war definition of addiction is a nineteenth-century medical-moral concept that was attached to a venerable word and used to promote the War on Drugs. It reduced the complex phenomenon of addiction to nothing more than a disease of excessive drug consumption accompanied by withdrawal symptoms and tolerance. It thus defined addicts as a separate group that could be pitied, despised, or cured, but – because they had the dreaded drug disease – could not be understood in the same terms as the rest of humanity. It created the category of 'addictive' drugs that must be eliminated at all costs. The spectre of addiction, in this sense, has helped to justify the War on Drugs for over a century.

Addiction, as it exists in human experience and in the traditional definition, cannot excuse a War on Drugs. Addiction is as likely to be a benefit as a curse. Moreover, when it is a curse, it most often has nothing to do with the drugs that are the object of the current War on Drugs. By restricting the term, the drug-war definition has denied the other aspects of addiction that modern research and everyday experience confirm: harmful addictions to activities that do not involve drugs; beneficial additive dedication that often lies behind human achievement; centrifugal addiction as a phase in healthy development that some of our students describe; and addiction as a temporary refuge when conditions become unbearable.

The traditional meaning of addiction, by contrast, readily fits with modern research and the complexity of everyday experience. It is compatible with the fact that people become 'given over' to, or 'overwhelmingly involved' with, involvements other than drugs, and that this capacity has empowered some people to produce great works of art, science, and physical prowess. Moreover, traditional usage also fits the fact that some forms of addiction are disastrous. Thus, the traditional definition implicitly acknowledges a close relationship between some of what is best and worst in the human potential. Addiction has to do with the great potential and the great frailty of human nature. It presents problems that call for the best of our understanding, subtlety, and appreciation of human diversity. These problems can never be solved with the brutish tools of war.

## DRUG ABUSE

There are many other terms in the lexicon of the War on Drugs that carry built-in justifications for the drug war in their definitions and customary usage. One of the most familiar is 'drug abuse.'

What precisely does drug abuse mean? For the most part, people use this term to describe drug use they do not approve of, and it therefore refers to different drugs and patterns of drug use in different contexts. According to Jaffe (1985, 532), 'The term conveys the notion of social disapproval, and it is not necessarily descriptive of any particular pattern of drug use or its potential adverse consequences.' Such a term can be used as a battle-cry to launch soldiers and citizens into battle, but it can never be used to increase understanding of the people against whom the battle is being launched, for it only says that they are bad. For these reasons, the term 'drug abuse' will not be used in this book.

## PHYSICAL DEPENDENCE

In drug-war parlance, some drugs are often said to cause 'physical dependence' or 'physical addiction.' These terms imply a kind of addiction that is especially severe and long-lasting because it is lodged in the body, as distinct from 'psychological dependence,' which is only in the mind. The logic of the War on Drugs demands that drugs that produce physical dependence must be banned by force because 'physical dependence' is almost impossible to overcome. But the concept of 'physical dependence,' in this sense, is more like a logical trick than a meaningful term. The belief that a permanent 'physical dependence' can be induced by exposure to a drug sounds suspiciously like the fear of possession by demons or, in earlier legends, the fear of Medusa and the other Gorgons that turned brave men who merely glanced at them into stone. Like the legends, the term 'physical dependence' has no substantial basis in medical research, although patient researchers have sought one for decades. Some of the relevant research is discussed in chapters 4 and 5.

Another source of confusion surrounding physical dependence is that the distinction between it and 'psychological dependence' assumes a sharp distinction between body and mind. Obviously, the mind and body must be separate entities for addiction to be able to reside in either one or the other, just as in Christian doctrine body and soul must be different entities to permit the soul to ascend to heaven after the death of the body. Most modern scientists and philosophers reject this 'dualism' in favour of 'monism,' which holds that mental terms and physical terms are simply different ways of describing the same indivisible unity. However, some of these same scientific scholars inattentively let the dualism creep back into their thought when they discuss 'physical' and 'psychological' dependence.

It is *persons* that become addicted, not minds or bodies. Lengthy experience with opiate addicts in Vancouver convinced me of the error of thinking of their habits as purely 'physical dependence.' Their addictions are manifest in the way they think about life and themselves and their 'craving' for the drug. Craving is a mental event. What can people mean when they talk about a 'physical craving'? Can a cell 'crave'? If the mind and the body are separate entities, then heroin addiction is lodged in both. So why would it be called a 'physical dependence'? On the other end of the spectrum, can anyone seriously believe that Peele and Brodsky's (1975) 'love addicts,' which many people would classify as 'only psychologically dependent,' feel their addiction in their minds, but not in their bodies? A conversation with a heavily smitten teenager will quickly reveal the truth about this phenomenon.

Some modern scholars have used the term 'physical dependence' in a more defensible way to refer to a state in which cessation of use of a drug produces 'withdrawal symptoms.' In this usage, 'physical dependence' is just a way of saying that a person is subject to withdrawal symptoms if he or she stops taking their drug. It tells nothing about whether the person is addicted. Jaffe (1985, 533) is quite explicit about this: 'It is possible to be physically dependent on drugs without being addicted and, in some special circumstances, to be addicted without being physically dependent.' However, this precise but unfamiliar usage is easily confused with drug-war parlance and misunderstood.

For these reasons, the terms 'physical dependence' and 'physical addiction' will be banished from this book. The people whom Jaffe (1985) and others label as 'physically dependent' will be described here simply as 'subject to withdrawal symptoms.'

## Conclusion

This chapter, in concert with the next five, is intended to refute some key justifications for the War on Drugs. Although more evidence will be presented in succeeding chapters, this one has introduced the possibilities that there is no drug epidemic in Canada (or anywhere else), that most drug use is non-addictive, and that many familiar terms, including addiction, drug abuse, and physical dependence, are fanciful spectres created to justify the drug war. The next chapter will examine drug-war justifications that specifically concern the prototypical devil-drug, heroin.

# 4    A fresh look at heroin

In this century, the great persuasive force of science and medicine has been artfully utilized to maintain public commitment to prolonged wars. Although the Nazis were not the only practitioners of this art, they provide the most notorious example. They stiffened the resolve of the German people through the terrible suffering of the Second World War with a theory of Aryan racial superiority that had a putative basis in genetic theory and medicine. The Nazis claimed that 'National Socialism is nothing but applied biology' (Nolan 1988). In a similar manner, public faith in the need for a 'War on Drugs' has been sustained for decades by apparently scientific claims about the effects of heroin. This chapter critically examines these familiar, supposedly scientific claims. The next chapter deals with similar claims about cocaine.

Conventional wisdom and drug-war propaganda take it as established scientific fact that heroin use causes irresistible euphoria, unbearable withdrawal symptoms, great physical damage, nearly irreversible addiction, and crime. An illustration of this doctrine in its full vehemence is the following excerpt from a United States Supreme Court ruling of 1962:

> To be a confirmed [heroin] addict is to be one of the walking dead ... The teeth have rotted out, the appetite is lost, and the stomach and intestines don't function properly. The gall bladder becomes inflamed; eyes and skin turn a bilious yellow; in some cases membranes of the nose turn a flaming red; the partition separating the nostrils is eaten away – breathing is difficult. Oxygen in the blood decreases; bronchitis and tuberculosis develop. Good traits of character disappear and bad ones

emerge. Sex organs become affected. Veins collapse and livid purplish scars remain. Boils and abscesses plague the skin; gnawing pain racks the body. Nerves snap; vicious twitching develops. Imaginary and fantastic fears blight the mind and sometimes complete insanity results. Often times, too, death comes – much too early in life ... Such is the torment of being a drug addict; such is the plague of being one of the walking dead. (Cited by Brecher 1972, 21)

These beliefs about heroin are used to justify harsh measures not only against heroin, but also against other drugs. Children must be prevented from using marijuana because it 'leads to heroin'; cocaine is a menace because it is 'more addictive than heroin'; and so forth.

This chapter is designed to provide a fresh look at heroin. The first section deals with pharmacological fundamentals. The second and third major sections discuss the pharmacological effects and societal effects of heroin and the other opiates. These sections will show that most of the supposedly scientific claims about these drugs that have been used to justify the drug war are either exaggerated, unsubstantiated, or untrue. This is not to say that heroin, or any other drug, is perfectly harmless. However, when the actual hazards of heroin are examined, it becomes clear that ordinary peaceful measures are sufficient to control them, and that, with its fierce repression of heroin users and traffickers, the War on Drugs actually causes much of the harm that it attributes to heroin.

Although the facts summarized in this chapter are taken from the best available scientific sources, readers may find some of them hard to swallow. I hope that those who do will be provoked to wonder if they might have grown accustomed to receiving something other than hard information, which usually requires some chewing.

## Basic Opiate Pharmacology

Heroin is one of a large family of drugs called 'opiates,' or sometimes 'opioids.' The family includes opium, morphine, and many other drugs. In equivalent doses, the pharmacological effects of most of these drugs are very similar to those of heroin, although none of them arouses the fear and horror among the public that heroin does.

The opiate family has several branches. Some opiates are extracted from opium poppies, some are synthesized artificially, some are manufactured naturally in the bodies of human beings and other vertebrates, and some exceptional synthetic opiates, the so-called antagonists, have exactly the opposite effect to the others and serve as antidotes to them. Most opiates are chemically classed as alkaloids, ring-shaped organic compounds known for their bitter taste. Besides opiates, the alkaloid group includes nicotine, caffeine, cocaine, and many other drugs with medicinal uses (Rodriguez, Cavin, and West 1982). Some opiates are not alkaloids but peptides. Peptides are short chains of amino acids. Although peptides are chemically distinct from alkaloids, peptide opiates and alkaloid opiates have virtually the same effects.

Like most psycho-active drugs, opiates are carried in the blood to the brain, where they exert their primary psychological effects. How they enter the bloodstream does not matter much – they can be injected, smoked, 'snorted' (that is, absorbed through the nasal membranes), swallowed, or taken rectally in a suppository. The effects are the same, although the route of administration affects the speed of action and the amount that is required to produce a given effect. For example, larger doses of opiates must be taken if the drug is swallowed rather than injected, because some of the dose breaks down in the digestive system before being absorbed into the bloodstream.

Like most drugs, the opiates have some side-effects and large overdoses can be fatal. As well, people sometimes become severely dependent on or addicted to them. Although these adverse effects are of the greatest concern to the War on Drugs, they are relatively uncommon in the normal course of legal and illegal opiate use.

There are particular areas of the brain called 'binding sites' where opiates attach themselves and generally exert their inhibitory influences on neurons. Different opiates bind to slightly different, but overlapping portions of the brain. The sites generally fall on the paleospinothalamic pain pathway, which mediates chronic pain, and on portions of the limbic system, which mediates emotion (Snyder 1977). These same areas are also 'reward centres' in the brain; that is, animals will press levers at high rates to stimulate these areas through implanted electrodes. Opiates also bind in some spinal-cord regions that are implicated in transmitting pain signals to the brain. Opiates are powerful pain-killers and tranquillizers because they inhibit the function of neurons involved with pain and emotion. Opiates, like all drugs, travel through the entire bloodstream and bind in numerous places other than their medically primary site. Opiates also bind, for example, on the large intestine and on the vas deferens in males.

There are hundreds of opiates, but the most important in the context of this book are the following.

## OPIUM

The dried juice of the unripe capsule of the opium poppy is called opium. Opium is about 10 per cent morphine, which is its major active factor, but it also contains codeine and traces of other psycho-active alkaloids. Opium is today generally consumed in a dried form called 'smoking opium,' or dissolved in alcohol to make paragoric or laudanum.

## MORPHINE

Morphine is an alkaloid that was first extracted from opium in 1806. It is a bitter-tasting, fluffy white powder. Because it has been in common medical use for so long, it serves as the standard against which all other opiates are compared.

## HEROIN

Heroin, also called diacetyl morphine or diamorphine, is a simple derivative of morphine made by heating morphine with acetic acid. The German pharmacologist Heinrich Dreser did the pioneering clinical research on heroin at Friedrich Bayer and Co., which introduced it commercially in 1898. Dreser found heroin to be a highly effective medication in the treatment of coughs, chest pains, and the discomfort of pneumonia and tuberculosis (Trebach 1982, 39). This effect was important because pneumonia and tuberculosis were the two leading causes of death at that time, prior to the discovery of antibiotics. Dreser recommended heroin to doctors on the grounds that it was stronger than morphine and safer than codeine. Because of its great potential, he derived his name for the new drug from the German word for 'heroic.'

An early report on the clinical use of heroin was written by Dr Floret, a physician: 'Approximately 60 patients [with respiratory diseases] have been treated by me with this drug so far. They all agreed that they noticed an immediate improvement and relief from the persistent cough immediately after taking the powder ... They also observed that the pains associated with the cough were reduced: "Doctor, the powder you prescribed was indeed very good. Immediately after taking the powder I felt relief, I had to cough a lot less and in general the cough improved a great deal after taking the powder" ' (cited by Trebach 1982, 40). On the basis of this kind of reaction, heroin was quickly adopted as a valuable treatment for pain and cough. Some physicians thereafter tried it as a treatment for relieving morphine withdrawal symptoms and published successful reports. Contrary to some reports, they did not, however, advocate its use as a long-term substitute for morphine in addicts (Trebach 1982, 41). For a time, heroin seemed to be regarded as an especially suitable medication for women, but after its image began to change, that concept disappeared (Trebach 1982, chap. 3).

Heroin is two or three times as strong as morphine, apparently because it crosses the membrane barrier between the blood and brain more quickly. The strength of a drug is sometimes offered as evidence that it is dangerous, but, in fact, strength indicates nothing more than the amount required to produce a particular effect. It takes about twice as much morphine as heroin to produce the same effects, but the maximum effects are essentially the same. In fact, heroin is reconverted to morphine before it binds to brain tissue, and therefore the effects of the two drugs are theoretically identical in equivalent doses. Although the important reactions to morphine and heroin are the same, the withdrawal following experimental addictions to morphine is somewhat more prolonged. Some experienced users cannot distinguish the effects of intravenous injections of the two drugs in the laboratory, and most find both acceptable for regular use. Other users, however, can distinguish the two drugs and claim to have a strong preference for one or the other (Martin and Fraser 1961; Jasinski and Preston 1986).

## CODEINE

Codeine, another opium derivative, is an alkaloid structurally similar to morphine but with less strength and a lower maximum effect. Lower 'maximum effect' means that there are some levels of pain that morphine and other opiates can relieve that cannot be relieved by any dose of codeine. As with most other opiates, non-medical use of codeine is prohibited under the Narcotic Control Act.

## METHADONE

Methadone is a synthetic alkaloid, not derived from opium, but chemically similar to morphine. Methadone was first synthesized in Germany in the Second World War as a morphine substitute, when the trade lines for natural opium were cut. It has sometimes been claimed that methadone's original name, 'dolophine,' was chosen in honour of Adolf Hitler, but this story has been disputed (Inciardi 1986, 146). Methadone was introduced to the United States as a prescription drug in the 1940s. Controls were tightened after a number of people became addicted to it. Under the name dolophine, it is sometimes said to be the drug referred to in the famous novel about drug addiction in American women, *Valley of the Dolls*.

In most ways, methadone is like the other opiates although it is synthetic. The chief difference is that some of its effects last longer than do those of morphine or heroin and that the period of withdrawal symptoms following chronic use is longer. Many addicts prefer methadone to heroin, saying it gives a better high (Agar and Stephens 1975). However, in a laboratory test, some addicts could not distinguish intravenous injections of heroin, morphine, and methadone (Jasinski and Preston 1986).

## MEPERIDINE

Like methadone, meperidine is a synthetic opiate alkaloid in common medical use, although not generally used for maintaining addicts. Demerol is a familiar brand name of a product containing meperidine. Meperidine has roughly the same pharmacological properties as heroin and morphine and the same binding sites. Some addicts say meperidine is not as satisfying as morphine or heroin. Meperidine was long thought to be non-addictive, but it is now recognized that some people become addicted to it, as they do to virtually all the opiates, except for the antagonists. In hostage-taking incidents at Canadian penitentiaries, convicts have sometimes included among their demands a supply of Demerol from the prison pharmacy.

## OXYCODONE

Oxycodone is much like morphine in strength, duration of action, and withdrawal symptoms, except that it is perhaps more effective orally (Jaffe and Martin 1980, 507). Oxycodone is a common street drug in Vancouver, usually under the brand name Percodan.

## PROPOXYPHENE

Propoxyphene is an opiate with an unusually low maximum strength, but it is medically useful in combination with aspirin for control of some types of pain. Darvon is a familiar brand. Some people have become addicted to it, even though it produces convulsions in large doses and tissue damage with repeated injection. Propoxyphene is not as medically valuable as codeine and is more expensive. None the less, it has been popular clinically because of 'unrealistic overconcern about the addictive potential of codeine' (Jaffe and Martin 1980, 521). Propoxyphene is specifically *excluded* by the Narcotic Control Act Schedule, which means that its illegal use is not subject to the strict penalties reserved for narcotics (Milligan 1982).

## ETONITAZINE

The unusual property of the opiate etonitazine is that it is about 1000 times stronger than morphine, and therefore 300–500 times stronger than heroin. In practice, this difference simply means that it is given in smaller doses, measured in micrograms rather than milligrams. Its potential importance is that it is an ideal drug for smuggling, because tiny quantities can be very valuable. It would seem an almost impossible substance to control by normal techniques. I know of no attempts to smuggle it yet, however.

## PURE ANTAGONISTS (NALOXONE, NALTREXONE)

Naloxone and naltrexone act as almost perfect antidotes for the other opiates (Jaffe and Martin 1980, 521), apparently by displacing them from their binding sites. In cases of opiate overdose, the antagonists counteract the opiate effect almost immediately. They have only minor effects on people who have not been treated with opiates and who are not under stress (Emrich and Millan 1982). Both naloxone and naltrexone are synthetic alkaloid opiates.

## MIXED AGONISTS-ANTAGONISTS (NALORPHINE, CYCLAZOCINE)

These drugs have the peculiar property of being both useful opiates (that is, 'agonists') and opiate antagonists. In fact, they are used medically in both capacities – as pain-killers in non-addicts and in the treatment for overdose in addicts (Julien 1981, 114, 115; Jaffe and Martin 1980, 521–2). Two special properties enable these drugs to act as both agonists and antagonists. Their agonistic activity is relatively weak, but they attach powerfully to the brain's opiate binding sites. Therefore, if an addict overdoses, an injection of nalorphine or cyclazocine will replace the heroin at the binding sites and, because the agonistic effect is less, relieve the opiate overdose. Either drug can, however, serve as an effective pain-killer for a non-addict with a low tolerance for opiates. Nalorphine is not, however, widely used as an analgesic because its peak effect is lower than other opiates and it can produce hallucinations.

## PENTAZOCINE

This mixed agonist-antagonist was synthesized specifically to produce a non-addictive opiate. It has weak antagonist as well as agonist effects. Addiction does occur, however, and for a time pentazocine, usually in the brand-name product Talwin, became popular with American addicts (Jaffe and Martin 1985, 522). When used in combination with tripelanamine, as it was during its period of popularity, it produces severe tissue damage that is not observed with heroin addicts in the same surroundings (Senay 1985). Pentazocine is prohibited in Canada under the Narcotic Control Act.

## ENDOGENOUS OPIATES

Endogenous opiates have the same effects as opiate drugs, but are synthesized internally in human beings and other vertebrates. These substances were not discovered until 1975. Because they are potentially so important in understanding pain, analgesia, and addiction, speculation about them has run far ahead of research.

The existence of endogenous opiates was predicted before they were actually discovered. The man basis for the prediction was the discovery of highly specific opiate binding sites in many vertebrate species. The binding sites not only exclusively accepted opiate molecules, but, even more specifically, accepted only one of the two forms. (Organic molecules occur in two mirror-image forms called stereo-isomers.) These facts provoked the imagination of scientists. Why would vertebrates have evolved a specific receptor for a drug that has only been used in a single species? Why would a salmon, for example, carry around a receptor for a drug that is inaccessible to it? Surely nature does not distribute complicated locks that can shut out pain without also giving out keys! A number of laboratories started hunting for opiates within the body. Because all opiates known up to that time were alkaloids, the search was led astray for a time.

In 1975 two research teams independently reported discovering brain extracts that attached to the opiate binding sites and mimicked the effects of morphine. The active molecules in these extracts were not alkaloids, as had been expected, but peptides. These were named methionine-enkephalin and leucine-enkephalin. Methionine-enkephalin is three times more powerful than morphine and leucine-enkephalin is one-half as powerful as morphine. These enkephalins occur naturally in the brain in the same areas that contain the binding sites for opiates.

A number of other endogenous opiates have been discovered since the original two. These include beta and gamma endorphin, which were first discovered in extracts from the pituitary gland, an endocrine gland that is attached directly to the brain. The endorphins are larger peptide molecules, but they contain methionine-enkephalin (Harber and Sutton 1984). That these endorphins are concentrated in an endocrine gland suggests that they may be released into general circulation, like other hormones. The enkephalins, by contrast, seem to be synthesized and utilized without leaving the brain (Hughes et al. 1980).

There are many indications that endogenous opiates are part of the normal system for control of pain and stress and that they work in the same way as opiate drugs. When injected they attach to the brain's opiate binding sites and produce analgesia (Emrich and Millan 1982). Experimental animals that have been deliberately subjected to stress and pain automatically release them. Laboratory animals that are chronically exposed to endorphins and then deprived show the signs of opiate withdrawal. However, the implications of these important discoveries are not as simple as it seemed at first. The relationship between endogenous opiates and addiction has proved difficult to understand. Almost immediately after the discovery of endorphins, new hypotheses appeared identifying endorphin insufficiency as the cause of opiate addiction. Although many people outside of the scientific community seem convinced that these hypotheses have been proved, there is no strong evidence to support them as yet. There are enough leads, however, to keep the possibility alive (Herz 1981; Way 1983).

The effects that a drug has when used in a particular way are its 'pharmacological effects' under those conditions of use. The effects the actions society takes towards a person because they use a particular drug – 'societal effects' – can be more powerful than the pharmacological effects of a drug, particularly when a War on Drugs is under way. Pharmacological and societal effects of opiates will be considered in the next two sections of this chapter.

## Pharmacological Effects of Opiates

Opiate drugs have both beneficial and harmful pharmacological effects, as do all drugs. Because the effects of opiates, like other drugs, are strongly influenced by the way in which they are used, the effects are described separately here for different patterns of involvement. This section on pharmacological effects will show that some of the familiar claims made about opiates in the War on Drugs propaganda have no scientific basis.

MEDICINAL EFFECTS IN CIRCUMSTANTIAL USE

Opiates are highly effective in circumstantial use by sick people. They were so highly regarded in the nineteenth century as remedies for pain, anxiety, cough, and diarrhea that some physicians referred to them as G.O.M. – 'God's Own Medicine' (Brecher 1972). Although opiates are normally prescribed by doctors in the Western world, they work as well when administered by folk doctors or by private individuals. In remote areas of Laos, for example, there are essentially no doctors and self-medication with locally grown opium is the only effective treatment for many diseases (Westermeyer 1982).

Opiate drugs do not cure diseases in the way that antibiotics do, but there are many cases where temporary relief of symptoms aids recovery. In other cases relief of symptoms is simply humane. Even in the industrialized world, after decades of pharmacological research, there are still no better drugs than the opiates for many purposes (Jaffe and Martin 1985).

## EUPHORIA

The word 'euphoria' is sometimes used with sinister overtones in the context of drugs, but the word itself simply refers to a state of feeling good or happy. Most people know that heroin and the other opiates can produce euphoria, but do not know that this effect only occurs under exceptional circumstances.

### Euphoria in Circumstantial Use

Opiates can produce strong euphoria when used to control physical pain, for example after surgery. In part, this euphoria results from relief when pain subsides, but some patients describe an additional component, a sense of warmth and optimism (Beecher 1959). There is a curious symmetry in the relationship of pain and opiate drugs. The opiates are an antidote for pain, and pain appears to be the natural antidote to opiates. For a person who has overdosed, for example, prolonged pain reverses the overdose symptoms (Jaffe and Martin 1985).

### Euphoria in Experimental Use

When they are used experimentally, opiates, including heroin, generally do *not* produce euphoria (Jaffe and Martin 1985, 498). Although this fact may be surprising to many people, it has long been known. Lawrence Kolb summarized it succinctly in 1925: 'Only in rare instances, if at all, does any one except the emotionally unstable, the psychopath, or the neurotic' experience positive pleasure from morphine (quoted by Beecher 1959, 334).

Because the fact that opiate drugs do not often produce euphoria in experimental use contradicts conventional wisdom, some of the evidence will be examined in detail. The best experiments were conducted in the 1950s and 1960s. They probably could not be done today, because of increasing restrictions on the use of opiates, even in scientific experiments. I will illustrate the findings with a well-known experiment by Beecher and his colleagues (1959, chap. 14).

Beecher brought twenty young male volunteers to the laboratory on several successive days and gave an injection of a drug on each visit. To minimize the effects of expectations on the results, neither the subjects nor the technicians who gave the injections knew what the drug was. This is called a 'double-blind' procedure. Each subject received the following drugs in random order: a sodium chloride placebo; amphetamine sulphate, in a dose of 20 mg for each 70 kg of body weight; heroin hydrochloride in doses of either 2 mg or 4 mg for each 70 kg of body weight; morphine phosphate at 8 mg or 15 mg for each 70 kg of body weight. These doses approximate the doses that would routinely be administered in a medical setting. Subjects were also given sodium pentathol, but these results are not important here and are omitted for simplicity. Subjects were observed through a one-way mirror for two hours after each injection, and filled out mood-evaluation questionnaires before each injection and 30, 60, and 120 minutes afterwards.

Because of the importance of this experiment to this chapter and the next, and because it is the best controlled of many experiments with similar results, the results appear in detail in table 5.

These results are best understood by comparing the responses to each drug with responses to the placebo. Table 5 show the effects of placebo and of amphetamine, heroin, and morphine in experimental use on young, adult, non-institutionalized males. The first line of the table shows that six of the twenty subjects had a 'euphoric' response to the placebo. For subjects to the placed in the euphoric column the number of their answers indicating a positive change after the injection had to be at least one greater than the number of their answers indicating a negative change; the 'mean score' of 23 indicates that the average amount of euphoria produced by the inert placebo was relatively small. Eight of the twenty normal subjects had a dysphoric response to the placebo, with an even lower mean score. The remaining six subjects had an exactly equal mood score before and after the injection and so were classified as neither euphoric nor dysphoric.

The results for amphetamine are dramatically different. The subjects all reported feeling an effect of the amphetamine injection and many were quite clear in expressing that it was a pleasurable effect, both in the formal questionnaire and in written comments. Fourteen of the twenty subjects gave an overall euphoric response to amphetamines and their mean score was much higher than the mean score for the placebo. Six of the twenty

TABLE 5
Responses to experimental drug administration

a) Questionnaire scores on mood items in twenty normal subjects

|  | Euphoric | | Dysphoric | | Group mean score | |
|  | No. | Mean score | No. | Mean score | Euphoric | Dysphoric |
|---|---|---|---|---|---|---|
| Placebo | 6 | 23 | 8 | 8 | 4 | – |
| Amphetamine | 14 | 43 | 6 | 30 | 21 | – |
| Heroin | 9 | 18 | 10 | 34 | – | 9 |
| Morphine | 8 | 16 | 10 | 44 | – | 16 |

b) Responses of normal subjects to questionnaire item on repeating drug experience

|  | Would like to repeat | Would not like to repeat | No feelings one way or the other |
|---|---|---|---|
| Placebo | 3 | 1 | 16 |
| Amphetamine | 14 | 2 | 4 |
| Heroin | 4 | 7 | 9 |
| Morphine | 2 | 9 | 9 |

c) Questionnaire scores on mood items in thirty 'post-addicts'

|  | Euphoric | | Dysphoric | | Group mean score | |
|  | No. | Mean score | No. | Mean score | Euphoric | Dysphoric |
|---|---|---|---|---|---|---|
| Placebo | 5 | 17 | 6 | 12 | 1 | – |
| Amphetamine | 20 | 32 | 5 | 14 | 19 | – |
| Heroin | 15 | 35 | 4 | 13 | 16 | – |
| Morphine | 22 | 38 | 3 | 4 | 27 | – |

d) Post-addict responses to questionnaire item on repeating drug experience

|  | Would like to repeat | Would not like to repeat | No feelings one way or the other |
|---|---|---|---|
| Placebo | 1 | 4 | 25 |
| Amphetamine | 16 | 3 | 11 |
| Heroin | 14 | 3 | 13 |
| Morphine | 17 | 2 | 11 |

subjects received overall dysphoric scores and their mean scores were also much more extreme than the placebo responses. In other words, the experimental subjects were very much aware of having taken a dose of amphetamine and about two-thirds definitely liked the feeling. Thus, amphetamine serves as an example of a drug that produces euphoria in experimental use.

The results show that heroin and morphine produced indifference or dysphoria in experimental use, rather than euphoria. Nine and eight of the subjects wound up in the euphoric-response column for heroin and morphine, which is slightly more than for the placebo, but their mean score, that is the degree of deviation from their mood before the injection, was actually *lower than the mean scores in response to the placebo*. Half of the subjects had an overall dysphoric response to heroin and morphine and their dysphoria scores were higher than for any drug in the experiment. This finding was confirmed by asking subjects after each injection if they would like to repeat the drug experience (see table 5, b). Most subjects either *did not* want to repeat the opiate experience, or didn't care one way or the other. The number who did want to repeat the experience was no greater than with the placebo. This shows, again, that the typical response to opiates in experimental use is indifference or dislike.

Beecher and his colleagues were aware of the discrepancy between the facts they had found in their laboratory and popular wisdom, and therefore performed a number of checks. To be sure the dose was high enough, they questioned the subjects about physical responses. Enough of the subjects reported minor physical responses to the higher doses of heroin and morphine to establish that the dose was being felt. To be sure that the dose was not too high to produce euphoria, a number of the subjects were asked to repeat the experiment with lower doses, but these were, as expected, too low to have any effect different from that of the placebo. Subjects were questioned orally after the experiment to ensure that they meant what their questionnaires indicated.

Beecher did find quite different effects of experimental use of opiates with addicted subjects, however. (He called them 'post-addicts' because they were addicted people in treatment. I prefer to refer to them simply as addicts because most people return to drug use after treatment.) The results in table 5 speak for themselves. Experimental use of opiate drugs has a generally euphoric effect in addicts.

It is possible that the laboratory environment somehow counteracted the normal euphoria produced by the opiate drugs in normal experimental subjects, but there are several reasons to doubt this explanation of Beecher's results. One is that the normal subjects did report euphoria after amphetamine injections under exactly the same laboratory conditions, and the 'post-addicts' reported euphoria after opiate injections under similar (but not identical) conditions.

Observations made under different conditions have confirmed Beecher's results. Westermeyer, an American who spent many years in Laos investigating opium use and addiction treatment facilities, has described the results of his investigation of experimental use of opiates, conducted outside of a sterile medical-school laboratory. He visited local opium dens with his friends on a few occasions and described the results as follows:

> Of my eight Caucasian fellow visitors, six did try smoking opium. None had ever used opium before, and to the best of my knowledge none has ever used it again. They inhaled relatively small doses, apparently more from curiosity and to say 'I smoked opium' than from any fervent wish to make this ritual part of their regular lives. All were married, in their thirties, employed, getting along well in their lives, and mostly in professional fields; and they did not live where they had ready access to opium or opium dens ... Among my adventuresome friends and acquaintances, a few non-smokers could not inhale the smoke deeply into their lungs and keep it there. A few others felt nothing after one or two inhalations. And a few more experienced some nausea and lethargy after finishing a pipe or two. None of them reported anything resembling pleasure or euphoria. One man having a bout of diarrhea at the time found that two pipefuls greatly relieved this condition (much as one would expect from a dose of the old nostrum, tincture of opium). I have followed the lives of these eight people (seven men and one woman) over a six-to-ten-year period since their smoking opium in one or another Laotian den. None has become an opium addict, or, for that matter, an abuser of any other substance. (Westermeyer 1982, 165–6)

It might be objected that it takes more than one or two exposures for the euphoric effects of opiates to be appreciated by experimental users, but this is not a sufficient explanation for Beecher's and Westermeyer's results. A careful report of experimental use of heroin over a period of several days that was reported in the *British Medical Journal* (Oswald 1969) included the following obvservations:

> We've been on heroin a week now, Stuart and I. Seven days of voluntary illness. And how ill we feel ... My personal view at present is just one made grey and utterly grim by heroin.
>
> The extraordinary thing is that it brings no joy, no pleasure. Weariness, above all. At most, some hours of disinterest – the world passing by while you just feel untouched.
>
> Even after the injection there is no sort of a thrill, no mind-expansion nonsense, or orgasmic heights, no Kubla Khan. A feeling of oppressed breathing, a slight flush, a sense of strange unease, almost fear unknown ... How can people want to take the stuff? To escape to all this – life must be hell if they can want to escape to all this ...
>
> It's a month now since we stopped the stuff, though some measurements continue. It's been wonderful to feel fit and to relish life again. To be once again in the regular sequence of clinics, wards, and teaching makes one realize the satisfaction within the routines of work. I'd taken some comfort during that week by quietly pottering in the garden, but how much richer is enjoyment now. The late October roses have liked this dry, still week, and the autumn foliage beside the river as I sit and look at it this Sunday afternnoon brings a greater peace than known to any poor devils who take heroin. We condemn them and despise them, but we forget to appreciate how fortunate we are to find our joy in life and not to be driven to escape it.

In seeming contradiction to these findings, euphoria appears to be common in the first opiate experiments of regular users of other psychoactive drugs (Le Dain 1973, 307). McAuliffe (1975) located seven university students who were frequent users of marijuana, LSD and various other drugs as well. He was able to question the members of this group after a session in which they got together to experiment with heroin. Five of the seven reported either euphoria or a mixture of euphoria and discomfort from the heroin, whereas the other two reported no euphoria.

About three-quarters of opiate addicts report having had either positive reactions or a mixture of positive and negative reactions on their first use (McAuliffe 1975). The following descriptions of first experiences come from New York City addicts:

It gave me like a sense of peace of mind. Nothing bothered me; it felt good.
Felt above everyone else – ready for Freddie – great.
I felt all right and more sure of myself. I got real sleepy.
I went to lay on the bed … I thought, this is for me!
And I never missed a day since, until now.
I felt I always wanted to feel the same way as I felt then.
I felt above everything. I felt I knew everything. I talked to people about
    interesting things.
Felt like heat was coming through my body and head. It made me forget
    all things.
Felt like nobody existed but me, like I was by myself.
(Chein et al. 1964, 157–8)

McAuliffe (1975) has suggested on the basis of the first experiences of experienced drug users and of people who subsequently became opiate addicts that Beecher's experiments are misleading. However, it seems to me more correct to make a distinction between experiments on randomly selected people, who represent the general population, and the relatively small number of opiate addicts and of people pre-selected by virtue of being regular users of prohibited drugs. Generally the former do not experience euphoria during experimental use of opiates.

*Euphoria in Casual and Regular Use*

Some of the people who experience euphoria when they experiment with opiates become addicted and others become casual or regular recreational users. Zinberg (1984) has systematically studied opiate use in what he calls 'controlled users,' the large majority of whom did not subsequently become addicted. In this group, the most frequently reported motives for opiate use were 'to enjoy the high,' 'to use for recreation,' 'to use for relaxation,' 'to socialize.' These appear to be descriptions of a euphoria that apparently sustains recreational opiate use.

Euphoria among casual and regular users would seem to be the basis for the popularity of opium dens in the past. Contrary to the popular stereotype of opium dens as the site of depravity and hopelessness, they seem to be generally places of quiet repose. W. Somerset Maugham visited an opium den in China in 1922 and, mindful of the stereotype, registered his surprised description of the reality as follows:

I was introduced into a neat enough room, brightly lit, divided into
cubicles the raised floor of which, covered with clean matting, formed a
convenient couch. In one an elderly gentleman, with a grey head and very
beautiful hands, was quietly reading a newspaper, with his long pipe by his
side. In another two coolies were lying, with a pipe between them, which
they alternately prepared and smoked. They were young men, of a hearty
appearance, and they smiled at me in a friendly way. One of them offered
me a smoke. In a third four men squatted over a chess-board, and a little
further on a man was dandling a baby (the inscrutable Oriental has a
passion for children) while the baby's mother, whom I took to be the
landlord's wife, a plump, pleasant-faced woman, watched him with a broad
smile on her lips. It was a cheerful spot, comfortable, home-like, and
cosy. It reminded me somewhat of the little intimate beer-houses of Berlin
where the tired working man could go in the evening and spend a peaceful
hour. Fiction is stranger than fact. (60–1)

## Euphoria in Dependent or Addicted Users

Euphoria is not the usual experience of dependent or addicted opiate
users. I have come to know a number of long-time, dependent methadone
users. They usually report that their methadone and, earlier in their lives,
their heroin, produced no euphoria at all, but rather relieved an oppressive
anxiety and prevented withdrawal symptoms. Often these dependent
users describe themselves as needing opiates to feel 'normal.' Many
addicted people report that although they experience some euphoria when
they receive an unusually large dose of heroin or morphine, their normal,
smaller doses are only sufficient to allay withdrawal symptoms – no
euphoria occurs. Some former heroin addicts have told me that they never
experienced any great euphoria from heroin use, but rather used it for
social reasons, particularly to maintain membership in a group of users,
or a relationship with a boy-friend.

Obviously, the relationship of opiate use to euphoria is complex, as it is
for other drugs as well. The Le Dain commission has provided what
seems to me one of the most concise summaries of this complex
relationship for the opiates, as follows: 'The subjective psychological
effects of opiate narcotics may vary considerably among different
individuals and situations. The once popular notion that morphine-like
effects are intrinsically so pleasurable that most persons who experience

them are promptly addicted has not been scientifically documented' (Le Dain 1973, 307).

## The 'Rush'

Another aspect of opiate euphoria is the so-called 'rush,' which has been described as an ecstatic, orgasm-like feeling in the lower abdomen following an intravenous injection of an opiate. The rush is described as a cherished experience by some intravenous users and clearly qualifies as a type of euphoria. Whereas the rush provides ecstatic moments for some opiate users, others have never experienced it at all. Heavily addicted street addicts can rarely afford enough opiates to produce more than a stabilizing effect. Although the intravenous injection is the well-established symbol of opiate addiction, many dependent and addicted users rarely if ever inject their drugs. Opium habitués in the nineteenth and early twentieth centuries typically drank opium in alcohol solutions. As well, American soldiers in the Vietnam War preferred to smoke heroin mixed with tobacco as long as the price of heroin was low. Needle use became widespread only when police action by the u.s. Army forced prices up. Therefore, although the rush undoubtedly exists, it is not an essential part of the opiate experience for many users, and may not occur at all for most.

### PHYSICAL HARM PRODUCED BY OPIATES

## Transient Side-effects in Regular Use

There are a number of 'transient' physical problems caused by regular dependent and addictive use of opiate drugs, that is, side-effects that disappear permanently when use of opiates is terminated. These effects include depressed breathing, 'pinpoint pupils,' constipation, depressed activity levels, excessive sweating, decreased sexual libido in both males and females, cessation of menstruation in females, withdrawal symptoms, and tolerance (Le Dain 1973, 308). These side-effects are a source of considerable discomfort to some regular opiate users, but result in no known permanent damage.

Withdrawal symptoms are the transient side-effect that figures most prominently in the War on Drugs rhetoric. They constitute a kind of illness that follows the cessation of opiate use after a period of regular use. Withdrawal effects are far less traumatic in reality than in the drug-war propaganda, although the evidence is not completely consistent on this topic. The symptoms of Vancouver addicts that I have observed during withdrawal are comparable to the flu. Most addicts describe them as similar to either a mild case or a serious case of the flu. Death during withdrawal from opiates almost never occurs (Hodding, Jann, and Ackerman 1980) except among the sick and malnourished (see Westermeyer 1982, 70, 90–4). By contrast, death during the more severe withdrawal from alcohol or barbiturates is more common (Kaplan 1983, 19). Opiate withdrawal is readily relieved with various drugs, particularly valium, alcohol, or clonidine, and by hypnotic suggestion or group pressure.

To give a full picture of this important topic, four separate ways of describing withdrawal symptoms are presented below. The first is from Canada's royal commission on the non-medical use of drugs, the Le Dain commission (1973), which described opiate withdrawal, following an exhaustive set of interviews and review of the medical literature, as follows: 'The classical, severe opiate narcotic withdrawal syndrome described above seems to be the exception rather than the rule; much milder, flu-like symptoms are typically described by clinicians and the drug users themselves. This may be due to the relatively low purity of street heroin in some areas, and the light and intermittent use patterns which have developed, but more likely reflects an overemphasis of extreme cases in the earlier literature' (Le Dain 1973, 318).

The second description comes from Goodman and Gilman's pharmacology text. Withdrawal symptoms are described there as a set of reactions that opiate addicts may experience 8–12 hours after cessation of opiate use. These include lacrimation (tearing), rhinorrhea (runny nose), yawning, and sweating. Later they may report restless sleep, dilated pupils, anorexia (loss of appetite), goose-flesh (which is apparently responsible for the slang expression 'cold turkey'), irritability, tremor, insomnia, depression, nausea, vomiting, intestinal spasm, elevated heart rate and blood pressure, chills and fever, abdominal and muscular pains, muscular spasms, and sometimes ejaculation in men and orgasm in women (Jaffe 1980, 547–8). Although this is a formidable list of torments presented in this form, a close examination will reveal that, with the exception of the last item, it is essentially a description of the flu. In both withdrawal symptoms and the flu, all the signs and symptoms do not occur in each case.

The third way of describing opiate withdrawal was provided by an addict who appeared as guest speaker in a small tutorial for a class of mine at the university. After establishing that he had been addicted to heroin and various other drugs for about twenty years, he was asked, among other questions, if it was true that withdrawal symptoms were not as serious as their media depiction would indicate. He answered by asking if anyone had been aware that he was undergoing withdrawal symptoms as he had been addressing the class. No one had guessed it although, in retrospect, his intermittent sniffing and tired appearance should have suggested it. The point he meant to make, however, was unmistakable.

Finally, one Vancouver addict, upon reading the information above, went to great lengths to convince me that the popular understanding of withdrawal symptoms is *not* exaggerated. He was sure that the addicts I had met before had simply not taken enough heroin. He described his own agonizing experiences, although it seemed to me that what he was describing was better understood as mental anguish, depression, and craving than as physical symptoms of withdrawal. The confusion about the severity of opiate withdrawal may result from ambiguity over whether mental anguish without tissue pathology constitutes withdrawal.

'Tolerance' is another transient side-effect of regular opiate use. The term refers to a diminishing effect of a given dose of an opiate with repeated administration. Like withdrawal symptoms, tolerance has been exaggerated and overdramatized in the rhetoric of the War on Drugs. Many regular opiate users develop very high levels of tolerance, but some develop relatively little, and many stabilize their intake without difficulty. It is not true that there is an ever-increasing appetite for opiates in most dependent or addicted users (Trebach 1987, 268).

### Irreversible Side-effects

Contrary to the conventional wisdom and to the War on Drugs propaganda, there are no known irreversible physical side-effects of opiate drugs.* This point was stated by the Le Dain commission as

---

* This topic has been extensively reviewed by Shepard Siegel of MacMaster University and I have drawn from his prodigious compilation of research in this summary.

follows: 'There appears to be little direct permanent physiological damage from chronic use of pure opiate narcotics' (Le Dain 1973, 309). British Columbia's Alcohol and Drug Commission states the point more clearly in a pamphlet printed for public distribution: 'Chronic use of pure opiate narcotics causes little or no permanent physical damage' (Province of British Columbia, 5). The word 'pure' in both of these statements is significant, because most street addicts cannot get pure drugs, and may suffer harm from the impurities. However, the deleterious effects of the impurities are not a pharmacological effect of opiates, but rather one of the societal effects that are imposed by making the pure drug unobtainable for many users. Societal effects of opiate drugs will be discussed in detail later in this chapter.

The conclusion that opiate drugs per se are not known to produce permanent physiological side-effects on the user is virtually unchallenged among medical researchers. It is based on decades of careful research on thousands of long-time opiate users. The basic facts are as follows:

1. Numerous people have gone through their entire adult lives dependent on opiate drugs without ever being discovered. Such cases are often revealed after their death by their family or by their private writings. In many cases, such people have been in excellent health and there is no indication for the group as a whole of any damage attributable to opiate drugs (Brecher 1972, 39).

2. In a classic study, 861 addicts were examined thoroughly in the Philadelphia General Hospital when they volunteered for treatment. Eighty per cent were addicted to heroin. The conclusion of the report was that 'addiction is not characterized by physical deterioration or impairment of physical fitness aside from the addiction per se. There is no evidence of change in the circulatory, hepatic, renal, or endocrine functions. When it is considered that these subjects had been addicted for at least five years, some of them for as long as twenty years, these negative observations are highly significant' (cited by Brecher 1972, 23).

3. It often has been noted that addicts are emaciated, but the Philadelphia study showed clearly that this, too, is not an effect of pharmacological origin. A subgroup of one hundred Philadelphia addicts was maintained on adequate morphine for a period of examination and testing. These addicts had been taking an average of 1260 mg of morphine or heroin per day, an enormous dose equivalent to about 40 'caps' by Vancouver standards (30 mg/capsule). Given free access to hospital food

their weight distribution became normal. Some were fat, some thin, most were normal.

4. Stevenson et al. in British Columbia gave extensive neurological and psychiatric examinations to addicts in prison and found no evidence of damage: 'As to possible damage to the brain, the result of lengthy use of heroin, we can only say that neurologic and psychiatric examinations have not revealed evidence of brain damage ... This is in marked contrast to the prolonged and heavy use of alcohol, which in combination with other factors can cause pathological changes in brains and reflects such damage in intellectual and emotional deterioration, as well as convulsions, neuritis, and even psychosis' (cited by Brecher 1972, 26).

Stevenson et al. also found no indication of personality deterioration (apart from that attributable to criminality and jail, and so on) or of IQ deterioration. In the latter case they were able to check childhood records against adult performance with no indication of deterioration (Brecher 1972, 26). Similar conclusions have been reported in other large-scale studies of personality and intellectual functioning in heroin addicts (see Brown and Partington 1942; Sapira 1968; Platt, Hoffman, and Ebert 1976).

5. Morphine has been in use for over a century and medical texts refer to it as a generally safe drug, except in patients with severe respiratory ailments, in whom opiate-induced respiratory depression can be dangerous (Jaffe and Martin 1985, 507). Likewise, observations of thousands of patients who have received substantial daily doses of methadone for up to fifteen years have revealed 'no direct injurious effects' (Jaffe 1985, 542). An expert committee of the U.S. National Institute on Drug Abuse on treatment for narcotic addiction concluded unambiguously: 'There was unanimous agreement that [methadone] is safe when used by physicians knowledgeable in the treatment of narcotic addiction ... Toxicity related to methadone during treatment is extraordinarily rare' (Cooper et al. 1983).

An American law professor, John Kaplan (1983), has disputed the claim that opiate drugs do not cause permanent damage. He has stated:

In the long term, heroin use, especially through intravenous injection, is not good for the addict's health. As we have noted, the British addicts, when they were receiving legal heroin, had a death rate even higher than that of American street addicts. So long as they continue intravenous administration, addicts will risk collapsed veins, hepatitis, and a whole series of physical ailments. Moreover, even though heroin seems relatively nontoxic, at least as compared to alcohol, we do not yet know the long-term physical effects of heroin addiction, even on a stabilized dosage and apart from the method of administration. The relatively sparse anecdotal evidence on this issue is not sufficient. The few case reports indicating that the long-term physical effects of medically stabilized heroin addiction are not serious cannot make up for the lack of controlled studies or careful examination of an adequate sample of users. (Kaplan 1983, 178)

Kaplan's argument is weak. He does not cite any direct evidence of the sort that would normally be used to show that a drug is dangerous, for example the kind of evidence that links tobacco smoking to lung cancer or alcohol use to cirrhosis of the liver. To my knowledge, and apparently to his, no such evidence exists. He claims that not enough research has been done on the sustained use of heroin, but he ignores the research on American heroin maintenance programs early in the twentieth century, mentioned above, and decades of clinical evidence that both methadone and morphine are safe drugs in sustained use.

The only fact he offers to support his position is that British addicts have a high death rate while maintained on legal heroin. Although the death rate of British addicts is in fact high, his interpretation of this fact is not valid. British addicts have never been merely typical citizens who happen to get maintenance doses of heroin, morphine, or methadone from their doctors. Many have severe health problems and self-destructive habits in addition to their heroin use. The high death rate among British addicts appears more related to the chaos of many of their lives than to the mere fact of their using opiate drugs.

Stimson and Oppenheimer (1982, 122–5) found that the major cause of death among British heroin addicts was overdose of opiates and/or barbiturates. Addicts appeared to overdose either because a shortage of prescribed methadone led them to use street drugs of uncertain strength or because despondency made them indifferent to their survival. The addicts who were most likely to overdose were those that Stimson and Oppenheimer called 'chaotic addicts' or 'junkies.' 'Those who were most chaotic when we first interviewed them in 1969, whom we called the "junkies," were, ten years later [likely to be] either abstinent, in prison, or dead' (129). Other addicts whose lives were running more smoothly showed little likelihood of overdosing and, therefore, a more normal death rate.

A case study provided by Stimson and Oppenheimer (1982) may illustrate the improbability that the high death rate among British addicts is caused by heroin *use* per se:

> Eddie Cox ... was brought up by his grandparents and finally drifted down to London in the early 1960s. He married another addict and together they lived ... a life that seemed to be wholly centred on drugs. In an effort to regularize their lives they moved down to Somerset ... but even in the country they remained involved with other drug users. He lost count of the drugs he was using and could not even remember what he had used the day we spoke to him. He was interviewed on a freezing January evening in an unheated room. The interview lasted two hours, during which the interviewer shivered from the cold and Eddie shivered from withdrawal. He was one of the few addicts who injected during the interview, putting the needle through his jeans into his thigh. He resisted any effort made to help him, with the exception of the offer of more drugs. He had no illusions about the possible consequences of his way of life and believed that he might die from his incautious use of drugs. 'Cocaine – if I couldn't get it legally I would get it by any way I could – even by killing. I can say from the bottom of my heart that this is the life I want to live and I'm living it ... It doesn't frighten me, death, because I'd rather be dead than be without drugs ... Because I am a chronic addict, I mean chronic. I've got a 'cancer' and I know it ... I have done nine cures, and I've been on a Section (under the Mental Health Act) for one year and I've still broken into three chemists during that Section.' The last time we saw him he was in a frightful state of health – thin, toothless, nose running, with recent scars from a knife fight, legs bandaged, intoxicated, and crying. He left the office where he had been interviewed and staggered across Denmark Hill to walk down to ... buy drugs ... A year later we heard that he had died. (127–8)

To take Eddie Cox's death as evidence that heroin is a physically damaging drug is to ignore everything else that was killing him. However, it would be foolish to claim that opiate drugs are totally harmless. It seems inevitable that all drugs, when studied long enough, will turn out to produce some unhealthful bodily alterations. However, whatever harm opiates may in the future be discovered to do will not justify the 'War on Drugs' as the old horror stories did. A discovery that chronic heavy use of the opiates is physically damaging would merely put them in the same category as nicotine, caffeine, ASA, alcohol, valium, and other drugs that people accept as *both* useful and dangerous. It may be useful to impose some controls on such substances, but it is obviously not necessary to impose war measures.

## FETAL DAMAGE PRODUCED BY OPIATES

There is no doubt that babies born to women who are addicted to opiates tend to be less healthy than babies of non-addicted mothers. In particular, they frequently are low in birth weight (Kandall et al. 1976), have a high incidence of meconium staining, and show signs of behavioural distress after birth that are attributed to opiate withdrawal (Ramer and Lodge 1975). Numerous other problems have been identified, especially during the first year of life (Householder et al. 1982).

However, the obvious conclusion that opiates taken during pregnancy damage the fetus is not as certain as it first appears. Because many opiate addicts live chaotic and unhealthy lives, it is difficult to assess the effects of opiates per se on their unborn children. Addicted mothers very often smoke and drink heavily, use other street drugs, suffer from malnutrition, receive inadequate medical care, suffer from chronic depression, and experience the stress and abuse associated with prostitution and street life. It is likely that all these conditions affect the health of their offspring (Finnigan and Fehr 1980; Klenka 1986; Reagh 1988). The effects of some of these conditions on unborn children are well documented. Heavy alcohol use, in particular, can produce 'fetal alcohol syndrome,' which involves low birth weight, permanent mental retardation, and other serious problems (Ritchie 1985, 375–6; Abel and Sokol 1987). Likewise, the evidence of fetal damage from maternal tobacco smoking is impressive (Martin 1982; Kleinman and Madans 1985).

There is a special problem in assessing the likelihood that maternal opiate use causes withdrawal symptoms in newborn children. Between 70 and 90 per cent of the babies of opiate addicted mothers born in the United States show some unusual degree of distress that is attributed to opiate withdrawal: restlessness, shrill crying, inability to sleep, hyperactive reflexes, tremors, poor feeding, vomiting, yawning, sneezing, and convulsions in severe cases (Householder et al. 1982). Such distress is usually interpreted, at least in the United States and Canada, as evidence that these are withdrawal symptoms produced in babies by their mother's drug addiction.

Judson (1973) has suggested a different view. In his report on heroin addiction in the United Kingdom, he pointed out that the reports of babies of addicted mothers being born with withdrawal symptoms come primarily from the United States, where heroin addicts are frequently malnourished or abused. He refers to studies showing that the proportion of disturbed or underweight babies born to female addicts is not higher than that for other underprivileged people in the United States. In England during the period prior to the mid-1970s, when medically prescribed heroin was provided for most addicts, addicted women were not much more likely to be underfed or abused than anyone else. Some English doctors of that period saw no evidence of withdrawal in babies born to addicted mothers under their care (Judson 1973). Moreover, the fact that a disturbed baby born to an addicted mother can be relieved with morphine injections does not necessarily mean that the baby is suffering from opiate withdrawal. Any disturbed baby can be relieved with morphine: opiate drugs were the most popular baby 'soothers' throughout the ninteenth century.

The best controlled research on this topic still falls short of providing a clear picture of the effect of maternal opiate use on unborn children. In one well-controlled study, Stimmel and Adamsons (1976) compared three groups of pregnant women: 28 were carefully supervised methadone patients, known not to be using other drugs; 57 were women using street methadone and/or heroin; and 30 were women with no illicit-drug history. The study was designed to separate the effects of simply using opiate drugs (in the 'supervised methadone' group) from the effects of using opiates plus being subjected to the stresses of street life (in the 'street opiate' group), and to compare both of these groups with a control group that had neither problem. The women were primarily Hispanic and black residents of East Harlem in New York City. Studies were done of the hospital records of their births and infant after-care. The controls were good, but far from perfect, for there was no control on smoking, drinking, or anxiety differences between the groups. Likewise, the opiate drugs used by the 'supervised methadone' and 'street opiate' groups were probably different, with the street-opiate group using more heroin and less methadone. Moreover, it was impossible for the staff to be unaware

TABLE 6
The condition of infants born to mothers who used opiates ('supervised methadone' group), mothers who used opiates and were subject to the stresses of street life ('street opiate' group), and a control group of mothers from the same neighbourhood ('no opiates' group)

|  | Supervised methadone (%) | Street opiates (%) | No opiates (%) |
|---|---|---|---|
| Fetal distress (tachycardia, brachycardia, or prenatal meconium) | 16.1 | 42.1 | 23.3 |
| Low birth weight | 22.6 | 26.3 | 3.0 |
| Serious neonatal complications | 16.1 | 40.4 | 23.3 |
| Irritability diagnosed as narcotic withdrawal | 58.1 | 50.9 | 0.0 |

of the background of the different patients, so their expectations could have influenced the results.

Table 6 shows that babies whose mothers use methadone are as healthy as babies whose mothers used no drugs at all in terms of 'fetal distress' (an index of several physiological indicators of severe problem) and 'serious neonatal complications' (another index). However, about a quarter of the infants in both opiate-using groups displayed low birth weights and over 50 per cent of the infants in both groups displayed symptoms of irritability that were diagnosed as 'narcotic withdrawal.'

Symptoms attributed to withdrawal were relatively mild, except in some infants whose mothers were heroin users. There was no correlation between presence of withdrawal and amount of methadone. Methadone children were followed up in a pediatric clinic. No growth abnormalities were noted, nor were any other abnormalities mentioned by the researchers. If the controls in this study were valid, it would mean that opiates produce low birth weight and irritability in babies, and that both effects are transient. It would also appear that opiates produce withdrawal symptoms, although they are usually mild. Thus, this study suggests that maternal opiate consumption adversely affects the fetus. However, the damage is relatively mild when compared, for example, with fetal alcohol syndrome, which includes permanent mental retardation, permanent hearing loss, and a number of physical deformities (Ritchie 1985; Abel and Sokol 1987).

THE OPIATES AS A CAUSE OF ADDICTION-NEGATIVE FINDINGS

The belief that exposure to heroin sooner or later causes addiction has been widely accepted throughout this century. Recent research, however, has shown that this familiar belief is wrong. Because the belief in heroin's great addictive liability has become almost an unquestionable truth, the evidence against it will be presented here in some detail.

Contrary to popular opinion, administering opiates to people who are organically ill does not cause addiction. In the United Kingdom, heroin is widely used as a medication for cough, diarrhea, and other illnesses. For example, in 1972 British physicians prescribed 29 kg of heroin, millions of doses, to medical patients. Careful examination of the British statistics on iatrogenic addiction revealed 'there is a virtual absence of addicts created by this singular medical practice' (Trebach 1982, 83). Twycross (1974) reported that cancer patients who were kept on heroin, often in very high doses, came off the drug easily if their cancer symptoms went into remission. Twycross stated that 'none of the patients reviewed became addicted' (197).

An American research team maintained post-operative patients on a bedside self-medication machine that delivered about 1 mg of morphine intravenously when the patient pressed a hand-button. The machine limited infusions to one every six minutes. Fifty patients were kept on the regimen for one to six days. The self-administered doses were considerably lower than the maximum the machine would allow. Rather than increasing as patients continued the regimen, the doses progressively declined (Bennett et al. 1982). There has been no problem of addiction or dependence with this device even in a small number of cases that were allowed larger doses over longer times (Graves, personal communication).

Several careful case studies have described people who have become casual or dependent users of opiates and have remained so indefinitely, in spite of their frequent exposure to opiates (Blackwell 1982; Zinberg 1984). Although estimates are uncertain on this topic, there are said to be about 3.5 million non-addicted opiate users in the United States and a half million addicts, a ratio of 7:1 (Trebach 1982, 3). These non-addicted users are no more likely to escalate to addictive use than to reduce their use or become abstinent. Zinberg has followed up a group of 'controlled users' of opiates 12–24 months after an initial interview. He was able to re-interview 60 per cent of the original group. Of these, 49 per cent were using drugs in the same way as at the first interview, 27 per cent 'had reduced use to levels below those required for them to be considered controlled users,' and 13 per cent were using more opiates than at the time of the first interview (Zinberg 1984, 71).

During the nineteenth century the availability of opiates in the United States and England was enormously greater than it is currently, yet the incidence of dependence and addiction never reached 1 per cent of the population and was declining at the end of the century before the restrictive laws were passed (Brecher 1972; Courtwright 1982). That is to say, even though people had free access to strong opiates in most pharmacies and grocery stores, and even though many people used them in large quantities, over 99 per cent of the population did not become dependent or addicted. In fact, opiate addiction is a rare condition in countries where opiates are more freely available in the twentieth century, including Mexico and Turkey (Kaplan 1983, 3).

If exposure engendered an irresistible craving for opiates, opiate addiction would be a permanent condition, because each new dose would fortify the already existing addiction. Only enforced abstinence might possibly disrupt this vicious cycle. But his view is false; large numbers of American junkies simply cease using opiate drugs on their own volition, a process that is sometimes called 'maturing out' (Winick 1962; Waldorf 1983). The best single source of evidence for this trend is the aftermath of large-scale heroin use by American soldiers in Vietnam. Extraordinary amounts of cheap, high-quality heroin were available to these soldiers. Some became addicted (as indicated by the presence of withdrawal symptoms, which were regarded by the army investigators as evidence of addiction). Many of the soldiers regularly injected doses of heroin much higher than would be available to 'junkies' in the United States. There was a great furore in the United States about the impact of these addicted men returning home, because it was assumed that they would be lifelong addicts (Brecher 1972). Fortunately, of those who had been 'addicted' in Vietnam, only 12 per cent re-established their habit, even temporarily, within three years after returning home (Robins, Helzer, and Davis 1975).

Why were these men able to discard their addictions? It was not because the army forced a period of abstinence on them, for many of these men received no treatment at all prior to discharge. Nor was it because heroin was unavailable in the United States, because the formerly addicted veterans reported finding ready access to heroin at home. Many reported casual, but not addictive, use (Robins, Helzer, and Davis 1975). Evidently addictions are not caused simply by past use of opiate drugs.

In spite of almost universal belief that exposure to opiate drugs causes negative addiction, there has never been any strong evidence to support it. For the most part, the belief is justified, if at all, by reference to either personal reports provided by heroin addicts and physicians or to experimental research on laboratory animals.

Personal reports of opiate addicts and physicians can be convincing (see Burroughs 1959; Courtwright, Joseph, and DesJarlais 1989, chap. 3). Many addicts claim to have been addicted practically from their first dose. Often, they describe the pleasure produced by the drug as irresistible and the withdrawal symptoms as unbearable. However, these reports do not constitute evidence that other persons who expose themselves to opiates would also become addicted. It seems more probable that opiate addicts, who form a tiny minority of the population, react to opiate drugs in an atypical way.

Controlled research, such as that described earlier in this chapter, shows that the vast majority of people who have been exposed to opiate drugs do not experience irresistible pleasure. In fact, most report displeasure or indifference. Long-time casual and recreational users of opiate drugs, who greatly outnumber addicts, do experience pleasure (Zinberg 1984), but obviously not enough to draw them into addiction. There are many people who manage to use heroin regularly, in spite of its great cost, and continue relatively normal lives as well (see Zinberg and Lewis 1964; Caplovitz 1976, especially his discussion of 'hidden addicts,' 7–8; Zinberg, Harding, and Apsler 1978). These people remain regular or dependent users, but do not become negatively addicted.

The most frequently cited evidence that exposure to opiate drugs causes addiction comes from animal research. Laboratory animals self-administer large quantities of opiates in some free-choice situations, both by drinking opiate-bearing solutions (Khavari and Risner 1973) and by pressing levers that inject opiates through a needle that has been permanently implanted in a vein (Weeks and Collins 1968). But these observations do not prove that opiates cause addiction. In the first place, the casual self-administration of opiates by laboratory animals bears little resemblance to the compulsive pursuit of drugs and 'overwhelming involvement' with them that defines human addiction. Several animal studies have shown that when the concentration of the experimental opiate solution is decreased or the number of responses required to maintain a given level of drugs in the body is increased, laboratory animals typically do not increase their rate of responding enough to maintain their accustomed level (Kumar and Stolerman 1977). It seems doubtful to some scholars that addiction has been demonstrated at all in laboratory animals (Thor 1972).

It is more likely that the self-administration of opiates in laboratory animals occurs primarily because there is little else to do in the barren laboratory environments in which such experiments are normally performed. A series of studies conducted a decade ago in the animal laboratories at Simon Fraser University support this interpretation. My colleagues and I designed a laboratory environment for rats that was far more roomy and comfortable than the usual solitary, metal laboratory cages that were then in use. We called our creation Rat Park. Rat Park was amply provided with wood chips for digging, tin cans for general recreational purposes, and other rats of both sexes for social and cultural activities.

Rats in Rat Park and in individual cages were given free access to water and morphine hydrochloride solution. In a series of experiments, isolated rats consumed up to sixteen times more morphine than did the animals in Rat Park. Under no circumstances did the Rat Park animals drink more. The differences in morphine consumption occurred in rats that had been exposed to morphine through prior forced consumption (Alexander, Coambs and Hadaway 1978) and in rats for which 'exposure' consisted merely of continuous availability of a sweetened morphine solution (Hadaway et al. 1979; Alexander, Beyerstein, Hadaway, and Coambs 1981). We have subsequently found that the differences in morphine consumption between the two environments can be replicated in some strains of rats but not others, but in no strains did the animals housed in Rat Park drink appreciable amounts of opiates, except in the special case where the solution was laced with sugar to the point of being sickeningly sweet, a taste experience that rats seem to find irresistible (Alexander, Hadaway, and Coambs 1988).

It is not clear why the rats behaved in this way. It could be that isolated housing is highly stressful to mobile social animals like rats, and that caged animals ingest opiates in an attempt to control the stress. It is also possible that animals in a social environment learn to avoid strong drugs because they detract from the levels of attention and co-ordination necessary to cope with their highly competitive environment, whereas isolated animals have no need to stay alert. But whatever the explanation turns out to be, these results explode the apparent support for the exposure orientation that has been drawn from the original studies of self-administration of opiate drugs in animals.

PHARMACOLOGICAL EFFECTS: CONCLUSION

In light of the relatively benign pharmacological effects of opiate drugs that have been found by careful research, how is it that society thinks of heroin in extravagant images reminiscent of medieval mythology – irresistible pleasure, unbearable punishment for yielding to temptation, poisonous effects on the body, and permanent enslavement after a few exposures?

I believe there are two major explanations for the mythicization of heroin in the public mind. The first is the incessant progaganda of the War on Drugs. In recent years, as the medical evidence has become better known, the media have become relatively reserved, compared to the hysterical claims about heroin that were common earlier in the century. However, the mythic view of heroin is sustained by dramatic media images and failure to mention the evidence of medical research on this topic.

The second reason for the ubiquitous misperception of heroin is that ruined specimens like Eddie Cox and the apparition from the U.S. Supreme Court decision cited earlier *do* exist. The disastrous lives of opiate users like these reinforce the belief that the pharmacological effects of heroin made them what they are. Logically, however, this is not a proper deduction. In a parallel example, there are many users of antibiotics who are conspicuously unhealthy, but it would be wrong to conclude that the antibiotic drugs are the cause of their condition, rather than an attempt to relieve a condition having a different cause. But if it is not heroin that makes 'junkies' unhealthy, what is it? This question will be considered in the next section.

## Societal Effects: How the War on Drugs Affects Opiate Users

Much of the destruction that is wrongly attributed to opiate drugs is actually caused by the War on Drugs itself. In Canada, the stringency of the law is such that heroin addicts can expect to spend a major portion of their lives in jail, to be arrested repeatedly and violently 'searched,' to be constantly anxious because of the unpredictability of these occurrences, to be poor because of the high black-market prices for their drugs, to be malnourished because they are poor, to be infected because they are unable to buy pure drugs or sterile paraphernalia for injections, to be unable to engage in normal work or family life because of the need to continually 'hustle' drugs, and to be demoralized by pointless and humiliating routines administered in the name of 'treatment.' Some examples of the violence that can be involved in these procedures were given in chapters 1 and 2.

Although it is hard to scientifically evaluate the effects of such experiences, it seems clear that each of them may cause grave harm to a person or, through a pregnant woman, to an unborn child. In concert, these kinds of experience can easily explain the ill-health and high mortality that characterizes heroin addicts. Edward Brecher summed up the situation as follows: 'Almost all of the deleterious effects ordinarily attributed to opiates, indeed, appear to be effects of the narcotics laws instead' (Brecher 1972, 22).

It is important not to push this argument too far. The War on Drugs clearly is a major cause of ill health among opiate addicts, but there are other causes as well. Many addicts are products of violent, unwholesome environments; many were depressed and self-destructive prior to becoming addicted. Addicts are apt to be heavy smokers of tobacco, heavy drinkers, and heavy users of valium, and to have poor diets (even when they can afford good food). This section is intended to show how the War on Drugs contributes to the ills that used to be regarded as pharmacological effects of opiate drugs, without denying the importance of other causes.

CRIME AND VIOLENCE

Some of the effects of the War on Drugs are officially interpreted to look like pharmacological effects of the drug. Crime is an example. A significant fraction of North American crime is committed by heroin users. The amounts of crime committed by some individual addicts are astronomical. A large proportion of violent criminals use heroin and other 'hard' drugs (Nurco et al. 1985; Inciardi 1986). To many people, these facts are sufficient to conclude that heroin use *causes* crime and violence. However, this conclusion is false, as most scholars who have examined the facts acknowledge, even if they may support the War on Drugs for other reasons (Brecher 1972; Fink and Hyatt 1978; Kaplan 1983, 51–8). None the less, the argument that opiates cause crime is widely accepted by the general public and supported by a few scholars. Therefore, it will be examined in some detail here.

The known pharmacological effects of opiates do not include dishonesty or violence. As this chapter has shown, opiates generally make dependent and addicted users feel well or 'normal' and, at most, somewhat happy and carefree. In higher doses it makes these people very drowsy. It is definitely not the right drug to administer with the intention of inciting a wave of violent crime. Prior to the War on Drugs, there was no particular association between opiate drugs and crime. Opiate drugs were plentiful and cheap, and most people used them in ways that were socially acceptable. The best-known groups of users in North America were probably Chinese labourers and Caucasian housewives (Brecher 1972). Some were treated with disdain for their unappealing habit, and a small minority became negatively addicted, slovenly and useless. But none of this had any connection with crime. Indeed, to regard the industrious, law-abiding, opium-smoking Chinese workers as a criminally inclined group would have been ridiculous. Where the Chinese were resented, it was for their virtues, not their vices.

The fact that opiates do not necessarily produce criminal activities can be substantiated in modern times by the existence of 'working addicts,' who make enough from legitimate employment to pay for their drugs and therefore have a minimal involvement in crime (Nurco et al. 1985). Likewise, many methadone patients live without crime in spite of large daily doses of their opiate drug. Finally, Chaiken and Chaiken (1982) identified a group of non-addicted heroin users in prison whose crime rate was no higher than that of non-opiate drug users or non-drug users.

Whereas crime is not a pharmacological effect of opiates, the War on Drugs created three important links between opiate drugs and crime. First, when the opiate supply was legally interdicted, some dependent people found they could not endure deprivation of their drugs, creating the demand for a black market. As enforcement reduced the competition and increased the expense of black-market vendors, prices sky-rocketed.

Those dependent users who were not wealthy enough to pay black-market prices were forced to choose between agonizing deprivation and crime, and some chose crime (Brecher 1972). However, these addicts avoided violence. The great majority of crimes committed to support heroin habits, then and now, are relatively minor ones such as running confidence games, prostitution, pimping, theft, cheque forgery, and drug dealing. A recent study of heroin-addict crimes showed that violent crimes (robbery and assault) constituted only 2 per cent of the total (Nurco et al. 1985). Similar results have been reported by Inciardi (1986, 127, 166).

A second link between opiates and crime was created as the War on Drugs forced the price of heroin ever higher. As heroin became very expensive and dangerous to obtain, it became a status item among criminals. Many found themselves learning about heroin and coming to prize it. Naturally, they were inclined to obtain their supplies by their established fund-raising method, crime (Kaplan 1983). A third link is the intrinsic violence of the black market. Heroin commands fabulous prices. Violent methods of competition can be used in the black market because it is not subject to legal controls.

Given these linkages, violence inevitably occurs among opiate users. However, the violence is clearly not a pharmacological effect of the drug, but an effect of the War on Drugs.

OVERDOSE

There are two separate events that are called overdose. One of these, which will be called 'pharmacological overdose' in this book, is the reaction to an overly large dose of a drug. In the case of opiates, the most dangerous effect of pharmacological overdose is respiratory depression, that is, a reduction in the rate of breathing. In most cases, pharmacological overdose is not fatal – the person breathes more and more slowly, struggles to stay awake, but falls into what appears to be a deep sleep with slow, laboured breathing. When the person awakens, he or she appears to be normal and may not recall passing out. In severe cases, however, death may occur from lack of oxygen.

Because of the development of tolerance, it is very difficult for addicted people to overdose. They can tolerate very high doses, far beyond the lethal threshold for non-opiate users (Brecher 1972).

Moreover, addicts are very knowledgeable about drugs and careful to test the concentration of any drug that they obtain, so that accidents are unlikely. In spite of this fact, drug overdose is a frequently reported cause of death among addicts (Stimson and Oppenheimer 1982, 125; Jaffe 1985, 542). This high frequency of reported overdose deaths occurs because there is a second type of death that is recorded as overdose on death certificates.

The second cause of death will be called 'overdose' in this book. The quotation marks call the appropriateness of the term into question, because although the term refers to deaths associated with the use of illicit opiates, it is not the result of taking too high a dose (Brecher 1972; Siegel, Krank, and Hinson 1987). In many cases, whereas the decedent is known to have developed tolerance, the dose that has been administered is too low to cause death in a tolerant person. In some cases, the decedent is known to have taken the same dose the previous day (Le Dain 1973, 314).

'Overdose' deaths are often very fast: sometimes the victims are found with the needle still in their vein. Pharmacological overdose, by contrast, is not at all rapid: Breathing gradually slows over many minutes as the person slowly drops off to sleep. The causes of 'overdose' deaths are still uncertain, but they probably include societal effects of opiate use. Some deaths may be caused by a slowly developing allergic reaction to the additives and contaminants that inevitably accompany black-market drugs (Brecher 1972; Lipski, Stimmel, and Donoso 1973). This conclusion seems probable because the likelihood of 'overdose' death following injection of pure pharmaceuticals in a medical setting is extremely low (Brecher 1972). Another cause of 'overdose' deaths may be that some addicts' health simply deteriorates to the point that the relatively minor stress of an opiate injection is too much to endure. In the study of deaths among French heroin users, cited in chapter 2, Ingold (1986, 87–8) attributed the deaths to an 'impaired general condition' rather than 'acute intoxication.' To a large extent, the 'impaired general condition' is attributable to the War on Drugs, since prior to the anti-narcotics laws, a great many habitual users of opiates were able to lead more normal lives. There are other credible explanations for the 'overdose' deaths that do not necessarily involve the life-style forced on opiate users by the War on Drugs (see, for instance, Siegel et al. 1982).

Whatever the actual cause or causes, however, many deaths ordinarily attributed to overdose are clearly not simple pharmacological effects of opiates. Therefore, they are avoidable, even among people who use large amount of opiates, if the appropriate precautions are discovered and publicized. However, publicizing safe ways of using opiates would be an unacceptable accommodation during a War on Drugs. Unless the threat of AIDS spreading to the non-addicted population changes this fact, it is likely that 'overdose' will continue to take its toll and that War on Drugs propaganda will continue to imply that these deaths are pharmacological effects of opiate use, rather than casualties of a futile war.

## Conclusion

Heroin, the ultimate devil of the War on Drugs propaganda for almost a century, is actually a respectable member of a valuable family of drugs. The opiates, including heroin, are medically indispensable and relatively safe, as drugs go. Heroin can be used in very unhealthy ways but, of course, so can many otherwise useful drugs and commodities. There is no reason to think that heroin is more physically damaging, more addictive, or more likely to incite violence than alcohol, tobacco, food, money, or love. Nor is heroin a short cut to ecstasy, except perhaps for short periods under unusual circumstances. Many of the widely publicized dangers that are associated with heroin in the public mind are in fact societal effects of the War on Drugs.

Exposing the heroin mythology robs the War on Drugs of some of its stongest justifications. However, in the last decade heroin has been replaced as the ultimate devil in the drug-war propaganda. The next chapter will discuss cocaine, the drug that has taken its place.

# 5    Cocaine:
# Dr Freud and
# Dr Gold

Cocaine is prominent in the propaganda that currently justifies the War on Drugs. Terrifying statistics and tragic personal stories about cocaine, especially in the form of 'crack,' fill the contemporary media. But is cocaine, in any form, actually such a menace? Or could it be another bogeyman, like glue, marijuana, heroin, and the others whose grossly exaggerated effects have justified the War on Drugs in past decades? Answering these questions requires an examination of the history and pharmacology of cocaine and related drugs. After these essential preliminaries, this chapter will evaluate three controversial issues: the extent of cocaine's 'addictive liability,'* cocaine's effects when it is used in moderate amounts, and the appropriate societal response to cocaine. The work of Dr Sigmund Freud and Dr Mark Gold will be used to frame these issues.

## Cocaine's History: From 'Gift of the Gods' to 'Evil Empire'

The cocaine-bearing leaves of the coca plant were used throughout South America for centuries in ways that supported the values of society, rather than threatening them. Cocaine itself acquired different meanings, however, after it was extracted and introduced to the world in the nineteenth century. It was at first regarded as a medical and social panacea and later as a drug that threatens morality, health, and social stability.

*The addictive-liability section of this chapter is modified from text originally prepared for *Social Pharmacology*, with Patricia Erickson as senior author.

## ANCIENT COCAINE USE

Signs of coca use have been found from Central America to Chile. From the time of the Incas to the present, its greatest use has been in the highlands of Bolivia and Peru (Grinspoon and Bakalar 1976, 70). In these harsh regimes, cocaine was chewed, used to make a tea, and probably smoked (Siegel 1982). Under the Incas, coca was cultivated in state-owned plantations for use in religious ceremonies including weddings, burials, and initiations. Although its use by common people was restricted, they had access to it as medicine, as a ceremonial drug, and as a special royal dispensation. Many people regarded it as a 'gift of the gods' (Grinspoon and Bakalar 1976).

## COCAINE AFTER THE SPANISH CONQUEST

The Spanish conquerors marvelled at coca. One wrote that it 'satisfies the hungry, gives new strength to the weary and exhausted and makes the unhappy forget their sorrows.' Another wrote: 'If there were no coca there would be no Peru' (Grinspoon and Bakalar 1976, 9). Almost from the start, however, cocaine provoked ambivalence among the Europeans. By the 1500s the Spanish bishops had condemned its use as idolatry, while the Spanish landholders were trading it, taxing it, and using it to extract work from underfed slaves. Its use spread greatly under Spanish rule, partly because the social controls of the Incas broke down and partly because the food-production system was disrupted – there was more need than ever for an effective appetite suppressant (Grinspoon and Bakalar 1976, 10–11). When South America finally became independent of Spain, coca use continued on a large scale. This usage was not generally regarded as a problem. Coca also became an important article of commerce. In 1850, for example, 8 per cent of the revenue of Bolivia came from coca trade.

Coca is still widely used by the rural lower class as an everyday drug to facilitate hard work, relieve hunger, and serve ritual functions (Morales 1989). Although blood levels of cocaine in modern *coqueros* are comparable to those found in North Americans who 'snort' refined cocaine in moderate amounts (Paly, et al. 1980), there is no resemblance between the regular cocaine use of *coqueros* and negatively addicted North Americans: 'The insatiable desire for the drug, paranoia and mental deterioration characteristic of cocaine addiction are not witnessed in the behaviour of the *coqueros* in their daily lives' (Hanna and Hornick 1977, 63). *Coqueros* apparently give up the habit easily when their nutrition is improved (Monge 1952, cited by Hanna and Hornick 1977).

There has been little local will to suppress coca use within cocaine-producing countries, but international agencies and the United States have applied mounting pressure against it. Under United Nations pressure, Peru and Bolivia both joined the Single Convention on Narcotic Drugs in 1961, which required the abolition of coca use within twenty-five years, that is, by 1986 (Wisotsky 1986). None the less, Peru still permits the legal production of coca for local use (Morales 1989). In recent years, enforcement efforts have become more violent and corrupt, with the influx of large amounts of u.s. money, technical advice, and, most recently, American troops. All indications are that the eradication effort has not and cannot succeed (Wisotsky 1986; Arnao 1988; Morales 1989).

In recent years, the destructive use of coca paste and other by-products of the illegal cocaine trade has been reported in the cocaine-producing countries, Columbia, Bolivia, Peru (Jeri 1986; Morales 1989), as well as in a cocaine trans-shipping country, the Bahamas (Jekel et al. 1986).

COCAINE AS PANACEA: DR FREUD'S DISCOVERY

The history of the coca leaf is strangely different from that of the tobacco leaf. Soon after the discovery of the New World, tobacco became a major article of trade as its use spread rapidly (Brecher 1972). By contrast, Europe and North America had little of coca other than fascinating tales. When some coca leaves were finally imported to Europe in the middle of the nineteenth century, the reports of its users were enthusiastic (Grinspoon and Bakalar 1976, 20).

In the 1860s, cocaine was chemically identified and isolated from coca leaves. It was then introduced into medical and recreational use in Europe and America. One of the early medical researchers in the United States, W.H. Bentley, reported that cocaine was useful in the treatment of morphine addiction, but the ultimate authority on this topic was Sigmund Freud, who became interested in cocaine in 1884. His pioneering research remained the definitive investigation of cocaine until about 1975, when a modern wave of cocaine research appeared (Van Dyke and Byck 1982, 131). Because Freud's role has been oversimplified and sometimes sensationalized, it is described here in detail.

As a struggling young doctor, Freud could hardly afford to buy cocaine, which had newly become available in the pure form. He felt that it was a promising drug, however, and pulled together the price of a single gram. When he got his tiny supply, he took 1/20 of the gram himself and gave some to his friend, Ernst von Fleischl, who was apparently addicted to morphine. Freud was delighted with cocaine's stimulating effects on himself and von Fleischl. He next used it successfully to treat a patient with 'gastric catarrh.' In his excitement over his initial findings, he wrote a letter to his fiancee suggesting that marriage might soon be possible and sent her some cocaine 'to make her strong and give her cheeks a red color' (Byck 1974, 7).

Freud knew that cocaine could be addictive when he wrote his first enthusiastic article about it, 'Über Coca,' in 1884. He described cocaine addiction as having 'a great similarity to the symptoms of chronic alcoholism and morphine addiction' (Freud 1884, translation in Byck 1974, 52). Notwithstanding this danger, and a few side-effects like burping and anesthesia of the mouth, Freud felt that the effects of cocaine were generally beneficial. Drawing mostly from his own experiences and the reports of friends and patients, he described the following psychological effect: 'exhilaration and lasting euphoria, which does not differ in any way from the normal euphoria of a healthy person. The feeling of excitement which accompanies stimulus by alcohol is completely lacking; the characteristic urge for immediate activity which alcohol produces is also absent. One senses an increase of self control and feels more vigorous and capable of work; one is simply normal and soon finds it difficult to believe that one is under the influence of any drug at all. This gives the impression that the mood induced by coca is due not so much to direct stimulation as to the disappearance of elements in one's general state of well-being which cause depression' (Freud 1884, 60).

Freud was fully aware of the effect of different patterns of use on the cocaine experience. In an 1885 article, he stated that the effect is barely noticeable to a person in excellent health who 'does not expect any special exertion thereafter' (Freud 1885, 114). However, an unhealthy, fatigued, or hungry person is strongly affected, being restored to full vigour and at the same time feeling euphoric. Apart from influences of setting on cocaine's effect, Freud recognized a difference in the way different people react. He felt that cocaine gave him, personally, 'a pure euphoria without alteration' (Freud 1885, 115), whereas some other users experienced a degree of intoxication, activation, and talkativeness, and still others apparently experienced nothing.

Freud did not feel that his increased effectiveness after taking cocaine was illusory, for 'so long as the effects of the drug persist, one can perform mental and physical work with great endurance and the otherwise urgent needs of rest, food and sleep are thrust aside' (Freud 1885, 114). As a physiologist, Freud was inclined to check his subjective observations with physical measures, so he experimented with the effects of cocaine on his own muscular strength (measured with a dynamometer) and his own reaction time. He found that both measures varied during the day. Although the form of the cyclic variation was consistent from day to day, the overall level varied between days in an unpredictable way. In effect, Freud found a way to measure the difference between what might be called a 'good day' and a 'bad day.' He reported that cocaine improved the muscular-strength and reaction-time values on bad days, but only up to the level of what they would normally be on an excellent day. Cocaine euphoria only occurred when these measurable physical benefits were being produced (Freud 1885).

Freud recommended cocaine as more than a tonic. He was captivated by its potential as a wonder drug. He wrote confidently of its use in the medical treatment of hysteria, hypochondriasis, melancholia, neurasthenia, tuberculosis, digestive disorders, anemia, typhoid fever, anorexia, mercury poisoning, morphine addiction, and alcoholism – although he pointed out that in many cases the necessary research had not yet been done (Freud 1884, 64; 1885, 116–17). Freud was vague about why cocaine should be used in the treatment of most of these problems, but for morphine addiction he was specific: cocaine made withdrawal distress more tolerable. He did not propose cocaine use as a substitute addiction, nor did he think addiction to cocaine would become a significant complication (Freud 1885, 117). However, the eventual outcome of the von Fleischl case led him, and others, to different conclusions, and eventually brought this part of his career to a halt.

Ernst von Fleischl was a brilliant doctor who was deeply admired by Freud. For ten years, von Fleischl had suffered from incurable pain, originating in the stump of a thumb that had earlier been amputated. He took huge doses of morphine to control the pain. To cure him of this apparent addiction, Freud introduced the 'withdrawal cure,' with cocaine to control the pain, in May 1884. The initial success was short-lived: 'But only a week later, in spite of the cocaine weaning him from morphia, Fleischl's condition was pitiable. After several vain attempts to get an answer to his knockings Freud procured help and he, Obersteiner, and Exner burst into the room to find Fleischl lying almost senseless with pain ...' (Jones 1953, excerpted in Byck 1974, 156–7). By January 1885 von Fleischl was taking a gram of cocaine every day and Freud first warned Martha against acquiring the habit, although he continued to send her cocaine. Von Fleischl eventually suffered a 'chronic intoxication' and ultimately a 'delerium tremens with white snakes crawling over his skin.' He died after six more painful years (Jones 1953, 153–8).

As more cases were reported, the horrors of negative addiction to cocaine captured the attention of prominent European doctors and, to his horror, Freud found himself accused of promoting a terribly addicting substance. In 1887 Freud, under growing public pressure, renounced injection of cocaine as a medical treatment. However, he insisted that cocaine addiction occurred only in persons that were already addicted to morphine, and that cocaine posed no threat of addiction to other patients (Freud 1887, 173). In the 1887 paper, Freud also acknowledged that cocaine sometimes produced irritating side-effects when used by eye and throat specialists: stupor, dizziness, increased pulse, irregular breathing, anorexia, insomnia, delerium, weakness. But these were rare and not seriously dangerous. The other problem he acknowledged was that some people experienced only the side-effects of cocaine and not the salubrious 'general reaction.' He could not predict who would experience which reaction.

Because of these problems, Freud wrote, 'I consider it to be advisable to abandon so far as possible subcutaneous injection of cocaine in the treatment of internal and nervous disorders' (Freud 1887, 175). Note that it was only cocaine *injection* that Freud abandoned. He continued to maintain that cocaine was harmless in oral use (Jones 1953, 198). At this point, however, Freud prudently ceased promoting cocaine and turned instead to hypnosis, hysteria, and psychoanalysis, which eventually gave him the fame he had sought.

Freud continued to use small quantities of cocaine himself, with favourable results and no addiction (Byck 1974, chap. 14). Ironically, he became seriously dependent on a drug, but it was tobacco, not cocaine (Brecher 1972). A recent book (Thornton 1986) has claimed that Freud's theoretical novelty in his psychoanalytic writing reflected paranoia produced by cocaine addiction. However, this seems to me an attempt to use guilt by association with cocaine, rather than logical argument, to discredit Freudian theory. Freud may well have continued to use cocaine covertly, as Thornton claims, but he obviously did not become negatively addicted to it. He maintained his productivity as a scholar, the loyalty of his family and friends, and a consistent public decorum.

Freud's colleague and rival Carl Koller established cocaine's place in modern medicine. Koller introduced cocaine as a topical anesthetic in eye operations where general anesthesia was impossible because the co-operation of the patient was necessary. Delicate, sensitive, lengthy operations carried on without anesthesia had been a kind of torture for both patient and doctor, but topically applied cocaine solved the problem miraculously. Koller's discovery provoked great interest in cocaine among physicians. William Halstead in the United States improved the technique by injecting cocaine into nerve trunks. Until the end of the nineteenth century cocaine was highly prized as the only effective local anesthetic. Around the turn of the century the first of the synthetics appeared (Grinspoon and Bakalar 1976, 23). At about the same time as Koller's achievement, another ophthamologist, Dr Arthur Conan Doyle, discovered that descriptions of cocaine use could fascinate readers and sustain their interest in the slow parts of the Sherlock Holmes mystery stories he was writing (Goldberg 1984).

Freud missed out on these important and lucrative discoveries although, to his somewhat smaller credit and benefit, he discoverd in these same years that cocaine could be used in the way some people use Alka-Seltzer: 'I have experienced personally how the painful symptoms attendant upon large meals – viz, a feeling of pressure and full-ness in the stomach, discomfort, and a disinclination to work – disappear with eructation [i.e., burping] following small doses of cocaine (0.025–0.05 g). Time and again I have brought such relief to my colleagues' (Freud 1884, 66).

By the 1880s coca and cocaine had become a panacea to many in the medical profession and were professionally recommended as a tonic for the nervous system, a cure for morphine and alcohol addiction, hay fever, head colds, stomach irritability, depression, and inflammations of the mucous membrane, a stimulant to athletic performance, and, when applied topically to numb the vagina, a preventative for masturbation in women (Grinspoon and Bakalar 1976, 23–4).

Coca was also promoted in quasi-medical forms. One of the most famous and fashionable was 'Vin Mariani,' a mixture of wine and coca-leaf extract. Although recommended as a general-purpose tonic, Vin Mariani was primarily dispensed through physicians. At one point its inventor maintained a list of three thousand physicians who had endorsed it. It won various prizes, including one in England as a 'wine for athletics,' and received testimonials from two superstars of the day, Thomas Edison and Pope Leo XIII. The pope 'habitually carried a flask of the wine at his belt.' It was also used by the czar of Russia, Jules Verne, Emile Zola, Henrik Ibsen, the Prince of Wales, General U.S. Grant, and Sarah Bernhardt (Grinspoon and Bakalar 1976, 25–6). Another quasi-medical form was Coca-Cola, invented by a Georgia pharmacist in 1886. It contained cola-nut extract (containing caffeine), coca extract (containing cocaine), and some citrous oils and soda-water. It was marketed in pharmacies as 'the intellectual beverage and temperance drink.' (Grinspoon and Bakalar 1976, 28). Cocaine was removed from Coca-Cola in 1903 (Grinspoon and Bakalar 1976, 78).

COCAINE'S DECLINE AND THE ASCENT OF DR GOLD

By 1890 four hundred cases of complications associated with cocaine use had been reported in the medical literature. The first reports of cocaine psychosis with tactile hallucinations ('coke bugs') appeared in 1886. In 1887 Erlenmeyer described cocaine addiction and labelled cocaine the 'third scourge of mankind' (Grinspoon and Bakalar 1976, 29–30). In the 1890s the habit of sniffing or 'snorting' cocaine became popular, making cocaine intoxication easy, fast, and efficient (Grinspoon and Bakalar 1976, 37–8).

Around the turn of the century, the decline in cocaine's status became precipitous. Increasingly severe penalties for cocaine possession and trafficking were enacted throughout the world. Canadian reaction against cocaine arose primarily in Ontario and Quebec, and was soon followed by legislation. The warlike character of the early Canadian cocaine rhetoric is unmistakable. In 1910, the *Canadian Pharmaceutical Journal* referred to cocaine as the 'dread evil' and the 'principal cause of the ruination of our young girls ... and ... the demoralization of young boys.' The archbishop of Montreal told the House of Commons that 'one is unable to take too severe measures against a plague which is still more terrible perhaps than that of alcohol' (Erickson et al. 1987, 13, 15).

In response to the uproar, Ontario banned the distribution of cocaine in 1908, except by prescriptions from pharmacists, physicians, veterinarians, and dentists. As well, the 1908 federal Proprietary and Patent Medicine Act banned the use of cocaine in patent medicines. Cocaine was treated more harshly under this act than any other drug – heroin, for example, could still be included in patent medicines as long as it was identified as an ingredient on the label. The 1911 federal Opium and Drug Act made it an offence to be in possession of cocaine as well as to import, manufacture, or sell it. The first American anti-cocaine state law was passed in Oregon in 1887, and the first federal law was the 1906 Pure Food and Drug Act. More severe legislation quickly followed.

The reason that the reaction against cocaine grew so fast is not clear. Of course, if the claims about cocaine's addictiveness and destructiveness to health and morals had been accurate, the reaction would have been reasonable, but there was little basis to validate the claims. Although cocaine addiction and cocaine psychosis did exist, they were always rare relative to the number of cocaine users. Even the period when cocaine was as cheap and available as Coca-Cola produced no evidence of large-scale problems arising from it (Grinspoon and Bakalar 1976, 161). Far more dangerous practices such as driving automobiles, playing hockey, and smoking cigarettes were objects of public concern and, eventually, of legal regulations, but not of the impassioned denunciations and total prohibition that cocaine provoked. It was probably true that criminals were likely to use cocaine, but criminals had been a problem long before cocaine became available.

If an epidemic of adverse effects did not cause society's violent attack on cocaine, what did? As in the case of the other drug prohibitions, various explanations have been suggested by scholars. In Canada, the determination of the medical and pharmaceutical professions to compete with the highly successful patent medicines provided one strong incentive for making cocaine only available through prescriptions (Erickson et al. 1987). Across North America the moral reformers were already in hot pursuit of 'demon rum' and 'Chinese opium.' These reformers saw cocaine, like the other demon drugs, as causing the growing personal and social disintegration around them. In 1914 the police chief of Atlanta, Georgia, blamed 70 per cent of local crimes on cocaine, and the District of Columbia police chief considered it the greatest drug menace (Grinspoon and Bakalar 1976, 38). However, the reformers presented little real evidence that cocaine use was a cause rather than a symptom of social disintegration.

Racial fears may have partly caused the violent reaction against cocaine in the United States. It was widely believed there that black men who used the drug were emboldened in their presumed relentless quest for white women. This image provoked alarm in a nation whose men grew up believing that black men had unusually well-developed sexual morphology that white women secretly admired. Moreover, some whites believed that blacks became invulnerable to bullets when they used cocaine, a belief that evidently aroused some insecurity (Grinspoon and Bakalar 1976, 39). Beyond racial fears, there were widespread reports that soldiers were taking cocaine in the U.S. Army and becoming overly talkative about military secrets as a result. This concern became especially worrisome in the pre–First World War climate, which included hysterical fears of a vast German spy network (Knightly 1975).

By the 1930s, cocaine was well on its way to infamy. However, it dropped from the centre of public attention between about 1930 and 1960. One reason for the hiatus was the great economic depression. Suddenly luxuries became unaffordable for most people and the attention of the media was diverted from sensational drug stories to economics. As well, amphetamines were invented and appeared on the market in 1932, providing a substitute for cocaine that was effective, cheap, and for a time socially acceptable (Grinspoon and Bakalar 1976, 47). During the period of quiescence between 1930 and 1960, cocaine use continued at a lower level, mostly at the fringes of society. Cocaine is mentioned in Cole Porter's song of that era 'I Get a Kick out of You' which, in its original version, contained the line, 'some get their kicks from cocaine.' Charlie Chaplin's 1936 film *Modern Times* contains a scene in which the hero sniffs a white powder in prison and becomes a comic superman. In this period an illicit distribution system for cocaine developed and it became popular among criminals (Grinspoon and Bakalar 1976, 48).

In the 1960s cocaine regained popularity, and infamy, for reasons that are difficult to understand fully. Its new popularity was connected with the 'hippie rebellion,' with the movement of South American people and culture into North America, and with changing attitudes towards drugs in general. The new popularity of cocaine renewed public concern, as manifested in stringent War on Drugs measures discussed in previous chapters. Following a series of escalations, the ultimate American cocaine prohibition, it seemed, was contained in the 1973 New York 'Rockefeller laws' discussed in chapter 1. These provided a mandatory life sentence for possession of more than two ounces of cocaine (Grinspoon and Bakalar 1976, 40–3). However, as chapter 1 showed, the severity of laws against cocaine and other narcotics has escalated again in the 1980s.

As cocaine regained popularity, the news and entertainment media focused attention on it, with a strange ambivalence. While the predominant message was negative, popular songs and films sometimes depicted cocaine positively, as a superlative illicit pleasure (Erickson et al. 1987). Other media depicted cocaine users as wealthy, glamorous, high-status individuals. At the same time, the media associated cocaine with evil, compulsion, and destruction. Perhaps the ultimate symbolic attack was a cover of *Newsweek* (Beck 1985) that identified cocaine with an 'evil empire,' a phrase previously reserved for American invective against the Soviet Union and, in Hollywood, for the realm of Darth Vader. But the media did not attack cocaine single-handedly. They were reinforced by government sources and by a number of scientists and physicians. A leader in the scientific community's participation has been Dr Mark Gold.

Dr Gold is a former member of the department of psychiatry at Yale Medical School and is currently the director of private hospitals in New Jersey and Florida specializing in the treatment of cocaine addiction (Kline 1985). He and his colleagues publish profusely in the professional literature on the psychology and physiology of cocaine and opiate use and on treatment for addiction. He has received prestigious awards for his research and public service. As well, Dr Gold is a perennial spokesman in the media for the view that cocaine is so serious a menace that militant public policy is required to control it. The title of Dr Gold's famous book *800-COCAINE* (1984) is also a long-distance toll-free telephone number that people in the United States may call for information about cocaine or to seek help if they feel their own use may be out of control. In turn, cocaine users contribute their experiences to Dr Gold's store of data.

Modern controversy over cocaine is neatly framed in the writings of the two bold young doctors whose work has now been introduced. Working a century apart, Dr Sigmund Freud and Dr Mark Gold both established their reputations by investigating cocaine. Both Dr Gold and Dr Freud were skilful physiologists, both undertook the study of cocaine soon after they left medical school, and both achieved fame for their studies of cocaine. Oddly enough, however, their conclusions about cocaine are diametrically opposed. It is at first hard to see how they could be describing exactly the same drug.

The differences between Gold's and Freud's positions can be summarized in the following three questions:

1. Is cocaine terribly addicting to experimental or recreational users (Gold) or is cocaine addiction rare and largely confined to previously addicted people (Freud)? This question is intertwined with the issue of whether there is an epidemic of problems growing from the current abundance of cocaine (Gold).

2. Is cocaine useless and dangerous when used non-addictively (Gold) or is it medically harmless and beneficial (Freud)?

3. Are warlike drug-control measures justified by the menace of cocaine (Gold) or should cocaine be eagerly explored as a potential blessing to humanity (Freud)?

Although current conventional wisdom supports Gold's position, the bulk of modern clinical, experimental, and historical evidence indicates that Freud was closer to the truth on the first two issues. On the third issue, I believe that Freud and Gold were both wrong. As in the last chapter, it is necessary to approach these contentious issues by way of a brief review of the basic pharmacology of cocaine and related drugs. Following this review, the chapter will take up the three key questions.

## Cocaine and Related Drugs: Some Basic Pharmacology

Cocaine is an alkaloid constituting about 1 per cent of the leaves of the plant *Erythroxylon coca*, a shrub that flourishes at high altitudes in the Andes Mountains of South America. The alkaloid cocaine is extracted and converted to cocaine hydrochloride for medical and non-medical use. Following conventional usage, the word 'cocaine' in this book refers to cocaine hydrochloride.

As with opiate drugs, it is impossible to talk about the effects of cocaine in a simple way. The effects of the drug are heavily influenced by the way it is used. This section will discuss the effects of cocaine hydrochloride when it is used in various ways, the effects of alkaloid cocaine and cocaine sulphate (which together will be called 'smokable' cocaine), and finally the effects of drugs that are used as substitutes for cocaine.

PHARMACOLOGICAL EFFECTS OF COCAINE HYDROCHLORIDE

*Circumstantial Use*

In circumstantial use, cocaine serves as an effective stimulant, local anesthetic, and appetite suppressant. Extensively used by physicians and dentists in the past, it has now been partly replaced by synthetic drugs with similar effects. It has by no means disappeared, however. It is still widely used as an anesthetic in eye, ear, nose, and throat operations by more than 90 per cent of American otolaryngologists (Goldberg 1984) and as a folk medicine in South America (Morales 1989). As happens with many drugs used in medical practice, hypersensitive reactions and other adverse complications sometimes occur, but they are relatively rare (Ritchie and Greene 1985).

*Experimental and Casual Use*

Cocaine can be administered as a recreational stimulant, usually by sniffing or 'snorting' it. Unlike opiate drugs, cocaine produces euphoria in experimental use (Van Dyke and Byck 1982). In a recent laboratory test of cocaine, the cocaine experience was described as follows: 'I feel as if something pleasant had just happened to me,' 'I feel less discouraged than usual,' 'A thrill has gone through me one or more times since I started the test,' 'I have a weird feeling,' 'Things around me seem more pleasing than usual,' 'I feel so good that I know other people can tell it,' 'I am bothered by a peculiar taste in my mouth,' 'I seem to be a changed person' (Van Dyke et al. 1982, 9). Experimental subjects also report feelings of vigour, relaxation, friendliness, and decreased appetite after taking cocaine. The depression of hunger appears to last somewhat longer than the euphoria (Resnick, Kestenbaum, and Schwartz 1977).

Although cocaine is clearly a more effective euphoriant than the opiates in experimental and recreational use, this does not, by itself, mean that it is addictive. There are many activities that can produce euphoria, like skiing, sex, and reading, but these are not addictive to the great majority of people, although each of them is addicting to some people.

In experimental tests, most subjects do not report dysphoria when the cocaine effect subsides (Post, Kotin, and Goodwin 1974; Fischman et al.

1976; Van Dyke et al. 1982). In one study, however, four of nineteen subjects reported 'feelings of anxiety, depression, fatigue, and wanting more cocaine' after a 25-mg cocaine injection, and two of five reported similar feelings after snorting 100 mg. It is unclear whether this study should be considered an investigation of 'experimental use' or of 'dependent use,' however, since the subjects were all heavy users (Resnick, Kestenbaum, and Schwartz 1977). Some recreational users report occasional depression after using cocaine outside the laboratory (Erickson et al. 1987).

Experimental and casual cocaine use typically increases heart rate, blood pressure, and body temperature (Fischman and Schuster 1980). Some users report other irritations including a dripping sensation in the throat and a burning feeling in the nose. The cardio-vascular stimulation and the side-effects last for only about an hour after cocaine is taken. In spite of recent exaggerated claims, moderate use of cocaine is unlikely to be physically dangerous. Because this is one of the key issues that divides Gold and Freud, it will be examined in detail later in this chapter.

## Heavy Use

Regular, dependent, addictive, and short-term heavy use of cocaine produce an intense stimulation. Heavy use can also produce unwanted side-effects including unpleasant hallucinations, feelings of paranoia, unpleasant tactile sensations called 'coke bugs,' repetitive behaviours, and severe depression after use. In the most severe cases, the unwanted effects resemble a short-term paranoid psychosis accompanied by convulsions. In addition to these experiences, excessive use of cocaine sometimes produces physical damage to the nasal tissues and kidneys, and extreme overdoses can be fatal. There is a recognizable sequence of reactions when a binge of heavy use ends, including a dramatic 'crash.' However cocaine does not produce physical withdrawal symptoms of comparable severity to those that follow heavy use of alcohol, barbiturates, or opiates (Grinspoon and Bakalar 1976; Gawin and Kleber 1986). Authorities differ on whether or not the aftermath of heavy cocaine use should be called 'withdrawal symptoms' at all.

Whether or not heavy cocaine use produces tolerance is also debatable. An 'acute tolerance' to the psychotropic effects of cocaine and to the elevations of heart rate and blood pressure has been reported during binges by heavy users (Fischman and Schuster 1980; Gawin and Kleber 1986; Ambre et al. 1988). But this tolerance may not persist until the next binge. By contrast, regular doses make experimental animals hypersensitive rather than tolerant to some of cocaine's effects (Fischman et al. 1976; Hinson and Poulos 1981).

## DRUGS RELATED TO COCAINE HYDROCHLORIDE

### Smokable Cocaine

The terms 'crack,' 'free-base,' 'coca paste,' 'rock,' 'basuco,' 'tangana,' and 'kete' refer to preparations containing the cocaine alkaloid or cocaine sulphate that have become popular in the 1980s. These forms of cocaine are typically smoked because, it is said, they can withstand heat better than cocaine hydrochloride. Because the large-scale use of these drugs is relatively recent, little systematic research has been done on them. Nevertheless, smokable cocaine is central in the ubiquitous horror stories in the current media. Smokable cocaine is said to stimulate erratic violent behaviour, to be extraordinarily addicting, and to be physically damaging or fatal to the user. Because these conclusions about smokable cocaine are similar to claims that were made earlier in this century about opium, heroin, marijuana, glue, and so on, they must be examined at length. This task is undertaken later in this chapter.

### Synthetics

A series of cocaine-like drugs have been synthesized as local anesthetics, beginning with procaine (a familiar trade name is Novocaine) in 1905. Lidocaine (familiar trade name, Xylocaine), tetracaine, and several others have since been added to this group. These are now widely used as substitutes for cocaine in local anesthesia. However, cocaine is still used as well, because of its unique virtue of constricting blood vessels as it anesthetizes (Ritchie and Greene 1985).

Although their chief medical use is as local anesthetics, there have been experimental trials of these synthetics as stimulants and euphoriants. In these experiments, the effects of the synthetics proved similar to those of cocaine (Van Dyck et al. 1982). In one experiment experienced users could not distinguish cocaine and lidocaine taken intranasally in the laboratory. Animals in self-injected experiments perform as much work to get injections of procaine as of cocaine (Van Dyke and Byck 1982). The ability of the synthetics to mimic the euphoriant effects of cocaine has been demonstrated in the black market. Illicit cocaine consumers often purchase synthetics or synthetic-cocaine mixtures, although they are usually told they are buying pure cocaine. Street 'cocaine' in Miami, for example, is usually cocaine hydrochloride mixed with lidocaine hydrochloride (Wetli and Wright 1979). Some samples of street 'cocaine' contain no cocaine at all, only mixtures of synthetics or amphetamines or both (Klatt et al. 1986).

## Amphetamines

Amphetamine was first marketed in 1932, under the trade name Benzedrine, and similar drugs have been introduced since. Their effects are remarkably similar to those of cocaine. Like cocaine, these drugs can be used as stimulants, appetite suppressants, and anti-depressives. They produce euphoria in experimental use as shown by Beecher's (1959) experiments discussed in the last chapter. As with cocaine, excessive amphetamine use can trigger a temporary paranoid psychosis (Brecher 1972; Fischman et al. 1976). The immediate effects of intravenous injections of cocaine and amphetamine are frequently indistinguishable to experienced users of cocaine (Fischman et al. 1976). (The effects later become more distinguishable, because the amphetamine effect usually persists longer than the cocaine effect.)

Like cocaine, amphetamines have been used as battlefield stimulants for soldiers. In the Second World War, Benzedrine was issued to soldiers by the British, American, German, and Japanese armies (Brecher 1972, 279). As far as I have been able to determine, the Canadian army issued Benzedrine only in small quantities to officers (Feasby 1953, 363; Mowat 1979).

Cocaine sold in the street is often mixed with amphetamines, as well as with the synthetics procaine or lidocaine (Van Dyck and Byck 1982; Grabowski and Dworkin 1985). Cocaine use diminished in North America at the time when amphetamines first appeared on the market at a lower price (Grinspoon and Bakalar 1976, 47). There are signs that the current American campaign against cocaine is leading to a major resurgence in the use of amphetamines (Gross 1988).

*Cathinone*

Cathinone is the active ingredient in khat, a leaf chewed by many inhabitants of Africa and the Middle East. In parts of these regions, khat grows wild and is picked by local residents for sale in town markets, along with other produce. Cathinone has only recently been extracted from khat, and has been found to be quite similar in most of its effects to amphetamines (Jaffe 1985a) and as reinforcing in animal research as cocaine (Johanson 1984).

Because cocaine is so similar in its effects to the synthetics, amphetamines, and cathinone, which do not arouse nearly as much public concern, it is clear that the 'cocaine problem' is not a simple consequence of cocaine's pharmacology. Rather, the problems grow from its unique history and its social meaning (Van Dyke and Byck 1982, 128). Therefore, the contentious issues introduced by Dr Freud and Dr Gold will be considered in a social as well as pharmacological context.

## Evaluating the Contentious Issues

Both the history and the basic pharmacology of cocaine suggest that the tales that are told about it in justification of the War on Drugs may be exaggerated. A full assessment of this possibility can be made by examining current research as it bears on the three contentious questions that were introduced earlier.

### ADDICTIVE LIABILITY AND THE COCAINE 'EPIDEMIC'

The first question concerns the addictiveness of cocaine. Freud thought that very few people, primarily those already addicted to morphine, were susceptible to cocaine addiction. Gold believes that cocaine is so addictive to people in general that its availability has precipitated a genuine epidemic of cocaine use and consequent addiction.

When the actual data on cocaine use and addiction are examined, it becomes clear that Freud was closer to the truth. In spite of widespread availability and declining prices, most people never use cocaine; of those who do, most use it only once or a few times; of those who become casual or regular users, most do not become dependent or addicted; of those who become dependent or addicted, most return to moderate use or voluntarily abstain without treatment; and of those whose addiction becomes serious enough to require treatment, most had lives that were marked by severe alienation or misfortune before they first used cocaine. None of this is intended to deny the horrors of severe negative addiction to cocaine, but rather to challenge the view that these horrors prove that cocaine is a highly addictive drug.

Establishing the facts about cocaine's addictive liability requires a review of several different kinds of research, because no single type is conclusive. The bulk of this research does not distinguish between different forms of cocaine or between different ways of administering it. Because snorting cocaine hydrochloride continues to be the common form of use (Erickson et al. 1987; Inciardi 1987; Johnston, O'Malley, and Bachman 1988), this research tells much about the addictiveness of this form of use, but less about the addictiveness of smoking or injecting cocaine. The information that specifically relates to smoking cocaine will be considered in a separate section.

## Survey Research

The American National Survey on Drug Abuse, which began in 1971 and continued every two or three years until 1985, randomly sampled residents of American households twelve years of age and over. The results indicate that the number of Americans who have ever tried cocaine nearly quadrupled between 1974 and 1982, going from 5.4 million to 21.6 million. The number of people who had used cocaine at least once during the year preceding the survey rose from 1.6 million to 4.2 million in 1982 (Adams and Durrell 1984). Cocaine use appears to have peaked by 1979 with indications of a levelling off in the early 1980s (Jaffe 1985a; Clayton 1985; White 1988). If the population of the United States is around 250 million, these results indicate that, at the peak, less than 10 per cent of Americans had ever used cocaine and less than 2 per cent had used it even once in the year that they were surveyed.

A second American national survey, conducted annually since 1975, involves a random sampling of high-school seniors. From 1976 to 1979, use of cocaine during the year preceding the survey doubled among these students, from 6 to 12 per cent. There were only minor fluctuations in subsequent years up to 1983 when 11.4 per cent used cocaine during the year preceding the survey (O'Malley, Johnston, and Bachman 1985).

Use of cocaine at least once during the 30 days preceding the survey also stayed almost constant since 1980 at about 5 per cent of the high-school seniors (O'Malley, Johnston, and Bachman 1985). There was a 'sharp downturn' in cocaine use in 1987, in both high-school seniors and previous graduates (Johnston, O'Malley, and Bachman 1988). In 1987, 6.0 per cent of high-school seniors had used it during the 12 months before the survey but not in the past month and 4.3 per cent had used it during the 30 days preceding the survey.

The 'addictive liability' of a drug is not a precisely defined term, but it could be reflected in the difficulty that people have in terminating their use of a drug. When high-school seniors who were considered recent users of cocaine were questioned in 1983, 3.8 per cent reported that they had ever tried to stop using cocaine and found that they could not, in comparison with 18 per cent of cigarette smokers (O'Malley, Johnston and Bachman 1985). A subset of this national sample of high-school seniors has been followed up over several years, producing this conclusion concerning the progression of cocaine use: 'Most of those who used [cocaine] in high school do not show a cross-time progression to heavier use in the three to four years following graduation, which suggests that dependence either develops rather slowly or develops with relatively low frequency among moderate and light users' (Johnston, O'Malley, and Bachman 1986, 221).

Other American surveys of more geographically limited populations have produced similar results and revealed some further patterns. Kandel, Murphy, and Karus (1985) randomly selected a group of people approximately twenty-five years of age in New York State. Of the 30 per cent of this group who had ever used cocaine, about 60 per cent had used it less than 10 times in their entire lives, 31 per cent had used it 10–99 times, 6 per cent had used it 100–999 times, and about 3 per cent (less than 1 per cent of the original sample) had used it 1000 times or more. Of those who had ever used cocaine daily, less than a quarter continued to do so in the year of the study (based on recalculation of data from Kandel, Murphy, and Karus 1985, 80–1).

Taken together, these American survey data indicate that cocaine is used by a minority of Americans and that only a small fraction of this minority uses very much. Of course, general population data like these tell little about special populations such as school drop-outs, in which more people may use cocaine and a high proportion may become addicted.

Canada has no ongoing national surveys of cocaine use. However, provincial surveys and various indirect indicators point to some increase in the uses of cocaine in Canada betwen 1970 and 1980 and to an average rate of use that is lower than that of the United States (Smart 1983). In Ontario, high-school survey data have shown that the number of students who have used any cocaine in the past 12 months has remained quite stable at around 4 or 5 per cent between 1977 and 1985 (Erickson et al. 1987, 51).

The Ontario Household Surveys have provided the only trend data available for Canadian adults (Smart and Adlaf 1988). As stated in chapter 3, the proportion of Ontario household survey respondents reporting ever using cocaine nearly doubled, from 3.3 to 6.1 per cent between 1984 and 1987. However, the change in the percentage that reported using cocaine at least once during the preceding 12 months was insignificant: 1.7 per cent in 1984 and 1.8 per cent in 1987 (Smart and Adlaf 1988, 34). Of those who had ever used cocaine, 95 per cent reported using it less than once a month in 1987.

A recent British Columbia survey conducted by the Co-ordinated Law Enforcement Unit (1987) reveals rates of experimental use higher than those in Ontario, but also indicates that most of those who have used cocaine do not become frequent users. Of a random sample of respondents from throughout the province, 11.2 per cent reported having used cocaine at least once in their lifetime. Of these, 56 per cent had used it less than 10 times in their lives, 36 per cent had used it 10–99 times, and 8 per cent (less than 1 per cent of the original sample) had used it 100 times or more. (These data are recalculated from the original report into a form comparable to data presented above.)

To my knowledge, the highest report of cocaine use in any single Canadian subpopulation not in treatment comes from students at Simon Fraser University in British Columbia. Of 107 students interviewed in one study, 40.2 per cent had used cocaine at some time in their life. However, when the behaviour of the students was examined more completely, there was no indication of high addictive liability. Only 4 of the 107 students had used cocaine at all in the 30 days prior to the survey, and none had used it daily during that period. One student reported having been dependent on cocaine in the past, but was no longer (Alexander 1985).

Thus, the Canadian and American survey statistics do not indicate that cocaine has a high addictive liability or that there is an epidemic of cocaine dependence or addiction. One could argue that there is an epidemic of having used cocaine at least once, if about 10 per cent of the American population and 6–11 per cent of the Canadian population can be taken as constituting epidemic proportions, but, as the surveys show, merely having used cocaine is associated with less than a 10 per cent chance of using it as often as 100 times. Dependent or addicted users would quickly use it more than this.

## Self-selected User Studies

There are a few studies in the world literature of cocaine users who were located through advertising or personal networks. Since these samples were not randomly selected, they do not represent all cocaine users. They are, however, likely to provide more in-depth information on users than would random surveys because the participants, being volunteers, are unlikely to conceal information from the interviewers.

In a study conducted in the San Francisco area, cocaine users who were initially interviewed in 1974–5 (Waldorf et al. 1977) were followed up after 11 years. Murphy, Reinarman, and Waldorf (1989) re-interviewed 21 of the original 27 respondents. There had been no formal contact with the respondents in the 11-year hiatus between interviews. The original sample was characterized as a 'naturally occurring friendship network' in which the age range was 16 to 51, the sex ratio was approximately 1:1, and most of the respondents were university students or graduates. In 1977, the investigators did not consider any of the 27 respondents to be addicted. Most were described as casual users, although four used daily.

The follow-up interviews revealed that all 21 respondents were gainfully employed, many in professional and managerial positions. However, some had experienced physical and psychological problems with cocaine when they began to use it more heavily and for longer periods (Murphy, Reinarman, and Waldorf 1989, 6). Eleven respondents reported having used cocaine daily at some point during the 11 years, but were no longer doing so. Seven of these 11 had reduced their consumption from as much as three grams a week to one-quarter gram or less, but continued to use in a controlled way. Four of these 11 had adopted abstinence after periods of heavy controlled use. Seven other subjects were characterized as 'continuous controlled users' who maintained moderate use patterns throughout the 11-year period. Two subjects had been continuous controlled users, but had eventually stopped using entirely for two and five years prior to the follow-up interview. One of the 21 original subjects was currently a compulsive user of cocaine.

This research provides much detail about the users' motivations for restraining their intake of cocaine. They mentioned the responsibilities of parenting, an avoidance of injecting or free-basing, health concerns, and a norm that 'small amounts on special occasions is the best way to enjoy cocaine' (Murphy, Reinarman, and Waldorf 1989, 26). With respect to addictive liability, this study suggests that one subject had developed a pattern of compulsive use and retained it for eleven years. The rest of the respondents retained, or lost and then regained, a pattern of controlled use of cocaine. For four of the respondents this 'pattern' meant abstinence.

Siegel (1980, 1985) recruited a group of 99 cocaine users in 1974 in the Los Angeles area and followed them for several years. All had been using one to four grams of cocaine per month for at least one year when the study began. Three-quarters of the participants were students, ranging in age from 21 to 38 years. The sample was 84 per cent male. Since the subjects were contacted every six months, close monitoring of use patterns was possible. From 1975 until 1978, all subjects remained social-recreational users, with occasional binges or 'runs' of intensified use that averaged about four hours in length. After runs, subjects invariably returned to social-recreational use; none was classified as a compulsive user. From 1978 to 1982, the 50 users still in the study showed less stability than in the earlier period. Whereas 25 were still classified by Siegel as social-recreational users of cocaine with occasional binges, 16 had become circumstantial-situational users (that is, used cocaine usually four or five times per week to enhance performance in specific situations at work or at play), four were classified as 'intensified daily users' (used cocaine daily to relieve stress or to maintain a desired level of performance), and five were classified as compulsive users (were overwhelmingly involved with cocaine), tending to use it in 24-hour binges; the five compulsive users were all free-base smokers. Thus, 9 out of 50 subjects, or 18 per cent, could be classified as either dependent or addicted users of cocaine. It must be stressed that this is not 18 per cent of typical cocaine users as they are known from survey studies, but from an original sample who had used 1–4 grams of cocaine per month for at least a year in 1974 and who were still using it almost ten years later.

A recent study of 160 non-deviant cocaine users and former users in the Netherlands was directed at establishing a reliable estimate of the dependency-producing properties of cocaine. The sample was 60 per cent male and the mean age was 30 years. All respondents had used cocaine at least 25 times and favoured the intra-nasal route. Of the 160 people interviewed, one-fifth had stopped using. About a third never exceeded a low level of use (less than half a gram per week). At the other extreme, 21 per cent of the sample had used over 2.5 grams per week at some point (Cohen 1987).

Cohen showed that, contrary to the popular stereotype, levels of cocaine use do not insidiously increase in most of those who use it for an extended period. He defined three levels of use: low (0.5 g/week), medium (between 0.5 and 2.5 g/week), and high (more than 2.5 g/week). His subjects classified their use during their first year, during the period of heaviest use, and during the three months immediately preceding the interview. Most subjects were classified as low-level users during the first year and again during the three months immediately preceding the interview, although some passed through a period of medium- or high-level use in the meantime. All of those classified as high-level users in the three months before the interview were also classified as high-level users during their first year of use. On the basis of retrospective descriptions of his respondents, Cohen concluded that the 'dependency producing characteristics of cocaine may have been overstated' (13). He found that subjects maintained controlled use by restricting their use to intra-nasal administration and to social settings. He also noted that some subjects 'progressed,' in a way that reverses the drug-war expectations of a drug with a high addictive liability, from heavier levels of use to lighter levels.

In Canada, Erickson et al. (1987) interviewed 111 cocaine users who had at least one experience with cocaine in the past three years. Attempts were made to attain a typical sample of users. Two-thirds of the respondents were males, the age range was 21 to 44, and all had been employed in the year prior to the interview. Nearly all respondents reported favouring the intra-nasal route of administration, and the average duration of time since first exposure to cocaine was seven years. While 58 per cent of the respondents had used cocaine less than 10 times in the previous year, a small minority (9 per cent) reported using it 100 or more times during that period. Less than half of the group had used cocaine in the previous month and, of these, only one-quarter had used it six or more times during the month.

Although quantities consumed on any single occasion were generally small, that is, six 'lines' or less over several hours, many of the respondents reported occasional binges of intensive use and 'runs' lasting two days or more at some time. Respondents reported considerable fluctuation in their consumption of cocaine. About half (51 per cent) reported more intensive periods of use in the past, usually of short duration and mainly in response to greater availability. Over half (61 per cent) reported cutting back on their cocaine use at some time and provided a variety of reasons including less availability, concern with physical risks and over-use, loss of interest, and life-style changes.

The subjects in this Canadian study were asked if they had ever experienced an uncontrollable desire or craving to use the drug. Almost half of the subjects reported never experiencing this feeling, 31.5 per cent said that they experienced it 'rarely' or 'sometimes,' and 19.8 per cent said that uncontrollable desire or craving occurred 'most times' or 'always' when they used cocaine. These experiential reports might suggest that one-fifth of the respondents are susceptible to cocaine addiction, yet only 3.6 per cent of the sample used cocaine as much as twenty times in the months of the interview. Apparently, most people who experience 'uncontrollable desire' find a way to control it.

Most of those interviewed by Erickson et al. were infrequent cocaine users who clearly were able to limit their use. Restricting use to party situations or special occasions, buying little or none at all, having a stable employment or domestic situation, and appreciating the risks of cocaine were some of the factors that appeared to reinforce its controlled use. Between 5 and 10 per cent of these Canadians developed very heavy or compulsive cocaine use at some time. The majority of those who had engaged in more intensive periods of cocaine use seemed to cut back on their own initiative. Seven individuals had sought treatment related to cocaine use, mainly for medical complications.

*Clinical and 'Hotline' Studies*

There has been a substantial increase in clients seeking help for cocaine problems in the United States and Canada (Kozel and Adams 1985; Schnoll et al. 1985; Community Epidemiology Work Group 1987, 1988; Firth 1988). This fact is sometimes taken to indicate a great addictive liability inherent in cocaine or the existence of a cocaine-addiction epidemic. However, this is not a necessary conclusion.

It is just as likely that the kind of disturbed people who were previously likely to receive treatment for alcoholism or other types of deviance have adopted cocaine use as the drug has become popular and relatively abundant. Clayton (1985) showed that clients who identify cocaine as their primary problem are 'likely to be abusing a number of other drugs at the same time' and to be 'essentially multiple drug abusers' (17). Drug addicts, including those addicted to cocaine, tend to suffer from anxiety, depression, hyperactivity, and other serious behavioural problems before becoming addicted (Newcomb and Harlow 1986; Newcomb, Maddahian, and Bentler 1986; Cocores et al. 1987; Tarter and Edwards 1987; PM, chap. 8). Therefore, it is likely that the people being institutionalized for cocaine addiction would be in other kinds of trouble if they did not have access to cocaine. A few patients with minimal experience with other drugs have been identified in treatment for cocaine addiction (Schnoll et al. 1985), but these are a small minority.

People who call cocaine 'hotlines' like 800-COCAINE (Gold 1984) report that cocaine is highly addictive for them, but it is not possible to draw conclusions about the general population of cocaine users from such data. Like clinical patients, these callers are likely to be facing a crisis situation related to cocaine use. For example, Gold reported that the average caller to his hotline spent $637(U.S.) on cocaine the week before the call. The typical Canadian user in Erickson, Adlaf, Murray, and Smart's (1987) study reported spending $50(Cdn) per month on cocaine, or less than $13 per week. The characteristics of a sample of 500 callers were found to be similar to those of clinical samples – most were heavy users, with about 40 per cent reporting a preference for intravenous use or smoking and over 90 per cent reporting adverse physical, social/financial, and psychological effects (Gold, Washton, and Dackis 1985).

Although clinical patients and hotline callers cannot be considered representative of the general population, they do provide evidence that there are people who find cocaine irresistible. A later section of this chapter is devoted to the implications of this fact.

## The Addictive Liability of Smokable Cocaine

It is widely reported in the media and the medical literature that smokable cocaine is much more addictive than intranasally administered cocaine hydrochloride. Crack, in particular, is frequently said to be 'instantly addictive' or the 'most addictive drug on earth.' There are eminent scholars who take these claims about smokable forms of cocaine seriously. However, other scholars point to the possibility that these claims are greatly exaggerated, for they are suspiciously similar to the unsubstantiated stories that were told about marijuana, glue, heroin, and cocaine hydrochloride when they first became matters of public concern (Brecher 1972; Inciardi 1986, chap. 1; Reinarman and Levine, forthcoming).

Smokable cocaine reaches the bloodstream much faster than does nasally administered cocaine hydrochloride (Paly et al. 1980). This in itself does not prove, as is sometimes claimed, that smokable cocaine is more addictive than other drugs. The speed with which smokable cocaine reaches the bloodstream is no greater than that with which smoked marijuana or nicotine, or intravenously injected cocaine hydrochloride normally enter the bloodstream (Paly et al. 1982).

Pharmacologically, the effects of smoking crack should be similar to those of smoking coca leaves because the active ingredient, the cocaine alkaloid, is the same. Of course coca leaves are normally chewed, resulting in a relatively slow absorption into the body, but they can be smoked. Parke, Davis and Company introduced coca-leaf cigars and cigarettes in 1885, and other drug companies introduced similar products, primarily as treatments for respiratory infections. Although cocaine was, in general, becoming disreputable in this period, these smokable forms were not the object of claims of instant addiction. In fact, they were publicly endorsed as mild and effective remedies by some users (Siegel 1982).

In spite of many media testimonials about the addictiveness of smokable cocaine, the only experimental evidence that I have found to support them comes from a single experiment on smoking coca paste in Lima, Peru. The subjects were all described as non-dependent 'occasional' users. All subjects (the total number does not appear in the report) became anxious before smoking, all expressed an 'extreme desire' for alcohol during the experimental sessions, and two described 'an inability to resist smoking' during the sessions (Paly et al. 1980). None the less, all subjects must have resisted smoking enough to stop voluntarily, since no injuries or deaths were reported even though the subjects were allowed as much coca paste as they wanted during two of the three experimental sessions in which each participated.

There is no statistical evidence of widespread use of crack or any other form of smokable cocaine in North America. Smart (1988) reported that

0.7 per cent of the respondents in an Ontario household survey reported ever using crack. Twelve per cent of those who reported ever using cocaine had ever used crack. In this same survey, 1.4 per cent of students had ever used crack, one-third of those who had ever used cocaine. In the United States, 5.6 per cent of high-school seniors surveyed have ever used crack (Johnston, O'Malley, and Bachman 1988).

People who have used crack do not report any exceptional desire to use it in the future. Inciardi (1987) reported that juvenile delinquents in Miami generally preferred cocaine hydrochloride to crack, because its effects lasted longer. Many of them used crack in addition to cocaine hydrochloride, however, because it was sold in smaller, cheaper doses. Inciardi also found that addiction to crack was rare among the delinquents he interviewed. The survey of 1987 American high-school seniors cited above suggests a similar conclusion. Although 5.6 per cent had tried crack, only 1.5 per cent reported use in the 30 days preceding the interview. Thus, crack did not cause 'instant addiction' in the great majority of people who tried it. The corresponding percentages for all forms of cocaine (mostly cocaine hydrochloride) were 15.2 and 4.3 per cent. Taken together, these data suggest that there is no difference in addictive liability between crack and cocaine hydrochloride.

The few crack users whom I have met have told me that crack is 'just cocaine,' except that it is faster-acting. They prefer cocaine hydrochloride and pay the larger amounts of money required to buy it.

Rapid increases in the addictive use of coca paste and other forms of smokable cocaine have been reported in the cocaine-producing countries, Columbia, Peru, and Bolivia (Jeri 1986; Morales 1989), and in the Bahamas (Jekel et al. 1986). These data have been used as the basis for arguing that, whereas coca-leaf chewing is a relatively benign habit, smokable forms of cocaine cannot be used without a high risk of addiction. However, this argument is flimsy. Alcohol remains everywhere the intoxicant of choice and the available quantitative data indicate that illicit-drug users in all three cocaine-producing countries utilize marijuana, tranquillizers, amphetamines, coca leaves, and inhalants like gasoline and paint thinner more often than smokable cocaine (Medina-Mora and Zavala 1988).

Moreover, it is impossible to say whether the surge in use of coca paste results from a greater addictiveness inherent in the drug or is a manifestation of dramatic social changes. For example, Peru faces social disintegration from several causes including ruinous inflation, uncontrolled violence by police, traffickers, and political guerrillas of the 'Shining Path'; widespread involvement of government authorities in illegal trafficking; government-sponsored dislocation of large numbers of people from traditional settlements into new regions; unprecedented wealth for large numbers of formerly impoverished people; and a powerful fad for American vices, including cigarettes and Scotch whisky (Morales 1989). Under such conditions, desperate people may find some refuge in powerful, relatively cheap, fashionable intoxicants that are by-products of the cocaine industry. A high proportion of the users of coca paste are street children or otherwise marginal people (Morales 1989).

In the Bahamas, several aspects of life have changed dramatically that may account for the increase in psychiatric patients whose condition is attributed to free-base cocaine. These include a lowering of the price of free-base cocaine to one-fifth of the former price of cocaine hydrochloride (or as low as one-eighth of the U.S. price), the disappearance of cocaine hydrochloride from the market (Jekel et al. 1986; Gawin, Allen, and Humblestone 1989), and the wholesale corruption and virtual takeover of the Bahamian government, including the prime minister, by cocaine-trafficking interests. The Bahamas have become a smuggling base, a centre for laundering money, and a safe haven for fugitives from American law. Wisotsky (1986) has described the Bahamas as 'a government captured by the cocaine trade.' The simultaneous demoralization of a country and the appearance of a cheap new drug may explain the dramatic increase of addicts to the new drug better than the hypothesis that the new drug is unusually addictive.

*Integration of Research Findings*

The data from surveys, self-selected user studies, and clinical studies, together with the limited information available on smokable cocaine provide no evidence that cocaine in any form has a high addictive liability or that an epidemic is under way. In Canada, in the Netherlands, and in the United States, the addictive liability of cocaine for most people has proved to be closer to what Freud thought it was than it is to what Gold thinks it is.

Part of the divergence of opinion about cocaine's addictive liability would seem to result from whether addictive liability is defined subjectively or behaviourally. Although most people who experiment with cocaine subsequently use it intermittently and moderately, if at all, some report that they 'cannot control' or 'can't handle' cocaine, and must therefore abstain completely, although they 'can handle' other licit and illicit drugs. Clinical patients and hotline callers often also describe cocaine as irresistibly addictive to them. Do these reports constitute evidence of a high addictive liability? I think not. It seems to me unwarranted to say that a drug has a high addictive liability if the great majority of people who have used it are not addicted, even if some of them find abstention to be the best way of controlling it.

Cocaine would appear to be an unusually appealing drug to many North Americans, just as 'junk foods' are unusually appealing foods. It is apparent that many people must control their intake or abstain from cocaine, just as many people control their intake or abstain from junk foods. People who are inclined to become addicted to drugs tend to prefer cocaine, just as people who are likely to become obese or bulimic are more drawn to junk foods than to Brussels sprouts or turnips. Likewise, people who become compulsively religious are more apt to be involved in an evangelical sect or a trendy cult than the United Church.

If this kind of appeal forms the definition of addictive liability, then cocaine is only one of hundreds of everyday substances and activities with a high addictive liability! There is no reason that I can find to suppose that cocaine exerts more control over North Americans than the other pleasurable commodities that surround us. Chapter 3 has introduced evidence that the likelihood of addiction to cocaine is considerably lower than that of addiction to junk food, sports, television, and so forth. This topic will be pursued in chapter 7.

If the relatively high current level of cocaine use is not an epidemic of addiction, what is it? I believe it is closer to being a *fad of conspicuous consumption*. To call cocaine use a fad is not to trivialize it. Fads exert powerful effects on people's motivations.

One subgroup that has been caught up in the cocaine fad is adventurous, young, affluent adults. For such people, 'coke is it': 'Some of the responses from the participants in our study indicate that the popular status which cocaine has achieved is one appealing feature of the drug. For instance, what someone liked most about their first experience was that they could now "brag about having done it." Someone else remembered that it meant that he was "now in the group." Another referred to the "thrill of just knowing I was doing coke." And someone made this analogy: "it's a special drug, like caviar." Still others said they tried it because it was "in vogue," "the chic thing to do"' (Erickson et al. 1987, 79). As with other expensive fads and fashions, the consequences for the great majority of participants are not dire, although a small fraction of the participants become negatively addicted or develop serious side-effects.

Perhaps even more than the young and affluent, fads attract socially marginal people who seek magical remedies to their problems. Because their need is greater, they are more likely to use cocaine excessively. The people who at other times in history would have become obsessed with marijuana, LSD, alcohol, sex, gambling, or political fanaticism may become negatively addicted to cocaine in the 1980s.

The idea that people who fall into cocaine addiction are socially marginal runs counter to the media portrayal of 'normal' people becoming addicted merely because of an ill-advised experiment. Chapter 8 will consider this crucial argument in detail. At this point, however, it may be useful to cite two time-honoured truths that are sometimes overlooked. One is that some people who appear successful are inwardly disaffected and desperate. Such people lead 'lives of quiet desperation' (Thoreau 1854/1942; St Augustine AD 397/1963; Woodman 1982). The other truth is that throughout history disaffected and desperate people have often fallen into compulsive involvements, chosen from the fashionable indulgences of the day. Plato (375 BC/1955) vividly described this tragedy. He depicted the 'master passion,' which could be directed toward wine, sex, or other indulgences, as follows:

The master passion runs wild and takes madness into its service; any opinions or desires with a decent reputation and any feelings of shame still left are killed or thrown out, until all discipline is swept away, and madness usurps its place ... When a master passion within has absolute control of a man's mind ... life is a round of extravagant feasts and orgies and sex and so on ... So that whatever income he has will soon be expended ... and next of course he'll start borrowing and drawing on capital ...

When he comes to the end of his father's and mother's resources ... he'll start by burgling a house or holding someone up at night, or go on to clean out a temple. Meanwhile the older beliefs about honour and dishonour, which he was brought up to accept as right, will be overcome by others, once held in restraint but now freed to become the bodyguard of his master passion … Under the tyranny of the master passion he becomes in his waking life what he was once only occasionally in his dreams, and there's nothing, no taboo, no murder, however terrible, from which he will shrink. His passion tyrannizes over him, a despot without restraint or law.

Thus, the collapse of human dignity in compulsive self-indulgence is a well-known tragedy that is as old as civilization. The pattern Plato described is essentially the same as that described by the most infamous 'cocaine addicts' of the twentieth century, such as Alistair Crowley and John Belushi (Crowley 1922/1972; Woodward 1984). To blame modern instances of this ancient tragedy on cocaine, rather than on the underlying despair that makes people vulnerable to the lure of excess, is to be seduced by the simplistic logic of the War on Drugs.

*Animal Research*

Often the conclusion that cocaine has a high addictive liability is based on studies of laboratory animals. This conclusion appears untenable in view of the contrary evidence from studies of humans, as cited above. However, the animal experiments are often given great credence, so they are examined in some detail here.

When animals are given intermittent opportunities to self-administer cocaine in the laboratory, there is little indication that cocaine has a high addictive liability. Many different mammalian species have been tested and some members of each will press levers to inject themselves with cocaine. The amounts they self-administer are moderate and controlled. If the concentration of the injected solution is raised, the animals generally respond proportionately less and if it is lowered they respond proportionately more. There are signs of stimulation from the drug, but convulsions from overdoses are rare (Johanson 1984). It is as if mammals find the drug appealingly stimulating, but naturally maintain the stimulation at a safe level.

When cocaine has been made available to animals around the clock, however, indications of high addictive liability have been reported. In

one experiment, two rhesus monkeys with no prior experience in drug
research were put in an apparatus where each lever-press produced
infusions of 0.2 mg of cocaine per kilogram body weight, around the
clock. The monkeys died in convulsions following massive consumption
of cocaine after three and five days. In another experiment, three
monkeys were put in cages where they were allowed to press only one of
two levers every fifteen minutes. One lever produced an infusion of
0.3 mg of cocaine per kg body weight and the other produced five 1-gram
food pellets. Over an eight-day experiment, all three monkeys chose
cocaine almost exclusively. Even on trials where they did not choose
cocaine, the monkeys did not press the food lever. The animals averaged
6–10 per cent loss of their body weight and displayed strange stereotyped
behaviours (Johanson 1984). In a recent experiment at Concordia
University, twelve rats were given a continuous opportunity to self-inject
cocaine. Ten injected significant amounts. The ten cocaine-using rats lost
an average of 29 per cent of their body weight and several experienced
convulsions. By the end of the thirty-day experiment, nine of the ten had
died (Bozarth and Wise 1985).

Such research is often interpreted as reflecting the fate of human beings
if cocaine were freely available. Cohen (1985) has stated: 'Under
conditions of access to large amounts of cocaine the human response
remarkably resembles that of the laboratory animal. Cocaine-dependent
humans prefer it to all other activities. They will continue using until they
are exhausted or the cocaine is depleted ... All laboratory animals can
become compulsive cocaine users. The same might be said of humans'
(152). However, generalizing these animal findings is dubious, for many
reasons. For example, monkeys are gregarious, active, curious animals,
with a great resistance to being handled or restrained. The same is true of
wild rats (Lore and Flannelly 1977) and, to a lesser extent, of their
laboratory-bred descendants. Cocaine self-administration studies isolate
such creatures in small cages, where they are surgically implanted with a
cannula and tethered twenty-four hours a day to the injection apparatus.
There is virtually nothing for these creatures to do in their solitary
confinement but to press a lever on the wall that produces a temporary
euphoric stimulation.

There is little basis for concluding that these animals would consume as
much cocaine in a more natural habitat. In fact, recent data indicate that
rats housed in isolation self-inject much more cocaine in daily self-

administration tests that rats housed more naturally in groups between self-injection testing sessions (Schenk et al. 1987). The observable behaviour of both animals and humans in their natural environments runs contrary to the insatiable cocaine consumption of isolated animals in the laboratory. No naturalistic observations of coca-leaf ingestion by animals were reported in a recent discussion of drug consumption in the wild (Greenberg 1983). In fact, the bitter taste of the alkaloid probably evolved as a defence against herbivores (Siegel 1985a, 217). The studies reviewed in previous sections show that most human cocaine users do not consume cocaine insatiably either, even though many wealthy North Americans and Europeans could afford lethal amounts of cocaine and many South Americans have free access to all the coca leaves they could take the trouble to chew. Nor did many people consume cocaine insatiably before 1906 when the original 'classic' Coca-Cola made cocaine cheap and as available as the nearest pharmacy (Grinspoon and Bakalar 1976, 161).

The failure of animals to eat in some experiments may be another sort of artefact. Cocaine is a potent appetite suppressant for animals as well as human beings (Papasava and Singer 1985). When, under conditions of continuous availability, experimental animals ignore their food and lose weight, the appetite-suppressing effects of cocaine provide a more parsimonious explanation than does a high addictive liability.

There is another line of animal research that is often cited as evidence of the great addictive liability of cocaine. This research concerns the effect of cocaine on the 'reward centres' of the brain. There are about three dozen such centres in the mammalian brain. Animals will press levers many, many times to activate circuits that stimulate these areas with small doses of electricity. Recent evidence indicates that at least one of these areas is also sensitive to cocaine and opiate stimulation (Wise 1984, 1988).

Current research indicates that reward centres in the ventral tegmentum, nucleus accumbens area can be stimulated in three ways: naturally, that is, by the stimuli arising from eating and drinking; electrically, by experimental stimuli introduced in the brain by implanted electrodes; and chemically, by cocaine and opiates. Because the cocaine and opiates act directly on the synapses or cell bodies of the reward centre, they presumably affect it more directly and powerfully than the sensations arising from food and water, which must be transmitted to the reward centre through a series of neurons. Therefore, the theory is that cocaine and opiate drugs are essentially irresistible (DuPont 1984, 39–40; Frawley 1987; Wise 1984, 1988).

A related theory builds on the finding that cocaine stimulates brain reward centres by increasing the activity of the neurotransmitter dopamine (see Koob, Le, and Creese 1987). There is evidence that this short-term increase in dopamine activity leads to a depletion in dopamine activity in the long term (see Trulson and Ulissey 1987), which is assumed to be the physiological basis of cocaine-craving in addicts (Dackis and Gold 1985).

This is sophisticated research. However, it does not prove that cocaine has a high addictive liability, but rather attempts to explain the mechanism of a high addictive liability *that is assumed to exist*. Contrary to this assumption, most people do not find cocaine at all irresistible and the small proportion who become compulsive users are usually able to moderate their use or abstain without professional treatment. It is obvious to many scientists that human addiction is too complex to be determined by the activities of a single reward centre in the brain or a single neurotransmitter, as these theories suggest (see Byck 1987; Barnes 1988).

*Cocaine's Addictive Liability: Conclusion*

The body of evidence relating to cocaine's addictive liability is large and difficult. In the end, however, cocaine has not been shown to have more addictive liability than the numerous other drugs and habits that people become addicted to, and there is no documented cocaine epidemic although experimental and casual use of cocaine has become something of a fad. Freud's view on this issue would appear closer to the truth than Gold's.

EFFECTS OF MODERATE COCAINE USE

On the question of whether moderate use of cocaine is useful and harmless (Freud) or useless and harmful (Gold), Freud was again closer to the truth. Excessive use of cocaine, like excessive use of other legal and illegal drugs, can cause serious damage or death. However, the great majority of cocaine users take the drug in moderate amounts, as shown above, and experience positive effects. Some moderate users experience side-effects, but they are generally minor. Both positive and negative effects of moderate use are summarized below.

## Positive Effects of Moderate Cocaine Use

Experimental and recreational users of cocaine do not feel 'stoned'; they feel more competent and confident. This fact is reflected in comments of Canadian users like the following:

> 'I like the energizing feeling.'
> 'It's a controlled high.'
> 'You can function.'
> 'It gives you confidence.'
> 'It makes you feel more comfortable with others.'
> (Erickson et al. 1987, 80)

It is possible that these perceived benefits are illusory. However, although controlled experiments are scarce, many careful observers have reached the conclusion that cocaine helps people do simple tasks, especially when fatigued or hungry, and that it helps performers of various sorts achieve the confidence that they need (Grinspoon and Bakalar 1976, 100–4; Wisotsky 1986). Cocaine measurably improves performance on simple physical tasks in North American people who are fatigued or deprived of sleep (Fischman 1984). South American Indians working to the point of exhaustion also had slightly better endurance and higher heart rates when chewing coca leaves than on non-coca trials (Hanna and Hornick 1977). There is also experimental evidence that chewing coca leaves affords some protection from exposure to the cold (Hanna and Hornick 1977).

As in Freud's earlier research, these modern studies suggest that cocaine is of little benefit to people who are well rested. Contrary to Freud's observations, however, cocaine apparently does not help with complex mental or learning tasks. Experimental subjects who are administered cocaine sometimes report some confusion and anxiety (Fischman 1984), although this result is hardly surprising in inexperienced subjects who cannot know what to expect from the drug they are given.

The stimulation from a moderate dose of cocaine can be as useful as the 'lift' from a cup of coffee, a short nap, or the satisfaction of a task well done. Of course, legal 'lifts' seem more proper than cocaine 'highs.' But outside the sheltered world of the well-fed and well-adjusted, for whom little naps and tasks well done are a realistic possibility, illegal highs may be a sensible recourse. Andean peasants used cocaine in this way for centuries without provoking alarm, until they fell under the searchlights of the War on Drugs.

Cocaine is widely regarded as an aphrodisiac (Grinspoon and Bakalar 1976, 104–8). Aphrodisiac qualities of cocaine are mentioned by users of both genders as being among their reasons for using the drug. Whether or not this effect is correctly labelled a benefit is a matter of taste, or perhaps mood, but clearly many people find it valuable.

*Negative Effects of Moderate Use*

Negative effects are relatively uncommon among moderate cocaine users. Less than 20 per cent of British Columbians who report using cocaine more than one time in their lives stated that they had experienced any negative side-effects (Co-ordinated Law Enforcement Unit 1987).

About 17 per cent of Ontarians who have used cocaine report that they either rarely or sometimes 'become violent or aggressive' and 23 per cent report that they rarely or sometimes 'feel that someone was out to get you' when they use cocaine. However, the remaining 83 and 77 per cent of these Ontario cocaine users *never* have these reactions. These adverse effects are less common in infrequent users than in heavier users (Erickson et al. 1987). Erickson et al. have identified several other adverse effects reported by moderate cocaine users in Ontario. The summary of cocaine's positive and negative effects is presented in order of frequency in table 7. These data show that a judicious cost/benefit analysis might rationally lead some people to adopt moderate cocaine use. Cohen's (1987) data on the advantages and disadvantages reported by cocaine users in Amsterdam suggest a similar conclusion.

The monetary cost of cocaine is high in North America, but moderate users do not buy enough to create a real financial burden. About half of the Canadian users in the study by Erickson et al. (1987) spent $50 or less a month on cocaine and only a quarter spent $100 or more per month. Many Canadians spend greater amounts on other forms of fashion or entertainment.

There is direct evidence that moderate doses of pure cocaine,

TABLE 7
Frequency of cocaine reactions among Canadian users (adapted from Erickson et al.
1987)

|  | Never | Rarely/ Sometimes | Most times/ always | Mean |
|---|---|---|---|---|
| *Reactions while using* | | | | |
| Energy | 5.4 | 16.2 | 77.4 | 4.0 |
| Talkativeness | 1.8 | 23.4 | 74.7 | 3.9 |
| Increased heart rate | 8.1 | 22.5 | 65.7 | 3.9 |
| Self-confidence | 7.2 | 26.1 | 66.6 | 3.7 |
| Restlessness | 7.2 | 42.3 | 44.1 | 3.5 |
| Increased sexual arousal | 10.8 | 44.1 | 44.1 | 3.3 |
| Dry mouth or throat | 9.0 | 52.2 | 37.8 | 3.2 |
| Acute insomnia | 18.0 | 42.3 | 38.7 | 3.0 |
| Nervousness | 14.4 | 57.6 | 27.9 | 2.8 |
| Self-consciousness | 37.8 | 54.9 | 6.3 | 1.9 |
| Buzzing in ears | 55.9 | 36.9 | 6.3 | 1.8 |
| Nausea | 53.2 | 43.2 | 3.6 | 1.7 |
| Lights in vision | 63.1 | 33.3 | 3.6 | 1.6 |
| Fuzzy vision | 64.9 | 30.6 | 4.5 | 1.5 |
| Paranoia | 76.6 | 23.4 | 0.0 | 1.3 |
| Aggression or violence | 82.9 | 17.1 | 0.0 | 1.2 |
| Hallucinations | 84.5 | 14.5 | 0.9 | 1.2 |
| *Reactions after use* | | | | |
| Congested nose | 9.0 | 58.5 | 32.4 | 3.1 |
| Unable to relax | 27.0 | 57.6 | 15.3 | 2.4 |
| Uncontrollable desire or craving to use | 48.6 | 31.5 | 19.8 | 2.2 |
| Chronic insomnia | 28.8 | 54.9 | 16.2 | 2.4 |
| Exhaustion | 30.6 | 54.9 | 14.4 | 2.3 |
| Sore or bleeding nose | 47.7 | 45.9 | 6.3 | 2.0 |
| Weight loss | 56.8 | 31.5 | 11.7 | 1.9 |

administered intranasally, are reasonably safe. Cocaine is routinely applied intranasally in doses of 200 mg or more in nasal surgery (Haddad 1983; Moore et al. 1986; Gordon 1987). These dose sizes are comparable to those typically taken by Canadian recreational cocaine users (Erickson et al. 1987) and the peak blood levels of cocaine following medical administration (Van Dyke et al. 1976) are comparable to those found following doses that produce a 'high' in experienced users (Javaid et al. 1978). A survey of plastic surgeons revealed five deaths (five one-thousandths of one per cent of the patients) and thirty-four severe, non-fatal reactions (three one-hundredths of one per cent of the patients) following 108,032 applications of cocaine in surgery (Feehan and Mancusi-Ungaro 1976). A recent case-study described an English woman who legally applied cocaine to her nasal membranes several times a day for the past 55 years. She is currently prescribed 3,150 mg of cocaine per week. At age 80: 'She appears to have suffered no ill effects from the prolonged use of cocaine in physical, psychological or social terms' (Brown and Middlefell 1989, 946).

Moderate injected doses of cocaine have also proved safe in experimental studies. Fischman and Schuster (1980) injected varying doses up to 200 mg of cocaine per hour intravenously into volunteers who were recreational cocaine users. These injections were repeated on several days, under varying conditions. Levels of cocaine in blood plasma up to 1.2 mg/L were recorded. Out of fifty subjects there was only one who had an adverse reaction, an 'intense anxiety attack associated with muscle contraction' that lasted about forty-five minutes. This study and others (Finkle and McClosky 1978; Barnett, Hawks, and Resnick 1981; Ambre et al. 1988) show that people regularly tolerate injected doses of cocaine that produce blood levels up to and in excess of 1.0 mg/L of blood, even though this level is often cited as the official minimum lethal level for cocaine (Wong and Alexander, forthcoming).

*Origins of Excessive Fear of Moderate Cocaine Use: Distortion of Medical Research*

In view of the relatively innocuous effects of moderate cocaine use, it is necessary to search for the source of the nearly universal conviction that such use of cocaine is highly dangerous.

There is no doubt that overdoses of cocaine can cause illness and death. The victims generally become excited and confused shortly after a large dose of cocaine, and subsequently undergo convulsions, depression, coma, and in severe cases, death from respiratory depression or, sometimes, heart failure. Overdose death usually occurs within a few hours. This syndrome has been well documented in human beings since the nineteenth century and can be replicated in experimental animals (Finkle and McClosky 1978; Smart and Anglin 1987).

Although there are many claims in the popular media and the medical literature that moderate doses are often fatal, there is little solid evidence to support them. After an extensive search of the literature, I have concluded that the widespread conviction that moderate user of cocaine is dangerous is based on horror stories about cocaine that are accepted uncritically and on medical research that is misinterpreted because of the presuppositions of the War on Drugs. The misinterpretation of medical research entails each of the following errors: (1) exaggerating the amount of sickness and death that is associated with cocaine; (2) gratuitously assuming that people harmed by using cocaine are moderate rather than heavy users; (3) neglecting indications that medical emergencies that befall heavy cocaine users could just as well have resulted from other drugs, activities, or pathologies of the users; (4) gratuitously assuming that cocaine users with medical emergencies following drug use have purchased unadulterated cocaine from street dealers; and (5) neglecting the fact that many other drugs and activities produce levels of danger comparable to those produced by cocaine. The occurrence of such elementary errors probably results from the great rewards bestowed by drug-war officials and the public on writers who generate anti-cocaine propaganda (Pollin 1985; Booth 1988). Under these conditions it is easy for scientific writers and others to misinterpret medical data.

Since 1982, the Drug Abuse Warning Network (DAWN) has reported dramatic annual increases (up to 200 per cent) in the frequency of 'emergency room mentions' of cocaine relative to other illegal drugs in many of the twenty-seven cities that it surveys (Community Epidemiology Work Group 1988). However, these DAWN data do not mean that cocaine has become a substantial health hazard. Cocaine is currently 'mentioned' only in 2.6 out of every thousand emergency-room visits (about a quarter of 1 per cent) in the DAWN cities (National Institute on Drug Abuse 1988). A mention does not mean that a drug necessarily caused the emergency-room visit, since each report may mention several drugs detected in a patient. Moreover, the fact that a patient has used drugs does not necessarily mean that drugs have caused his or her illness (National Institute on Drug Abuse 1988, 269). In addition, the DAWN cities do not represent the United States as a whole, which has a substantial rural and small-town population (National Institute on Drug Abuse 1988, 1).

Similarly, although cocaine is currently mentioned in 14.4 of every thousand deaths (about 1.5 per cent) reported to DAWN through medical examiners in the DAWN cities (National Institute on Drug Abuse 1988,

236), these mentions do not mean that cocaine causes this proportion of American deaths. Medical examiners may mention several drugs in connection with a single death, so cocaine is certainly not the cause in all of them. Most routine deaths are not reported to medical examiners, so this is hardly a sample of typical American deaths. Most importantly, there is no detailed information in the DAWN studies to show that any significant proportion of the emergencies and deaths are related to moderate cocaine use, or that the 'cocaine' used by any of the decedents was free of common black-market adulterants.

A well-known article by Wetli and Wright (1979) provides a more detailed example of careless logic used to attribute lethality to moderate cocaine use. This article, entitled 'Death Caused by Recreational Cocaine Use,' was published in the *Journal of the American Medical Association* and has been widely cited since. However, it contains no evidence whatsoever that justifies the ominous assertion in its title.

By searching the records of the Dade County Florida (Miami) coroner's office between 1969 and 1978, Wetli and Wright located sixty-eight people who had cocaine in their body at the time of death. However, their conclusion that even this relatively small number of deaths was 'caused by recreational cocaine use' was not warranted. Virtually all of the bodies contained other drugs besides cocaine, particuarly the synthetic lidocaine, which is 'usually' mixed with street cocaine in Miami (Wetli and Wright 1979). Heroin, barbiturates, alcohol, valium, and numerous other drugs were also found in the blood of these bodies, so there was no possibility of determining the effect of cocaine by itself. In fact, 29 of the 68 deaths were officially attributed to 'multiple-drug intoxication.' Fifteen of the remaining 39 deaths were officially attributed to 'trauma,' including automobile accidents, drowning, and gunshot wounds.

Of the 24 remaining cases, five were shown to be traffickers who died when cocaine-laden condoms burst inside their bodies or when they swallowed massive doses to conceal them from the police and a sixth apparently overdosed to commit suicide. In the end, Wetli and Wright succeeded in documenting 18 people over a ten-year period (less than two per year) who *could have* died from recreational cocaine use. However, not one of these was actually shown to be a recreational user, rather than a dependent or addicted person. It is entirely possible that none of them was a recreational user! In fact, this study involves all five errors of interpretation mentioned above.

Numerous similar problems inhere in newer studies from Dade County (for example, Mittleman and Wetli 1984). One of these studies (Wetli and Fishbain 1985) is remarkable in that all seven cases of death attributed to cocaine had less than the official minimum lethal level in their bloodstream. In some instances the level of cocaine in their blood was less than the peak plasma levels of some medical patients receiving intra-nasal cocaine as a local anesthetic during surgery, as reported by Van Dyke et al. (1976) and lower than the peak plasma levels of some experienced coca-leaf chewers as reported by Paly et al. (1980). All seven 'recreational cocaine users' in this study fought violently with police (or, in one case, paramedics) at the time of their apprehension, at least three showed indications of a history of 'drug abuse,' and another had 'several arrests for trafficking' (Wetli and Fishbain 1985, 874–8). Again, there was no credible demonstration that *any* of them was a recreational user.

There is little evidence that deaths officially attributed to cocaine in Canada are actually caused by it. My colleagues and I have been unable to find evidence that more than one of 29 people whose deaths were attributed to cocaine by the Vancouver *Province* in 1987 and 1988 were only moderate users. In fact, coroners' records indicated that most were long-time addicts to intravenous heroin, cocaine, alcohol, and other drugs. As well, we could find no basis for confidence that cocaine actually caused the deaths of more than a few of the 29 people, although the coroners identified cocaine as the official cause of death in 20 of the 29 cases. In most of the cases, long-term deterioration from a criminal and dissolute life style seems more likely to account for the deaths (Wong and Alexander, forthcoming).

A spate of case studies arguing that recreational cocaine use causes heart attacks is based on similarly dubious logic. For example, a recent article in the *Journal of the Canadian Medical Association* (Rollingher, Belzberg, and Macdonald 1986) has attracted media attention in Canada (Gifford-Jones 1986), although it is based on a single case. A 24-year-old man was hospitalized for a serious heart attack that required several days' hospitalization after a single dose of street cocaine, while his friends, who took similar doses, only experienced euphoria. The young man injected an unknown amount of street cocaine dissolved in tap-water directly into a vein. No chemical analysis of the drug or the man's blood is provided.

Interpreting this study as evidence that cocaine is an extraordinarily dangerous drug requires ignoring at least two critical questions. First, did this patient really purchase cocaine? A Los Angeles study found that only

58.3 per cent of street-cocaine samples contained cocaine alone. About 19.2 per cent contained no cocaine whatsoever. A total of fifteen different stimulant drugs were found in street 'cocaine samples' (Klatt et al. 1986). Second, was this young man really a moderate user? He 'denied any previous abuse of illicit drugs' (Rollingher, Belzberg, and Macdonald 1986, 45), but his denial is doubtful. Intravenous injection of cocaine is almost never chosen for a first illicit drug experience. In British Columbia, 99.4 per cent of those who have used cocaine have used cannabis as well. Less than 2/10 of 1 per cent of cocaine users in British Columbia reported injection as their first method of using cocaine (Co-ordinated Law Enforcement Unit 1987, 36, 49) and these are probably intravenous users of other drugs. Thus, although it cannot be disproved, it appears highly unlikely that this young man's story is accurate and there is no substantial evidence that his heart attack was caused by cocaine at all.

There are are similar methodological problems with the other North American case studies that attribute heart attacks to cocaine use (Kossowsky and Lyon 1984; Schachne, Roberts, and Thompson 1984; Howard, Hueter, and Davis 1985; Pasternak, Colvin, and Bauman 1985; Isner et al. 1986; Edwards and Rubin 1987; Haines and Sexter 1987; Ascher, Stauffer, and Gaasch 1988; Wang et al. 1988). The greatest problem is that the number of reported cases is so few compared with the millions of North Americans who have used cocaine at least experimentally, a point noted by Sternberg et al. (1989, 522). Most of the dozens of studies in the literature report only a case or two. Moreover, in the majority of cases, the patients had other risk factors for coronary disease. A majority were smokers, used other illicit drugs, and many had obstructive coronary artery disease (Bates 1988).

Although many authors of the studies cited above assert that cocaine produced the heart attacks that they studied, most point out that the evidence for this conclusion is equivocal even when they are discussing heavy rather than moderate users. For example, Haines and Sexter (1987) state 'no causal relationship between cocaine use and myocardial infarction has been shown' (1326). Devenvi and McDonough (1988) and Sternberg et al. (1989) have pointed out the weakness of attributing heart attacks to cocaine when so many other factors in these patients could be responsible. In a thorough review, Bates (1988) states, 'It is not possible to unequivocally state that cocaine abuse causes myocardial infarction' (441).

Because cocaine is a strong heart stimulant, it is certainly probable that it increases the likelihood of heart attacks to some degree in people with high blood pressure or pre-existing heart damage (Mittleman and Wetli 1987), and it could well produce cumulative damage that eventually leads to heart attacks (Sternberg et al. 1989). However, the actual incidence of such events is evidently so low that it is difficult to prove that it occurs *at all* with certainty.

Brain hemorrhages and other neurological damage have been associated with cocaine use in some recent studies (Golbe and Merkin 1986; Kaye and Fainstat 1987; Lowenstein et al. 1987; Tuchman et al. 1987; Wojack and Flamm 1987; Mody et al. 1988). These six studies reported a total of thirty-eight cases. In many there was documentation of neurological defects pre-existing the trauma that was associated with cocaine use, indications of the concomitant use of other strong drugs, or indications of a history of heavy cocaine use. A few of the patients claimed to be recreational users or to have used cocaine for the first time before the neurological problem developed, but these claims must be regarded as dubious without confirmation.

There are isolated reports of cocaine precipitating panic attacks (Aronson and Craig 1986; Rosenbaum 1986; Pohl, Balon, and Yergani 1987), aortic rupture (Barth, Bray, and Roberts 1986), pulmonary edema (Cucco et al. 1987), liver damage (Perino, Warren, and Levine 1987), intestinal gangrene (Mizrahi, Laor, and Stamler 1988), transitory kidney failure (Herzlich et al. 1988; Lombard, Wong, and Young 1988), exacerbation of the symptoms of Tourette's syndrome (Factor, Sanchez-Ramos, and Weiner 1988), and other relatively obscure problems. The significance of these reports remains to be seen. It seems judicious to conclude at this point that use of cocaine might produce a variety of severe adverse reactions on rare occasions, especially in conjunction with other drugs and in persons with pre-existing pathology. However, this conclusion would simply put cocaine in the same category as most other drugs that are in daily, legal use. The infrequent adverse reactions produced by cocaine appear to be comparable in frequency and severity to those produced by many other common drugs, including legal opiates and ASA (see Gilman et al. 1985; *PM*, chap. 6).

Siegel (1980a) has commented on dangers associated with many legal cocaine substitutes such as 'Zoom,' 'Yocaine,' and 'Cokesnuff.' These substitutes contain strong drugs including tobacco, caffeine, ephedrine, and procaine. Siegel suggests, 'The reports of adverse effects and the rarity of such reports in users of pure cocaine suggest that the "real thing" is less problematic in normal patterns of use than many of its substitutes' (1980a, 817).

Normal prudence would argue against even moderate use of cocaine during pregnancy, but the existing studies on the health of infants whose mothers used cocaine during pregnancy do not demonstrate that the mothers were only moderate users. Rather, the studies often suggest that they were dependent or addicted (Acker et al. 1983; Chasnoff et al. 1985; Critchley et al. 1988; Little et al. 1989). Donovito (1988) in a letter to the *American Journal of Obstetrics and Gynecology* commented on the lack of control in such studies and suggested that fetal harm attributed to cocaine might just as well be due to alcohol use during pregnancy. There are recent controlled studies that clarify this issue to some extent. Cocaine-dependent mothers have significantly more birth complications and their infants a significantly higher perinatal death rate and a higher rate of genito-urinary tract malformations than do users of other illicit drugs (Chasnoff, Burns, and Burns 1987; Ryan, Ehrlich, and Finnegan 1987; Chasnoff, Chisum, and Kaplan 1988). Controlled studies indicate that cocaine administered to a pregnant animal reduces the uterine blood flow, which would be a likely cause of spontaneous abortion (Woods, Plessinger, and Clark 1987). However, none of these studies demonstrates that moderate cocaine use during pregnancy is hazardous.

*Origins of Excessive Fear of Moderate Cocaine Use: Smokable Cocaine*

Currently, the popular media and some professionals claim that crack, free-base, and coca paste are far more damaging than other drugs, including cocaine hydrochloride. This claim accounts for much of the fear that surrounds moderate use of cocaine. The claim must be regarded as questionable for the reasons that were outlined in the discussion of the addictive liability of smokable cocaine above. It is impossible to say whether the harm that has recently been associated with coca-paste use in the cocaine-producing and trans-shipping countries results from a greater harmfulness inherent in smokable cocaine or is a manifestation of social disintegration in these countries.

However, it can be said with certainty that some of the widely reported North American evidence that crack and other forms of smokable cocaine are exceptionally dangerous is simply false. For example, *USA Today* attributed 563 deaths to cocaine and crack in the first six months of 1986. On the basis of careful study of the official government reports and available medical literature in the United States, Trebach (1987) published the following response:

> I have searched. My assistants have searched. We have gone through
> many government reports. We have quizzed government statistical experts.
> We have yet to discover one death in which the presence of crack was a
> confirmed factor ... (12)
>    All of the claims about the great rise in crack deaths *for the first months of*
> *1986,* such as that reported by *USA TODAY* and other major media voices,
> were false. Even more significant, none of the leading goverment drug-abuse
> officials, who knew the claims for 1986 to be false, felt any responsibility
> to tell the public the truth. (11)

Two years after Trebach wrote these passages, Ostrowski (1989) was forced to a similar conclusion: 'In recent years, the cocaine derivative crack has become the drug of the moment. In spite of the fact that crack is a more pure and potent form of cocaine, there is little evidence that its use has increased cocaine fatalities. The author was unable to obtain statistical information about crack fatalities in phone calls to the National Institute on Drug Abuse, the 1-800-Cocaine Hotline, or the New York State Division of Substance Abuse Services' (49).

There are some claims in medical journals that crack, free-base, coca paste, and other forms of smokable cocaine are significantly more harmful than cocaine hydrochloride (Siegel 1985; Washton, Gold, and Pottash 1986; Honer, Gewirtz, and Turey 1987; Isaacs, Martin, and Willoughby 1987; Levine et al. 1987; Manschreck, Allen, and Neville 1987; Mody et al. 1988). However, apart from the well-established fact that smokable cocaine reaches the bloodstream faster than orally or nasally administered cocaine, these articles offer little data to support their claims. The authors seem to have relied on uncritical assumptions about evidence, including all five of the logical errors that were mentioned above. At least one set of medical researchers has complained in print about the uncritical way in which crack was assumed to be the cause of harm in a case where the harm could have resulted from other aspects of the patient's life-style (Levine et al. 1987).

In one of the most convincing of these articles claiming that crack is extraordinarily dangerous, Honer, Gewirtz, and Turey (1987) found considerable differences between the frequencies of various adverse consequences in users of crack compared to users of cocaine hydrochloride. However, they found similar differences between users of crack and users of free-base. Crack and free-base are both forms of smokable cocaine and their pharmacological effects should be very similar. However, these two forms of cocaine are typically used by people of very different ages and socio-economic status. The young, poor people who usually buy crack may well be more unhealthy than the older, more affluent people who are likely to buy free-base. Similarly, the differences in adverse effects between users of crack and users of cocaine hydrochloride are just as likely to be caused by age and socio-economic factors as by pharmacological factors.

A report from a cocaine-abuse treatment program indicated that free-base smoking was not associated with more problems in the patients than either snorting or injecting cocaine hydrochloride (Gawin and Kleber 1985). Craig (1988) compared scores on numerous psychological-deviance subscales for men in treatment for free-base cocaine addiction with those of men in treatment for heroin addiction. The free-base users had generally lower deviance scores, although the differences were small.

There are reports that prolonged exposure to cocaine smoke (like other forms of smoke) produces at least temporary respiratory problems (Itkonen, Schnoll, and Glassroth 1984; Kissner et al. 1987; Tashkin et al. 1987; Weiss et al. 1987; Rebhun 1988). There are single case reports attributing a lung hemorrhage and a case of pneumonia to free-base smoking (Patel, Dutta, and Schonfeld 1987; Murray et al. 1988). There are also reports that the forced deep breathing and mouth-to-mouth smoke exchange sometimes associated with free-base smoking may result in a painful chest problem called pneumodiastinum (Salzman, Kahn, and Emory 1987; Wiener and Putnam 1987). However, these studies only confirm that smoking is a relatively dangerous way of administering drugs, as is the case with legal drugs like nicotine as well (Benowitz 1988).

## Origins of Excessive Fear: Exaggerating the Effects of Heavy Use

The real dangers of chronic, heavy use of cocaine may have contributed to the excessive fear of moderate use in the current popular wisdom. There is no doubt that serious damage occurs in some heavy cocaine users, including overdose, ulceration of the nasal septum, psychotic episodes, delusions, violence, and possibly liver damage and convulsions (Smart 1983, 81; Spotts and Shontz 1984). Although these problems can be fatal, they more usually disappear when cocaine use ceases.

As well as being largely transient, these problems may be less frequent among heavy users than public information on the topic proclaims. Chitwood (1985) studied adverse effects in a South Florida sample of which the majority were receiving treatment for 'drug abuse.' In the subgroup of this sample that reported the highest level of cocaine use, only 10 per cent of the patients had ever experienced a cocaine overdose, 11 per cent had experienced ulceration of the nasal septum, and 29 per cent had experienced lack of sexual interest. Gold (1984) reports a much higher incidence of adverse reports in a sample of five hunderd cocaine users who called his national 'cocaine hotline.' Of these cocaine users, 82 per cent reported chronic insomnia, 76 per cent chronic fatigue, 60 per cent severe headaches, 58 per cent nasal problems, and 55 per cent poor sexual performance.

## Gaining Perspective on Moderate Use

I do not mean to claim that harm never results from moderate use of cocaine. All drugs, including cocaine, can hurt people. However, the existing research does not justify the claim that using cocaine in moderation is an unusually dangerous practice.

When a person dies as a result of jogging, playing squash, driving a car, or engaging in sexual intercourse, it provides a good reason for people who engage in these activities to reassess the pros and cons. It does not provide the occasion for a 'War on Jogging' or any of the others. The kind of research that has been taken as serious proof that cocaine regularly causes heart attacks and other dire consequences in moderate users only really proves, again, the existence of an extraordinary, warlike mentality. This kind of thinking forfeits a normally critical perspective to embrace spurious justifications for the War on Drugs.

### COCAINE: SCOURGE OR BENEFACTOR?

The third difference in the outlooks of Drs Gold and Freud is the tone of their writings on cocaine. Dr Gold treats cocaine as something evil and discusses it only within the context of pathology and control. Dr Freud, by contrast, was uncharacteristically lyrical in his description of the drug and its effects. In his proposals that cocaine be used to cure most diseases and improve most human activities, Freud appeared to be proposing cocaine as a welcome benefactor and saviour from the stress of life. Since these opposing views are more matters of feeling than fact, there is little research that can offer a direct resolution of this issue. However, it seems to me, upon reflection, that both views are clearly wrong.

Contrary to Gold's view, cocaine cannot hurt us much. It is a stimulant that can be used in destructive ways, but it is very unlikely to lead to addiction except in people who are already in deep trouble. The great majority of people who try cocaine find it possible to use it in a generally beneficial way, or to leave it alone. The percentage of users that are harmed by it is probably comparable to the percentage for participants in other stimulating but socially acceptable activities.

Freud was also wrong. Cocaine is not the great chemical saviour he thought it was – it is just a stimulant and stimulants do little more than enable people to borrow from psychic reserves that have to be paid back later. Sometimes such loans are useful, even pleasurable, but, as saviours of mankind, they don't measure up. In a study of hospitalized, depressed patients it was found that single injections of cocaine often produced euphoria or tearful reminiscences that might be useful in helping patients gain insight. However, relatively long-term oral administration of cocaine did not seem generally helpful. One patient appeared to improve, one became more depressed, and the rest reported no effect or mixed effects (Post, Kotin, and Goodwin 1974).

No drug can make people feel alert, healthy, and alive for very long. The only hope for a persistent sense of well-being is the patient cultivation of courage, honesty, friendship, realism, hard work, and so forth. The promises of the ancient homilies are far more valid than the magical promise that cocaine held out to Freud. Cocaine has potential medical applications (Byck 1987, 10) that might be investigated further if not for the War on Drugs atmosphere, but there are no signs that it can be the panacea that Freud imagined.

In sum, cocaine is not very important. It neither causes the problems that wrack our times, nor can it rid us of them. Rather, the abundance of refined cocaine is another one of many complexities of a technological age. It may improve our lives to a degree, if we learn to use it wisely. However, using it wisely could turn out to mean not using it at all. Like atomic energy, supersonic air travel, and so on, it is too early to know if it can be domesticated.

In this century we have over-reacted to the dangers of cocaine with a futile attempt to ban it from the earth. As a result of this new extension of the War on Drugs, cocaine has become available to children and adults, without regulation, in the strongest forms. Under these conditions, some people have harmed themselves with cocaine in spectacular ways that alarm society still further. We have responded to the new alarms by further escalating the War on Drugs.

This comedy of errors is not funny. It stains the earth with blood and corrupts the fragile institutions of democracy. Worst of all, it diverts our attention from the real causes of the misery and violence that surrounds us. Cocaine is not a significant cause of crime, violence, addiction, heart disease, brain damage, unhealthy babies, student apathy, low productivity, or terrorism in the Third World. It is the destructive illusion that we can relieve these deeply rooted problems by attacking cocaine that is the real danger related to cocaine in our times.

# 6    ASA-like drugs

ASA and similar drugs stand on the other end of the continuum of social acceptability from cocaine and the opiates. The War on Drugs is built on the presumption that addictive, toxic drugs like heroin and cocaine must be understood in an entirely different way from medications like ASA. However, this chapter is intended to show (1) that there is far less difference than most people think between the ASA-like drugs and the socially unacceptable ones, and (2) that serious drug-use problems, which have arisen with the ASA-like drugs, can be handled peacefully and rationally. This may seem too much ado about innocuous headache remedies. However, the power of ASA-like drugs for both good and ill is greater than most people realize. Physical diseases, dependence, and addiction associated with ASA-like drugs are deadly serious problems.

As in the previous two chapters, it is necesary here to discuss a family of similar drugs rather than a single one and to consider their history rather than just their current usage. As well, understanding the pharmacological effects and dangers of ASA-like drugs requires surveying diverse patterns of use. Thus, this chapter assesses these drugs by the same standards that were applied to the opiates and cocaine in the previous two chapters.

## History of ASA-like Drugs

The Reverend Edmund Stone reported to the Royal Society of London in 1763 that willow bark was useful in treating fevers. The Reverend Mr Stone made this discovery after acidentally tasting willow bark and discovering it was bitter, like quinine, which he knew to help in the treatment of malaria. He reasoned that, since willow trees grow in damp ground where diseases like malaria originate, and since willow bark tastes like quinine, it would probably cure fevers. In spite of his medieval logic, willow bark did relieve the symptoms of his patients (Flower, Moncada, and Vane 1985). Willow bark contains salicylic acid, a chemical precursor of acetylsalicylic acid, the compound known in Canada as ASA. Willow bark is not the only folk medicine that contains salicylates (that is, compounds related to ASA). The perianal scent glands of the beaver contain a substance called castorium that had been used to treat headaches and fever for centuries (Franco 1931) and was a major Canadian export through the Hudson's Bay Company. Castorium too is said to contain salicylates, although it may have many other active ingedients as well (Newman 1985).

The modern era for ASA-like drugs began in 1874, when it was discovered that salicylin, a chemical extract of willow bark, relieved rheumatic fever (Collier 1963). Subsequent pharmacological research and development culminated in the commercial introduction of ASA under the trade name Aspirin by the Bayer company in 1899 (Flower, Moncada, and Vane 1985). Coincidentally, this was only a year after Bayer introduced heroin commercially, in 1898.

ASA went on to become the most widely used medicine in the world, its use doubling and redoubling in every country. Americans consume 50 million pounds of ASA per year (Phillips 1988). By my calculations this is the equivalent of 279 325-mg tablets for each of 250 million Americans each year. As well, ASA is or has been offered unobtrusively in numerous products including Alka-Seltzer, Anacin, Bufferin, Cope, Darvon, 222, 282, 292, Excedrin, and Vanquish (Wenger and Einstein 1970). Among students interviewed at Simon Fraser University, about 97 per cent have used ASA-like drugs at least once in their lives, 47 per cent used at least one in the thirty days preceding the interview, and 3 per cent are currently using them daily (Alexander 1985).

Use of ASA-like drugs is particularly high in Australia for some reason. A comment published in 1907 asserts 'what the drink habit is to men in Australia, the headache powder is to women' (Murray 1980, 9). In Queensland, 16 per cent of women and 10 per cent of men use ASA or a similar drug daily (Murray 1980).

In spite of the invention of many drugs with similar effects, ASA itself remains the most widely used and prescribed of the lot. Because the most common over-the-counter analgesics contain ASA and drugs whose effects mimic it, the medical literature sometimes refers to these analgesics collectively as 'aspirin-like' drugs (Flower, Moncada, and Vane 1985). In this book these drugs will be referred to as ASA-like drugs. ASA-like drugs include acetaminophen, which is the active ingredient in Tylenol and many other over-the-counter preparations, and phenacetin, formerly the active ingredient in Excedrin. These two drugs have been in use since the late nineteenth century, but have never been as commercially successful as ASA, partly because they are not as effective in controlling inflammation.

This chapter will discuss these ASA-like drugs collectively, and will also discuss some key differences between ASA, acetaminophen, and phenacetin. It begins with a summary of the beneficial and harmful pharmacological effects of these drugs in different patterns of use and then discusses the phenomenon of addiction to them.

## Beneficial and Harmful Pharmacological Effects

The effects of ASA-like drugs can be measured in the brain, peripheral nervous system, and many other parts of the body. Although they have diverse physiological effects, their potency as medications is thought to occur because they inhibit the biosynthesis of prostaglandins, chemical agents that are manufactured and released by injured cells. There are several types of prostaglandins that collectively produce pain, fever, and inflammation, the same trio of effects that ASA-like drugs counteract. ASA-like drugs will not counteract these effects when they are produced by injection of prostaglandins, indicating that the ASA-like drugs prevent the synthesis of prostaglandins rather than acting as antagonists (Flower, Moncada, and Vane 1985). Like most drugs, ASA-like drugs have beneficial effects and harmful ones. Their effects will be discussed in relation to circumstantial use of moderate amounts, circumstantial use of large amounts, experimental use, and recreational use.

### CIRCUMSTANTIAL USE: MODERATE DOSES

Moderate doses of ASA-like drugs, a few tablets per day, are immensely valuable in circumstantial use. They relieve mild-to-moderate pain without interfering with thought or concentration. This effect makes them

preferable to opiate drugs as analgesics in many situations. They have a
lower maximum effect, which makes them generally less effective in
treating intense pain, even in massive doses (Julien 1978). However,
there are some types of intense post-operative pain for which ASA-like
drugs are effective (Flower, Moncada, and Vane 1985). ASA itself is the
most effective of all orally administered non-opiate analgesics in
combating cancer pain (Tuttle 1985).

Besides relieving pain, moderate doses of ASA-like drugs also reduce
fever effectively. Normal doses do not affect body temperature in people
without a fever, even those whose body temperature is elevated by
exercise or hot temperatures (Flower, Moncada, and Vane 1985).
ASA-like drugs are also extremely effective in reducing swelling, so
effective that they remain the main treatment for rheumatism, rheumatoid
arthritis, and rheumatic fever, as they have been for a hundred years.
Acetaminophen and phenacetin are not as effective anti-inflammatory
drugs as ASA, but diflunisal, a salicylic-acid derivative, is highly effective
(Flower, Moncada, and Vane 1985). Although moderate doses of ASA
sometimes suffice to control pain of inflammatory diseases harmlessly,
larger amounts are often required. The effects of these larger doses are
considered in the following section of this chapter.

Although universally prescribed, ASA-like drugs usually do not cure
disease but merely relieve symptoms. For example, in the case of
inflammation, 'aspirin-like drugs provide only symptomatic relief from
the pain and inflammation associated with the disease and do not arrest
the progression of pathological injury to tissue' (Flower, Moncada, and
Vane 1985, 687). In addition to controlling symptoms, however, daily
doses of ASA-like drugs may prevent heart attacks and stroke, both of
which are sometimes caused by formation of clots, which is inhibited by
ASA-like drugs (Flower, Moncada, and Vane 1985).

There is some controversy about ASA's psycho-active effects in
circumstantial use. There is no scientifically documented basis for its use
as a sedative or relaxant (Wenger and Einstein 1970). Anacin (ASA and
caffeine) has been advertised as a 'tension reliever,' but a U.S. court
investigated these claims, found them without substance, and in 1978
ordered a $24 million advertising campaign to correct the misconception
that had been spread by earlier advertising (Hughes and Brewin 1979).
However, some consumers stubbornly deny the judicial conclusion that
ASA does not act as a mild sedative and cold remedy. For example,

American students cite tension relief and cold relief among the main reasons for taking ASA (Krupka et al. 1978, 917). I have heard first-hand reports of Canadian auto-production workers who consume handfuls of ASA from the factory dispensary daily, washed down with Coca-Cola, believing that this combination combats pain and fatigue and provides a lift.

In addition to the great value of ASA-like drugs, they can also produce serious harm, even in moderate circumstantial use. The major harm arises from hypersensitivity and combination effects.

## Hypersensitivity

In some individuals, one or two ASA tablets produce adverse effects in the form of a severe allergic-like responses: hives, runny nose, asthma, and rarely extreme illness and death (Collier 1963; Wenger and Einstein 1970). Gastric hemorrhage also occurs in some cases. This hypersensitive reaction occurs following a small dose, and previous trouble-free ingestion of ASA is no guarantee against future hypersensitivity. Flower, Moncada, and Vane (1985) have cautioned physicians prescribing ASA-like drugs as follows: '*Hypersensitivity to aspirin* is a contraindication to therapy with any of the drugs discussed in this chapter; administration of any one of these could provoke a life-threatening hypersensitivity reaction reminiscent of anaphylactic shock' (679). I have not been able to determine whether sudden deaths due to hypersensitivity to ASA are more or less common than the sudden deaths that occasionally occur with cocaine and heroin as described in chapters 4 and 5. Such statistics are unavailable and would be difficult to interpret in any case, since ASA-like drugs are generally consumed under different conditions than are cocaine and the opiates.

## Combination Effects

Harmful side-effects, many of which are severe, have been shown to occur when ASA-like drugs are used in combination with any one of dozens of other drugs (Murad and Gilman 1985). Combination effects are unpredictable, partly because they occur only in some people and partly because new drugs are developed constantly with no way to foresee their combination effects. The following is a newspaper account of a severe, but not fatal, case:

A 29-year-old Canadian sign painter remained in fair condition Wednesday as he waited for word on whether he would get his Christmas wish – to see his children.

Martin Ramsay of Scarborough, Ont., hoped that the tiny telescope doctors implanted in his eye could restore the sight he lost from an allergic reaction to penicillin and aspirin.

The team at Park Ridge hospital, led by chief surgeon Dr. James Aquavella, ended 6½ hours in the operating room Tuesday with words of hope for Ramsay.

'I think he has a good chance,' Aquavella said after the surgery.

Ramsay, the father of three children who until last year operated his own business, went blind after taking penicillin for a minor ear infection and aspirin for a subsequent fever.

The combination of the common drugs dried up Ramsay's mucous membranes, forming an opaque wall of puffy, red scarred flesh over his eyes and damaging his heart, kidney and ears.

Moments before Ramsay was wheeled into surgery, Aquavella sat on his bed and spoke with his mouth close to Ramsay's near-deaf ear.

'You'll be able to sleep,' the surgeon told Ramsay, easing the man's fear that boring a hole through the cornea to the centre of the eye and installing a miniature plastic telescope would bring sleepless nights because one eye would always remain open.

'When you sleep, you'll turn it off subsconsciously,' the doctor said.

Aquavella said the operation was done only in hopeless situations. He said he has performed 34 such operations in the last two years with a more than 50-percent success rate.

Aquavella initially planned to insert the telescope in Ramsay's left eye because the right eye still perceived light from dark.

But on the operating table, Aquavella found the left eye too damaged and, after a quick consultation with Ramsay's wife, Marianne, inserted the telescope, the thickness of a pencil, into the right eye. (Vancouver *Province* 1979, B4)

## Clotting

The length of time it takes a bleeding wound to clot is significantly longer in people who have taken ASA-like drugs. Even a single dose of ASA (two tablets or 0.65 g) almost doubles experimentally measured bleeding time for a period of four to seven days. For that reason people are advised not to take ASA-like drugs before surgery.

The harmful effects described above are all produced by moderate doses of ASA-like drugs. There are other dangers when these drugs are used in larger amounts.

CIRCUMSTANTIAL USE: HIGH DOSES

Many people use large amounts of ASA-like drugs daily, usually to control pain. This type of use is sometimes medically prescribed and sometimes adopted without medical advice. In either case there are serious dangers associated with it.

*Intoxication*

'Salicylism' is a kind of intoxication that occurs after repeated doses of fifteen to twenty adult ASA tablets/day, although the dose required to produce intoxication varies considerably among people. Symptoms of salicylism include dizziness, ringing in the ears, diminished hearing, headache, mental confusion. There is a more powerful form of intoxication called 'encephalopathy' because the effects on the brain are indicated by an abnormal EEG. Such symptoms as 'mental confusion, restlessness, incoherent speech, vertigo, tremor, delirium, hallucinations, convulsions, and sometimes coma may occur'. The mental disturbances may simulate alcohol intoxication and have been called a 'salicylate jag,' which is a rather depressive and unhappy experience (Wenger and Einstein 1970, 763; see also Schwartz 1984). Apparently a key cause of the mental effects is a sharp reduction in blood glucose.

*Internal Hemorrhage*

Regular heavy use of ASA and other salicylates can also produce serious intestinal effects. These effects, however, do not result from the use of phenacetin or acetaminophen. Patients taking regular doses of ASA often complain of 'heartburn, nausea, vomiting and abdominal discomfort' (Wenger and Einstein 1970, 763). These complaints are accompanied by measurable inflammation of the stomach and duodenum, along with vascular contractions, erosions, ulcerations and hemorrhage into the stomach (764). Such results are partly overcome if the ASA is administered with a large dose of antacid, that is, 'buffered.' However, stomach acidity is not the whole problem, because the intestinal damage can also be produced by injecting salicylates. Apparently the action is partly produced by inhibition of prostaglandin synthesis in the stomach as well as by local irritation from the ASA's acidity (Flower, Moncada, and Vane 1985).

About 60 per cent of patients taking regular heavy doses of ASA over a long period show increased blood in the feces produced by gastro-intestinal bleeding from multiple acute ulcerations, although the rate of bleeding is generally low. '70% of adults who take aspirin regularly (and many brand-name products contain aspirin) lose about a pint-and-a-half of blood every year from intestinal bleeding' (Coleman 1975, 148). In severe cases the blood loss is critical enough to require transfusions, but stops when ASA taking is stopped. In less severe cases it leads to anemia. How serious the latter is, however, is not conclusively known. According to Coleman (1975), 'one of the commonest major emergencies of clinical practice is massive hemorrhage of the upper g.i. tract ... and aspirin [is] one of the commonest causes of these hemorrhages' (148).

*Liver Damage*

This occurs primarily in patients receiving ASA-like drugs in prolonged heavy doses. There are usually no detectable symptoms as the problem progresses, but accumulating liver damage may eventually prove fatal. One form of this problem is Reye's disease, a rare but often fatal consequence of infection with varicella and various strains of influenza virus. The fatal liver damage is thought to be associated primarily with salicylate use and the U.S. surgeon general has therefore advised against the use of salicylates in children with chicken-pox or flu (Flower, Moncada, and Vane 1985).

*Kidney Damage*

Probably the most severe danger of heavy use of ASA-like drugs is permanent kidney damage. This problem was not recognized until 1953, although it had previously been evident that kidney disease was becoming more common (Murray 1980). Chronic interstitial nephritis is a progressive kidney disease caused by a bacterial infection of the kidney. It is particularly insidious because there are few symptoms until severe kidney failure occurs, although the disease can be detected earlier by laboratory tests (Wenger and Einstein 1970, 771; National Institutes of Health 1984). This disease is particularly common in women who take large doses of over-the-counter analgesics daily over long periods, and is likely to be associated with gastro-intestinal tract disorders, anemia, and emotional disturbance. When it occurs in association with ASA-like drugs, this disease is sometimes called 'analgesic abuse nephropathy.' One study showed that the incidence of kidney damage was seventeen times higher in heavy users of ASA-like drugs than in non-users. The incidence is higher in regions where the use of ASA-like drugs is unusually high, including the American southeast, Australia, and Switzerland. Complete kidney failure occurs most often in Switzerland, with fifteen cases per million population per year (National Institutes of Health 1984).

Current knowledge does not tell how much analgesics, or even exactly what kinds, cause the disease. The best indications are that (1) 'a substantial proportion' of regular, heavy users show at least moderate loss of kidney function' (2) the condition is caused by a mixture of ASA and/or phenacetin and/or actominophen rather than by any one of them alone; and (3) there is little danger associated with infrequent use, or even regular use as prescribed by a doctor (National Institutes of Health 1984).

An earlier series of European studies led to the conclusion that analgesic abuse nephropathy might be caused primarily by phenacetin (Murray 1980). The indication was strong enough that Anacin, which for years was advertised as a combination of three 'wonder ingredients' – phenacetin, ASA, and caffeine – was reduced to two, ASA and caffeine. But more recent evidence is that phenacetin was not the sole culprit because the incidence of analgesic abuse nephropathy was not reduced in countries that banned phenacetin (Murray 1980; National Institutes of Health 1984). Recent evidence suggests that phenacetin and acetaminophen in combination may be the chief culprits (Sandler et al. 1989).

*Suppressed Immune Response*

Large doses of ASA-like drugs inhibit the normal protective mechanisms of the immune system. 'Several different mechanisms are involved including suppression of antibody production, interference with antigen-antibody aggregation, inhibition *in vitro* of antigen-induced release of histamine, and nonspecific stabilization of changes in capillary permeability in the presence of immunological insults' (Flower, Moncada, and Vane 1985, 684).

## Fetal Damage

Extremely high doses of ASA administered to pregnant animals cause deformities in offspring. Chronic high-dose therapy in pregnant human females with rheumatoid arthritis increases the length of gestation and prolongs labour. This action seems to be associated with inhibition of prostaglandin synthesis, which plays an important role in facilitating birth (Flower, Moncada, and Vane 1985). However, 'there is no evidence that therapeutic doses of salicylates cause fetal damage in human beings, and their use in moderation in pregnancy does not appear to be contraindicated' (Flower, Moncada, and Vane 1985, 684–5).

## Overdose

Overdoses of ASA-like drugs are often fatal. The fatal dose of ASA for an adult is 10–30 g or 30–90 regular ASA pills. The cause of death in such cases appears to be respiratory acidosis, metabolic acidosis, hyperthermia, dehydration, and occasionally kidney failure. Generally overdose deaths from acetaminophen are attributed to liver failure. Lethal doses of phenacetin are associated with cyanosis, respiratory depression, and cardiac arrest (Flower, Moncada, and Vane 1985). In the United States, 'ASA is said to be second only to digitalis as the leading cause of drug related hospitalization' (Phillips 1988, 2), although in DAWN cities in 1987 cocaine was the most frequently mentioned drug in emergency-room visits. Acetaminophen and ASA combined were fourth (National Institute on Drug Abuse 1988, 26). As in the case of methadone- and cocaine-related deaths discussed in earlier chapters, however, many of the figures relating ASA-like drugs to hospitalization appear to come from case studies where alternative causes cannot safely be ruled out (see Fiscina 1986).

## Miscellaneous Effects and Unanswered Questions

There are other metabolic effects of large doses of ASA-like analgesics that are of unknown importance to health, but that may prove harmful in individual cases. For example, ASA and other salicylates increase the rate of breathing, inhibit energy metabolism in a number of ways, affect blood-sugar levels, cause the release of adrenalin, probably cause the breakdown of proteins, and have a number of effects on the thyroid gland (Flower, Moncada, and Vane 1985).

The half-life of ASA in the body, in the form of its active salicylate metabolites, varies between three and thirty hours, with the longer half-life occurring at the higher doses (Flower, Moncada, and Vane 1985). The medical significance of this fact is not clear, although the fact that marijuana has a long half-life in the body is often mentioned in the War on Drugs literature as a matter of great concern.

Fever reduction is one of ASA's well-known virtues, but it could be a hazard as well. 'Little is known concerning the relationship between fever and accelerating of immune processes; it may at times be a protective physiological mechanism' (Flower, Moncada and Vane 1985, 688).

EXPERIMENTAL AND RECREATIONAL USE

ASA is often the first drug that children experiment with and is sometimes used as a recreational drug by teenagers and adults. Over the years, several people have described their recreational use of ASA to me. It is apparently used primarily in conjunction with Coca-Cola. Used in this way, it is said to reduce pain and to produce a psycho-active effect that is only vaguely described. I know of no formal studies on these practices or on their physiological effects.

DEPENDENT AND ADDICTIVE USE

The physiological effects of ASA-like drugs on dependent or addicted people who use large doses appear to be similar to the effects on people who use large doses circumstantially. The larger question, of course, is whether dependence or addiction to ASA-like drugs exists in the same sense as dependence and addiction to the drugs that are the targets of the War on Drugs.

## Addictive Use of ASA-like Drugs

The following cryptic story from the *New York Times* suggests that severe addiction to ASA-like drugs may be a reality:

Since the funeral of Howard R. Hughes, there has been much speculation
on the cause of his death. Some associates said an addiction to the
tranquilizer Valium was the direct cause, while others said it was an
addiction to the pain-killer codeine.

Now the reclusive millionaire's personal physician, Dr. Wilbur Thain, has
finally talked about Mr. Hughes, and he says that what led to the decline
and death of his patient was massive doses of aspirin.

'He was taking large doses of the aspirin-like analgesic, up to 20 to 30
tablets a day,' Dr. Thain said in an interview in American Medical News,
a publication of the American Medical Association. 'It was the aspirin that
killed him.' (*New York Times* 1979, B4)

This view is supported by studies of less famous people as well. Although
the majority of users of ASA-like drugs, like users of illicit drugs, take
them in moderation, some users become dependent, addicted, and negatively addicted. Heavy addictive use of ASA-like drugs can be fatal.

The medical literature is ambiguous about what term should be applied
to compulsive use of ASA-like drugs. For example, Flower, Moncada, and
Vane (1985) say the ASA-like drugs 'do not cause dependence' (677).
However, the same chapter goes on to discuss the fact that 'the abuse of
analgesic mixtures has been linked to the development of renal injury'
(678) and 'it is possible that chronic abuse of any aspirin-like drug or
analgesic mixture may cause renal injury in the susceptible individual'
(679). It is unclear from such statements what constitutes 'abuse.' This
section will show that severe cases of 'abuse' of ASA-like drugs fit the
definition of negative addiction given in chapter 3 and that less severe
cases fit the definitions of dependence and addiction.

Compulsive use of ASA-like drugs first came to public attention
in Europe. A Swiss watch factory provided workers with a phenacetin-
caffeine-antipyrene mixture to control headaches (antipyrenes are sedative, fever-reducing drugs). In the Swedish town of Huskvarna a similar
concoction, Dr Hjorton's Powder, was being sold. In both places, the
mixture of ASA-like drugs became popular, to the point of being given as
gifts, taken at parties, and spread on sandwiches. At the same time,
severe kidney disease became common (Murray 1980). A number of
people were treated for dependence on these mixtures. The typical patient
treated for dependence was a 35–45-year-old housewife who might also
be employed in a factory. Male patients were also likely to belong to the

same age group and to be factory workers or craftsmen. These patients typically had been taking 8–20 pills per day for 5–7 years. Seventy per cent of these drug-dependent patients displayed some signs of kidney dysfunction (Kielholz and Ladewig 1977).

The patients also displayed acute intoxication in which they acted 'befuddled' and either hyperactive or apathetic. 'They bump into objects and may even fall, thus sustaining typical injuries. Haematomas can usually be seen on the face, the shoulders, and on the pelvis' (Keilholz and Ladewig 1977, 668). When drug use was terminated, withdrawal symptoms began within 12–48 hours, lasting for ten days in the 'acute phase' and two to four months in a 'protracted phase.' Symptoms included headache, problems in sleeping, mental unrest, muscular twitching, rheumatic pains in the limbs, anxiety, depression, diarrhea alternating with constipation, vomiting, delirium, hallucinations, and grand mal seizures. The more severe withdrawal symptoms seemed to correlate with the use of higher doses (Kielholz and Ladewig 1977).

The patients usually stated at first that they were taking the pills to control pain, most often headaches, but the pain was described only vaguely. After extensive interviewing, the patients revealed themselves to be deeply troubled people, unsuccessful, insecure, depressed, and isolated. Their pain appeared to be largely psychosomatic, as it 'had a habit of worsening after they had suffered losses or disappointments, and ... a change of environment, a pleasant experience, or success at work caused the pains to disappear temporarily' (Kielholz and Ladewig 1977, 670).

The authors of this Swiss study concluded that the heavy use of analgesics seemed to serve an adaptive function for the patients, as follows: 'It is quite understandable that, to combat their psychosomatic symptoms, these patients resort to analgesics and hypnotics, which are on sale everywhere and are claimed to be completely safe and harmless. The persons who take them certainly have no desire to become dependent on drugs, nor do they consciously wish to escape from reality; they are merely trying to treat themselves so that they can keep going and live free of the symptoms that afflict them' (670).

Murray (1973) studied all fifty-six patients with kidney damage attributed to ASA-like drugs that were attending a kidney unit in Glasgow between 1969 and 1971. All patients displayed a degree of kidney failure and there was a high incidence of gastro-intestinal bleeding, peptic ulcer, and chronic anemia characteristic of the analgesic abuse syndrome. Of the fifty-six, five were too sick to be interviewed. All patients had taken at least 1 g of analgesic daily for three years. The average quantity admitted to was six preparations daily for twenty years. The most common preparation was 'Askit Powders,' which contain 550 mg ASA, 400 mg phenacetin, 110 mg caffeine, which was roughly the equivalent of one-and-a-half ASA tablets, a phenacetin tablet, and a cup of coffee.

Murray provided highly detailed studies of these addicted patients. His case studies suggest several ways that the addictive patterns were similar to those associated with more familiar drugs of addiction, like the opiates, cocaine, and alcohol:

1. Only two patients had a detectable medical basis for using the drug (arthritis).

2. The dose to which patients initially admitted was always an underestimate. This misinformation often had led to past mis-diagnoses of the cause of their kidney conditions. According to Murray: 'Few patients volunteered information about their analgesic habits, and 19 denied analgesic consumption – in some cases even after analgesic nephropathy had been proved radiologically. Patients universally minimized the extent and duration of their analgesic intake. Although in a few cases analgesic taking had been concealed even from spouses, relatives' estimates of the analgesic intake were usually more accurate and were often three or four times higher than the patients' estimates' (267).

3. Of the fifty-six patients, 'at least thirty-one had continued their analgesic habit against family and community opposition. In some cases the family had hidden or destroyed the analgesics and in a few the patients were not given sufficient money to buy the drugs ... Family opinions ranged from "she seems to need them" to "she's an addict" or "she's doped silly with Askit"' (267). Few of the personal physicians of these people knew of their habit, although some of the shopkeepers who sold them did, and had refused to sell more. In these cases, the patients sometimes sent relatives or children to get them. The following is a sample case:

(Case 2) A 51-year-old spinster ... over the previous 3 months her blood urea had risen from 50 to 290 mg/100 ml [that is, her kidneys were not functioning effectively]. She remained confined for a week and required haemodialysis 3 times, but thereafter renal function began to improve.

Past history revealed gastro-intestinal bleeding, gastric ulcer, and chronic anaemia and a nervous breakdown.

She admitted taking 3 Askit a day since her teens, but a friend volunteered that her normal dose was 20 daily. As she had been banned from all the local chemists and shops, she sent workmates to get the analgesics ... She also took daily purgatives, hypnotics, and phenobarbitone, and stated that both her mother and an aunt 'took more Askit than me'; her mother had had renal disease for many years, and the aunt had died in uraemia. (Murray 1973, 268)

4. Like people who are negatively addicted to prohibited drugs and alcohol, the analgesic-nephrectomy patients showed many signs of other problems in life. They tended to come from disturbed families, to have 'passive, neurotic, and introverted' personalities, to smoke and drink excessively, and to use other 'psychotropic medications' (Murray 1980, 12–13). These facts were confirmed in seven independent studies that Murray (1980) cited.

5. Like the development of alcoholism and other negative addictions in later life, the development of negative addiction to analgesics is a lengthy process. Kielholz (1970) has described this process as follows: 'Only after several years of habituation and corresponding dose increases do the patients realize that side by side with the analgesic effect the drug now has a chiefly invigorating, stimulating, apparently performance-enhancing action. From then on they can no longer do without this secondary effect' (cited by Murray 1980, 12).

6. Murray described a vicious cycle similar to that described for other addictions. It appeared that the more people took of the drug, the more they needed. When this vicious cycle could not be broken, the patients sometimes died. According to Murray: 'The large amounts consumed cause symptoms of intoxication for which further analgesics are taken and if they try and stop they develop caffeine withdrawal headaches. As anaemia and uraemia ensue the psychotropic effects become even more desirable and a vicious cycle of decreasing health and increasing intake of analgesics is established. When advised of the dangers of analgesics in their condition at least 20 continued their ingestion unabated. In 13 of the twenty renal function deteriorated and 7 died in uraemia' (Murray 1973, 12).

In a separate study of patients admitted to a psychiatric hospital in

Glasgow, 8.8 per cent of 181 patients were found to have consumed more than 1 kg of ASA or phenacetin during their lifetime, with an average consumption of 3.3 kg of phenacetin and 5.12 kg of ASA. Only one of these patients had symptoms that seemed (at least to the patient) to justify the high dose of analgesics, that is, migraine headaches. Instead of medical complaints, the patients' explanations for their use included statements that the analgesics calmed them down, or helped them 'get my strength back.' Eight of the patients described themselves as 'addicted' to ASA preparations. About a fifth of the patients were known to continue to use ASA-like preparations secretly in spite of having been told of the dangers involved and in spite of an attempt to impose total prohibition by the hospital staff (Murray, Timbury, and Linton 1970).

These patients were compared with psychiatric patients who did not report extensive use of ASA-like drugs. The analgesic users, most of whom were middle-aged women, were more likely to be diagnosed as neurotic, depressed, personality disordered, or addicted (to other drugs) than as manic depressive or schizophrenic. They were also more likely to show evidence of digestive, kidney, or urinary-tract ailments and high blood pressure.

The data from the Glasgow psychiatric patients suggest that the potential prevalence of dependence and addiction to ASA-like drugs is high. If 8.8 per cent of all psychiatric patients are compulsive users of these drugs, as was true in this study, then the number of people involved world-wide would be very large. Of course it is possible that Glascow is, like Switzerland, a place where addictive use of ASA-like drugs is, or was, unusually large.

A final perspective on addiction to ASA-like drugs may be provided by Truman Capote's sensational case study of the murder of a Kansas family, published in book form as *In Cold Blood* (1965). One of the murderers, Edward Perry, was a chronic compulsive user of ASA, which he claimed to use to control pain in his legs that persisted from an automobile accident. However, the 'pain' was at least partly psychosomatic, for it flared up regularly in times of stress. This of course, does not mean that ASA incites violence, although it is almost certain that, had Perry's drug of choice been heroin or cocaine, his crimes would have been blamed on those drugs.

Whereas these studies establish that people can develop dependence and negative addictions to ASA-like drugs, they provide no real understanding of how the process occurs. This is a difficult matter to fathom, since most people experience no euphoria when they take an ASA-like drug. Murray (1973, 1980) provides some facts that seem relevant, but no integrated understanding of the addictive process. He reports that those patients who did stop taking the analgesics beyond the initial period of withdrawal symptoms improved their health and behaviour and frequently reported, paradoxically, that their headaches improved. The disappearance of headaches following cessation of headache medicine has been reported in other studies as well. If the headaches are caused by the caffeine that always seems to be found in the preparations to which people become addicted, then it is conceivable, as Murray suggests, that these people unconsciously choose such preparations *because they cause headaches* and therefore provide an excuse to take more of the ASA-like drugs that are combined with the caffeine.

As with the opiates, these drugs do have positive mood-altering effects for the small proportion of the population that becomes compulsive users of them, even though they do not for most other people. Of Murray's 56 patients in the 1973 study, 24 felt the analgesics had mood-altering properties, 6 found them stimulating, 9 took them as sedatives, 4 thought they were both, and 5 couldn't exactly describe the mood-altering property. Of 56, 22 claimed they took the analgesics for headaches, but some of these also described a mood-altering property.

In the end, the fact that people can become addicted to ASA-like drugs remains mysterious. Later chapters will delve further into the psychology of addiction in general. Obviously, an adequate theory of addiction should be able to explain addiction to ASA-like drugs as well as to the better-known drugs.

Whereas the problem of dependence and addiction to ASA-like drugs has been documented extensively in Europe, it has received little attention in the North American medical literature apart from scattered case studies. One possible reason for this inattention is that there are many more drugs available in North America, so that the counterparts of people addicted to ASA-like drugs in Europe would have access to tranquillizers, opiates, or other drugs that could serve their purposes better. The other possibility is that North American physicians put neurotic, middle-aged people with kidney problems in a different diagnostic category that does not focus attention on their consumption of analgesic drugs. There are indications in the very recent literature, however, that North American physicians are beginning to describe a large-scale problem of dependent and addictive use of ASA-like drugs (Phillips 1988).

## Conclusions

The facts summarized above suggest some general conclusions about ASA-like drugs. Because this is also the end of a cycle of three chapters about three types of drugs, some conclusions about drugs in general will also be suggested. Naturally, general conclusions would be better founded if other drugs in addition to opiates, cocaine, and ASA-like analgesics had been reviewed, but this book must move on to other major topics and these three very diverse drugs can at least illustrate some major themes.

1. The dangers of sudden death and overdose are as real for ASA-like drugs as they are for heroin and cocaine, in spite of ASA's great value and its innocuous reputation, although it is impossible to make precise statements about their relative likelihood. Clearly, all drugs must be used with caution. However, in moderate doses, the pharmacological risks associated with all three drugs are quite small.

2. Because of the risk of gastric, liver, and kidney damage, it seems likely that regular, heavy use of ASA-like drugs is more physically harmful than comparable use of many other drugs, including the opiates. Therefore, people who find themselves becoming addicted to ASA-like drugs are in serious danger. If they cannot find an alternative to addiction, they should at least seek a different kind of drug to use.

Is it, therefore, better to be addicted to heroin than to ASA? Probably not, because of the enormous societal hazards that are brought on by addiction to heroin. None the less, this conundrum does further illustrate the harm done by the War on Drugs. Within the War on Drugs mentality it would be absurd and reprehensible to urge people to switch from ASA addiction to heroin addiction. But, when the pharmacological hazards of the two kinds of drugs and the personal histories of people who have been dependent on them for long periods are compared, the suggestion becomes reasonable on health grounds. The War on Drugs mentality, in this case as in others, makes a rational decision unthinkable.

3. Drug problems can be faced without hysteria. The very real problems associated with ASA-like drugs are a matter of concern within government and the medical profession. Reasonable measures have been

taken to reduce the problems, still recognizing the basic value of the drugs. For example, Australia attempted to control the problem of analgesic abuse nephrectomy by banning phenacetin, on the supposition that it was the toxic analgesic. This policy, unfortunately, did not reduce the problems arising from analgesic use in Australia. Other countries, observing this effort, did not declare a world-wide war on phenacetin, but tried other measures. The chief one seems to be a general recognition of the potential dangers of ASA-like drugs and a tendency to prescribe them more sparingly, and to avoid prescribing them for certain conditions, such as flu in children, where serious consequences are suspected (Mitchell et al. 1982). Phenacetin is no longer being prescribed in Canada, although other ASA-like drugs are still in use. Such quiet measures, unknown to most of the public, can minimize drug problems.

4. People need to know much more about drugs – schools should provide real drug education. Existing drug education seems to publicize the good qualities of some drugs and the dangers of others. Yet an informed person would surely need to have a balanced perspective on the pros and cons of all drugs, so that sensible choices can be made.

5. It is easy to be deceptive about drugs. There are, as this chapter shows, real dangers associated with ASA-like drugs. It would be easy to distort this information by publicizing gory case studies of the worst harm associated with ASA-like drugs and leaving out the great benefits and minimal harm that most users enjoy. Likewise, it would be easy to create the idea that there is a connection between ASA-like drugs and crime by publicizing the number of violent crimes committed by people who used ASA. Although such distortions would be laughable in the case of ASA-like drugs, exactly this kind of disinformation has become commonplace with the opiates and cocaine.

# 7   Addiction without drugs

Justifications for the War on Drugs represent it as a way of protecting society from the horrors of negative addiction. However, if drugs are involved in only a small proportion of negative addictions, as chapter 3 suggests, then even a successful War on Drugs could not substantially lessen the problem of negative addiction. The claim that drug addictions account for only a small portion of the problem of addiction may seem to be stretching a point, in spite of the evidence summarized heretofore. People generally speak of everyday addictions to exercise, chocolate, their soap opera, people they love, and so on, in a more light-hearted way than they speak about the horrors of alcoholism or cocaine addiction. Non-drug addictions are a favourite topic of contemporary humour.

In most cases, this light-heartedness about non-drug addictions is warranted. Everyday habits, dependencies, and addictions to non-drug activities are usually not serious problems, just as corresponding levels of involvement with drugs are usually not serious problems. In fact, chapter 3 shows that positive addictions can make an important contribution to the quality of a person's life. But full-blown negative addictions to everyday, non-drug activities do occur. Even though most such addictions do not entail the criminal hazards that addictions to prohibited drugs do, they can be fully as disastrous medically, psychologically, and socially (Peele 1981; Orford 1985), and are much more common (Alexander and Schweighofer 1988).

This chapter is an attempt to go beyond the half-real and humorous approach in order to examine negative addiction without drugs as a serious social problem. The first section of this chapter uses physical exercise as an example. This is an arbitrary choice – gambling, love, sex, religion, or work would serve just as well, for the existence of devastating negative addictions to these activities is also well documented. However, rather than multiplying examples, the second section of this chapter is a biographical study of a single person with at least three addictions, of which only one involved a drug, tobacco. The life of James M. Barrie, the author of *Peter Pan*, has been selected to illustrate the cruel severity of negative addiction even when illegal drugs and criminality are not involved. Barrie's life also illustrates the way drug and non-drug addictions interrelate and the functions they serve.

## Exercise

There were 3.5 million runners in Canada in 1981 (O'Hara 1981) and 30 million in North America. Running is big business and good exercise – yet there are persistent dark rumours that it does a lot of harm. Is 'running addiction' a joke or a serious problem? As with drugs, there is a range of involvement with exercise from simple experimentation to casual and harmless use to negative addiction. Again, as with drugs, the effects of exercise depend greatly on the pattern of involvement.

### CASUAL AND REGULAR RECREATIONAL USE OF EXERCISE

A little exercise generally makes people feel better. Controlled measurements show that a vigorous 24–40-minute work-out reduces anxiety for the following 20–30 minutes (Francis and Carter 1982). Prolonged anxiety reduction and a sense of general well-being is reported by many people who exercise regularly, but this longer effect is hard to measure precisely. Indications from a large number of independent studies are that the benefits can be demonstrated most clearly in people who were more than normally anxious and depressed or unusually out of shape at the start of exercising (Browman 1981; Francis and Carter 1982). In this regard, the effect of exercise is similar to the relief produced by heroin, cocaine, and ASA-like drugs, as discussed in chapters 4, 5, and 6. There have been demonstrations that exercise programs can relieve clinical depression and depression in alcoholics.

In addition to the benefits, there are injuries and hazards that are caused by regular exercise in some people. Over fifty injuries have been associated with running alone, and the list is growing. These injuries include shin splints, muscle cramps, tendonitis, black nail, Morton's neuroma, runner's nipple, jogger's amenorrhea, heel spurs, ruptures of the Achilles tendon, stress fractures, heat exhaustion. frost-bite, dog bite, and traffic accidents (O'Hara 1981). Unfortunately, there are individuals who are biomechanically unsuitable for exercise and cannot exercise without injury. Exercise programs may also precipitate anxiety attacks in patients with a diagnosis of anxiety neurosis (Browman 1981).

## DEPENDENT AND ADDICTIVE EXERCISING

Public attention was drawn to the addictive potential of exercising by William Glasser's popular book *Positive Addiction* (1976). Glasser originally coined the term 'positive addiction' to refer specifically to addictions to running and meditation. He contrasted these with 'negative addictions' to harmful activities like drinking and using heroin. Glasser assumed that it was the activity or substance, rather than the type of involvement, that determined whether an addiction was positive or negative. He assumed that running, being a healthful habit, could only lead to positive addiction and that people who need addictions would be better off to choose positive than negative ones.

Unfortunately for exercise enthusiasts, this formula proved too simple. In 1979, three years after Glasser's book, William Morgan, a professor of physical education at the University of Wisconsin, wrote an influential article entitled 'Negative Addiction in Runners' in a sports medicine journal. The title obviously contradicts Glasser's thesis that addiction to exercise is always positive.

Morgan showed that, although running can be used in a moderate recreational way, it can also be used in a harmfully addictive way, and he specifically argued that addictive use can be just as destructive as addictive use of opiates. According to Morgan, 'Running should be viewed as a wonder drug analogous to penicillin, morphine, and the tricyclics. It has profound potential in preventing mental and physical disease and in rehabilitation after various illnesses have occurred. However, just like other wonder drugs, running has the potential for abuse, and the runner who appears in the physician's office on crutches or in a wheelchair as a result of the crippling effects of excessive running can be compared to the hard-core drug addict who overdoses. Running is a form of negative addiction in the case of the hard-core exercise addict' (Morgan 1979, 58).

Morgan went on to describe the progression whereby some people become negatively addicted to running. He stressed its similarity to the progression from experimental use of a drug to negative addiction. Morgan noted that the first few experiences with running may not produce anything resembling euphoria, and that the beginning runner's motivation usually comes from will-power and grim resolve. Many beginners drop out, although some continue on to become casual or regular recreational runners. Some, however, develop negative addictions.

Those who are in the process of developing a negative addiction to running show three signs. The first is a loss of interest in their family and family responsibilities as more and more time and concentration is used up in running. Typically, a person runs three to four hours per day at this point. Second, the person becomes more self-directed and less concerned about his or her vocation. The negatively addicted runner is no longer concerned with achievements or promotions. 'Such a point of view ... may not only limit professional growth, but it can actually jeopardize one's employment' (Morgan 1979, 62).

The third and most definitive sign, according to Morgan, is a lack of concern with the runner's own bodily health. This result presents a paradox, because good health, presumably, was the motivation for exercising in the first place. Morgan describes this sign as follows:

> The final test of whether or not exercise addiction exists occurs when the runner is told that he or she must stop running because of a medical problem. As with the alcoholic who continues to drink or the heroin addict who continues to mainline when told that such behaviour will result in impaired health, the [addicted] runner continues to run. Such runners realize that continued abuse will cause further damage, but they need the exercise high. At this point exercise addicts risk self-destructing – and some do precisely that. My clinical experience has been that serious runners begin to move inwardly and adopt unconventional priority systems when they reach about 100 miles a week. Runners in this range risk self-destructing in much the same way that chronic drug abusers risk overdosing.

Morgan points out that the amount of running is not a definitive sign of addiction. Some runners complete 100–125 miles per week without showing the neglect of family, work, and their own health that marks negative addiction. These runners are 'well-adjusted psychologically ... and if necessary they can stop running for a time without withdrawal symptoms' (62–3). Some of these people are somewhat compulsive about their running habits, but on the whole the effects are positive. In the vocabulary of this book, these people would be described as dependent or addicted, but not negatively addicted. By contrast, there are people running as little as 30–50 miles per week who are negatively addicted.

Morgan illustrates his points with a series of case studies. For example:

Case 2. A 35-year-old professor ran 1 or 2 miles a day because everyone was doing it. He eventually worked up to 5 miles a day, and he ran daily for approximately 12 months even though the pain in his feet became nearly intolerable at times. He constantly urged himself to 'work through the pain' to continue, and his cognitive strategy appeared to be one of dissociation, which has previously been noted in some distance runners. In his words: 'At five miles or so into my daily run I developed a sense of invincibility – I was truly indestructible in that transcendent state. The cares of the day would quickly pass at about 5 miles, and nothing bothered me. I guess you could say I was omnipotent at that point. Even though I learned to work through the pain during my runs, the pain following my runs became more and more excruciating. I had to walk downstairs backwards in the morning. I knew something was wrong, but I just could not give it up – it felt too good – it meant too much – I had to have it. Finally, I awoke one morning and was unable to even go downstairs backwards! I visited an orthopedic surgeon who asked me 'Where did you put your Achilles tendon?' I had to undergo surgery to reconstruct the damaged foot. Even though the surgery was quite success-ful, I can no longer run, and I walk with a limp.' (63)

I will add a case study from my own experience, because it provides a more personal view to supplement that of a professional observer who sees patients more in terms of their symptoms. My friend, who will be called Charlie, was a Hong Kong Chinese, older than the average student when he came to my university in his first year. He had a lovely wife and daughter, lots of personal charm, but low self-esteem and little confidence outside of the areas of casual socializing and athletics. He was a liquor importer whose former business had flourished for a few years in spite of his lack of formal education, primarily on the strength of his intuition. However, eventually the business failed and Charlie brought his family with him to university in Canada.

I believe he exercised three to four hours every day. I became his tennis partner for one summer. We played every morning at 7:30, after which I went to work and he went on to a few more hours of various athletics. He was quite aware that his excessive athletic involvement was interfering with his school work, his family life, and ultimately his health, but he had a series of humorous ways of changing the topic and continuing with his excessive habits. He sometimes explained that he had to work very hard in the morning because of his guilt over the night before. He spent most of his nights drinking, smoking, and socializing with his friends or in the student pub. Sometimes he would drink and smoke at home, sitting with stereo earphones driving loud music into his head for hours. At the pub or at home he was lost from the world of adult responsibilities, and he felt guilty in the mornings about the wasted time and the harm the drugs were probably doing to his body. He seemed to feel he could work through the guilt by severely exercising his body.

He eventually appeared to lose the respect (but not the love) of his wife and daughter and finally had to leave the university because of failing marks. Now ten years later, his family is still together, although his wife and teenage daughter regard him as something of a clown. His wife still supports the family as a legal secretary, and he contributes by part-time work, but little else. He cannot exercise any more because he continued his strenuous schedule against his doctor's repeated orders until it was no longer possible to exercise. He can still walk, although with a limp.

## THE CAUSE OF NEGATIVE ADDICTION TO EXERCISE

What causes negative addiction to exercise? At least two distinct possibilities are discussed in the sports-medicine literature. One is that exercise addiction is a kind of disease growing from the body's exposure to endogenous opiates produced during exercise, much in the way heroin addiction is said to be caused when 'the body develops a physical need' for exogenous opiates. The other is the possibility that unhappy people rely on exercise as an escape and a substitute for otherwise unappealing lives. The next chapter will consider these two ideas in the broader context of addiction in general, but here they will be examined in this special case.

## A Physiological Explanation of Exercise Addiction

Endorphins and the so-called runner's high are often discussed in the popular media. The idea that exercise addicts have become hooked on the high produced by their own endorphins is familiar to many people. In fact, there is now good evidence that endogenous opiates released during sustained exercise do produce a mild euphoria, but there is no evidence that these endogenous opiates cause exercise addiction. The phrase 'runner's high' has become so familiar that many people take it for granted, but it is more a faddish hyperbole than a reality. For most people, the euphoria that comes with regular exercise is not a 'high' that in any way resembles the elation that sometimes accompanies alcohol or marijuana use. Rather, exercise typically produces a sense of accomplishment and relaxation, but the effects are subtle, and sometimes only recognized when a person has stopped exercising for a time. Allen (1982) has suggested that the phrase 'runner's calm' would be more accurate for the great majority of people who exercise. (It remains possible, however, that, as in the case of heroin, there is some intense euphoria that is rare and known only to addicted people.)

The role of endogenous opiates in producing the runner's calm is still being worked out. Various endogenous opiates are released during strenuous exercise (Harber and Sutton 1984; Howlett et al. 1984). However, some authorities doubt that enough endogenous opiates are produced to have much of an effect on mood (Harber and Sutton 1984). Injections of beta-endorphins have been found to change the mood of psychiatric patients, but the quantities required appear to be much larger than those produced by running (Moore 1982).

The most direct evidence, until recently, suggested that endorphins were not involved in the production of the runner's calm. In one study, fifteen runners of marathon quality were given a 'mood-state check-list' before and after running an average of 10.9 miles. On some occasions, they were given an injection of either water or 0.8 mg naloxone right after running and checking off the mood-state check-list. Then they were asked to check off the mood-state list again in fifteen to twenty minutes. Naloxone, as explained in chapter 4, is an opiate antagonist and therefore essentially an antidote for endorphins. Both the naloxone group and the placebo group improved their moods after their run. The naloxone injections did not eliminate the mood elevation, as might be expected if it had been caused by a release of endorphins (Markoff, Ryon, and Young 1982).

However, the newest evidence appears to have rescued the hypothesis that endogenous opiates are responsible for the runners calm. Allen and Coen (1987) at Simon Fraser University had twelve men run forty-five minutes on a treadmill in the laboratory. On two of the runs the men received a total of 10 mg of the opiate antagonist naloxone, 5 mg before the run began and 5 mg through a catheter in a continuous drip while they were running. On the other two runs the men received placebo injections. The men who received the naloxone injections did not feel better after the run, as reported on carefully constructed mood inventories. The men who received the placebo injections did feel better. Allen and Coen (1987) suggest that the reason naloxone apparently prevented a mood shift in their study, but not in the earlier ones, was that they injected the antagonist *before the run began*. They suggest that the mood change may be triggered by endorphin release, but once triggered may be self-perpetuating. Therefore, the antagonist given after the run in the earlier studies may simply have been administered too late to prevent the response from being established. They conclude that runner's calm may be instigated by endorphin release after all.

Although Allen and Coen's experiment implicates endorphins in the runner's calm, it does not establish any definite link between running addiction and endorphins. More generally, the apparent role of endogenous opiates in instigating the euphoria associated with exercise for many people does not automatically implicate endogenous opiates in exercise addiction. As chapter 4 showed, exposure to pharmaceutical opiates does not produce addiction in the great majority of human beings, and there is no reason to suppose the endogenous opiates are more addicting than their exogenous counterparts. Futhermore, if exercise addicts are really endorphin addicts, they could satisfy their craving with opiates just as well as exercise. However, I have found no evidence of exercise addicts turning to opiate drugs even when they become physically debilitated, although an emotionally crippling 'athlete's neurosis' has been described in physically incapacitated athletes (Sachs and Pargman 1983). Nor have I ever met a heroin addict who could satisfy his cravings for heroin with exercise. The two types of addiction do not appear in the least interchangeable.

*Motivational Explanation of Exercise Addiction*

A different cause of negative addiction to exercise has been suggested by

Morgan and by Michael Sachs, formerly of the Université du Québec à Trois-Rivières. Like Morgan, Sachs describes extreme absorption with exercise in a way that clearly fits the overwhelming involvement concept of addiction. He also recognizes a clear distinction between 'positive addiction' and 'negative addiction' to running (although he sometimes uses a different terminology), and believes that negatively addicted runners should seek therapy. Positive addiction to running serves to integrate the addicted runner's life and make him or her function better because of the relaxation and bolstering of self-esteem that it provides (Sachs and Pargman 1979, 150). Positive addiction continues because of these psychological benefits as well as benefits to health and social life. By contrast, negative addiction to running interferes with important aspects of the runner's life and in severe cases may precipitate marriage breakup, social isolation, and loss of employment. People engage in this destructive life-style because it provides escape from reality and a sense of self-esteem that cannot be attained in other ways. Failure to exercise in negatively addicted runners leads to extremes of guilt, anxiety, neurosis, and withdrawal symptoms (Sach and Pargman 1979, 1983). Sachs has supported these ideas with reference to various lines of research, including a study by Baekeland (1970) who attempted to pay regular runners not to run in order to study exercise deprivation. He found that many would not stop exercise for the money he offered and that some said they wouldn't stop for 'any amount of money' (Sachs and Pargman 1979, 145).

Further insight into how people become negatively addicted to running can be drawn from a study by Folkins and Wieselberg-Bell (1981) of participants in the Western States Endurance Run, which is said to be the most demanding race in the United States. The race covers one hundred miles over the crest of the Sierra Nevada mountains. The total altitude gain over the course exceeds three miles and the total descent is about four miles. Temperatures can vary along the trail from freezing to over 100°F. The participants run through the night, carrying flashlights to light the trail. By the end of the race, the runners are suffering from low blood sugar and dramatic weight losses. Many report hallucinations, paranoid thoughts, and errors in judgment (Folkins and Wieselberg-Bell 1981, 120).

Forty-six of the forty-nine participants in one year's race agreed to psychological testing before they ran the race. Participants, particularly those who managed the entire hundred-mile run, received high scores on 'psychopathic deviance,' schizophrenia, and depression scales of the Minnesota Multiphasic Personality Inventory, although the group means were within the clinically normal range. The authors characterized the personalities of the participants as follows: 'A degree of emotional shallowness in relation to others, especially sexual and affectional behaviors ... To the extent that these individuals tend to exhibit some of the traits which characterize the psychopath, they may also experience some of the loneliness and sadness experienced by the psychopathic personality ... Overvaluation on exercise and undervaluation of other sources of satisfaction, such as work and family, could leave many vulnerable to psychological difficulties in later life (Folkins and Wieselberg-Bell 1981, 125–6).

Negative addiction to running serves such depressed people as a kind of substitute for the normal pleasures and responsibilities of life, and may therefore be continued compulsively as a desperate means to maintain some kind of integrity. This interpretation, however, goes beyond the data. The test scores could just as well reflect a result of exercise addiction as a cause of it. The question of cause will be considered from a different angle of attack through a case study of the life of James M. Barrie in the next section of this chapter.

## James M. Barrie, Addict

James M. Barrie, the author of *Peter Pan*, was negatively addicted to at least two pursuits that did not involve drugs and to tobacco (Alexander 1982). His life, which has been the object of considerable biographical study, is uniquely suited to illuminate the tragic nature of negative addiction in which drugs are not a primary feature. His voluminous and exquisitely precise writing provides lengthy descriptions and analysis of his own addictive involvements. His writings are supplemented by extensive biographical sources. Since Barrie died in 1937, his life provides a view of the entire history of an addicted person, an advantage not found in current case studies. Barrie's life illustrates the tragic cruelty of negative addiction, even in the case of a publicly successful person whose addictions involved neither illegal drugs nor criminality.

Barrie's life serves to illustrate two additional qualities of negative addiction which, I believe, apply whether drugs are involved or not. First, Barrie's addictions were functional, primarily serving as a substitute for attainments that he deeply desired but could not achieve. Second, Barrie's addictive involvements encompassed a shifting complex of habits. Therefore, his life suggests the possibility that the traditional idea of addiction as fixed on a single drug or activity may be too narrow. It could be argued that Barrie's unique life rules him out as a typical representative of anything – that he was an oddity. However, the universal appeal of his writing, especially *Peter Pan*, suggests the opposite. He embodied and expressed much that is universal.

EARLY LIFE

James M. Barrie was born to a relatively prosperous weaver's family in an obscure Scottish village. His next older and highly gifted brother, David, was his mother's favourite until age thirteen, when he died in a skating accident. Barrie's mother was laid low with grief and hardly even recognized Barrie, then six, for months afterwards. She mourned David for the rest of her long life, her chief comforts being a growing relationship with Barrie and the belief that, since David had died a child, he would remain happy in childhood forever. In Barrie's words: 'She lived twenty-nine years after his death ... but I had not made her forget the bit of her that was dead; in those nine-and-twenty years he was not removed one day farther from her. Many a time she fell asleep speaking to him, and even while she slept her lips moved and she smiled as if he had come back to her, and when she woke he might vanish so suddenly that she started up bewildered and looked about her, and then said slowly, "My David's dead!" or perhaps he remained long enough to whisper why he must leave her now, and then she lay silent with filmy eyes. When I became a man ... he was still a boy of thirteen' (cited by Birkin 1979, 5).

As a child, Barrie fostered his relationship with his mother by wearing David's clothes, imitating his posture and whistle, and trying to remind her of him. He also questioned her extensively about her own youth and avidly read fantasy and adventure books with her. Her intense involvement with this relationship, together with her preaching the sanctity of motherhood and her derogation of adult sexuality, led one biographer to characterize her as 'an emotional boa constrictor' (Dunbar 1979). Barrie's devotion to his mother and to motherhood in general became one of his lifelong trade marks (Mackail 1941).

## ADULTHOOD

Barrie had a strong aversion to growing up. He expressed this conflict, particularly as it concerned sexuality, in many ways, including poignant entries made in his personal notebook while at university that have been collected by Birkin (1979, 12). He grew very slowly. At seventeen, barely five feet tall, he had not begun to shave, but had apparently finished growing, and found himself a matter of little consequence to the opposite sex. He became painfully shy. He was deeply hurt by his lack of sex appeal. Using a fictional name, 'Anon,' he said of himself:

> Did Anon ever hear ladies discussing him for the briefest moment ... ?
> Alas, his trouble was that ladies did not discuss him ... I remember (I should
> think I do) that it was his habit to get into corners. In time the jades put
> this down to a shrinking modesty, but that was a mistake; it was all owing
> to a profound dejection about his want of allure. They were right those
> ladies in the train; 'quite harmless' summed him up, however he may
> have writhed (or be writhing still) ... If they would dislike him or fear
> him it would be something, but it is crushing to be just harmless ... In
> short, Mr. Anon, that man of secret sorrows, found it useless to love,
> because after a look at the length and breadth of him, none would
> listen. (Cited by Birkin 1979, 12)

His overwhelming concerns were clinging to his childhood and attracting women, but his overwhelming involvement, at this stage of his life, was work. Barrie graduated from university in 1882 as an MA. By 1887 he was at the top of the literary profession in London, contributing articles to virtually every prestigious periodical in England. He reached this status by producing barrages of articles on diverse popular topics, by enduring rejections and personally charming hesitant editors, and by prodigiously rewriting. By 1890, eight years after completing university, he had published six books, almost completed another, and produced a mountain of published and unpublished journalistic writing. During part of this same period he had produced two newspaper articles a day and four columns a week. Barrie's work was not limited to writing. He was also active in civic societies and charity, and was a diligent social climber who, despite his humble origins, consorted with the great figures of his day. He attended church twice or more on Sunday (Mackail 1941; Wright 1976).

Why did he work so hard? Birkin writes: 'Hard work took Barrie's mind off his increasing bouts of depression, when he would "lie awake busy with the problems of my personality"' (16). Barrie was depressive and morose throughout his life, suffering chronic headaches and recurrent nightmares. His writing makes it clear that his overwhelming involvement with work served as a substitute for sexual fulfilment. In the following passage, he says this explicitly, referring to himself in the third person: 'If you could only dig deep enough into him you could find first his Rothschildean ambition, which is to earn a pound a day; beneath that is a desire to reach some little niche in literature but in the marrow you find him vainly weltering to be a favorite of the ladies. All the other cravings he would toss aside for that; he is only striving for numbers one and two because he knows with an everlasting sinking that number three can never be for him' (cited by Dunbar 1970, 71).

In other writings he takes the next obvious step and feminizes work: 'The most precious possession I ever had [was] my joy in hard work. I do not know when it came to me – not very early, because I was an idler at school, and read all the wrong books at college. But I fell in love with hard work one fine May morning ... Hard work more than any woman in the world, is the one who stands up best for her man' (cited by Birkin 1979, 16). He also feminized work in one of his novels: 'Ah work, work, there's nothing like it. The sparkling face of her when she opens your eyes of a morning and cries "Up, up, we have a glorious day of toil before us." I have run back to her from dinners and marriages and funerals. How often she and I have sat up through the night on tiptoe, so as not to wake the dawn' (cited by Wright 1976, 23).

In fact, Barrie did run from his own marriage back to work, and in another direction as well. When he was thirty-four he married a beautiful actress, then starring in one of his plays. The marriage was childless and essentially sexless, according to the guarded account in his notebooks and his wife's statements after their divorce (Dunbar 1970). His tormented ambivalence is detailed in his novels. Before his marriage he wrote a novel about a man who couldn't bear to marry and, afterwards, one about a man whose marriage was failing because he could not experience sexual passion for his wife. The protagonist in the latter novel says:

If we could love by trying, no one would ever have been more loved ...
He knew it was tragic that such love as hers should be given to him; but

what more could he do than he was doing? Ah, if only it could have
been a world of boys and girls ... He could not make himself anew. They
say we can do it, so I suppose he did not try hard enough. But God
knows how hard he tried ...

He was a boy only. She knew that, despite all he had gone through, he
was still a boy. And boys cannot love. Oh, is it not cruel to ask a boy to
love? ... He gave her all his affection, but his passion, like an outlaw, had
ever to hunt alone. (Cited by Birkin 1979, 40)

After his marriage failed, Barrie continued his formidable output of
work and also developed a series of intense involvements with children,
especially little boys. He became famous for his ability to charm children
in endless games and stories and to lose himself interacting with them.
Some of the most powerful passages in his writing describe his deep
feelings for little boys (see Birkin 1979, 73–6). There are no indications
that his relationships with boys were ever overtly homosexual, but there
are innumerable indications of an 'overwhelming involvement' (Mackail
1941). A contemporary friend noted: 'Aug 12 (1908). Mr. Barrie arrived
in the evening. He was quite talkative at dinner ... We talked a great deal
of Sylvia's boys and it is extraordinary to see how they fill his life and
supply all his human interest' (cited by Birkin 1979, 168).

'Sylvia's boys' were the five sons of Arthur and Sylvia Davies who,
after the death of their parents, became Barrie's adopted sons. Arthur
Davies had succumbed after a lingering death from cancer with Barrie in
constant, devoted attendance as a family friend. Upon Arthur's death,
Barrie essentially took over responsibility for the boys as well as
increasing his filial devotion to their mother, Sylvia, who however, also
died of cancer, three years later. According to Birkin (1979), Barrie
became the boys' guardian through an act of forgery. Sylvia wrote a short
will, but it was not legally witnessed. Barrie found it in her papers and
produced a hand copy for the family. It was a true copy, except that the
name 'Jenny,' mentioned as caretaker for the boys, was changed to
'Jimmy,' the family's name for Barrie.

Barrie attended Sylvia daily during her last few months of life and
revealed afterwards that she had promised to marry him if she survived.
Much of Barrie's personality and relationship to the boys comes through
in the later thoughts of one of the brothers, Peter, on the possibility of
the marriage.

Others may well say, and doubtless did, that it would have been the
most natural thing in the world: that she was already more intimate with
him than with any other living being, that he had adored her for years
and loved her children, that she was taking so much from him that she
could scarcely refuse if that was what he wished, and in fact it was
much the best solution. All this is true enough. But I think that to Jack
[another brother] ... the thought was intolerable and even monstrous;
so much so that he could not refrain from expressing himself in the
most forcible manner to that effect when [Barrie] in an unguarded moment
spoke to him of it. To me too, I confess, the idea of such a marriage
is repugnant. Up to a point, perhaps, this is mere sentimentality ...
But it does seem to me that a marriage between Sylvia, the widow, still
so beautiful in her forty fourth year, of the splendid Arthur, and the
strange little creature who adored her and dreamed, as he surely must have
dreamed, of stepping into Arthur's shoes, would have been an affront,
really, to any reasonable person's sense of the fitness of things. And I do
not believe that Sylvia seriously contemplated it ... Let me not be
thought unmindful, in writing what I have written, of the innumerable
benefits and kindnesses I have received, at one time and another, from
the aforesaid strange little creature, to whom, in the end, his connection
with our family brought so much more sorrow than happiness. (Cited by
Birkin 1979, 192)

A sense of the negatively addictive nature of the attachment between
Barrie and his adopted sons is provided by a close friend of Michael, one
of the five sons, during his college years:

Michael took me back to Barrie's flat a number of times, but I always felt
uncomfortable there. There was a morbid atmosphere about it. I remember
going there one day and it almost overwhelmed me, and I was glad
to get away. We were going back to Oxford in Michael's car, and I said,
'It's a relief to get away from that flat,' and he said, 'Yes it is.' But the
next day he'd be writing to Barrie as usual ... It was an extraordinary
relationship between them – an unhealthy relationship. I don't mean
homosexual, I mean in a mental sense. It was morbid, and it went beyond
the bounds of ordinary affection. Barrie was always charming to me,
but I thought there was something twisted about him. Michael was very
prone to melancholy, and when Barrie was in a dark mood, he tended

to pull Michael down with him ... I remember once coming back to the flat with Michael and going into the study, which was empty. We stood around talking for about five minutes, and then I heard someone cough: I turned round and saw Barrie sitting in the ingle-nook, almost out of sight. He'd been there all the time, just watching us ... He was an unhealthy little man, Barrie: and when all is said and done, I think Michael and his brothers would have been better off living in poverty than with that odd, morbid little genius. Yet there's no doubt that Michael loved him; he was grateful to him, but he also had an affinity with him that ran very deep. (Cited by Birkin 1979, 282–3)

Michael drowned at Oxford in 1921. Those most acquainted with the circumstance of Michael's death recorded suspicions that it was a suicide (Birkin 1979). Barrie never recovered from Michael's death. He was a broken man, although he pursued various other consuming involvements until his own death in 1937. The eldest adopted son, George, Barrie's original favourite, died in the war in 1915. Peter, the adopted son who was so repulsed by the possibility that Barrie could have married his mother, eventually committed suicide in 1960.

As well as his non-drug addictions, Barrie was addicted to tobacco. One of his early books was entitled *My Lady Nicotine* (Barrie 1892). It is a droll but unmistakable description of an overwhelming involvement with tobacco, presented in a favourable light. The title feminizes tobacco, as his other writing in that period feminized work, and throughout the text he favourably compares the merits of tobacco to those of marriage, although he was not yet married at the time he wrote it. At some point his involvement with tobacco became a clearly negative addiction. He remained an incessant, heavy smoker of pipes and cigars throughout his life, in spite of medical warnings and a chronic, racking cough. He tried unsuccessfully to give tobacco up (Mackail 1941).

THE FUNCTION AND STRUCTURE OF BARRIE'S ADDICTIONS

Barrie's life and writing suggest that the primary function of his addictions was to compensate for unbearable failures at growing up and sexuality, rather than to satisfy an irresistible attraction to work, little boys, or tobacco. He substituted overworking, over-involvement with childish fantasy, and oversmoking for what he really wanted.

Barrie's addictions also functioned as a source of his creative genius. In *Peter Pan*, Barrie personified all three of his major addictions. Peter was inwardly yearning to grow up, but too terrified to abandon childish fantasy. At the end of the narrative, when Peter is about to return to Never-Never Land, Wendy and Mrs Darling each make entreaties to him, which the ever-present Barrie interprets in the stage-notes:

WENDY. (*making a last attempt*). You don't feel you would like to say anything to my parents, Peter, about a very sweet subject?
PETER. No, Wendy.
WENDY. About me, Peter?
PETER. No (*He gets out his pipes, which she knows is a very bad sign. She appeals with her arms to MRS. DARLING*).
MRS. DARLING. (*from the window*). Peter, where are you? Let me adopt you too. (*She is the loveliest age for a woman, but too old to see PETER clearly*).
PETER. Would you send me to school?
MRS. DARLING. (*obligingly*). Yes.
PETER. And then to an office?
MRS. DARLING. I suppose so.
PETER. Soon I should be a man?
MRS. DARLING. Very soon.
PETER. (*passionately*). I don't want to go to school and learn solemn things. No one is going to catch me, lady, and make me a man. I want always to be a little boy and have fun.
(*So perhaps he thinks, but it is only his greatest pretend.*)
(Barrie 1928, 154–5)

At other points in the play, as well, Barrie reveals Peter Pan's fear of growing up, primarily through the stage directions. The curiously analytical stage directions make it clear that Peter Pan is a tragic figure. He is vain, overwhelmingly involved with fantasy, indifferent about his own physical survival, and out of touch with people, physically and emotionally. There are also several hints that Peter, inexplicably, has a great affinity for his nemesis, Captain Hook.

Captain Hook serves to personify the other two of Barrie's major addictions. Hook, like Barrie, was a hard smoker. According to Barrie's stage instructions, '*A holder of his own contrivance is in his mouth enabling him to smoke two cigars at once'* (Barrie 1982, 52). Barrie, of course, managed only one, but his cigars were renowned for their bore and potency. Hook showed many signs of an ambivalent workaholism, perhaps a trait not normally associated with pirate captains. At one point he delivers a short soliloquy:

> HOOK. (*communing with his ego*) ... All mortals envy me, yet better
> perhaps for Hook to have had less ambition! O fame, fame, thou glittering
> bauble, what if the very [he is interrupted] ... No little children love
> me. I am told they play at Peter Pan, and that the strongest always chooses
> to be Peter ... that is where the canker gnaws. (125)

Barrie's muliplicity of overwhelming involvements suggests that the term 'addiction' might be too singular. For example, a specialist in drugs might reasonably identify Barrie as a 'tobacco addict,' but it would be an incomplete diagnosis. Smoking was only part of Barrie's addictive complex. Had tobacco been successfully prohibited, he would no longer be identified as a 'tobacco addict,' but his addictive complex would almost certainly have continued to dominate him as it did when Michael Davies was taken from him by a premature death. Barrie was devastated, but not delivered from addiction. He turned to absorbing alternative involvements including, it seemed, his own protracted and dramatized grief itself. Others included writing, public-speaking projects, and other personal relationships that he expanded to addictive proportions. As well, late in life he developed an inordinate fondness for heroin, which had been prescribed for him during numerous illnesses. His doctors and friends eventually felt they had to deny his requests of the drug (Dunbar 1970).

An addictive complex such as Barrie's cannot be considered as a fortunate life-style – Barrie was miserably unhappy, despite his fabulous literary and social attainments. Throughout his life he was subject to deep depression, chronic headaches, and recurrent nightmares. He was an object of pity and amusement to his friends, but also of some distaste, as the quotes earlier reveal. He was loved by many but, it seems, mostly for his fame, intermittent boyish charm, and great financial generosity. His biographies suggest tormented loneliness, especially in his later years.

## Heroin Addiction and Addiction in General

Is it really valid to compare exercise addiction and Barrie's various compulsions to drug addiction? Or, is this comparison merely an academic exercise? Readers will make up their own minds, of course. In considering this issue, I find it useful to reflect on the heroin and methadone addicts that I have known for many years in Vancouver. Part of this time I have worked as a family therapist, but the larger amount of time I have known these addicted people as fellow members of a local organization, the Concerned Citizens Drug Study and Education Society, which is devoted to protecting addicts against the excesses of the War on Drugs. I have learned much from these addicted people, for their lives bear little similarity to the stereotypes of heroin addicts that were part of my earlier education. It has gradually dawned on me over the years that, like James M. Barrie, the primary problem for these addicted men and women is an inability to find a satisfactory place in society. Eventually, they lose hope that such a place can ever be found. Heroin addicts display this hopelessness when they are 'wired on heroin,' when they are using methadone, when they are drinking beer, and when they are not using any drugs at all. They talk endlessly about the injustices worked on them by the legal system and various bureaucracies, but the great majority cannot find any time for constructive work to remedy the problem. Such a simple thing as sending a form letter to an MP creates great complications and sometimes insuperable difficulties. This same incapacity carries over into all aspects of their lives: most cannot find time for a job, or for their children. Even the responsibilities of a normal friendship are usually beyond their reach.

Addicts' time is often taken up by seeking and using heroin, which is convenient for their purposes because its illegality makes obtaining it hard, and thus time-consuming. If the heroin is not available there are many other tasks that become more important than dealing with reality. These can include watching television, endlessly talking about their problems, seeking help from others, and 'getting their act together' (which usually means making unrealistic plans). If they have an irresistible craving in common, it is a craving to find a substitute for personal social integration, through excessive involvement in activities that are casual amusements for the majority of people. The pre-nineteenth-century term 'addicted to intemperance' seems more apt than the nineteenth- and twentieth-century term 'heroin addiction.' This concept of addiction is confirmed, at least in my mind, by the readiness with which 'junkies' switch to other drugs, particularly alcohol, valium, and barbiturates, when opiates are not available. It is also revealed in the ugliness of the language they use to describe their apparent 'drug of choice.' Heroin is horse, skag, dope, and 'shit' in everyday addict language, hardly terms that would be chosen for an irresistibly attractive substance. Barrie's life suggests to me that these dynamics can apply to people who are outwardly successful as well as to those who are outcasts.

A major drawback of the term 'addiction,' even in its traditional usage, is its singularity. The term implies being given over to a single thing, as a slave is given over to a single master. In fact, negatively addicted people are most likely to have a complex of addictions and others at the ready in case there should be an additional need. They appear given over to avoiding or finding substitutes for the complications and stringencies of normal life through compulsive involvement with one or more of the activities that serve most people as temporary diversions.

## Conclusions

This chapter, with its diverse content, suggests some conclusions that are specific to negative addiction without drugs and some that are relevant to the issue of addiction in general.

1. Negative addiction to exercise and numerous other activities that do not centre around drugs can be as destructive as negative addicition to drugs.

2. The objects of a person's addictions may shift from time to time, especially as difficulties with one of them arise. The various components of an addictive complex may have little in common, except that they serve a common function for the addict. If their primary function is avoiding a conflict or failure, then any absorbing activity appears to serve the purpose.

3. As with drugs, there are many more users who benefit from activities like exercise, work, fantasy, and so on than there are users who are negatively addicted.

4. Negative addiction without drugs is a major problem, but one that has been obscured by society's collective obsession with drugs.

This chapter and previous ones have nibbled at the question of how negative addiction is caused. This is a complex and controversial issue, but because it is central in the ideology of the drug war, it will be addressed more formally in the next chapter.

# 8 The causes of negative addiction

This chapter will attempt to discredit what is perhaps the most powerful justification for the War on Drugs, the widely accepted view that drugs *cause* negative addiction.* Conventional wisdom and drug-war doctrine identify certain 'addictive drugs' that, once taken, induce eternal addiction and associated criminality in vulnerable people. It follows logically that traffickers in addictive drugs must be eliminated mercilessly, just as malarial mosquitoes must be destroyed to protect a defenceless public. It also follows that Draconian legal controls can be exercised over drug users and addicts, since their deviant behaviour is a manifestation of disease, rather than a constitutionally protected pursuit of happiness. Because this view interweaves medical and criminal themes, it is here called the 'disease/criminal model' of negative addiction.

Because it is now an integral part of the drug-war definition of addiction, the disease/criminal model may seem the only possible explanation of how negative addiction occurs. In reality, however, it is only a particular viewpoint that has become dominant at this period in history. An alternative view is that negative addiction is a way people adapt to serious problems if they can find no better solution. According to this 'adaptive model,' the immediate cause of negative addiction is not a drug but a situation so dire that addiction is the most adaptive response a person can muster. From this viewpoint, no disease or criminality is necessarily involved. The adaptive model obviously lends little support to the War on Drugs.

* This chapter was jointly authored with Julian Somers.

Discrediting the disease/criminal model is more complex than the tasks undertaken in earlier chapters. This chapter will attempt to show that the adaptive model is a better way to look at addiction by developing the following points: (1) both models provide logically coherent accounts of the cause of addiction, but they are based on fundamentally incompatible assumptions; (2) both models have been known for centuries and have ancient, pre-scientific roots in Western philosophy; (3) the disease/criminal model is explicitly used to justify the harshest aspects of the War on Drugs, whereas the adaptive model has more humane implications; (4) the weight of current empirical evidence runs contrary to the disease/criminal model; and (5) there is strong empirical evidence to support the adaptive model.

This chapter will discuss the causes of negative addiction only. Experimental use, circumstantial use, casual use, regular recreational use, and dependent use of drugs are probably better explained in other ways. Although the two models of negative addiction can explain other forms of deviant behaviour including crime and madness, that application will not be undertaken here.

## Two Incompatible Accounts of Addiction

This section analyses the two models of addiction by breaking them into their component hypotheses. It shows that each provides a theoretically coherent account of negative addiction, but that they are logically contrary, that is, they cannot both be correct.

### THE DISEASE/CRIMINAL MODEL

The disease/criminal model represents a familiar explanation of negative addiction that pervades War on Drugs thinking as well as the doctrines of many therapeutic agencies and of Alcoholics Anonymous. According to this view, susceptibility to addiction is caused either by a genetic predisposition or by faulty upbringing, or by both. Exposure of a susceptible person to drugs, especially during periods of environmental stress, eventually causes addiction. The addiction progresses and eventually causes economic dependence, family breakdown, self-hate, criminality, and so on. This model is schematized in figure 3, panel a.

In different variations of the general disease/criminal model, different causal factors are emphasized. One common variation, which will be

a) Disease/criminal model

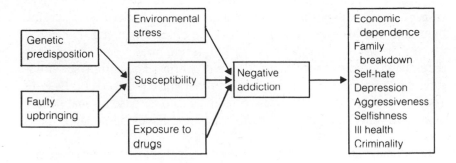

b) Disease/criminal model (exposure orientation)

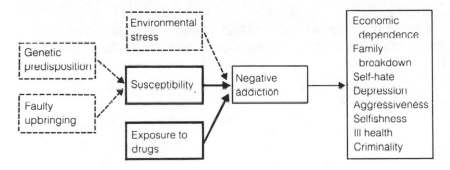

c) Disease/criminal model (genetic predisposition hypothesis)

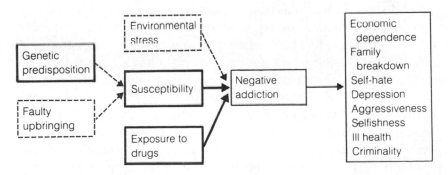

Figure 3

called the 'exposure orientation' in this book, treats exposure to addictive drugs as the primary cause of addiction and regards all or most people as susceptible. The exposure orientation can be schematized by enlarging the 'exposure to drugs' component of the disease/criminal model and making the others correspondingly small (see figure 3, panel b). This is the essential theme of several well-known theories of addiction (see Goldstein 1979; Bejerot 1980; Lindesmith 1980; Gold and Rea 1983; DuPont 1984) and is implicit in the view of addicts as otherwise normal people who have failed to 'just say no' to drugs and have consequently been 'hooked.'

In another variation on the disease/criminal model, genetic predispositions are stressed as the primary determinants of susceptibility (see Goodwin 1985). Exposure becomes somewhat less important, since it is said to cause addiction only in genetically predisposed people. This variation, which will be called the 'genetic-predisposition hypothesis,' is schematized in figure 3, panel c.

In another familiar variation, 'faulty upbringing' is emphasized as the cause of susceptibility (see Milkman and Frosch 1980) rather than genetic factors. This view was popular earlier in this century when addiction was frequently attributed to an 'addictive personality,' and is currently being revived by a popular movement called Adult Children of Alcoholics (Robinson 1989).

## THE ADAPTIVE MODEL

The adaptive model explains negative addiction as a way of adapting to a dire situation. Like the disease/criminal model, the adaptive model can be represented as a set of causal hypotheses, shown in figure 4. According to this model, combinations of social and constitutional problems sometimes result in a failure of psychosocial integration, that is, in people not finding a way to live in society that is satisfactory both to society and to themselves. Failure of psychosocial integration is a grave emergency because it gives rise to depression, despair, ostracism, and suicide. Therefore, the threat of integration failure incites urgent efforts to achieve psychosocial integration or, failing that, to find a substitute life-style.

Substitute life-styles do not provide the abiding satisfactions of psychosocial integration, but they do provide a basis for survival and the possibility of trying again to achieve fuller integration in the future.

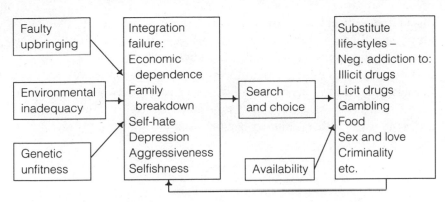

Figure 4  Adaptive model

People who cannot achieve psychosocial integration cling to their substitute life-styles resolutely, even at the cost of their reputation and health. This condition constitutes the persistent 'centrifugal' impulse that was indentified as the essence of negative addiction in chapter 3. According to this view, people adopt the life-style of an addict only because it is adaptive. It may, in some situations, provide more hope for survival than the unbearable social and psychological void of no identity at all. In other situations, immersion in the banal addict subculture may be less destructive than total isolation. In others, chronic intoxication, although unhealthful, may provide vital distraction from a crippling preoccupation with a sense of personal failure.

The claim that harmful drug addictions are *adaptive* may seem outrageous in the atmosphere of the War on Drugs. In other contexts, however, the idea that harmful behaviour is sometimes adaptive is familiar and accepted. Consider, for example, the use of ordinary wooden crutches. People who have been required to use them know that they can cause painful blisters on the hands, bruises in the armpits and even serious accidents. None the less, crutch use is *adaptive* for many injured people because their alternatives, that is, putting weight on the injury or staying in bed, are worse. With time and social support, people can learn to use crutches skilfully, although they are never more than a poor substitute for natural locomotion. When people find better alternatives, they readily abandon their crutch habits. In other words, in a dire situation, whether it is a broken leg or a failure of psychosocial integration, it is often adaptive to choose the lesser evil, even though such a choice would be maladaptive under other conditions. For some people the dire situation may last a lifetime. In the first case, such a person would normally be described as crippled, in the second, addicted.

As with the disease/criminal model, there are numerous variations of the adaptive model, each emphasizing different causes of integration failure, different functions that substitute life-styles can serve, and different reasons that addicted persons cannot find socially acceptable ways to adapt.

## THEORETICAL DISTRACTIONS

Although understanding the cause of negative addiction is crucially important to formulating rational drug policy, the theoretical dissonance between the two models of negative addiction has not been resolved, in part because a number of unhelpful ideas have obscured the issue.

### Combining Models

The biggest obstacle to resolving the theoretical conflict has been the idea that the two models can be either accepted simultaneously or amalgamated. In fact, most theories of addiction in the contemporary scholarly literature combine elements from both models (see theories summarized in special issues of the *Journal of Drug Issues*, 1987, no. 2, and the *Journal of Abnormal Psychology*, 1988, no. 2). However, these combinations are logically untenable.

The two models are not merely different ways of saying the same thing. Rather, they are logically incompatible in at least six fundamental ways. First, the disease/criminal model depicts negative addiction as a disease (or 'pathology,' 'syndrome,' 'disorder,' 'illness,' or 'maladaptive behaviour'). In contrast, the adaptive model does not depict addiction as any sort of disease, but as an adaptive substitute life-style.

A second difference between the two models is that a critical cause-and-effect relationship is reversed. 'Drug addiction' is seen as *causing* a host of problems in the disease/criminal model, but in the adaptive model it is seen, at least initially, as *resulting from* the same problems. The adaptive model recognizes that an addiction may later introduce new problems or exacerbate some of the problems that preceded it as indicated by the feedback arrow in figure 4.

A third difference is that the disease/criminal model depicts an addicted person as under external control (of a drug, a genotype, or a traumatic childhood) or simply 'out of control.' The adaptive model portrays addicted people as actively controlling their own actions. In other words, the disease/criminal model takes an essentially deterministic view of addiction, whereas the adaptive model takes a purposive view.

A fourth difference is the importance of exposure to drugs. All variations of the disease/criminal model accord exposure to the drug a causal role in the development of addiction. By contrast, all forms of the adaptive model accord the major causal role to an individual's adaptive drive in a dire situation, with a particular drug merely serving as the focus of a substitute life-style if it is conveniently available.

Fifth, similar components in the two models are construed differently. For example, 'environmental stress' in the disease/criminal model is termed 'environmental inadequacy' in the adaptive model, reflecting a more critical view of the social environment. Likewise, 'genetic predis-position' means something quite different from 'genetic unfitness,' as this chapter will later show. Even the arrows in the schematic drawings of the two models have somewhat different meanings, since some of those in the adaptive model imply a final cause rather than a material or efficient cause.

Sixth, the two models draw on different aspects of biology. The disease /criminal model draws from the medical and physiological traditions whereas the adaptive model draws from evolutionary biology. These traditions have been conceptually separate throughout most of the history of biology, although in their modern forms they are more reconcilable (Mayr 1982, 571).

When the various differences are considered together, the incommen-surability of the two models becomes undeniable. A person behaving adaptively is not a patient in need of medical treatment; adaptation is not disease; addiction cannot be both primarily the cause and primarily the effect of the behavioural problems that go with it; a behaviour cannot be both in a person's control and out of their control at the same time; exposure to a drug cannot be both an important cause and merely a logical necessity; and the disparate world-views implicit in the two models cannot be maintained simultaneously.

Each model constitutes a coherent whole. When parts from the two are combined, coherence dissolves and conceptual fog inevitably rolls in. Rational understanding cannot be based on contradictions.

The common view that adaptive factors explain initial drug experimentation but that addiction itself develops though a disease process (see Hochhauser 1980; Wikler 1980) might appear to combine the two models coherently, but it does not. The adaptive model is not a model of drug experimentation, but a model of the addictive process itself. Therefore, this putative sequential combination of the models is actually just an acceptance of the disease/criminal model, augmented by the observation that people are behaving purposefully when they try drugs in the first place.

'Multifactorial models' may appear to amalgamate the two models by depicting addiction as the result of numerous factors from both models that act more or less independently to contribute to the final outcome. However, multifactorial models lack theoretical structures that enable assessment of the interrelationship of causal factors and they evade the issue of how factors that are logically incompatible can coexist. Multifactorial models are so complex and formless that they generally produce more muddle than insight (Tesh 1988).

Historically, scientific advance has often required that some competing models be completely rejected in favour of a single conception that captures the imagination of society and the scientific community (Kuhn 1970, chap. 9; Mayr 1982). Of course, there have also been crucial syntheses in the history of science as well, but it is by no means true that all scientific divisions of opinion are resolved by synthesis.

*Physical and Psychological Addiction*

It sometimes appears that the disease/criminal model describes 'physical addiction' and the adaptive model describes 'psychological addiction.' However, both models include physical and psychological terms. As explained in chapter 3, the argument over whether addiction is 'physical' or 'psychological' has proved to be a futile one that should be abandoned (Marlatt 1985, 368–9). Addiction is a human life-style. As such, it can be described in both physical and pyschological terms.

*'Free Will'*

Although the concept of 'search and choose' in the adaptive model implies that a person is purposefully choosing between alternatives, it does not necessarily imply 'free will.' On the contrary, the adaptive model implies that people's choices are very much affected and limited by previous experiences, by formative events of life, and by heredity. 'Free will vs. determinism' is a convoluted, ambiguous issue (Taylor 1967) that can only obscure the comparison of the two models of addiction.

## Responsibility

The difference between the two models is not, as sometimes alleged, that the disease/criminal model treats negative addiction as an illness, whereas the adaptive model treats it as a sin or crime by assigning responsibility to the addicted person (Gold and Miller 1987; Miller and Gold, forthcoming). In fact, the disease/criminal model has traditionally served as the justification for punitive policy, as this chapter will later show. Contrariwise, it is not true that the adaptive model denies that negatively addicted people have a serious problem. The adaptive model treats negative addiction as a cause for alarm, but not as a medical or criminal condition.

## Origins of the Two Models

The view of addiction as a disease is sometimes regarded as a modern scientific achievement that supplanted an ealier criminal view of addiction (see Inciardi 1986, 108–9; Gold and Miller 1987). Indeed, shifts between disease and criminal emphases have been hotly debated in recent years (see Solomon and Green 1982, 89; Trebach 1987; Fiffen and Lambert 1988). However, from a longer perspective it is clear that the disease and criminal emphases have been closely related throughout the history of Western civilization and that the adaptive view has been conceptually separate from both.

ANCIENT ROOTS

The current disease/criminal model is the modern form of an ancient view of harmful excess as either medical, criminal, or both, with the emphasis changing from one to the other at intervals. Aristotle formalized this disease/criminal view. In his *Nicomachean Ethics* (circa 330 BC/ 1925, book 7), he presented a complex analysis of various forms of excessive behaviour, some of which involved simple violence and some of which were equivalent to negative addiction. He identified two causes of such excess. One was an affliction that takes possession of individuals against their will and for which they cannot be considered fully blameworthy. Aristotle likened this 'incontinence' to the disease epilepsy, adding that it is a curable condition. On the other hand, 'self-indulgence' or 'vice' is a permanent, incurable badness that does not involve any loss of control but is instead deliberately wicked. Thus, negatively addicted people are either sick or bad. In either case, their actions are harmful, and societal intervention is required to control them. This Aristotelian analysis is compatible with the disease/criminal model.

The roots of the adaptive model are equally ancient. In the *Republic*, Plato described the natural development of self-destructive 'master passions' that are clearly instances of negative addiction (Plato, circa 375 BC/1955, 377–95). He identified the young men who develop master passions as those who have failed to find meaningful, stable values in declining democratic societies. Although at some points he described these young men in ways that were compatible with the disease/criminal model, at others he depicted them as acting understandably given the vacuum created by the spiritual uncertainty of the times and the weakness of their families and the larger culture. Thus, he stated the essence of the adaptive model.

Plato's adaptive view is clearer, although more generally stated, in his *Protagoras* (circa 390 BC/1956, 89–92). In this work Plato argued that it is impossible for men to knowingly act against their self-interest (as addicts appear to do when they are perceived as 'out of control'). It would follow that people who are not ignorant of the consequences of their actions must be acting in accordance with their self-interest, that is, adaptively, even if they do not appear to be.

About eight hundred years after Aristotle and Plato, St Augustine conveyed the essence of *both* the disease/criminal and adaptive models in his *Confessions* (circa AD 397/1963). The disease/criminal model is implicit in Augustine's description of his own excessive sexuality and his mother's youthful over-indulgence in alcohol as 'diseases' to be 'cured.' He explained their causation in terms that suggest a force that is both beyond a person's control (as is disease) and wicked (168, 174). In the same work, St Augustine utilized an adaptive view in his analysis of the habitual drunkenness of a beggar in Rome as a natural and adaptive response to the hopelessness of his situation (119–20).

The disease/criminal model has been influential throughout history, but was not predominant in the English-speaking world before the nineteenth century. This is reflected in the work of John Locke, the major English-language philosopher of the eighteenth century. Although he was not always consistent, Locke generally viewed the kind of life-style that is here called negative addiction (particularly chronic drunkenness) as an error in living caused by insufficient reflection on the consequences of one's own actions (Locke 1690/1959, 335–58), a view that supports neither of the two models directly.

## EVOLUTION OF THE MODERN DISEASE/CRIMINAL VIEW OF ADDICTION TO ALCOHOL

Between about 1780 and 1830, the temperance movement successfully popularized the disease/criminal model of drunkenness as set forth in a pamphlet originally published by Dr Benjamin Rush. Rush's views have been summarized as follows: 'Rush argued that distilled liquors were physically toxic, morally destructive and addictive. Regular drinkers ... ran the serious risk of many diseases ... they also tended to engage in many forms of antisocial, immoral and criminal behavior. Further ... regular drinkers become 'addicted' to alcohol, and he described alcohol addiction in the full contemporary sense of the term: those addicted experience uncontrollable, overwhelming and irresistible desires for drink ... Finally, Rush called this condition a 'disease' and recommended total abstinence as the only remedy for the addicted individual' (Levine 1984, 110). Like earlier forms of disease/criminal analysis, temperance language mixed moralisms and medical jargon. At the same time that alcohol became 'demon rum,' excessive alcohol use became a 'disease' called addiction or, later, alcoholism. In parallel developments, madness came to be seen as both a disease and a moral failure, leading to the establishment of a new medical speciality, 'moral medicine.' Later, un-employability also came to be viewed as both a moral failing and a genetic defect (Rose 1985, chaps. 2–3).

The fully modern form of the disease/criminal model of alcoholism appeared in the 1930s when Alcoholics Anonymous added the concept that some individuals have a genetic predisposition to alcoholism (Levine 1984). AA also emphasized the deterministic aspect of the disease/criminal model by making the idea that an alcoholic was 'out of control' and 'powerless' predominant in their doctrine. The AA version of the disease/criminal model was subsequently given the blessing of science by Jellinek's famous research at Yale University. There was a close relationship between AA and Jellinek's work: 'Jellinek did his studies using Alcoholic Anonymous members and translated their experiences and views into scientific and medical terminology and categories' (Levine 1984, 117).

The popularization of the AA view of addiction would appear to have again shifted the emphasis away from criminality. But recent court decisions in the United States have changed the balance again. In a recent case before the U.S. Supreme Court, two American veterans claimed extensions of their eligibility for educational benefits beyond the usual ten years on the grounds that the disease of alcoholism, for which both men had been repeatedly hospitalized, prevented them from using their benefit within the normal time-span. When the case reached the Supreme Court, the Veteran's Administration argued that there are two kinds of alcoholism. Secondary alcoholism is 'secondary to and a manifestation of an acquired psychiatric disorder,' that is, a disease. Primary alcoholism is 'willful misconduct,' that is, criminal. The Veteran's Administration pointed out that it spends $100 million a year on alcoholism treatment and rehabilitation, but it cannot pay disability benefits to people because they are 'compulsive drinkers' (Holden 1987).

The Supreme Court upheld the definition of primary alcoholism as 'willful misconduct' on 20 April 1988. It conceded that 'primary alcoholism' may not always be willful, but that 'the VA stance falls within the bounds of reason given the amount of controversy over the subject' (Holden 1988, 597). Thus, the disease/criminal model of addiction, in its current form, confers an obligation to seek treatment on addicted people without a corresponding immunity from responsibility for the effects of the supposed disease.

THE MODERN VIEW OF ADDICTION TO OTHER DRUGS

Although the disease/criminal model of addiction was most conspicuously applied to alcohol in the nineteenth century, it was applied to other drugs as well. For example, opium had been widely used for thousands of years and excessive use was usually regarded as simply unfortunate before the nineteenth-century 'discovery' that habitual use was a disease as well as a moral failure. The disease/criminal model was applied to opiate drugs in the 1870s by the German scholar Eduard

Levenstein and others (Sonnedecker 1963). It gained popularity as pressure for stringent opiate prohibition began to strengthen in England and the United States (Musto 1973; Berridge and Edwards 1981). As with alcohol, the disease of opium addiction, as displayed by opium 'fiends,' was soon discovered to be the cause of all social problems.

In the twentieth century, prominent researchers have explained the use of marijuana (Jones and Jones 1977; Staats 1978; DuPont 1984), cocaine (DuPont 1984; Gold and Dackis 1984; Dackis and Gold 1985) and other illicit drugs in disease/criminal terms. Chronic use of these drugs is widely regarded as a disease and, at the same time, blamed for society's ills and subjected to extraordinarily stringent controls.

## The Disease/Criminal Model as Justification for the Drug War

From the early nineteenth century, proponents of the War on Drugs have often used the disease/criminal model to justify warlike measures (Clark and Cahalan 1976; Grinspoon and Bakalar 1976; Aaron and Musto 1981, 139; Szasz 1985, 1987; Gold and Miller 1987). This section will provide contemporary examples of these justifications and show that a very different approach is suggested by the adaptive model.

### DISEASE/CRIMINAL JUSTIFICATIONS FOR THE DRUG WAR

Supporters of the drug war are apt to regard addiction as a fatal disease that is spread by the criminal actions of drug traffickers and by the irresponsibility of drug users. Because the supposed disease is perceived as a major cause of society's problems, and because it perennially threatens to reach epidemic proportions, war measures against traffickers and users can escalate without limit.

It is part of Western tradition that epidemics warrant stringent measures to protect the public. During epidemics of various contagious diseases over the last few centuries, it has seemed legitimate for authorities to quarantine ships, prevent people from entering and leaving towns on pain of death, seize and incarcerate people who show signs of the disease, and, in extreme cases, kill people suspected of transmitting the disease. At times, suspected disease transmitters have included prostitutes, grave-diggers, lepers, and Jews (Tesh 1988, chap. 1).

Recent Canadian government announcements of moves towards a

'zero tolerance' policy, a major escalation of the War on Drugs, were justified in disease/criminal and epidemic terms, as reported in the *Globe and Mail*: 'Uncompromising, "zero-tolerance" measures to stem illegal importation of drugs may be needed in Canada, Revenue Minister Otto Jelinek said yesterday ... Last month, Prime Minister Brian Mulroney promised tough new measures to deal with what he described as the "scourge" of drugs. Mr. Mulroney said the drug problem in Canada is worse than $2\frac{1}{2}$ years ago when he was accused of exaggeration for saying there was an "epidemic of drug abuse in Canada." Mr. Jelinek said yesterday that Mr. Mulroney is "a hero ... for saying there is an epidemic"' (Koring 1989).

Recent debates on 'drug legalization' profusely illustrate the use of disease/criminal thinking as justification for drug prohibition (see *The Economist* 1988, 4–6; *Time* 1988, 14–16). Robert L. DuPont, former head of NIDA in the United States, alluded to neurophysiological theories of drug addiction in the following statement in a letter to the editor of *The Economist* (1988): 'While education and persuasion play a potent role in reducing the acceptability of drugs ... they are insufficient in the face of the powerful biological effects of these drugs on the central nervous system. The solution is a tough minded policy that identifies and punishes drug use in five areas: at school, at work, behind the wheels of vehicles, for parolees and probationers, and for teenagers at home' (4, 6).

Mark Gold has used the disease/criminal model to justify war measures in criticizing a recent article of mine: 'Just as vaccinations for infectious agents are used commonly to prevent infectious diseases, preventative measures to prevent the predisposition and exposure to drugs are important. Drug testing, drug education, law enforcement, and education regarding alcohol and drugs are not an infringement on people's rights, as suggested by Dr. Alexander, any more than are vaccinations' (Gold and Miller 1987, 7).

The genetic aspect of the disease/criminal model has been used to justify extraordinary measures as well. Because this model identifies a genetic predisposition to addiction as an important part of the cause, it appears sensible that people who have alcoholic relatives (or relatives with any other addiction) should be forced into preventative treatment, whether they show any signs of addiction themselves or not. It is justifiable to abrogate normal civil rights when the likelihood of contracting a severe disease is certified by medical science. This practice appears to be spreading in the United States, as discussed by Peele (1985).

The disease/criminal model readily serves to justify grossly misleading propaganda. From this viewpoint, people must be afraid to experiment with drugs in the same way they should fear experimenting with the AIDS virus. It is not a matter of first concern that the basis of the fear be true – the intent is to prevent the catastrophic spread of illness, and the truth may be too complex to instil the kind of reflexive horror that is needed. There will be time enough for truth when the epidemic threat is past.

In the climate of the present drug war, the word 'treatment' is sometimes a euphemism for coercion, as shown in chapter 2. The disease /criminal model is often invoked to justify such coercive treatment. Current law in British Columbia provides an example. The Heroin Treatment Act provides the legal framework for taking complete control over people thought to be addicted to heroin. The act is written in a mixture of medical and legal language.

Under the act (which is not currently being enforced), people suspected of being narcotics users may be required by a policeman to attend an 'area co-ordinating centre' (all quotes are from British Columbia's Heroin Treatment Act 1978, c. 24). There they can be detained, without charge, warrant, or trial, for three days and required to submit samples of their blood and urine for analysis. Refusal to attend the centre or to provide bodily fluids constitutes 'an offense' under the act, which subjects the offender to legal punishment. If an 'evaluation panel' reports that the person is 'in need of treatment' (the act specifies no criteria whereby this decision is to be made), the person is placed in mandatory 'treatment' for three years, at which point he or she is termed a 'patient.'

The act makes no provision for 'patients' who are cured in less than three years to be released from treatment. At the discretion of the director, and the board of review, some or all of these years may be spent as 'detention in a treatment centre' or in out-patient treatment in a clinic or under 'supervision and direction of such a kind and of such duration as a director may require.' Charges may be laid against patients who defy the act or refuse a 'requirement or direction' given by any employee of the provincial Alcohol and Drug Commission. Nothing in the act prevents a patient who is released from treatment after three years from being immediately sent into treatment again, via the 'area co-ordinating centre.' (In fact, discussions in the act's planning phase made it clear that multiple terms were envisioned by its authors.) Thus, this act allows for indefinitely long detention without a trial.

The Heroin Treatment Act was legally challenged on the grounds that it was not really medical, but a criminal law, and thus a provincial infringement of exclusive federal jurisdiction over criminal law. However, in spite of the extraordinary character of the treatment, the Supreme Court of Canada ruled that 'the dominant characteristic of the Heroin Treatment Act was the medical treatment of drug addiction' (*Schneider v. the Queen* 1982).

In other cases, the disease/criminal model has been used illogically, apparently to rationalize a treatment it does not really justify. In a recent article, for example, following a lengthy explanation of cocaine addiction as a disease caused by the capacity of cocaine to deplete the dopamine in the brain, Dackis and Gold (1985) proposed a plan for treatment. However, there is no real relationship between the coercive treatment that was proposed and the dopamine-depletion hypothesis, although the two topics are presented contiguously in the text as though the hypothesis justified the treatment. The following excerpts show that the proposed treatment draws more inspiration from the War on Drugs mentality than from a physiological theory:

An effective inpatient program should generally last at least 4 weeks and address the psychological, social, and lifestyle factors associated with the compulsive cocaine use. Initially, the patient must relinquish control to the treating staff and follow direction while slowly engaging in a drug free peer group with structured outpatient aftercare treatment provided to foster long-term recovery.

When hospitalization does not appear to be indicated, outpatient treatment can be started immediately. The goal of treatment should be complete abstinence from all mood-altering chemicals (including alcohol, marijuana, etc.) and adoption of a drug-free life style ...

Specific and sensitive urine testing is essential to the success of outpatient treatment. Throughout the entire course of treatment, urines should be tested regularly for cocaine and other commonly abused drugs ... Patients are generally relieved to find that urine testing is mandatory. Urine testing helps to identify patients who are either unable or unwilling to stop using cocaine and those who switch to other drugs. Patients should be encouraged to report any instances of drug use before it is detected in the urine so that discussion of the issue can take place as soon as possible to maximize therapeutic gains. Consequences for drug-positive urines should be clearly stated at the outset of treatment. Although a rare or infrequent 'slip' may occur during the course of treatment, this relapse should call for a revision of the patient's treatment plan. This revision may entail more frequent visits, completion of a specified drug-free period verified by urine tests or a period of hospitalization before resuming in outpatient treatment. (Dackis and Gold 1985, 474)

In the same article, Dackis and Gold do suggest some specific physiological treatments based on their dopamine-depletion theory of cocaine addiction. These treatments appear in a section entitled 'Experimental treatment,' and the subsequent text makes it clear that the physiologically based treatments have at most a secondary role.

Beyond justifying the coercive treatment programs, the disease/criminal model has provided the justification for a huge investment in more conventional, relatively non-coercive professional treatment for addiction. If addiction is an intractable disease, it obviously requires treatment by professional specialists. However, this huge conventional-treatment apparatus has produced no substantial evidence of success and much evidence of demoralization among therapists and patients (see *PM*, chap. 2). By depicting addiction in such a way that professional treatment seems necessary, the disease/criminal model produces a cruel paradox. Addicted people are pushed into seeking medical treatment that is unlikely to work for a condition that may not be a disease in the first place. This is a formula for increasing helplessness.

Urine-testing appears to be spreading to Canada from the United States. The disease/criminal model can be used to justify this new indignity on the basis that the use of addictive drugs is a sign of an existing or imminent incapacitation from the disease of drug addiction. By this logic, employees who fail the urine tests that are imposed on them by their employers should be disciplined or forced into treatment for their 'illness.' However, the data reviewed in this book would suggest that most employees with illicit-drug residues in their bloodstream probably use the drug casually or recreationally and without deleterious effects on their work. Some users of stimulants might reasonably point out that, under the conditions of fatigue or stress on the day of the test, their performance was likely to benefit from the drug, rather than be harmed by it. Of course, some of the people making such arguments would be concealing their harmful drug use, but the majority – experimental, circumstantial, casual, or regular users – would likely be correct.

## DRUG CONTROL POLICY – AN ADAPTIVE VIEW

Whereas the disease/criminal model serves to justify the harsh and futile measures that constitute the War on Drugs, the adaptive model points in a different direction. From an adaptive viewpoint, punitive measures directed at traffickers and users are not only ineffective, but counter-productive.

If the War on Drugs miraculously eliminated illicit drugs from the face of the earth, more harm than good would result. Most people use illicit drugs, like other artefacts of modern technology, moderately, safely, and beneficially. People become drug-addicted because, at the time, they are capable of no better substitute adaptation for themselves. Eliminating illicit drugs would help neither moderate users, nor addicts, nor society. Therefore, drug-control policies that grow from the disease/criminal model are intrinsically harmful, no matter how effectively they are executed and no matter how benevolent the people who carry them out. Furthermore, from an adaptive viewpoint, harsh coercive treatment is most likely to exacerbate drug addictions. People adopt substitute adaptations because they have failed to put together a satisfactory adult life-style. Therefore, afflicting them with additional stigmatization, guilt, and confinement can only worsen their problems and is therefore likely to intensify their addictions.

From the adaptive viewpoint, pushing addicted people into conventional treatment is also a dubious policy. The essential task for an addicted person is pulling together a satisfactory life that does not require heavy involvement in substitute adaptations. Help with that task can be provided by friends, neighbours, and community leaders, all of whom know the difficulties of attaining integration, just as well as it can be by professionals. All of these avenues are blocked, however, by the dominance of the disease/criminal model and its insistence on professional treatment.

For people who are not addicted, the drug-control policies that derive from the disease/criminal model can only reduce their options to use drugs reasonably. Opiate drugs, for example, are of great value to the sick, but their use is greatly limited by the fear engendered by the disease/

criminal model. Countless people in desperate pain have been pointlessly denied the use of opiate drugs, or have denied themselves these drugs because of unfounded fears of addiction (Trebach 1982; Zinberg 1984). Many of the illicit drugs could be used in beneficial or pleasurable ways if they were more accessible.

Essentially the adaptive model suggests that an abundance of drugs is one of many fruits of technology that perplex this incredible century and that people must learn to use drugs by the same sort of trial-and-error process by which we are learning to use automobiles, computers, and televisions. In each case, there have doubtless been people who urged their prohibition, but society as a whole has recognized that these popular technologies cannot be rejected at will. Instead they must be domesticated. By a slow process society must learn the appropriate values and rules to regulate their use, and must learn how to convey these values to the young.

Under any future policy, there will inevitably be some misuse of drugs. However, people are basically concerned with their survival and happiness and, given the opportunity to learn, will come to use new technologies in a generally beneficial way. This viewpoint does not suggest that there should be no legal controls, but that such controls should be of a normal sort, designed to minimize problems rather than eradicate an enemy, and that the controls should be changed if they prove to do more harm than good.

## Empirical Weaknesses of the Disease/Criminal Model

In spite of the fact that the disease/criminal model is often regarded as a scientific viewpoint, the empirical evidence supporting it is weak. The enormous body of relevant evidence can only be touched upon here, but the widely publicized claims of empirical support for the two major variations of the disease/criminal model will be considered in some detail.

### THE 'EXPOSURE ORIENTATION'

Until a few years ago, there was an almost universal belief among the general public and in the scientific community that exposure alone was sufficient to cause addiction to certain drugs. This variation of the disease/criminal model, the 'exposure orientation,' was illustrated above in figure 3, panel b. In spite of the earlier certitude, it is now clear that there is no solid empirical support for the exposure orientation, and much to contradict it. Some of the evidence against the exposure orientation as it applies to heroin and the other opiate drugs was summarized in chapter 4. There it was shown that most people who experiment with these drugs do not experience irresistible pleasure, that withdrawal symptoms are generally not the unbearable experience that the propaganda depicts, that most users are not addicted, and that people who do become addicted, including numerous American soldiers from the Vietnam War, most often terminate their addictions without treatment. The anecdotal and animal studies that appear to support the exposure orientation were reviewed and the support they provide was shown to be weak.

Some of the evidence against the exposure orientation as it applies to cocaine was summarized in chapter 5. In spite of the ubiquitous claims that cocaine hydrocholoride and smokable cocaine have an extremely high addictive liability, most users do not become dependent or addicted and those who do generally seem able to terminate their addictions without professional help. Again, the chief source of support for the exposure orientation appears to be media stories and over-generalization of animal research. (For further discussion of the evidence against the exposure orientation as it applies to the opiates and cocaine see Fingarette and Hasse 1979; Alexander and Hadaway 1982; Falk 1983; Zinberg 1984; Peele 1985; Cohen, forthcoming; and Erickson and Alexander, 1989.)

The exposure orientation has been applied to other drugs besides heroin and cocaine. The temperance movement spread the doctrine that all alcohol users eventually become addicted. The same doctrine was spread concerning marijuana in the twentieth century by drug-war activists and by some respected scientists (Jones and Jones 1977; Nahas 1979). However, in both cases it has long since become obvious that the vast majority of users of these two drugs do not become addicted to them or to any other drugs as a consequence (Le Dain 1973). The exposure orientation looks even weaker when other forms of addiction are considered. Although serious, sometimes fatal, negative addiction does occur to aspirin-like drugs, as discussed in chapter 6, it seems impossible that exposure is the cause. If it were, addiction to these drugs would be virtually universal, rather than a rarity.

The exposure orientation does not seem more applicable to the case of negative addiction to habits that do not involve drugs at all, such as love, work, and gambling. No exogenous chemical is present to subvert the body's metabolism. Because of the overwhelming weight of dissonant evidence, proponents of the exposure orientation have been forced to modify their position. Currently they argue that illicit drugs cause addiction, but only in certain persons whose identity cannot be predicted in advance (DuPont 1984). In recent years this argument has usually been advanced in the form of the genetic-predisposition variation of the disease/criminal model.

## The Genetic-Predisposition Hypothesis

The data refuting the exposure orientation can be easily reconciled with the disease/criminal model if it is assumed that only people with genetic predispositions are susceptible to negative addiction to a particular drug. The genetic-predisposition hypothesis has been described with great conviction in numerous popular reports. For example, a poignant *Newsweek* article contained the following lament:

> How could this have happened to me? I live in a good neighbourhood and have beautiful children, a successful husband and go to mass every Sunday. I've been to college and read and pray and lead a good life, yet I contracted Jellinek's disease [i.e. alcoholism].
>
> As I began to realize the scope of my illness, I was plunged into grief, for never again would I be like ordinary people. I railed against my God for having done this to me, and I shook my clenched fist at my genes, my heredity, my father, for had I not been programmed long before my birth to be a Jellinek victim? (Fitzgerald 1983)

The following quote from the *New York Times* makes the case in the form of a review of recent scientific developments:

> Discoveries are coming out in such rapid-fire succession that many experts see the dawn of a new age of enlightenment, wherein alcoholism will be proven to have a tapestry of subtle biological causes. Though the disease may be set in motion by environmental and/or psychological factors, alcoholics fall prey to their illness because their metabolisms, due to either genetic predisposition or to the effects of heavy drinking, differ distinctively from those of nonalcoholics.

'The drunk memorialized by Eugene O'Neill and Tennessee Williams –
the undisciplined soul who drinks out of soul sickness – is disappearing
behind the curtins,' says Dr. Nicholas Pace, one of the nation's leading
alcoholism treatment specialists and founder of Pace Health Services in
Manhattan. 'If we thought yesterday's alcoholic was haunted by internal
conflict, we know that today's is primarily haunted by his liver.' (Franks
1985, 48)

In spite of the popular appeal of this hypothesis, there is no strong
evidence to support it. By most accounts, the strongest support for the
hypothesis over the last decade has come from two teams of American
investigators, headed respectively by George Vaillant and Donald
Goodwin. Some of Vaillant's strongest data compare the prevalence of
alcoholism among men with no alcoholic relatives to that of men with
several alcoholic relatives. If genes can confer a susceptibility to
alcoholism, more of the men with several alcoholic relatives should
become alcoholic. Indeed, in two large, carefully studied samples, only
10 and 14 per cent of the men with no alcoholic relatives became 'alcohol
dependent' at some time in their adult lives, whereas 29 and 34 per cent of
men with several alcoholic relatives did so.

However, Vaillant judiciously pointed out that these data are more
equivocal than they seem at first glance, and certainly not as powerful as
his uncritical supporters have assumed. The men with several alcoholic
relatives very likely grew up in homes where alcoholism and the related
tensions were much more prominent, so environmental influences cannot
be separated from genetic determinants. There is no way in the framework of Vaillant's naturalistic research to rule out the influence of family
environment.

Moreover, ethnicity provided an alternative explanation for Vaillant's
findings. In the core city sample, where ethnic backgrounds were a
prominent aspect of life, ethnicity was highly correlated with frequency
of alcoholism. For example, Irish-American men were much more likely
to become alcoholic than Italian-Americans or Jews. Vaillant attributed
this ethnic effect to subcultural differences in attitudes towards drinking
and drunkenness. Obviously, this factor could have accounted for part of
the correlation between alcoholism prevalence and number of alcoholic
ancestors. Italian-Americans, for example, are apt to have both few
alcoholic relatives and a low likelihood of alcoholism for cultural

reasons, regardless of their genes. When Vaillant controlled this factor, by looking separately at each ethnic group for the relationship between alcoholism and the number of alcoholic relatives, the correlation was greatly reduced. In fact, the correlation disappeared in some of the ethnic groups.

Clearly, this evidence provides very weak support for the genetic predisposition hypothesis. Vaillant (1983) acknowledged this fact, but maintained that stronger support for the hypothesis could be found in Goodwin's famous adoption studies, which provide a more substantial opportunity to control environmental factors. However, when Goodwin's research is examined closely, it provides no better evidence for the hypothesis than Vaillant's.

Goodwin clearly subscribes to the genetic-predisposition hypothesis (Goodwin 1979, 1985), but there are many problems with the supporting data he and his co-workers provide. First, in general, the research is not the same high quality as Vaillant's. For example, the classification of people as alcoholic is based on interviews conducted in Danish in Copenhagen, transcribed into English, and then diagnosed by an American psychiatrist in St Louis. The frequency of alcoholism determined in this way is, in some of the studies, then compared to the Danish estimates of alcoholism in the general population, which is obviously determined in a different way, although the Danish method is not explained in the studies (see Goodwin et al. 1974). Obviously, there are too many differences in the two methods of determining the prevalence of alcoholism for comparisons of data obtained in this way to be regarded as strong evidence.

Another serious problem is that Goodwin et al. found differences that can be attributed to heredity only in males. The strongest finding is that 15 per cent of male offspring of alcoholics that had been adopted by non-alcoholic parents were diagnosed as currently being alcoholic, whereas only 4 per cent of adopted males whose biological parents were not alcoholic were so diagnosed. The results for females actually ran *contrary* to the genetic-predisposition hypothesis, although the differences did not reach statistical significance (Goodwin et al. 1977). The restriction of the key finding to males is overlooked in most generalizations that are drawn from the data, including Goodwin's own statement of conclusions (Goodwin 1979). Subsequent to Goodwin's research, Bohman, Sigvardsson, and Cloninger (1981) found evidence of a hereditary factor in females. There was a higher incidence of alcohol abuse in adopted daughters of alcoholic mothers (6.7 per cent) than in adopted daughters of non-alcoholic mothers (2.3 per cent). However, as with Goodwin's research, there are serious methodological problems with this study. In a recent review, Searles (1988) pointed this fact out with unusual emphasis: 'It is remarkable that the results of these studies have been accepted with virtually no critical examination. This may be due to the complex and perhaps intimidating statistical analyses performed on the data. Subsequent publications and reviews, then, usually report only the positive results, without reference to methodological and theoretical concerns ... Close examination of these studies reveals several methodological problems that require an adequate response before the results can be accepted' (159).

Whereas the data furnished by the foregoing studies are widely cited as support for the genetic-predisposition hypothesis, they demonstrate, at most, a weak effect. They indicate that the vast majority of adopted children of alcoholics do *not* become alcoholic. In fact, *these data fit better with the adaptive model than they do with the genetic-predisposition hypothesis*. From an adaptive point of view, genetic unfitness of many sorts may hinder a person's efforts towards psychosocial integration. If integration failed because of any genetic problem, the person would be likely to adopt alcoholism or some other form of addiction as a substitute adaptation. This view predicts the kind of weak, non-specific inheritance of alcoholism that the studies above have reported. The adaptive interpretation of these data finds additional support in other types of research on alcoholism as well.

Alcoholics have special temperamental traits that are measurable before they begin to drink. These include hyperactivity, heightened sociability and social aggressiveness, emotionality, and short attention span. Although these traits are sometimes viewed as specific temperamental antecedents of alcoholism, people with these traits are also prone to other behavioural problems, including hysteria, borderline personality, bulimia, anorexia nervosa, 'drug abuse,' gambling, and antisocial personality (Tarter, Alterman, and Edwards 1985; Tarter and Edwards 1987). Therefore, it does not seem like a specific inclination to drink that is inherited by 'genetically predisposed' people, but something more general.

Furthermore, whereas the relatives of alcoholics are somewhat more likely to become alcoholic, the same can be said of the relatives of people afflicted with hysteria, borderline personality, bulimia, anorexia nervosa, antisocial personality, and schizophrenia – they are more likely to be *alcoholic* as well (Tarter, Alterman, and Edwards 1985). Again, these data are contrary to the notion of a specific predisposition to alcoholism and compatible with the adaptive interpretation given above.

Recently, biological markers have been identified among people who are relatives of alcoholics. These include unique brain-wave patterns, depressed levels of alcohol-metabolizing enzymes, and unusual sensitivity to alcohol (Schuckit 1984, 1987). Reviews of the literature concerning these biological markers have not provided much support for the genetic-predisposition hypothesis, however. For example, Peele (1986) concluded that 'it is typical of research in this area that distinctive electroencephalogram patterns have been found in each investigation of descendents of alcoholics but that no two sets of results have coincided' (65). Conflicting data have also been reported with respect to biochemical sensitivity and reactions to alcohol (Searles 1988) as well as rates of alcohol metabolism and enzyme levels (Mendelson and Mello 1979). Furthermore, it is unclear at present how such factors as sensitivity to alcohol and rates of metabolism would be expected to influence an individual's drinking behaviour. Mendelson and Mello (1979) point out that while 'faster rates of alcohol metabolism could lead to more frequent and copious alcohol consumption ... slower rates ... would prolong intoxication – a condition sought by persons with alcoholism' (913). Although his work is often cited in support of the genetic-predisposition hypothesis, Schuckit himself has noted that 'no generally accepted biological marker of a vulnerability to alcoholism has yet been identified' (1987, 307).

The genetic argument is often made in a racial form. It is claimed that North American Indians are genetically predisposed to alcoholism and that this predisposition explains the high alcoholism rates among them. However, although some metabolic differences between racial groups in reactivity to alcohol have been found, the results have not been consistent. Moreover, native Indians are genetically similar to Orientals, having reached the Americas by way of a relatively recent migration from Asia. Many Indians and many Orientals show the so-called 'oriental flush' when they drink. Yet Orientals living in North America have relatively low rates of alcoholism, whereas native Indians have high rates (Peele 1985, 106–7).

A more parsimonious primary explanation for the high alcoholism levels among native Indians may be the simple fact that the indigenous cultures of these people have been corrupted by an alien invasion. Psychosocial integration is difficult in their devastated indigenous cultures, which have little to offer, and in the alien white culture, which is unwelcoming. This view, which fits the adaptive model, has been stated by authorities on Indian culture (May 1982; Mohatt 1972). If this adaptive explanation were correct, it would be expected that native Indians would tend towards heavier use of all drugs rather than just alcohol. This does seem to be true. Although there is great variation from band to band, North American Indians are susceptible to heavy use of most illicit drugs (Liban and Smart 1982; Smart 1986). Also in accordance with an adaptive interpretation, Liban and Smart (1982) showed that most of the differences between the drug consumption of Indian and white students in Ontario disappeared when the students were carefully matched for geographic location and socio-economic conditions.

Devastating epidemics of addiction in racial groups that are genetically distant from Indians have been attributed to difficulty of psychosocial integration. Such racial groups include Australian aboriginals following the European invasion of their homeland (Chatwin 1987, 157) and American blacks who were part of the massive migrations from the rural south to the alien culture of the urban north (Courtwright, Joseph, and DesJarlais 1989, 16–17).

Two additional points about the genetic-predisposition hypothesis should be mentioned. One is that several extended, recent critiques have expressed scepticism about the evidence for the genetic-predisposition hypothesis (Murray, Clifford, and Gurling 1983; Peele 1986; Zucker and Gomberg 1986; Searles 1988). The second point is that research on no other drug besides alcohol has provided even the equivocal support that has been mustered for a genetic predisposition towards drug addiction. For example, the well-known research on strain differences in the opiate consumption of mice (see Horowitz et al. 1977) is of dubious relevance. There is no clear connection between simple consumption of opiates by animals and addiction – addiction is a complex event involving, by almost any definition, more than simple consumption of a drug.

## Empirical Support for the Adaptive Model

Evidence for the adaptive model can be found in diverse sources including clinical studies, quantitative research, and scientific theory in several fields. Although it is not conclusive, it is stronger than that which has been mustered in support of the disease/criminal model.

## INTEGRATION FAILURE AS THE PRE-CONDITION FOR ADDICTION

A central hypothesis of the adaptive model is that integration failure is a necessary pre-condition for addiction. The model maintains that people who cannot achieve psychosocial integration are likely to shield themselves from incapacitating depression, isolation, or suicide by seeking out substitute adaptations including negative addiction.

This view has been stated in different terms by major figures in modern psychology, sociology, and psychiatry, including John Dewey (1922), Sigmund Freud (1929), Alfred Adler (1934/1954), Erik Erikson (1963, 1968), Robert K. Merton (1957), and Carl Rogers (1980). For example, Erickson's cross-cultural and psychoanalytic research revealed a series of stages in human development, each of which requires the integration of a person's needs with society's demands. Erickson found failure of integration at any of the successive stages to be harmful, and accumulated failures to be potentially disastrous.

Erikson's best-known stage is 'identity achievement,' which generally occurs in the late teen-age years. To achieve identity, people must create a personal and public definition of themselves that integrates the opportunities offered by their society with their unique personality traits and instinctive drives. Failure in this stage of integration leads to a potentially destructive 'identity crisis.' A prolonged identity crisis may be relieved, in Erikson's terms, by the adoption of a 'negative identity' or 'pseudo-identity,' such as delinquency, fanaticism, or drug addiction. These sorts of identity provide some of the vital satisfactions of identity formation, especially when the substitute identity is supported by a deviant subculture composed of like-minded people. However, many substitute identities are socially condemned or physically harmful if they continue too long. Erikson's theory is not limited to the problems of teenagehood. Instead, it suggests that there are many stages of psychosocial integration beginning early in childhood and persisting until old age. Therefore, 'integration failure' can occur at any time during the life cycle.

Various kinds of social-science research have shown that the conditions that are likely to lead to integration failure are correlated with the occurrence of negative addiction. For example, the family backgrounds of addicted people frequently include sexual abuse, incest, parental delinquency, physical violence, too much or too little parental control, emotional cruelty, and overdependence of parents on offspring (Chein et al. 1964; Braucht et al. 1973; Alexander and Dibb 1975; Helzer, Robins, and Davis 1975/76; Wurmser 1978; Yeary 1982; Browne and Finkelhor 1986). In addition, there are frequently direct indications of prior integration failure in people who become addicted. Visible temperamental problems that are likely to precede addiction include depression, hyperactivity, reduced attention span, heightened emotionality, alienation, personal insecurity, anxiety, conflict with parents, sense of meaninglessness, and perceived loss of control (Peele and Brodsky 1975; Kielholz and Ladewig 1977; Tarter, Alterman, and Edwards 1985; Newcomb and Harlow 1986; Deyken, Levy, and Wells 1987; Peele 1987; Tarter and Edwards 1987).

Whereas no one of these 'risk factors' alone is a powerful predictor of later addiction, people who display several of them are more likely to later become addicted (Bry, McKeon, and Padina 1982; Timmer, Veroff, and Colton 1985; Tucker 1985). Of high-school students who reported none of ten 'risk factors' at the first interview, only about 1 per cent reported heavy use of any drugs one year later, whereas of the students who reported seven or more risk factors at first interview, 28 per cent were heavy users of 'hard drugs,' 56 per cent were heavy users of cannabis, and 34 per cent were heavy users of cigarettes one year later. The relationship between risk factors and later drug use held up when partial correlations were used to control for drug use at the time of the first interview (Newcomb, Maddahian, and Bentler 1986).

Relapses to addiction following treatment frequently occur in situations that suggest integration failure. Interviews with patients who relapsed following treatment for alcoholism, smoking, heroin addiction, compulsive gambling, or overeating revealed that the majority of relapses occurred during 'negative emotional states.' Relatively few relapses could be associated with withdrawal symptoms or spontaneous craving for drugs (Marlatt 1985a, 1985b).

A variety of minor biological abnormalities have been found to accompany a higher probability of alcohol addiction, including low platelet monoamine oxidase levels, EEG abnormalities, hormonal abnormalities, and tremor (Tarter and Edwards 1987). Even left-handedness and a family history of left-handedness appear to correlate with the severity of alcoholism (London 1986). The fact that such an extraordinary diversity of minor problems correlates with later addiction fits the adaptive model, if it is assumed that almost any deficit, even a minor one like left-handedness, increases the likelihood of integration failure to some degree.

One indicator of integration failure among adults is unemployment. There are many reports that alcoholism and other substitute adaptations are frequent among the unemployed (Smart 1979; Kirsch 1983, 59–61). Of course, unemployment may be a result of problem drinking as well as a cause. However, case-studies of workers conducted three years after a 'plant closing' in Saltville, Virginia, provide clear evidence that unemployment can increase smoking and alcoholism, as well as a variety of other personal problems. Because the abrupt closing of the factory threw all the workers out of work, it is clear that unemployment led to addiction, rather than the other way around (Strange 1977). Unfortunately, this study provided no count of the total number of workers who responded to their abrupt dismissal in an addictive manner.

The view that failure to achieve integration can provoke actions as desperate as addiction fits the thinking of the existential philosophers as well as social scientists. Much existential writing depicts the agonized groping of people who cannot achieve a sense of integration with their society, and their consequent fascination with neurosis, madness, suicide, and sexual deviance (see Sartre 1938/1964; Genet 1943/1963; Tillich 1952, 71–4). Such analyses may provide an introspective view of the state of 'search and choice' that follows integration failure and of the appeal of deviant substitute adaptations under those conditions.

The hypothesis that integration failure is a pre-condition for substitute forms of adaptations is compatible with biological theory as well as social and existential theory. When any animal population is stable because of limited resources, many of the developing individuals in each generation cannot be 'recruited' into the 'adult population' (Krebs 1978). For example, among territorial birds, the adequate food-producing areas are marked off into breeding territories. Those who do not gain a territory are unable to reproduce, although they may survive by adopting strategies that would not be adaptive in individuals who have acquired a territory. The non-recruited individuals may acquire a territory later if a natural disaster depletes the breeding population (Wynne-Edwards 1986). From this theoretical viewpoint, addiction can be understood as one of the strategies that a member of the human species might display when failure of recruitment (that is, integration failure) has occurred or is imminent. For example, addiction could serve to remove the individual from competitive situations in which defeat is almost certain, thus preventing injury and creating an opportunity to survive away from an inaccessible adult population and be available later, should an opportunity to join it arise.

Finally, the view that integration failure is a pre-condition of addiction and of other personal tragedies is implicit in the modern public health and 'primary prevention' literature (Albee 1986). Cassell has stated this view succinctly: 'A remarkably similar set of social circumstances characterizes people who develop tuberculosis and schizophrenia, become alcoholic, are victims of multiple accidents, or commit suicide. They are individuals who for a variety of reasons ... have been deprived of meaningful social contact' (quoted by Albee 1986, 893).

## THE FUNCTIONS OF ADDICTION

The adaptive model depicts negative addiction as serving diverse adaptive functions for addicts. Many clinicians and other observers of human behaviour have analysed such functions, describing addictions as well as other deviant life-styles as helping individuals to gain power over others (Adler 1933/1954), control aggressive impulses (Khantzian 1974), prevent neurotic disintegration of the ego (Wurmser 1978), provide a substitute 'career' where legitimate opportunities are few (Coombs 1981), provide an 'illusion of potency and social recognition' for suppressed people (Dewey 1922, 148), control the pain of chronic physical illness (Westermeyer 1982, 140–4), reduce tensions that threaten to split up a family (Alexander and Dibb 1975), alleviate crippling personal insecurity (Peele and Brodsky 1975), energize people who are chronically depressed (Khantzian and Khantzian 1984), control intolerable self-hate and guilt (McFadden 1987), fill spiritual vacuums (Woodman 1982), regain an intensity of feeling that has been repressed during childhood (Miller 1981), reduce the pain of life in repressive civilizations (Freud 1929), and achieve many other, more idiosyncratic goals (Davis et al. 1974; Khantzian, Mack, and Schatzberg 1974).

Some scholars see North Americans addicts in general as 'self-medicating,' that is, using drugs addictively in order to control catastrophic emotional problems and physical pain (see Peele 1978; Khantzian and Khantzian 1984). Zinberg reported that 85 per cent of 'compulsive' (addicted) opiate users reported 'to alleviate depression' as a motive for their opiate use (1984, 76). The most frequently reported motive for the non-addicted users was 'to enjoy the high.' This 'self-medication view' also gains credibility from the observation that cancer patients and others with uncontrollable pain often become obsessed with narcotic prescription drugs, and appear addicted to others (Tuttle 1985, 122).

## ADDICTION AS A FORM OF CONTROL

The adaptive model depicts addicts as responding purposefully and adaptively to their environment. If this view is correct, they are not out of control, as assumed by the disease/criminal model. Many addicted people publicly claim to be out of control, but these claims require scrutiny because they represent such effective defences against blame and guilt. Moreover, addicted people are often convinced they are out of control by treatment agencies and accused of denial if they say otherwise.

A large number of experimental studies have shown that severe, chronic alcoholics given unlimited access to alcohol in a controlled setting typically do not drink 'to oblivion.' Instead they moderate their drinking for many reasons, for example, to reduce the discomfort of anticipated withdrawal symptoms or to obtain small monetary rewards offered by experimenters (Mello and Mendelson 1972; Fingarette 1988). Alcoholics allowed to drink for two days in the midst of a treatment regimen were able to stop drinking again when the period of allowable drinking ended, even though they were free to leave treatment and continue the binge (Pattison, Sobell, and Sobell 1977, chap. 5). In another study, alcoholics given free access to 32 oz of liquor per day for nine to twelve days maintained remarkably stable blood-alcohol levels. They accomplished this by varying their consumption of both alcohol and food and generally not consuming all the alcohol available to them (Mello and Mendelson 1971). The alcohol intake of alcoholics appears to be under the same kind of control as other types of behaviour.

ADDICTION AS A TEMPORARY CONDITION

If addiction serves as a way of adapting to integration failure, it should cease if psychosocial integration occurs later. This deduction from the adaptive model contradicts the view that addiction is a permanent condition, which is part of many variations of the disease/criminal model.

There is now overwhelming evidence that addiction to alcohol and other drugs is often transient and frequently disappears without professional treatment, an event that is sometimes called 'maturing out' (Winick 1962; Robins and Murphy 1967; Pattison, Sobell, and Sobell 1977, chap. 6; Zinberg, Harding, and Apsler 1978; Blackwell 1982; Schachter 1982; Vaillant 1983; Alexander and Schweighofer 1988; Cohen, forthcoming). Of course, addiction sometimes persists for a lifetime. This fact does not contradict the adaptive model if it is assumed that, in such cases, successful integration was never achieved.

ADAPTATION AS A 'LESSER EVIL'

When only harmful alternatives are possible, the adaptive model assumes that it is adaptive to choose the 'lesser evil,' even though it is harmful. This use of the term adaptive is accepted in modern behavioural theory outside of the field of addiction. For example, Vaillant, in his book *Adaptation to Life* (1977), pointed out that a self-deceptive ego defence mechanism like 'denial' may help a person adapt to especially difficult circumstances by censoring thoughts that are too threatening, even though denying reality entails a harmful inflexibility. Other commonly used 'coping mechanisms' have obviously detrimental effects. These include overeating, undereating, 'Type A' behaviour, and excessive denial of reality (Roskies and Lazarus 1979). The adaptive model would add negative addiction and other substitute adaptations to this list of harmful, but none the less adaptive, coping behaviours.

This view of adaptiveness is also compatible with evolutionary theory. A fox caught in a leg-hold trap might behave adaptively by gnawing off its own foot rather than dying of starvation in the trap. This behaviour would only appear maladaptive to a short-sighted observer who could not discern the trap beneath the snow. Even addicted persons may not clearly see the hidden trap that incapacitates them, but may only perceive an inexplicable attraction to their harmful behaviour.

Addiction sometimes causes premature death. However, even this fact does not necessarily indicate that the behaviour is maladaptive in general. A similar danger inheres in other emergency responses. For example, the 'General Adaptation Syndrome' is a complex of physiological responses that is adaptive because it protects the body from severe stress. In cases where the stress persists too long, however, the adaptive syndrome sometimes causes 'diseases of adaptation' that can be fatal (Selye 1976).

This is not to imply that all self-destructive behaviours are adaptive. Evolutionary biologists might think of a self-destructive behaviour as 'maladaptive' if it were caused by a deleterious mutation or if it had evolved under one set of conditions and then become dysfunctional when the species' environment had changed. But such maladaptive traits would tend to be eliminated rapidly through natural selection. Therefore, behavioural capacities that have been relatively common throughout long historical periods, such as addiction in human beings, would normally be considered adaptive by evolutionary biologists unless some reason to think differently was apparent (Symons 1979, 46; Bock 1980; Darwin 1981/1981, 381; Mayr 1982, 132).

Hibernation is a familiar instance of a costly adaptive process. Hibernation protects animals from the harshness of winter or other environmental stringencies through a pre-programmed reduction in food intake and diminution of metabolic activities. This protective retardation of function comes at the cost of weakening the hibernating creatures, taxing their physiological systems to the limit, and making them vulnerable to predators. Yet hibernation and other lengthy types of 'animal anorexia' are recognized as adaptive in large numbers of vertebrate species (Mrosovsky and Sherry 1980). According to the adaptive model, addiction, like hibernation, occurs when an individual cannot meet the demands of the environment and survives by adopting a diminished mode of functioning until the opportunity for more complete activity reappears.

Another parallel between hibernation and addiction is the apparent involvement of opiates in both activities. There is evidence that the pattern of physiological responses that accompany hibernation is made possible by the release of endorphins and terminated by endogenous anti-opiate substances (Margules 1981). Human beings do not literally hibernate of course. However, the adaptive model proposes that they may use addiction analogously as a shelter from the demands of a too harsh reality. Opiate addicts have been described in psychiatric writing in terms that are surprisingly analogous to hibernation: for instance, 'the user must withdraw periodically to find relief from a life that is too stressful, complicated, and demanding. Opiates pharmacologically induce a primitive state characterized by peace, contentment, and serenity' (Spotts and Shontz 1982, 960).

## THE INTERCHANGEABILITY OF ADDICTIONS

An implication of the adaptive model is that the prohibition of a substitute life-style will result in a person choosing another, unless the integration failure that maintains the substitute life-style is simultaneously amelio-rated. My own experience with heroin addicts is that they respond to periodic short supplies of heroin by redirecting their addictions to alcohol or valium. McGlothlin and Anglin (1981a) have shown that former patients whose methadone program had been shut down for administra-tive reasons consumed much more alcohol and heroin than patients who continued to have access to legal methadone.

A related implication of the adaptive model is that a person might respond to integration failure with several substitute adaptations, rather than a singular addiction. This scenario fits well with the recent observation that 'polydrug abusers' are more common than addicts to a single drug (see Tarter and Edwards 1987, 75). Cook (1987) has shown that self-reported addictions among university students tend to cluster in particular individuals. The average student who reported addiction to one habit also reported addictions to three or more others. The concept of the 'addictive complex' was introduced to describe this phenomenon as part of the case study of James M. Barrie in chapter 7.

## Beyond Simple Empiricism

In spite of the vast accumulation of empirical and theoretical knowledge, no resolution of the theoretical conflict between the two models of addiction has been achieved. There are firm supporters of each and the majority seem content to mix them, in spite of their logical incompatibil-ity. This section will argue that the reason for this stalemate persists because the task of resolving the conflict lies beyond the powers of simple empiricism.

Modern history and philosophy of science have shown that all science is built on broad assumptions that cannot be empirically proved or disproved (Foucault 1970; Kuhn 1970; Lakatos 1978; Mayr 1982). Various historians and philosophers have given these sets of assumptions different names. I will refer to them here as 'frameworks,' which is simplification of Carnap's (1952) term 'frameworks of entities.' Other scholars have called them 'paradigms,' 'disciplinary matrices' (Kuhn 1970), 'epistemes' (Foucault 1970), the 'protected hard core of research programmes' (Lakatos 1978), or simply 'theories' (William James 1906/1963; Feyerabend 1978; Hacking 1983; Tesh 1988). Although frameworks must fit empirical observations, they are not adopted or sustained entirely on empirical grounds. On the contrary, their acceptance is determined to a great degree by the consensus of scientists prior to extensive empirical investigation, by their practical utility, and by the broader concerns of society.

Although historians of science generally agree that social influences affect the choice of scientific frameworks, they differ sharply on whether or not this *should be* so. I am persuaded by those who believe that social influence on the choice of frameworks is both inevitable and desirable (see Becker 1963; Gergen 1985, 1987; Howard 1985; Tesh 1988). Social influence on frameworks is inevitable because scientists are human beings, enmeshed in society. To believe that one's own views on deeply emotional issues could be coldly objective and detached would seem to be an indefensible vanity for a scientist or anyone else. Beyond being inevitable, social influence on the development of scientific frameworks is desirable. If it did not occur, the immensely powerful force of empirical science could become an unleashed menace unconstrained by its impact on human welfare.

Social influence on frameworks takes nothing from the rigour of science. Once a framework has been adopted, scientists explore its consequences using rigorous empirical methods. In fact, frameworks make rigorous science possible by defining basic terms and rules for a scientific community (Kuhn 1970). On the other hand, a framework is nothing but an empty verbal construction until it is filled in with careful empirical research. Therefore, the two phases of scientific development, framework evaluation and empirical research, are completely dependent on each other.

I believe that the disease and adaptive models are frameworks rather than empirically testable hypotheses, for they are ancient conceptions built on conflicting metaphysical assumptions about the nature of human beings, as shown earlier in this chapter. If the two models are indeed frameworks, the conflict between them cannot be resolved by solely empirical methods. Instead, a broad exploration of their history and social implications is a necessary and proper aspect of their evaluation.

When the disease/criminal and adaptive models are evaluated in terms of their social implications, that is, treated as frameworks, the superiority of the adaptive model becomes clear on at least three grounds that have been discussed in this chapter. First, although the disease/criminal model is often regarded as the more 'scientific,' this model did not originate in science or medicine at all. Rather, its current popularity can be traced to the influence of the moralistic culture of the nineteenth century and of professional interest groups. Second, although the disease/criminal model has been ascendant for over a century, it has not led to theoretical understanding, prevention, or effective treatment of addiction, in contrast to other human problems that were claimed by nineteenth-century medicine. Third, although it is sometimes justified on humane grounds, the disease/criminal model has been used to rationalize the most Draconian aspects of the War on Drugs, whereas the adaptive model has more humane policy implications.

If the adaptive model is so clearly in accord with the values of humane society, and if the empirical evidence tends to favour the adaptive model over the disease/criminal model, then why is the disease/criminal model currently the more popular of the two?

The ultimate issue may be courage. Adopting the adaptive model requires giving up the belief in an easy fix for horrendous social problems that is promised by the disease/criminal model, and, instead, facing up to their fearsome complexity. The adaptive model spoils the dream of controlling social ills simply by punishing and treating people who use drugs. For health professionals, the adaptive model means giving up the monopoly on treatment and the unjustified claim to privileged, expert knowledge about addiction. For scientists, the adaptive model means giving up an engagingly simple deterministic metaphysics and coming to grips with a purposive organism whose passion for life sometimes guides it into addiction. It also requires giving up the view of an entirely empirical science in which accumulated data automatically become the rungs of a ladder to useful knowledge. Instead, it requires accepting the historical reality that scientific frameworks are built upon social, ethical, and esthetic foundations. For society as a whole it means giving up the comfortable allegiance to the social structures of the present and acknowledging a need for major changes at times in history when large numbers of people cannot survive without substitute adaptations.

On a personal level, accepting the adaptive orientation requires the courage to accept the personal responsibility that the disease/criminal model disclaims. The disease/criminal model portrays the dreadful problem of addiction as caused externally, by perniciously addictive drugs, genetic accidents, and psychiatric traumata. It suggests that help must come from others – police who will stem the flow of evil drugs, pharmacologists who will discover antidotes, doctors who will discover treatments, and geneticists who will protect the next generation. It implies that parent groups may protect their children by organizing to 'fight drugs,' but need not worry about the far more difficult issue of raising healthy, well-integrated children in an unhealthy, chaotic world.

The adaptive model can only be accepted by people who have the courage to acknowledge their own part of the responsibility for society's problems and to face the cost of the solutions that will be necessary. If something is to be done about addiction, comfortable people must allow the reconstruction of social institutions that are too cold and harsh for many of those who must use them, parents must find ways to give their children the confidence and skill to function effectively, and all people must struggle to define attainable goals for themselves, lest they find their diversions more attractive than their impossible dreams.

# 9 Alternatives to the War on Drugs for Canada

Although no good comes of it, and although its justifications are in tatters, society continues and expands the drug war. The most recent American drug slogan, applauded by some Canadian politicians, has been 'zero tolerance.'

In part, people cling to the War on Drugs because they cannot envision clear alternatives. As in conventional wars, they seem convinced that the only alternative to blind persistence is surrender (see Inciardi 1986, 203–17). However, this chapter will show that there are reasonable alternatives to continuing the drug war. My thesis is that peaceful measures, by replacing war measures, can reduce the terrible tolls of war and ameliorate the problems that the war measures were intended to solve.

Two cautions should be mentioned before this task is undertaken. First, no quick fix is proposed. On the contrary, the problems of current society call for patience and resolve rather than magical solutions. The alternatives that are proposed here may seem tedious, but they have more substance in the long run than the flashier propositions of the drug warriors. Second, there is some public sentiment that drug-law enforcement should be de-emphasized in favour of 'legalization,' 'drug education,' 'prevention,' and 'treatment,' but there are treacherous ambiguities in each of these alternatives. Legalization is sometimes a call for a reflexive abandonment of all attempts to control drugs by society, growing from frustration and a feeling that drug users deserve the evil consequences that will follow. Such a policy shift is as simplistic as the War on Drugs. The most likely consequence would be a period of chaos followed by reimposition of even more Draconian drug laws. Genuine drug education and treatment can be valuable, but in current parlance 'education' and 'prevention' often refer to anti-drug propaganda and 'treatment' often refers to current bureaucratized, ineffective methods of control. When the terms are used in this way, the debate is pointless because, as chapters 1 and 2 show, education, prevention, and treatment are part of the War on Drugs, not alternatives to it. This chapter proposes more fundamental changes of direction. Like chapter 2, this one deals successively with prohibition, propaganda, and treatment.

## Alternatives to Drug Prohibition

When society can let go the impossible dream of eliminating drugs by force, it will awaken to the possibility of using the law and other agencies of social control to minimize harmful drug use. Ending drug prohibition does not mean legalizing needles in school-yards or pure cocaine in corner stores. Society regulates most commodities, and there is no reason for drugs to be an exception. Anthropological studies indicate that traditional societies may allow unregulated use of some drugs, but they regulate others, and prohibit still others entirely. The ones that are controlled in one society may be prohibited or unregulated in others and vice versa (Blum and Associates 1969, chap. 8).

Ending drug prohibition means that drug use, like other potentially dangerous activities, will be regulated in normal, non-warlike ways. Such regulation can be divided into two basic types: legal regulation and social control.

### LEGAL REGULATION

It would be naïve to suggest a codified legal alternative to present drug law. Effective law evolves gradually. However, it does seem realistic to suggest generalizations that could underlie new drug laws.

### Regional Control

Drug regulations should be as local as possible, rather than determined by national and international law. Earlier chapters in this book have shown that drug use is not an epidemic disease or a moral cataclysm that requires intervention on a national or international scale. Rather, non-medical drug use is more reasonably regarded as a matter of life-style that communities and provinces can regulate, as they regulate land use, Sunday closing laws for stores, educational curricula, recreational facilities, and so forth. As community standards change, regulations change accordingly, with minimum strain. By contrast, drug regulations imposed by a distant federal government or by an obscure international treaty make no sense in many localities and can be enforced only by violence, if at all (Nadelmann 1987, 24–5).

Criminal law is a federal responsibility in Canada, but this fact is not an insuperable obstacle to regionalizing drug regulation. The Canada Temperance Act of 1878 allowed cities and counties to decide the legality of the sale of alcohol by local plebiscite (Spence 1919, 124). This provision led to the prohibition of alcohol in various cities and counties, and eventually in all ten provinces. The advantage of the local option was that prohibition was instituted relatively easily when a locality felt the need for it and later modified or replaced in accordance with local experience. Eventually, all the provinces found prohibition unworkable and replaced it with alternative forms of control (Smart and Ogborne 1986). Regionalization of alcohol regulation may account for the lesser stress and violence with which Canada, compared to the United States, slipped into and out of alcohol prohibition.

In a broader sense, the history of alcohol regulation in both the United States and Canada can be viewed as a demonstration of the effectiveness of regional control. United States and Canadian alcohol regulation can be divided into three phases. In the first phase, which lasted from the earliest European settlements until about 1840, alcohol was considered a basic commodity. Its use was regulated primarily by individual conscience and local custom. Consumption was high by modern standards. In the second phase, beginning around 1840, alcohol came to be viewed as 'demon rum,' which was said to cause most of the burgeoning social problems of the nineteenth century. The increasing societal control in this second phase culminated in violent national prohibitions in both countries around the time of the First World War.

The third phase began with the failure of prohibition and is still in progress. This phase is not simply a return to the first. Instead, individual conscience and local custom are now bolstered with strict local, provincial, and state regulations on the sale of alcohol. For example, in

British Columbia a new neighbourhood pub cannot be opened unless the local residents indicate support for it in a referendum. Local controls are backed by federal control over manufacturing, advertising, and distribution. There is little need for regulation beyond the national level. The third phase is obviously not utopia, but it is a dramatic improvement over the first two – people drink less than they did in phase one and social costs are less than they were in both previous phases.

If regional control were introduced for psycho-active drugs, one might anticipate that most Canadian cities and counties would probably retain the current prohibition. However, some localities might choose to permit the possession and sale of some currently illicit drugs or to open Dutch-style 'coffee houses,' where marijuana or some other tolerated drug could be used. Other communities would probably attempt to prohibit all drugs, including alcohol and tobacco. Such regional controls would probably be much more respected than the present ones, and if they proved unworkable, they could be readily changed.

No doubt drug-war propaganda can generate images of such a system creating enclaves of sin and degradation that would poison the rest of the country, but this view contradicts history. Regional control has worked well where it has been tried.

Marijuana legalization for personal use in Alaska, decriminalization in several other American states, and de facto legalization in the Netherlands continue to seem reasonable to the people directly involved and have done no visible harm to bordering states and provinces (Kaplan 1983, Cohen 1988).

Alaska replaced marijuana prohibition with legal regulation in 1975, becoming the only American state in which possession of up to four ounces of marijuana and cultivation for personal use are not against the law. Possession of larger amounts remains illegal, although penalties for conviction are relatively mild by American standards. Although this policy is viewed with alarm by proponents of the War on Drugs, it seems to be working well, and the Alaska legislature has not voted to reinstate marijuana prohibition, in spite of annual hearings by committees of the state legislature on the topic. Even the Alaska state police, in their submission to the most recent hearings, saw little problem with the current law. The police took the position that they would support re-criminalization of marijuana to bring the state's laws into accord with the other American states, but they would not feel justified in enforcing new marijuana legislation, because they could not see that marijuana posed a police problem (Laird Funk, 1988, personal communication). Moreover, there have been no reports in British Columbia, which shares a long border with Alaska, of a mass exodus of citizens across the line to take advantage of the availability of marijuana since 1975.

In Alaska, statewide legalization of the possession and cultivation of marijuana for personal use is accompanied by prohibition of the sale of alcohol in some counties (Zeese, 1987). Only time will reveal how well this unusual arrangement serves the needs of Alaskans, in their unique environment. If it does not serve well, local voters are liable to change it quickly. It is just as reasonable in my mind for counties to ban the sale of marijuana and allow alcohol, provided it is done in the spirit of making sure the laws change quickly if they do not work.

The Dutch experience with de facto legalization for over a decade has been particularly instructive, although it has been distorted by misleading reports and rumours originating outside of the Netherlands. Chapter 2 summarized the ample evidence that the Dutch experience has been a success domestically. Moreover, there is no evidence that Dutch marijuana laws have spread pharmacological corruption in the rest of Europe.

Are New York's Draconian 'Rockefeller laws,' discussed in chapter 1, an example of local option run amok, producing violent, unenforceable laws? I think not. New York State with its seventeen and one-half million people is hardly a locality. Its population is two-thirds as large as Canada's and its cultural diversity is comparable. Drug laws that might be respected in an upstate farming community would make no sense in Harlem; laws suitable for eastern European immigrant settlements in New York City might seem foreign in the suburbs or on an Indian reservation. New York needs many sets of drug laws, not just one. By the same logic, it seems impossible that a single set of drug laws could be simultaneously appropriate for Montreal, Winnipeg, Indian reserves in the Yukon, and British Columbia's Slocan Valley.

Drug laws must conform to the natural divisions between communities of shared values. Sometimes very small units like Indian bands require local regulations and in other cases relatively homogenous nations like the Netherlands can utilize a single set of drug laws. Though localized drug laws might be hard to organize in the urban sprawls of the east, much of Canada is fertile ground for such an approach.

If the history of drug legislation follows the same course as that of alcohol legislation, the current period of Draconian drug prohibition may prove to be a transition between unregulated use of the illicit drugs and the adoption of a set of more reasonable regional regulations.

Even local powers to regulate drug use should probably not be absolute. Perhaps people should retain a kind of inalienable right to produce and consume organic drugs, like alcohol and marijuana, in their own homes, even if the local community bans their sale and public use. Such a provision would provide a reasonable refuge for nonconformists from the tastes of the majority. It would also recognize the undesirability, and impossibility, of legislating people's most private acts in their homes. On such topics there are no universal truths. The suitability of such constitutional rights ultimately must be debated within the context of each country's tradition of individual freedom.

*Pragmatic Law*

The last two decades have shown that legal trial-and-error with mild punishments can reduce smoking without creating great resentment, sending people to prison, arousing unrealistic expectations, or whipping up prohibitionistic zeal. Legislation in this spirit has been introduced in many parts of Canada and the United States. Simply raising taxes on cigarettes is responsible for the steady decline in Canadian consumption since 1982, according to business analysts (*Globe and Mail* 1985). Such constructive use of law engenders respect rather than disobedience.

Some more recent anti-smoking legislation is more extreme. The new Vancouver 'clean air' by-law, supposedly 'the strictest in the country,' sets a harsher, less pragmatic tone. It prohibits smoking 'in any public place' in Vancouver, and stipulates a maximum $2000 fine for offenders (Mullens and Flather 1986, A1, A7). It is conceivable that the new Vancouver law goes beyond the balance point where the benefits are exceeded by the costs. The law may create resentment among confirmed smokers, may engender disrespect and disobedience, may create animosity between supporters and opponents of the law, may create unnecessary hardship through imposition of large fines, and may generate unrealistic expectations ('The bylaw ... ensures no citizen involuntarily breathes second-hand smoke in any public place' Mullins and Flather 1986, A1, A7).

If the law is generally beneficial, it will help to control the drug problem by encouraging people to smoke less and lessening the discomfort that their smoking creates for others. If it is not beneficial it should be repealed or ignored and, in the long run, little harm will have been done. The danger in this situation is that the law will fail and, instead of being repealed, will be progressively strengthened to the point where tobacco becomes one of the enemies in the War on Drugs. In fact, there are some disturbing signs that smoking controls are already moving in a dangerous direction. Some anti-smoking groups in Canada have explicitly adopted a military vocabulary, have promulgated grossly exaggerated claims about the harm that tobacco can do, and have launched shrill ad hominem attacks on dissenters (Gilbert 1986, 1987; Chambers 1987; Hadaway and Beyerstein 1987).

When the facts are well understood, I believe, it will become obvious that drug laws must move in the opposite direction, if they are to be effective. Legal controls on illicit drugs can move into the domain of pragmatism, like most of the existing laws that control the use of tobacco and alcohol.

## Controlled Distribution

A form of legal regulation that has proved effective is limiting distribution to the least dangerous forms of drugs. For example, pure 100-per-cent alcohol is not sold in Canadian liquor outlets, with good reason – it is dangerously flammable, caustic, and poisonous. Instead alcohol is marketed in the more dilute form of beer and wine and, at a higher price, spirits that usually contain about 40 per cent alcohol. Phenacetin is no longer marketed as a headache remedy in Canada because of its connections with addiction and kidney problems, but ASA and acetaminophen are still readily available (see chapter 6).

The same kind of sensible logic would suggest that a city like New York, which has proved entirely unable to eliminate the supply of opiates by force of violence, might do better to distribute them in relatively safe forms. Such a program might allow heroin and morphine to be prescribed to addicts as well as methadone. It might allow private doctors to prescribe for patients who do not need clinic supervision. In addition, legal access to smoking opium through regular drug stores might provide a safe, cheap source for recreational opiate users and for addicts who wanted to give up needle use.

Within the War on Drugs mentality, of course, controlled distribution of opiates seems completely unrealistic. However, this is because of false assumptions that drug prohibition is effective (see chap. 2), that opiates cause physical harm (chap. 5), and that exposure to opiates causes negative addiction (chap. 8). In view of the facts that have been reviewed in earlier chapters, it seems clear that the regulated availability of relatively mild forms of opiates could not do a fraction of the harm to New York City that is done by the black market, police corruption, and unsterile drugs.

If there is an unquenchable appetite for cocaine in some localities, why not supply it in a relatively mild, safe form? Conceivably, this approach might mean putting cocaine back into a cola drink. This truly 'classic' cola drink could be marketed through drug stores (as Coca-Cola was when it contained cocaine) in areas that decided to allow cocaine distribution. Such a change would allow people who feel they must have cocaine to administer it in a mild, but effective form. Present-day drug laws essentially guarantee that cocaine is only used in expensive, often impure street mixtures designed for injection or smoking. Contemporary laws have also stimulated the development of legal but unsafe cocaine substitutes. By contrast, orally administered cocaine, used in moderation, is relatively safe (see chap. 5), in spite of the fearsome claims about it in the current media. By providing regulated purchasing and marketing system, controlled distribution can eliminate much of the demand for a black market and the attendant violence and corruption.

SOCIAL CONTROL

Social control is a powerful way of restraining human behaviour that does not involve legal procedures. Social scientists have observed that social pressures and fears of health consequences are more potent obstacles to drug consumption than legal deterrents (Solomon, Single, and Erickson 1988, 374). Various forms of social control will be discussed below.

*Righteous Indignation*

People who smoke tobacco in public places get a powerful message through no smoking signs and the disapproval of others. Every smoker who has been subjected to the righteous indignation of offended non-smokers (especially the insufferable former smokers) knows how powerful social control can be.

*Role Models*

Arnold Trebach has observed that skier Steve Podborski, by shunning
skiing events sponsored by a tobacco company a few years ago, did more
to fight drug addiction than the entire Canadian drug-enforcement
establishment. I believe Trebach's observation is astute. (See *Vancouver
Sun* 1983.)

*Creating Roles*

'Designated driver' programs have been instituted by the Keg restaurants
and more recently by a major distiller. The designated driver in any group
of restaurant patrons is offered free non-alcoholic drinks for the evening,
with the understanding that he or she will chauffeur the others safely
home. This sensible technique not only provides help in getting
celebrants home safely, but also creates a recognized social role for those
who choose not to drink. It has the approval of the Mothers Against Drunk
Driving and the Canadian Association of Chiefs of Police Research
Foundation (Parton 1985).

*Social Controls over Illicit Drug Use*

Social control could reduce problems associated with illicit drugs as well
as with alcohol and tobacco. The War on Drugs, however, partly shields
illicit drug users from this powerful influence. The drug war forces people
to conceal illicit drug use, for fear of arrest. Users of illicit drugs are
further shielded because War on Drugs propaganda persuades the public
that they are 'out of control.' If this were true, then attempts at social
control would be futile. The shield can be removed. It is not necessary to
make the use of illicit drugs a criminal act that must be concealed.
Moreover, the claim that illicit drug users are 'out of control' is baseless.
Instead of being 'out of control,' people use illicit drugs to achieve the
ends they desire (see *PM*, chaps 4, 5, 8).

   Communications media could function as an agency of social control
rather than as the purveyor of drug-war propaganda. The great persuasive
power of the media could be used to urge those who use drugs to avoid
situations where use is dangerous or socially inappropriate and to learn
safe procedures from experienced users. This approach would require

giving up the fiction that illicit drugs cannot be used by reasonable people and that users are necessarily 'out of control.' However, it would not prevent the media either from advocating non-pharmacological routes to the experiences that drug users seek, from warning users of the real pharmacological hazards of drugs, or from conveying the message that the majority of society disapproves of illicit drugs.

## The Limits of External Control

Reasonable legal regulations and social controls can reduce harmful drug use to some extent. Further reduction requires something other than external pressure, that is, ameliorating societal pressures that incite harmful drug use and helping people deal with problems that they are unable to master alone. When external controls are escalated beyond the limits of their effectiveness, they only create misery.

## Alternatives to Drug-War Propaganda

The obvious alternative to drug-war propaganda is valid information. As chapter 2 showed, propagandistic misinformation makes it impossible for people to respond intelligently to problems associated with drugs. When misinformed, even thoughtful, humane people can mistake windmills for dragons. By contrast, valid information enables people to make intelligent decisions about both social policy and their own use of drugs.

Disseminating valid information about drugs necessarily means telling the whole truth, that is, the benefits of drugs as well as their costs and dangers and the way that the majority uses them safely as well as the way that the minority does not. A truthful presentation would convey the disapproval of the majority of people about using drugs and about styles of living that are symbolized by certain drugs, but it would not cheapen this legitimate concern with bogeyman images.

Like other homilies, the simple admonition to tell the truth ignores many complexities, which will be considered next. First, what is the valid information that is likely to be useful to the public? Second, what are the barriers to providing valid information about drugs? Third, what are the best channels for introducing the truth? I hope that discussion of these complexities will show that telling the truth about drugs is possible as well as desirable.

USEFUL INFORMATION ABOUT DRUGS

Previous chapters have summarized a well-established body of information about drugs that contradicts the War on Drugs doctrine. The following summary is meant to show that this body of valid information can be summarized in a concise, non-technical way for public consumption. Some of the statements in this summary will seem outrageous in the current atmosphere. However, all parts of it are founded on solid evidence discussed in previous chapters. The information will be summarized here under two headings: current drug-related problems and practical knowledge for dealing with drugs and drug-related problems.

*Current Drug-related Problems*

Current rhetoric concentrates fearful attention on the 'drug problem' or the 'drug epidemic' – but what precisely is meant by these terms? Informing the public requires replacing the vaguely defined 'drug problem' with a description of the several problems associated with drugs. These can be summarized as follows:

1. The Problem of Conflicting Values. There is a painful conflict of values concerning drugs in society. A majority of Canadians feel that neither children nor adults should use the illegal drugs. But other Canadians and many people of other cultures ridicule this abstemious view. Drugs provoke one of the intense value conflicts that fracture contemporary Canadian society. Informing the public that there is a legitimate conflict of values at issue makes possible a search for reasonable accommodations.

2. The Problem of Addiction. Addiction can be tragic – in extreme cases it can destroy self-respect, wreck families, ruin health, cause death, and weaken society. However, the War on Drugs propaganda has distorted this problem. In Canada, the greatest danger of harmful drug addiction comes from legal drugs, primarily alcohol, tobacco, and caffeine (Smart 1983; Alexander 1985; *PM*, chap 3).

Beyond drugs, people become addicted to habits like exercise, work, gambling, love relationships, compulsive eating, and so on. Negative non-drug addictions are at least as common and certainly as dangerous as addiction to illicit drugs (Peele and Brodsky 1975; Morgan 1979; Orford 1985; Alexander and Schweighofer 1988; *PM*, chaps 3, 7).

There are few precise figures on the prevalence of drug addiction, but the indications are that there is less of it than is suggested by the War on Drugs propaganda. By all accounts the most frequent addiction is to alcohol. It is generally assumed that 5 per cent (sometimes 10 per cent) of North Americans are alcoholic, but there is no real basis for this estimate. In fact, there are authoritative claims that the figure is a serious overestimate (Cahalan 1987, 16–18). Moreover, any sort of national average is relatively unimportant. Addiction rates almost certainly vary significantly among different segments of the population.

3. The Problem of Health Hazards. Heavy drug use can cause serious health hazards, whether the user is addicted or not. A regular drinker, for example, can have cirrhosis of the liver without being addicted to alcohol. Billions of dollars are spent in Canada on health problems induced in part by drugs: lung cancer, emphysema, heart disease, cirrhosis, analgesic abuse nephrectomy, intestinal ulcers, pancreatic cancer, and so on (Lalonde 1974). The Alberta Alcohol and Drug Commission estimates that 20 per cent of patients in Alberta acute-care hospitals are there for a condition 'related to or aggravated by' their alcohol use (Skirrow 1985). As with addiction, most of these diseases are associated with legal, not illegal drugs (see Lalonde 1974).

4. Drug-related Crime. Murder, reckless driving, home and industrial accidents, family violence, robbery, rape, fighting, suicide, industrial vandalism, and so on occur disproportionately among heavy drug users, especially users of alcohol (Nurco et al. 1985). Even though the War on Drugs propaganda unquestioningly asserts that drugs *cause* drug-related crime (see Gray 1972, 1982; Quayle 1983), the assumption is gratuitous. It is possible that both heavy drug use and the misbehaviour associated with it result from another underlying cause, like desperation or alienation.

For example, whereas drunk drivers have more accidents than sober drivers, people who have drunken-driving convictions also have more offences and accidents when they are sober than the rest of the population (Walker 1986). Apparently, the same qualities that make these people drink heavily also make them likely to have accidents when they are sober. As well, the destructive tendencies of violent people might be expressed at other times if alcohol and drugs did not trigger them (Wishnie 1977; McLellan et al. 1981). The widespread belief that heroin, cocaine, and marijuana incite massive amounts of deviant behaviour is not supported by evidence on the pharmacological effects of these drugs, although there is evidence that substantial crime and deviance grow from the prohibition of these illegal drugs and the consequent black marketing and smuggling (Brecher 1972; *PM*, chaps 4, 5). Even though drugs may be only one of many causes, drug-related crime remains a serious problem. It is most 'related' to alcohol, which is closely associated with violence in North America.

5. The Problem of Cost. In view of the unanswered question about the degree to which drugs cause drug-related problems, the economic cost of drugs to society is impossible to know (Maynard, Hardman, and Whelan 1987). *Newsweek* claims a $25.8 billion annual cost to the u.s. economy due to drugs (Brecher et al. 1983). Other American estimates put the costs for theft, enforcement, and treatment for heroin alone at $10 billion per year or more (Kaplan 1983, 2–3; *Time* 1988, 16). Staggering estimates of the cost in Canada have been made public recently. An analysis in the *Globe and Mail* claims that Canadians spend $10–12 billion per year on illicit drugs, $15 billion on drug-law enforcement, $7 billion on drug-related health care, and $10 billion on economic costs, including absenteeism (Appleton and Sweeny 1987). The magnitude of some of these Canadian figures has been challenged by independent economic analysts (see Ward 1988), but there has been no public resolution of the issue. However, even if these figures are exaggerated by a factor of ten or twenty, which would seem likely given the history of War on Drugs propaganda, the real cost to the economy would be immense. Health and social costs associated with legal drugs contribute much of the cost, but illicit drugs figure prominently in the economic part of the problem because of the huge expense of futilely striving to stamp them out of existence.

6. The Problem of Normal Drug Use: A Questionable Concept. Is normal, socially acceptable drug use harmless, or is it an important drug problem? For example, what about the millions of Canadian coffee and tea consumers who ingest 60 to 400 mg of caffeine daily for several decades of their lives? Such people (I am one) continuously bathe their metabolisms in caffeine. Can this practice by totally harmless? If very large amounts of caffeine raise the likelihood of heart attacks, cancer, and other diseases, then might not small amounts do subthreshold damage that is revealed when a person is stressed or begins to age (Gilbert 1988)? There is mounting evidence of important interactive effects of caffeine, nicotine, and alcohol consumption on health (Istvan and Matarazzo 1984). Do not small problems such as these become weighty when they

are multiplied, first by dozens of commonly used drugs and then by 25 million Canadians?

Is there not a serious loss in self-esteem that comes with the realization that one needs a drug like tobacco so much that one takes it in spite of the likelihood that it will ultimately prove harmful or fatal? Many people report significantly reduced self-esteem arising from what seem to others like minor, legal dependencies. The fragility of self-esteem appears to be one of the major problems of our times. Just how much harm does 'normal' drug use do in this regard?

Finally, the amount of land used to produce drugs for normal, legal use is immense. At a time when 800 million people in the world have 'grossly inadequate food' (Graham 1986), how many millions of acres in the Third World go to produce coffee, tobacco, and tea for Canada? Surely far more than are needed to produce our cocaine, heroin, and marijuana. In Ethiopia, people starve by the thousands while the small amounts of fertile farmland and almost all the modern agricultural technology are used to produce coffee for export (Kumar 1988). Can it be more important that Canada imports a few hundred kilograms of cocaine per year than that it imports, mostly from hungry countries, over 100,000 metric *tons* of coffee and almost 20,000 metric tons of tea (United Nations Department of International Economic and Social Affairs 1988; Royal Canadian Mounted Police 1988)? How many Canadian acres that might grow food for a hungry world are used to produce tobacco or grain for Canadian whisky and beer instead, with minimal nutritional benefits? When food became strategically important during the War of 1812 and a century later during the First World War, national alcohol prohibition was enacted in Canada (Smart and Ogborne 1986) – but is not the need for food far greater now? Moreover, could not land used to produce drug crops at least lie fallow to prevent the massive wind erosion that relentlessly despoils the Canadian prairies?

I do not hope to incite war on legal drug use. The point is that a balanced perspective is required to determine which parts of the enormous consumption of drugs are the most harmful. Once the simplistic logic of the War on Drugs is discarded, it will become possible to face up to painfully difficult issues.

7. The Problem of Missing Information. A crucial drug problem is the lack of essential information. Although enough is known to inform the public better than before, much more needs to be known to enable wise

action. This problem grows from Canada's dependence on American sources for news, entertainment, and scientific data. Canadian researchers have shown that even accurate American data often do not apply in Canada, because of different patterns of drug use in the two countries (Smart 1983, 58, 60; Erickson et al. 1987). Valid policy cannot be derived from imported statistics.

*Practical Knowledge*

The list of contemporary drug problems given above is only part of the valid information about drugs that can be publicized as an alternative to drug-war propaganda. The other major part is practical knowledge drawn from science, clinical research, and everyday experience that can help people make decisions about using drugs. The following is a list of eleven well-established facts about drugs and addiction that could be useful.

1. People should treat all drugs with great caution. Legal ones, especially tobacco, alcohol, and caffeine, are at least as dangerous and addicting as illegal ones, and should be treated accordingly (*PM*, chaps 3–5). Even benign drugs like aspirin can pose serious dangers and must be used with caution (chap. 6).

2. Any negative addiction is a sign of a serious underlying problem that requires attention (chap. 8). However, the addiction itself is only a way of adapting to the problem – therefore forcing a person out of an addiction prematurely may do more harm than good.

3. If a person becomes negatively addicted, it should not be a cause for despair or panic, because many people get over serious negative addictions, including addictions to tobacco, alcohol, cocaine, and heroin. It is not true that 'once and addict, always an addict' (chaps 8, 9).

4. Serious addictions that do not involve drugs, such as addictions to gambling, sex, or television, are no less destructive than drug addictions and pose a greater threat, since they are more prevalent (Alexander and Schweighofer 1988; *PM*, chap. 3, 7).

5. At the same time, dependence and harmless positive addictions occur in almost everybody's life. Even if they involve illegal drugs they may continue indefinitely without cause for alarm, although they occasionally change into negative addictions (chap. 3).

6. If drug problems arise, trusted friends are the most likely source of help. In most cases, professional treatment adds little to the natural

maturing process and the support provided by friends and relatives (chap. 2).

7. There is no need to be seriously concerned over experimental or casual drug use in oneself or others, even if illicit drugs are involved. Negative addictions usually do not develop in casual users (chaps 3–6).

8. Recreational use of licit and illicit drugs provides a stimulating, relaxing, sexy, enlightening, and friendly experience for many people (Huxley 1963; *PM*, chap. 3). Moderate use of drugs may confer tangible benefits as well. There is good evidence in the medical literature that moderate use of alcohol is associated with lowered risk of myocardial infarction, improved quality of life in the elderly, and beneficial stress relief (Turner, Bennett, and Hernandez 1981).

9. There are good alternatives to using drugs for pleasure and there are serious dangers of arrest and imprisonment associated with all the illegal drugs even when their use is beneficial (chap. 1).

10. Although experts can provide general information, there are far too many new drugs and drug combinations for experts to know much about their individual effects now or in the near future. People who experiment with drugs are essentially on their own.

11. All information about drugs broadcast on television and through the other media must be evaluated sceptically, for most of it is one-sided, distorted, or simply false (chap. 2).

### BARRIERS TO VALID INFORMATION ABOUT DRUGS

Canadians normally assume that people behave most intelligently when they are well-informed. Therefore, efforts are made to provide as much information as possible about new, potentially dangerous technology. This approach seems natural for hazardous products like automobiles, power tools, gunpowder, household chemicals, and computers. Why then does society fear the truth about drugs, in the face of a cherished tradition of intellectual freedom?

### Propaganda-induced Fear

War propaganda is designed not only to generate fear of the enemy but also to generate distrust of *the truth itself*. Truth has been called the 'first casualty' of war (Knightly 1982). In wartime, news reporting and scientific research come under direct government control. Unwanted facts are seen as weakening the resolve and ruthlessness that are required to achieve victory. Questioning authority on the essential issues is seen as reckless. The War on Drugs endlessly proclaims that illicit drugs are so powerful that people lose control if they experiment with them. Telling people truths about drugs that contradict this doctrine might encourage them to experiment, and thus condemn them to a horrible fate, if the doctrine were in fact true. Thus, propaganda incites fear of valid information.

## Fear of Drug Education

People who fear the truth about drugs sometimes refer to studies that appear to show that drug-education programs based on providing valid information in the schools have increased drug use among students. However, the finding that drug-education programs increase drug use is by no means universal. Some studies of drug-education programs have found that they produce decreases, rather than increases, in student drug use depending on the type of program and on the pre-program drug-use patterns of the students (Blum et al. 1978; Schaps et al. 1980; Hanson 1982).

More important, the simple observation that drug education provokes drug use in some children provides no valid argument against drug education. Normally, increased experimentation would be considered an indication that a course in school had effectively stimulated students' interest and that students would have been taught to experiment safely and would benefit from the experience. Of course, this normal reasoning violates the War on Drugs mentality, which insists that there is no such thing as safe experimentation with drugs. However, as previous chapters have shown, the great majority of North Americans who experiment with drugs do not suffer any adverse consequences.

It is true that children who have their first drug experiences before age fifteen are more likely to have later drug and alcohol problems than are children whose first use occurred later or not at all (Robins and Przybeck 1985). However, this fact does not prove that youthful experimentation stimulated by drug education would cause harm to most children. Those who experiment at an age when experimentation is strictly proscribed also tend to have problems with drunkenness, school discipline, depression, stealing, vandalism, family antisocial behaviour, and so on (Robins and

Przybeck 1985). Naturally, children with such backgrounds are more likely to get into trouble later on, but there is no basis to conclude that their early drug use per se is the cause of these later problems, or that such problems are likely to be instigated by educated experimentation with drugs.

## Insufficient Research as a Basis for Withholding Information

There is another argument for fearing the truth about drugs. It is sometimes argued that more research must be undertaken before any really authoritative conclusions can be publicized. This argument claims that scientists and scholars must be silent until they are positive. Such intellectual timidity is unconscionable. This century abounds in technology that is dangerous and largely untried. Making intelligent use of the available information is people's best hope for coping. If scholars shrink from supplying this information, they abdicate their best opportunity to help.

## HOW CAN THE TRUTH BEST BE INTRODUCED?

War on Drugs propaganda is a distortion of the truth, but the fear it has generated is genuine and must be given consideration. Because of this fear, the truth about drugs cannot be announced precipitously, but must be allowed to emerge from hiding a little at a time. Two of the gateways through which the truth can be cautiously admitted are schools and homes, but the crucial portal is the mass media.

## Schools

Universities provide a traditional haven for free discussion, under the protection of 'academic freedom.' University courses often expose students to facts that they find shockingly dissonant with conventional wisdom. Nineteen years of teaching courses on addiction at Simon Fraser University have served me as a personal experiment on how people respond to valid information about drugs. My lectures have been based on the standard academic literature in psychology, history, medicine, and sociology. Inevitably, much of the information I present flies in the face of the opinions that students have formed earlier.

I have found that the majority of students are shocked by basic facts about drugs that normally do not reach them, and many change their views dramatically. Many who change feel appalled at the smoke-screen of misinformation that has previously clouded the issue for them. Many students argue against the information that I introduce to them, but even these come to acknowledge that the issue is more complex than they had thought.

I cannot believe that students in my courses become addicted or otherwise depraved as a result of being exposed to new ideas. Arnold Trebach (1987) has systematically investigated the effects of his own, similar university courses. Responses to his questionnaires indicated that most of his students felt their personal drug use or non-use was unaffected by his course. Some did report an effect, though: 2.8 per cent reported increased drug use and 11.3 per cent reported decreased use. In two cases, Trebach's course, in conjunction with some personal advice, seems to have helped students control serious drug problems.

I do not mean to claim that university courses like mine and Trebach's convert all students who attend. My course enrolments are high, but some students recoil. Some display powerful passive resistance, complaining bitterly about being 'brainwashed' or 'only given one side of the issue.'

Greater than the individual barriers of resistant students are those barriers imposed by the War on Drugs mentality on the universities. Students often joke about the possibility of a 'laboratory course,' in which they would take measured doses of drugs. Why does this possibility seem incongruous? Laboratory courses effectively prepare students to handle other dangerous but useful things including toxic chemicals, electricity, and bacteria. I am not suggesting anything unusual, but rather something normal – supervised 'hands-on' experience and supervised experimentation. Somehow, however, learning methods that are conventional in other areas seem out of the question with drugs. This barrier is a logical consequence of the distortions that serve to justify the War on Drugs, particularly those concerning the toxicity of illegal drugs and the cause of negative addiction. Until this barrier is removed, the truth about drugs remains interdicted, and higher education is, to that extent, hobbled by the War on Drugs.

Public schools are far more constrained than are universities by the War on Drugs mentality. Canadian drug educators have told me that many apparently innocuous scientific facts about drugs are *verboten* in the class-room. In some schools, drug educators are not allowed to acknowledge the existence of illicit drugs by asking the children questions about them. Children tell their parents, fearful parents tell principals, and principals are passionately devoted to keeping their schools out of trouble. The school-yard gate is closed to valid information about drugs, but wide open to War on Drugs propaganda.

Schools are more than information dispensaries. They are also agencies of social control. This role is natural and proper. Schools should teach community standards about drugs. But these efforts need not preclude the truth. The effectiveness of schools as agencies of social control erode when schools sacrifice their credibility by dispensing propaganda and banning valid information.

*Homes*

Parents can tell their children the whole truth about many sensitive topics, including drugs, and children need exposure to their parents' experience of the world in order to be equipped for its challenges. Many parents have personal experiences with illicit drugs that are apt to be more useful to their children than the distorted generalizations of the War on Drugs. Moreover, most parents are best qualified to judge how and when to introduce complex ideas to their children so they are most likely to be understood. However, there are blocks against imparting this knowledge. In an age of uncertainty, parents may lack the confidence to reveal their personal experience. Somehow professionals seem better qualified to talk about drugs. Parents may find it hard to own up to behaviour that is condemned by drug-war propaganda, even though they know that it distorts reality.

*Mass Media*

The mass media are powerful determinants of public opinion. But, with the partial exception of CBC Radio, the Canadian media seem committed to the War on Drugs mentality. Obviously, the War on Drugs cannot end until they change their line. Herman and Chomsky (1988) have argued that the mass media are firmly controlled by large corporations and government and will not stray from official policy. Therefore, they propose that people wishing to provide something other than propaganda must develop their own media, such as community radio and television stations. It may be, however, that this perception of the media is too pessimistic, and that change can be expected in cases where official views on a particular topic have proved bankrupt. Hints of possible change in the media treatment of drugs are appearing in the newspapers, if only in the comics. Recent strips of Doonesbury, Bloom County, Kudzu, and Tank MacNamara illustrate that it is becoming possible at least to laugh at the War on Drugs in the news media.

*Good and Bad Myths*

In this analysis, I have not forgotten that parents, educators, and the media sometimes function as purveyors of society's vital myths, rather than questing after the Holy Grail of absolute truth. Absolute truth is not the issue here. The myths conveyed by drug propaganda need to be discarded not simply because they are untrue, but because they are harmful.

## Alternatives to War on Drugs Treatment

Finding alternatives to prohibition and propaganda can undo some of the harm caused by the War on Drugs, but cannot ameliorate the terrible problems of addiction and violence that instigated it. Although treatment has proved ineffective, it cannot simply be abandoned without replacement.

Four types of alternatives to existing drug treatment are discussed in this section. These are medical dispensation of prohibited drugs, non-professional help for addicts, expansion of the involvement of social-science professionals in areas where they are uniquely valuable, and social change to prevent drug addiction and other forms of deviance from developing.

### MEDICAL DISPENSATION OF DRUGS TO ADDICTS

Once the War on Drugs mentality abates, many regions will probably seek ways to provide adequate supplies of prohibited drugs to long-term addicts. Such policies will prevent needless suffering and avoid the depradations of a black market. In Canada, physicians are the most likely agents for supplying needed drugs to addicted people, but there is an impediment to their serving in this capacity. Current drug-war doctrine depicts addicts as criminal geniuses, capable of tricking naïve physicians into prescribing excessive quantities of drugs that the addicts then peddle to non-addicted customers (see Goldman 1987). However, this doctrine contradicts history and current experience. Where doctors prescribe narcotics to addicts, they generally provide a valuable service both to society and to the addicts involved (O'Donnell 1969, cited in Brecher 1972, chap. 13; Waldorf, Orlick, and Reinarman 1974; Trebach 1982; Fazey, unpublished; *PM*, chap. 2). I have learned after working closely with heroin addicts and their physicians for nearly two decades that addicts are seldom geniuses and physicians are seldom simpletons. Moreover, modern recording systems make it easy to detect and control the occasional foolish doctor.

The capability of physicians to prescribe for addicts could be enhanced with a clear definition of their role and a guarantee that they would not be subject to harsh penalties if their medical judgment in some cases contravened community expectations. These are the normal conditions of medical practice outside of the drug-war zone.

## NON-PROFESSIONAL HELP FOR ADDICTS

A second alternative to the expensive, ineffective, and sometimes harmful professional treatment that addicted people receive is non-professional help. This section will describe examples of effective help for addicts from communities and non-professional organizations. It will also discuss why non-professional help is as effective as it is and some steps towards deprofessionalizing help.

### Community Help

The best example that I have found of an effective community response to addiction comes from the Indian reserve at Alkalai Lake in British Columbia. There, a mixture of local initiatives and locally controlled professional interventions spanning the period from the early 1970s to the present have revitalized a community where alcoholism, violence, child abuse, sexual abuse, accidents, and illness had been rampant. Alcoholism and violence have dwindled from near universal problems to rarities (Hodgson 1987; M. Wright, personal communication, 1988).

The people of Alkalai Lake approached their alcoholism problem on many levels. These included showering social approval on people who gave up drinking; providing a house for band members who decided to continue their schooling; reintroducing traditional spiritual practices such as sweat lodges; reintroducing the band's language through the schools; withholding the welfare cheques of alcoholics and instead issuing vouchers that could not be exchanged for alcohol; offering petty offenders a choice between accepting treatment for alcoholism and facing legal charges; laying charges against bootleggers; creating employment by opening a local logging operation and a store on the reserve; organizing support groups for victims of physical and sexual abuse; caring for the families and fixing up the homes of people who left the reserve for treatment; and establishing AA groups and social-skills training programs on the reserve. All of these efforts were embedded in a matrix of native spiritualism and traditionalism that provided an explanation for what was happening in familiar terms. Professionals and law-enforcement officers were involved, but they were under the control of the band, rather than representing autonomous, external institutions.

Similar community efforts on reserves at Tache and Anahim Lake, BC, have produced equally dramatic results, although the programs are too new to evaluate adequately. The Tache program is only three years old and the Anaheim Lake program is less than a year old. These programs have made less use of external professional treatment institutes and more use of native counsellors on the reserve (Hodgson 1987).

## Non-professional Institutions

Non-professional institutions can offer sensible, effective help to addicted people. For example, a Toronto group called 'Beat the Street' has set out to teach literacy to street people, particularly prostitutes and drug addicts. In a world of signs, maps, and computers, millions of illiterate Canadians are crippled and therefore prey to poverty, despair, and escapism through drugs and crime. It seems inescapable that effective literacy training will create alternatives to destructive drug use (and other forms of social deviance) for some of these street people. By contrast, conventional therapists struggle to make people quit drugs when their illiteracy blocks any real integration. Unfortunately, 'Beat the Street' appears to be desperately underfunded (CBC Radio, 17 Nov. 1985).

Another non-professional institution is Rehabilitation of Metropolitan Addicts (ROMA ) in England. ROMA's concept is that drugs are not really at the heart of addicts' problems. Rather, addicts need help in getting jobs, caring for their families, maintaining friendships outside of the criminal subculture, and so forth. ROMA offers such help in a hostel for addicts in London. Given support, respect, and guidance (when requested), addicts pay their rent, hold jobs, develop relationships, and, if they feel they can, stop using drugs.

This program flourished in London in the 1960s and early 1970s because addicts were allowed to get the drugs they needed, including heroin and cocaine, through legal prescriptions (Trebach 1982). When the drug supply was largely restricted to oral methadone by new policies in the 1970s, many addicts could not longer meet ROMA's requirement that residents not use illegal drugs. However, ROMA still functions successfully with residents who can function on the drugs that are legally available. It seems obvious, however, that the effectiveness of ROMA is limited by the new British War on Drugs mentality that prevents many seriously addicted people from obtaining drugs legally. However, a philosophy similar to ROMA's has been adopted by some professional treatment institutions in Britain. Such treatment programs do not segregate addicts in separate facilities or make their addiction the focus of attention. Instead, attention is directed to the addicts' needs for housing, employment, training, and so on, and they are not necessarily required to give up drug use to receive the services they need (Spurgeon and Black 1987).

'Portage' in Montreal is a Canadian non-professional 'therapeutic community' that has similarities to therapeutic communities around the world (Ferrier 1985). Portage uses a highly structured system of discipline and status. Addicts are harassed and intimidated into conformity. Their feelings are expressed during abrasive group therapy sessions that all residents must attend. Although this rough approach limits membership, Portage and similar institutions have been life-savers for many addicted people. There have been many controversies around therapeutic communities in other places, especially Synanon in California and Le Patriarche in France, for they occupy a strange border zone between community and cult, and between treatment and ideology. Their status in the future is hard to predict.

The best known of the non-professional institutions is Alcoholics Anonymous, or 'AA.' AA has numerous spin-off organizations including Narcotics Anonymous, Cocaine Anonymous, Overeaters Anonymous, and even Emotions Anonymous and Sexaholics Anonymous. All these groups employ a similar rigid, semi-religious philosophy (the 'twelve steps') and promulgate a disease model of addiction that is not acceptable to some addicted people. But for countless others these groups have provided crucial help. There are no statistical demonstrations of the efficacy of AA. Moreover, its anonymity makes it almost impossible to design research that could provide such a demonstration (Glaser and Ogborne 1982). None the less, no one can reasonably ignore the ubiquitous personal testimonials of 'recovering alcoholics' who testify that AA literally saved their lives.

Unfortunately, the distinction between Alcoholics Anonymous and professional treatment has been blurred in recent years. After many years of denying the effectiveness of AA, many therapeutic and enforcement bureaucracies have now taken it upon themselves to force people into joining. They often withhold individual therapy or social services until people join AA. Obviously, forcing people into therapy groups against their will has little to do with nurturing the innate healing process, with establishing a warm relationship, or with helping people to see their problems as ordinary solvable ones rather than pharmacological diseases. The traditional AA doctrine wisely stated that the choice to join must come from within (Alcoholics Anonymous World Services, Inc. 1976, 564), but AA now accepts people who have been required by outside agencies to attend (Alcoholics Anonymous 1987). Whereas it is difficult to see how forcing people into AA could help them, it is easy to see how it could do harm. Only certain types of alcoholic are able to benefit from AA – middle- and upper-class people with relatively stable lives before becoming alcoholic and a religious, guilt-motivated world-view (Ogborne and Glaser 1981). Other people not only do not benefit from AA, but are frequently harmed by the experience (Glaser and Ogborne 1982).

## Why Non-professional Help Works

Chapter 2 showed that people who are treated for addiction by conventional professional psychotherapy recover no faster than those who are not treated. This pattern can be seen as an indictment of professional treatment, but may be better understood as an indication of the success of what is sometimes called the 'natural healing process.' Although recovery without extensive professional intervention is sometimes called 'spontaneous recovery' by professionals, such recoveries often require great personal effort and patience, as well as intelligent, creative help from other people. This natural healing process is a fundamental, inevitable thrust of human life that requires no external instigation, and has been observed in many types of mental patients (Ansbacher and Ansbacher 1956; Mahoney 1985). Quantitative research has documented the importance of the natural healing process in successful psychotherapy. The single most important contributor to success in psychotherapy is the strength of the client's motivation to change. The second most important factor is a warm, trusting relationship between client and therapist. By contrast, the particular techniques that a therapist learns in professional training make little or no difference (Bergin and Lambert 1989, 80; Stiles, Shapiro, and Elliot 1986).

Obviously, non-professional helpers have as much access as professionals to the addicted person's motivation for success and are just as able to establish a warm relationship. Moreover, non-professionals are apt to be more available, affordable, and interested than professionals. Non-professionals do not know the elaborate techniques used by some professionals, but these have little measurable importance.

The most important contributor to success, the patient's motivation, is often crushed in professional treatment because professional treatment agencies are trapped in the War on Drugs mentality. For example, I have rarely, if ever, heard patients in British Columbia methadone treatment centres express a wish to stop using methadone. The reason, I believe, is that BC methadone patients are incessantly urged, or forced, to quit using methadone before they are ready. The War on Drugs mentality assumes that patients must be forced to quit. This attitude subverts the patients' all-important healing motives. Clients are too concerned with getting the methadone they need from their clinic to be able to focus on more fundamental problems. In contrast, Dutch professionals involved in methadone treatment have described the greatest eagerness of their patients to withdraw from methadone (Noorlander 1987). I have seen this first-hand at a treatment centre for heroin addicts in Rotterdam. The patients in the centre were under no great pressure to quit heroin use and none at all to quit methadone. Yet they expressed great concern about getting off methadone and other drugs as soon as possible.

The adaptive model of drug addiction (*PM*, chap. 8) also helps explain why non-professional help can be so powerful. More than anything else, addicted people need help in the crucial task of achieving psychosocial integration. Such help is not merely palliative, but is fundamentally important, because sustained integration failure is the essential reason that people become addicted in the first place.

Reliance on non-professional help may seem naïve to those who have seen severely addicted patients in crisis situations, which may require immediate professional intervention in the form of organic treatment, sedation, or restraint. But most addicted people are not in this kind of condition. Most live empty, dreary lives without such crises. Many draw away from their addictions without any professional intervention, much less the dramatic interventions necessary in crisis cases.

This is not to say that non-professional help can cure drug addictions overnight, solely through good will and common sense. By the time addictive problems are recognized, the underlying problems are probably severe and a great deal of time, effort, and insight are required. However, a caring, well-informed friend may well do more for an addicted person than a professional specialist.

## Legal Obstacles to Non-professional Help

Perhaps the greatest virtue of non-professional institutions is that they do not have a legal monopoly. If they are not effective, they must change, or see their clients disappear. Professional therapists are not subject to this discipline, because their professional organizations work diligently to establish legal monopolies that eliminate competition, and often force addicts into their treatment whether it works or not. In this way they impose themselves and reduce the opportunity for non-professional help to take place.

For example, the British Columbia Psychologists Act reserves the use of the title 'Psychologist' to people who are members of the BC Psychological Association and who have passed a professional accreditation examination. The effect of this law is that anyone hired as a psychologist within the province must fit a particular professional mould, defined by the membership requirements of the professional association and by the accreditation examination. If addicted people seek help from a psychologist, but find that psychologists who fit the professional mould cannot help them, they have no alternative – no other kind of psychologists can legally practise in British Columbia. Patients are free to seek out practitioners who are not psychologists, but their services are not provided under the provincial medical insurance plan, whereas the services of a psychologist are covered by 'extended benefits' packages, to a limited extent. (Services of a psychiatrist are covered by BC medical insurance, but these, too, are professionally defined and regulated.) Moreover, the words psychologist and psychiatrist carry specific meanings that people understand. Titles that are not protected by professionalizing legislation, like 'Gestalt therapist' or 'Jungian Counselor,' do not sound as reputable.

If the treatment provided by BC Psychological Association-type psychologists were demonstrably better than help provided by friends from the addict's community or by non-professional institutions, then this legal monopoly might be justified. However, there is no body of evidence showing that professional psychologists offer a superior service. I believe legislation like the Psychologists Act should be revised. Rather than defending a legal monopoly on psychological treatment of addicted people, psychologists might better serve society by encouraging and empowering non-professional helpers. This is not an attempt to put my fellow psychologists out of work. Those who can help people will always be in demand. They need no legal monopoly. The rest of us psychologists have other important work to do. My fear is that psychologists and their professional associations may be seduced by the promise of wealth and security into an unwholesome involvement in the War on Drugs.

REDIRECTION OF PROFESSIONAL EFFORTS

Whereas the present professionalized treatment system is ineffective and self serving, there is much that professionals such as psychologists can do to ameliorate drug-related problems.

*Identifying Successful Treatment*

The professional monopoly on treatment could be replaced by a professional system for identifying truly effective practitioners and types of intervention to the public. Some therapists and organizations, whether professionally trained or not, can help addicts. Obviously, such therapists and organizations deserve recognition. Psychologists and other professionals have the skills to identify effective therapists and organizations and to publicize them.

*Handling Special Cases*

There are special cases where professional psychotherapists are needed. Professional psychiatrists and psychologists have the confidence and training to undertake extensive personality rebuilding where it is needed and where there is time and money enough to support the process. This kind of professional help may be indispensible for people who have been scarred by child abuse and other horrors that go beyond the patience of most non-professionals to unravel. Professionals can also provide help to addicted people who require professional standards of confidentiality or who are too isolated to obtain effective support from their friends and community.

Sometimes addiction originates in the family itself (Alexander and Dibb 1975; Stanton, Todd, and Associates 1982), and it may be vital to turn to a professional who has the authority to try to change the relationships of an entire family, as well as the habits of the addict, although evaluation studies of family therapy have not, in my opinion, yet provided adequate evidence that it works well in cases of drug addiction.

*'Minor Problems'*

Professional psychotherapy tends to be effective in helping people deal with relatively minor problems that they have failed to solve on their own, including fears, compulsions, school problems, and lack of assertiveness. Such problems are far less serious than negative addiction, but there is an important relationship between them and negative addiction. People who fail in solving relatively minor problems become vulnerable to addiction and other sorts of deviance if the minor problems interfere with their achievement of psychosocial integration (*PM*, chap. 8). Therefore, professional psychotherapists have a crucial role to play with troubled people in preventing the development of addiction.

*Aiding the Natural Healing Process*

Professional 'community psychologists' sometimes provide short, practical training programs to concerned community members to enhance their ability to prevent drug problems and help people deal with them if they recur (Rappaport 1976). Other professionals attempt to analyse the reactions of community organizations to drug problems and to formulate principles that lead consistently to success (Dorn, Jones, and South 1988). Still other professionals have put themselves at the service of an indigenous community movement, as in Alkalai Lake. These professional interventions support the natural healing process. There is a risk, however, that professional status can intimidate community amateurs into merely imitating professional techniques, rather than following their own inclinations. It may require an unusual sensitivity for a professional to support or analyse a naturally occurring social process without inadvertently gaining control over it and thereby destroying its essential value.

SOCIAL CHANGES

I believe that the greatest opportunities to ameliorate drug problems do not lie in attempting to treat afflicted individuals, but in attempting to change society in order to lessen the frequency of negative addiction and other forms of deviance. Serious drug problems arise in people who have difficulty achieving or maintaining integration. Therefore, the Canadian thinkers whose work is most relevant to drug addiction are those who are concerned with helping people with the difficult task of attaining psychosocial integration. An admirable group of scholars, some of whose work is cited below, is seeking ways to use institutions like schools and businesses to engender a sense of confidence and power in people.

This work, obviously, has implications beyond drug problems. In the words of one educator: 'We will not solve our problems with intoxicants unless we change the conditions in which we live and grow, but there are also more important reasons for making these changes. The same conditions that make populations susceptible to the types of self defeating behaviours briefly described here also create susceptibility to authoritarian cults and the appeal of apocalyptic events and mortal violence ... There is a hunger for clear solutions, a sense of power and certainty, and it is being filled by simple-minded visions based on the thrill of power without perspective ... There will be no return from that ultimate self-defeating behavior' (Low 1982, 331).

Since empowering people is not part of the tradition of most bureaucracies, ingenious innovations have been devised to transform institutions to make them serve this vital function (see Gibbons 1974;

Low 1978, 1982; Canadian Intramural Recreation Association 1985; Skirrow 1985).

The Canadian Intramural Recreation Association (CIRA) had undertaken a major program to expand participation in intramural sports in Canada. Recognizing that sports contribute powerfully to the development of health, confidence, and competence, CIRA is addressing the problem that the traditional system of competitive athletics eventually excludes, even from intramurals, the majority of school-children who cannot perform at superior levels. There isn't time for physical-education teachers to organize enough sports programs for all students. CIRA's program is a training program for teachers and students designed to develop student leaders who will organize intramural sports that de-emphasize competition and focus attention on maximum participation, exercise, and fun (CIRA 1985). Since its introduction in 1985 this program has been highly successful in increasing student participation in both leadership and sports. Over a thousand Canadian schools are participating. Although there is no specific attention to drugs in this program, its potential for reducing drug addiction is clear. Successful participation in sports is a major aid in achieving psychosocial integration for many young people.

The most comprehensive program of which I am aware is that undertaken by the Alberta Alcohol and Drug Abuse Commission (AADAC) to reduce problem drinking among adolescents. This program starts with the assumption that adolescent drinking can be normal and healthy, and is in any case unavoidable. Within this framework, efforts are made to reduce the amount of alcohol consumed, the age of onset of drinking, and the problems that arise (Skirrow 1985). AADAC produced a series of media presentations including high-quality radio and television messages, and a magazine distributed free to teenagers. These materials said little specifically about alcohol. Rather, they emphasized awareness of the normalcy of growing independence during adolescence, of the relationships between normal adolescent development and alcohol use, of the way adolescent development is influenced by peers, of ways to socialize and communicate that do not involve alcohol, and of the facilities available through AADAC. In addition to media advertising, AADAC provided a co-ordinated program of local community projects and educational materials for schools.

This approach had a measurable effect on Alberta teenagers. Over a two-year period from 1981 to 1983, during which a sample of Alberta adolescents was compared with a sample of Manitoba adolescents, Alberta adolescents showed greater declines in drinking, especially among 12- to 13-year-olds, less drinking in unsupervised settings, and less trouble with police (Skirrow 1985). Follow-up data indicated continued measurable benefits of the program until 1986 (Thompson, Skirrow, and Nutter 1987). However, many of the gains lessened in 1987, a change that coincided with the phasing-out of the radio and television campaign in 1986 for budgetary reasons (Thompson 1988). In the electronic age, the media may be essential in any large-scale effort to influence people.

*Health Promotion*

Harmful use of drugs is not entirely an individual problem. Healthy bodies and socially acceptable behaviour come naturally to people who live in physically and emotionally wholesome surroundings, and are difficult to achieve for those who do not. These conclusions were set forth by the First International Conference on Health Promotion in Industrialized Countries, held in Ottawa late in 1986. This conference, sponsored by the World Health Organization, Health and Welfare Canada, and the Canadian Public Health Association, was based on the proposition that the essential requirements for health (where 'health' is taken to include not becoming addicted to drugs) include peace, shelter, food, income, a stable ecosystem, sustainable resources, social justice, and equity (MacLennan 1986).

Of course, it is difficult to meet these requirements. However, from this point of view, drug addiction and numerous other health problems could at least be reduced by diverting the billions of dollars wasted on the War on Drugs to social changes that promote health and therefore make people less likely to over-use drugs. Such programs would include teaching literacy, providing shelter for homeless juveniles, providing school lunches for children who are too hungry to learn, settling the land-claims cases that stultify the development of many native communities, finding meaningful work opportunities for teenagers, and supporting community economic development.

This is a health concept with deep Canadian roots. A key document in the world literature on this topic, *A New Perspective on the Health of*

*Canadians*, was written by Marc Lalonde (1974) when he was minister of health. An update of this concept was presented to the recent health-promotion conference by Jake Epp, current minister of health and welfare (Epp 1986). Canada was among the first countries to establish a health-promotion directorate within the government.

Although health promotion is a strongly Canadian concept, it is often ignored in Canada. The day that this paragraph was being written, the *Vancouver Sun* reported that the city of Vancouver had turned down a motion to provide funds for lunches in Vancouver schools, even though an estimated six hundred children go to school hungry every day in Vancouver (Cox 1988). Funding for Vancouver school lunches has also been turned down by the provincial and federal governments, apparently on grounds that the responsibility should be taken by another level of government, or by the parents. Meanwhile, the six hundred children are left with their hunger pains. The probability that they will learn what they need to know to achieve psychosocial integration is almost inevitably diminished. Correspondingly, the probability that they will turn to deviance or negative addiction as a substitute is increased. It is a bizarre ramification of the War on Drugs mentality that governments can quibble over the petty cost of school lunches for a few hundred children while wasting millions of dollars on anti-drug propaganda.

A FINAL QUESTION

Is it naïve to approach the dreaded scourge of drug addiction with such mundane tools as local ordinances, free dissemination of information, and school lunches? I think not. The true naïveté is the drug warriors' faith in simple, coercive solutions to deep social problems. The alternatives proposed here address what is superficially called the 'drug problem' at a greater depth.

People cannot be forced to behave with decorum and moderation in a chaotic, inhospitable world. Therefore, the most important action that government can take to quell drug problems is to govern well, in the interest of all the people. Likewise, the most important action parents can take is to satisfy the important needs of their children, their community, and themselves. Bureaucratic controls like drug-law enforcement and drug treatment can be of help if they are locally sponsored and mild in their application. Propaganda cannot help at all.

This analysis leaves a final, essential question unanswered: If the arguments against the War on Drugs and for these alternatives are valid, why were such alternatives not adopted long ago? It is my belief that the War on Drugs cannot be ended until this final question is confronted. I believe that dealing with this question requires an analysis of the deepest motives of those who carry out the War on Drugs, those who sanction it by acquiescing to its violence and illogic, and those who resist it by using the forbidden substances. Such a psychological analysis is obviously not a minor undertaking, but it will be attempted, with some trepidation, in the final chapter of this book.

# 10 Why the War on Drugs continues and how it can end

The first nine chapters of this book have developed four theses: (1) Canada is an active participant in a genuine war directed against drug users and merchants; (2) this War on Drugs is a cruel and costly failure; (3) much of the popular wisdom that is used to justify the War on Drugs to the public is unsubstantiated or wrong; and (4) better ways to respond to drug-related problems are available. But these four theses inevitably prompt a final question: Why does this futile crusade continue in spite of all reason?

The thesis of this final chapter is that the War on Drugs persists because drugs have come to symbolize deep psychological needs, conflicts, and fears for much of society. In other words, the War on Drugs is not fundamentally about drugs. I hope that unmasking the needs, conflicts, and fears that underlie the drug war will lessen its credibility and hasten its end.

This is a psychological rather than a political analysis. Although there is little doubt that the drug war is used as a means of achieving political goals by inflaming the public, I do not think this fact can be used to explain its existence. In my way of thinking, it is more fully explained in terms of fears and conflicts that, at this time in history, make people vulnerable to those who set out to inflame them against illicit drugs and drug users. It is this primary cause, the psychological vulnerability, that I hope to explain in this chapter. To elucidate the motives that underlie the drug war it is first necessary to classify people into groups of participants, then to explore the motives of each, and finally to show that these motives can be satisfied in ways that do not necessarily entail a War on Drugs.

## Combatants in the War on Drugs

DRUG WARRIORS

The War on Drugs is supported, for the most part, by earnest, intelligent people. They can be called 'drug warriors' without insult because they openly and conscientiously support warlike measures against drug users and suppliers. Drug warriors whom I know personally include worried parents, former drug addicts and their spouses, physicians, psychotherapists, narcotics policemen, and some concerned citizens who have no personal experience with illicit drugs or drug problems. Proponents of the War on Drugs are sometimes depicted as twisted puritans, tormented by other people's innocent pleasures. However, most of those who carry out the drug war do not fit this caricature. Depicting them thus is no more useful than depicting all people who use prohibited drugs as 'drug abusers.'

There must be hidden reasons for the enduring zeal of the drug warriors, because the obvious explanations are not adequate. Their zeal cannot come from a rational analysis because, as the earlier chapters of this book have shown, the drug war does not stand up to rational analysis. Moreover, their enthusiasm for the drug war does not have a rational feel to it, but feels more like a dogmatic foreclosure of reason. Similarly, their enthusiasm cannot be explained by the ubiquitous propaganda. People are not fooled by propaganda for very long. Otherwise, totalitarian regimes that control state media would never fall. Similarly, vested interests cannot fully explain the persistent zeal of the drug warriors. Many drug warriors do not belong to groups that profit from the drug war. The deeper sources of the drug warrior's zeal will be discussed below.

RESISTERS

Throughout the long history of the War on Drugs, there have been millions of people who have used illicit drugs in defiance of it. Although drug warriors often characterize these people as drug abusers or addicts, these descriptions are unwarranted. Most resisters are not addicted or likely to become addicted. Their only abuse is defiance of the drug war. Greed is not their primary motive – most drug users are not traffickers except in the special inclusive way that the term is defined in the drug laws. These people will be called 'resisters' in this chapter, because they knowingly violate a strong prohibition of their society, often at great risk.

Recently, a substantial number of academics, jurists, doctors, businessmen, politicians, and other concerned citizens have joined the resistance to the War on Drugs. These new resisters generally have little interest in personal drug use, but find themselves nevertheless appalled by the War on Drugs. I consider myself one of this group.

OTHER PARTICIPANTS

Although drug warriors and resisters constitute the bulk of the cast in the drug-war drama, several other groups must be considered to complete the list.

*Villains*

To clarify the picture of the majority of drug warriors and resisters, I have omitted the small number of genuine villains – hypocrites, killers, and torturers – who also carry out or resist the drug war. The cruelties of such people are manifestations of their personal torments. By contrast, the motives of the larger numbers of drug warriors and resisters whom I have learned to know over the past nineteen years are more ordinary and constructive. Of course, each side in the drug war identifies the other side with its villains rather than with its more typical members, but this contumely must be ignored if the psychology of the war is to be understood.

*Double-Standard Bearers*

Some people are *both* drug warriors and drug users. Elvis Presley, for example, was negatively addicted to prescription drugs that he obtained quasi-legally through his private physician. None the less, one of Elvis's prized possessions was a letter from U.S. president Richard Nixon, naming him as a special agent in the War on Drugs (Goldman 1981). People who are negatively addicted to drugs tend often to support war measures against drugs other than their own drug of choice, and sometimes against their own drugs as well. Alcoholism is a major occupational hazard among narcotics police. I have met some regular marijuana users who applaud stringent War on Drugs measures against cocaine.

*Neutrals*

Finally, the majority of people have no interest in the War on Drugs, and therefore play only a small role in it individually. These people, quite reasonably, concern themselves with more important issues. They have little wish either to protect their own right to use illicit drugs or to restrict others. However, neutrals cannot escape wars. The drug war's expense deprives the neutrals economically, while its cruelty undermines the civility of their society. Moreover, both drug warriors and resisters court them assiduously. At this time in history, neutrals are much more likely to be moved by the powerful images of the drug warriors. Because of their great numbers, even half-hearted support of the War on Drugs by neutrals as a group lends great strength to it.

## Motives of Drug Warriors and Resisters

The convictions that I will express here about the motives that sustain the War on Drugs come from almost two decades of close involvement with both drug warriors and resisters. I have striven to see the world through the eyes of both. I have invited their comments on my own emerging ideas about their motives. I have checked my conclusions about motives against their behaviour. Through this process, I have become convinced that drug warriors and resisters use the War on Drugs to cope with the same set of emotional problems. The two most important of these problems are (1) the need to blame someone for the unremitting evil and cruelty in the world and (2) the painful conflict between opposing needs for societal control and for individual autonomy. Although social scientists have identified other motivations for the War on Drugs and for persecution of social deviants in general (see Becker 1963; Harris 1974; Girard 1977; Berridge and Edwards 1981; Pfohl 1985; Ericson, Baranek, and Chan 1987, chaps 1, 2), I am convinced by my observations that the two bases mentioned above run the deepest.

### BLAMING

Chapter 1 argued that a major cause of the War on Drugs in the nineteenth and early twentieth centuries was a need to find a scapegoat to blame for society's problems. I believe that this same need to blame comprises a major motivation of both drug warriors and resisters at present. The world provides a daily horror show of physical and emotional violence. Some of this violence entails direct attacks perpetrated by criminals, disappointed lovers, soldiers, guerillas, religious fanatics, reckless drivers, police, parents, spouses, and so on. Some of the direct violence is self-directed mutilation or homicide. Some of the violence is indirect, as when citizens of wealthy nations engage in gluttonous, banal 'consumerism' in full view (through the news media) of hundreds of millions of impoverished, often starving people in the Third World. Some violence is not directed against persons, such as the physical destruction of the earth's fragile ecosystems. Through it all, the denials and hypocrisy of public figures petrify hope for improvement.

What causes these horrors? This is the eternal conundrum of Job and his descendants. Throughout history, people have tried to answer the riddle by blaming groups of other people. There are at least three functions that blaming serves.

First, blaming and attacking the scapegoat provides a feeling of at least doing something about a threatening situation. Inaction feels worse than erroneous blaming, because inaction eventually leads to debilitating stupor, whereas error at least leaves people capable of more promising courses of action in the future.

Second, identifying someone else as the cause of terrifying problems is one way of escaping the blame oneself (A. Freud 1946; S. Freud 1922/ 1955). The need to escape blame seems transparent, for example, in parents whose teenagers have become delinquent. They shield themselves from their terrible sense of guilt by using drugs as a scapegoat for their family's tragedy. They recite like catechism the theory that the drugs cause their children's delinquency. If their teenagers are not known to use drugs then they ingeniously seek to prove that *hidden* drug use is the cause of their actions. In turn, they blame their children's drug use on traffickers, on the irresistible addictiveness of the drugs, on the international Mafia, and so forth. All of this protects them from the more parsimonious but painful explanation that their family has failed to surmount the obstacles that impede growth and integration of children in a troubled world.

Third, blaming functions to organize and mobilize the emotions of a society. Terrifying problems become manageable when the evil derives from a single source. Anti-Semites pin the problems of the world on Jews and Zionists. Similarly, Communists blame revisionists and American imperialists; fascists and conservatives blame Communists; and Christians blamed witches, heretics, and Satan worshippers for centuries. Modern North Americans blame 'pushers,' 'druglords,' 'narcoterrorists,' or just 'drugs,' along with the traditional scapegoats of the past.

When the public feels overwhelmed by problems, it punishes its scapegoats, often on a massive scale. Jews have been persecuted in this way throughout European history. Likewise, the Inquisition set out to improve the world by torturing and burning heretics and witches. In this century, Communists have tried to solve their social problems by killing or 're-educating' revisionists in the Stalinist purges and the Chinese Cultural Revolution; fascists try to solve theirs by torturing and killing Communists in Latin America.

In a parallel way, the War on Drugs will mark a unique period in history in which, at times (including the present), one-third of all the people in American federal prisons were convicted of nothing more than being 'narcotics users' or 'narcotics dealers' (Musto 1973, 204; *New York Times* 1987, cited by Ostrowski 1989, 20); in which huge federal 'narcotics farms' or 'hospitals' imposed maximum-security confinement in the name of treatment on people, many of whom had been convicted of no crime at all (Musto 1973, 205–6); in which police brutality towards addicts was tacitly accepted throughout the world, including Canada; and in which the public-information industries pumped a litany of terrifying misinformation into children's minds.

When society needs scapegoats, it doesn't matter too much if nobody is at hand who truly belongs to the group that has been singled out. For example, along with genuine heretics, the Inquisition tortured and killed old widows who were merely a financial burden on the rest of the population (Spanos 1978). It also destroyed people on the evidence of denunciations wrung from other victims under torture (Harris 1974). The House Un-American Activities Committee prosecuted people as Communists whose membership in the Party was an idealistic experiment. The Stalinist purges found 'dissidents' who were as loyal to Stalin's regime as they could possibly be (Solzhenitsyn 1985). The Nazis defined as Jews people whose biological and cultural taint of Jewishness was negligible. Sartre (1948/1976) has suggested that anti-Semites 'create' Jews to meet their needs for victims.

Similarly, the War on Drugs punishes and treats 'drug abusers' whose use of drugs is completely harmless or even beneficial. Chapter 1 showed how urine tests and *agents provocateurs* are used to scoop up people who are in no sense addicts or traffickers, and in some cases are not even drug users. Such judicial short cuts do not arouse great concern, because persecuting scapegoats can serve symbolic functions even when some of the victims are innocent, as long as they are punished in the name of controlling drug abuse. Thomas Sowell has observed, 'Policies are judged by their consequences, but crusades are judged by how good they make the crusaders feel' (Sowell 1987, 74).

There is often a symbolic connection between the group that is chosen as scapegoat and the evils for which they are blamed. Thus, heretics seemed to symbolize the loss of orthodoxy that was truly undermining the Church in the Renaissance; in some loose sense their horrible punishments could seem warranted. Jews, because of their traditional role in Europe as money-lenders, could symbolize the economic barbarism that was ravaging Weimar Germany when Hitler was gaining power.

It seems to me that drugs serve as the current scapegoat because they so well symbolize the genuine chemical menace that faces modern society. Contemporary civilization threatens to toxify and corrupt itself and the earth with pesticides, nuclear waste, industrial chemicals, chemical and biological weapons, legal drugs, sewage, growth hormones, and so forth. Even though the problems caused by these chemical products are easily seen, it appears impossible to control them, because their countervailing benefits seem great to society as a whole and to powerful vested interests. This deadly chemical dilemma is neatly exorcised by seeking to destroy a set of illicit drugs that are presumed to be highly toxic and also cause people to lose control of themselves. These illicit drugs become the poisons that threaten civilization.

As earlier chapters have shown, there is little evidence that illicit drugs cause any substantial amount of harm. Likewise, there is little evidence that illicit drugs cause anybody to go 'out of control,' although the chemical threats named above are, in fact, out of control. But illicit drugs offer little benefit to a majority of citizens and the people who use them are often socially marginal and, therefore, defenceless. It would seem that drug users, like other scapegoats, provide a substitute for destroying a problem that is too large to handle.

Most people's involvement in scapegoating is not active, but passive and symbolic. Most Germans were not actively involved in the mass murder of Jews, but were inspired and aroused by the doctrine that their troubles could be ended by exorcizing the Jewish menace and by the festival of symbols that glamorized the slaughter. The death camps themselves were hidden from the view of ordinary citizens. Similarly, most North Americans are not physically involved in any of the day-to-day violence of the War on Drugs, but they see, and revel in, glamorized versions of these achievements on the nightly news or, in even more fictional form, on the incessant crime shows.

In spite of all the enthusiasm it has aroused for centuries, scapegoating does not benefit society. Instead, the horrors of persecution are added to the horrors that instigate it.

Blaming has been used throughout the War on Drugs by resisters as well as drug warriors, although the drug warriors are currently much more successful in gaining acceptance for their version. The following is an example of blaming by resisters: 'It is corrupt to the core. It is rotten in its essence, unsound in its nature, wrong in principle, unchristian in character and undermines the foundation on which all human liberty rests. It is conceived in ignorance, engendered in hypocrisy and bolstered up by a shameless distortion of facts. It is a curse to the nation, a blight to the country and a disgrace to the statute books wherever adopted. It breeds disloyalty to the flag, contempt of the power that brought it into being and generates wholesale disregard for the law. It shatters national unity, foments civil strife and would take 27,000,000 enforcers to make it effective' (cited by Gray 1972, 209). In this case, the putative cause of society's ills is not drugs or alcohol but *alcohol prohibition*. The source of this message is an editorial originally printed in *St. Peter's Messenger*, a Catholic newsletter published in Manitoba in 1925, as prohibition in that province was nearing its end.

Other modern attempts to blame society's ills on the drug war can be found in the modern literature of the anti-drug-war movement. For example, the newly formed Anti-Prohibition League, of which I am a member, included the following passages in its 'Political Resolution' adopted in Rome, in April 1989: 'The modern version of prohibition has turned great cities into battlefields, without safeguarding those whom it was intended to protect ... Freedom itself is rapidly being undermined by the enforcement of the laws against drugs, to win no advantage for individuals or for society.'

Blaming is only part of the explanation for the actions of drug warriors and resisters. It explains the need to persecute, but it does not explain why the drug warriors find drug users such an appealing target. It tells more about drug warriors than about resisters, because resisters do not spend as much of their time blaming. The next section considers another, perhaps more powerful, kind of motivation that drug warriors and resisters share.

CONFLICT OVER POWER

In addition to needing scapegoats, drug warriors and resisters manifest intense conflicting needs for societal control on the one hand, and for individual autonomy on the other. Bertrand Russell (1949) has described the social origins of conflicting needs for societal control and individual autonomy:

> From the fifteenth century to the present time the power of the state as
> against the individual has been continuously increasing, at first mainly
> as a result of the invention of gunpowder. Just as, in the earlier days of
> anarchy, the most thoughtful men worshipped law, so during the period
> of increasing state control there was a growing tendency to worship liberty
> ... And the exigencies of total war have persuaded almost everybody
> that a much tighter social system is necessary than that which contented
> our grandfathers ... Individual initiative is hemmed in either by the
> state or powerful corporations, and there is a great danger lest this should
> produce, as in ancient Rome, a kind of listlessness and fatalism that is
> disastrous to vigorous life.' (18)

In the 1980s, both individual autonomy and societal control seem profoundly threatened. People seek new guarantees of personal freedom, such as those provided by the Canadian Charter of Rights and Freedoms. Freedom and democracy are icons of our times, dramatically materialized in 1989 as a styrofoam Statue of Liberty in Tien An Men Square, Beijing. At the same time, people are desperate to bolster fragile national economies, military defences, and precarious world order. These essential social complexes require predictable human components – the antithesis of personal autonomy. Modern communications technology and computers offer means of monitoring and controlling human components more effectively than ever before. 'Permissiveness,' 'liberal,' and even 'civil liberties' became terms of opprobrium in the last American presidential election. It is hard to see room for both individual autonomy and societal order in the face of such intense needs for both.

However, both personal autonomy and societal control are indispensable to human development. Erik Erikson (1963) has shown how, at each stage in children's development, society and the parents must foster their burgeoning autonomy, but must also constrain it within practicable boundaries. The balance is a delicate one and neither the need for autonomy nor the need for the security provided by reasonable social control can be ignored without disastrous effects.

The same conflicting needs for autonomy and control are powerfully felt in adults. A threat to personal autonomy is a threat to a person's claim to self-respect and dignity, and ultimately to one's existence as a human being. A threat to society's capacity to exert control is a threat of chaos, anarchy, and destruction.

Tillich (1952) has described the conflict in existential terms. He describes personal anxieties during periods of social disintegration and change as follows: 'Non-being, in such a situation has a double face, resembling two types of nightmare ... The one type is the anxiety of annihilating narrowness, of the impossibility of escape and the horror of being trapped. The other is the anxiety of annihilating openness of infinite formless space into which one falls without a place to fall upon ... Both forms of the same reality arouse the latent anxiety of every individual who looks at them. Today most of us do look at them' (68).

This conflict is a crucial social issue as well as a personal problem. Russell (1949) has pointed out that each society must continually shift the balance between individual and societal power to respond optimally to the changing conditions that confront it. In war, for example, societal control must predominate, as recognized in Canada's War Measures Act. In times of expansion and development, individual prerogatives and power must be at a maximum. It appears that the USSR currently seeks to increase its productivity by increasing individual autonomy whereas the United States seeks to respond to the fear of losing its political supremacy in the Western world by decreasing individual autonomy, as witnessed by its move towards conservatism in religion, education, and legal policy. I believe that the U.S. position as unquestioned world leader in promoting the War on Drugs manifests this same restrictive trend.

People seem to resolve the dilemma of mutually exclusive needs for personal autonomy and societal control by embracing one of these needs compulsively, while angrily denying the other. Where compromise is out of reach, a black-or-white choice must be made. Similar polarization surrounds many social issues that involve strongly held but incompatible needs, for example, the polarization in the recent Canadian election that opposed the need for economic growth promised by free trade to the need for national sovereignty.

*Power Needs of Drug Warriors*

Drug warriors embrace the need to reinforce societal control and to suppress personal autonomy. Their mood is dark because the impulses for personal autonomy that they seek to suppress in others are ones they know well in themselves, but deny or subdue. Their stance fits the general pattern that has been named 'authoritarianism' by social psychologists and studied intensely over the last thirty years (Adorno, et al. 1950; Altemeyer 1988). People who receive high scores on a psychological test of 'right wing authoritarianism' also favour harsh treatment for drug addiction, although this has become difficult to detect in recent years because such a large proportion of the population agree on the need for harsh punishment for drug users (Altemeyer 1989).

Illicit drugs are ideal targets for people who fear individual autonomy, because drugs have a real potential to increase personal power against societal control, at least temporarily. When used at the right times, drugs like LSD and marijuana really do facilitate extraordinary, marvellous ways of seeing the world, as testified by serious intellectuals like Aldous Huxley (1963). Under their influence, social conventions may seem arbitrary and individual expression may seem all-important. Drugs like cocaine and the amphetamines really can mobilize concentration and endurance during crisis periods, which is why they have been used so massively by national armies, athletes, and racehorse owners. However, when controlled by socially marginal individuals they can energize antisocial behaviour. Drugs like heroin can engender a dreamy indifference to severe distress, thus making extreme mental or physical pain bearable. Being resistant to pain makes people less responsive to the physical and emotional punishments that society dispenses, and therefore more difficult to control.

Most drug warriors do not oppose personal use of drugs that enhance the social order. Thus, they are relatively unconcerned over caffeine used to help people function alertly at work; nicotine used to enable people to endure difficult kinds of work; or alcohol and other depressants used to help people sleep so they can return to their jobs in the morning. The prototypical drug warrior, Harry W. Anslinger, architect of many Draconian American drug-enforcement policies, arranged regular supplies of opiate drugs for an addicted senator and for a society matron in Washington, DC (Trebach 1982, 141). This extraordinary inconsistency can be understood if it is recognized that the senator and the society matron used the drugs to sustain them in positions at the apex of societal control in the United States, so their drug use could be condoned and even supported by the ultimate drug warrior.

Drug warriors do not appear concerned over drug use by institutions of societal control, such as mental hospitals which require that some patients take strong psycho-active stimulants and depressants with clearly deleterious side-effects or prisons that have administered powerful drugs to seemingly dangerous criminals (Pfohl 1985, chap. 4). Nor do drug warriors worry much about the reliance of their national armies on amphetamines to energize men for battle, or opiates to relieve the wounded and get them back into action, on alcohol and marijuana to facilitate 'rest and recreation,' or on LSD to aid in interrogations. Armies, too, are agencies of societal control as opposed to personal autonomy.

Rather than argue directly against the desirability of personal power and autonomy, the rhetoric of drug warriors obscures the underlying issue by incessantly denying that personally empowering use of illicit drugs is possible. Instead, drug-war propaganda attributes great power to drugs, but claims that drugs appropriate this power themselves by inevitably causing users to 'lose control.' But chapters 3 to 8 have shown that there is no substantial basis for this claim. Like other powerful forms of technology, drugs, as they are normally used, increase people's autonomy and power. People use drugs to make themselves alert when they need to be alert, to make themselves relax when they want to relax, and so on. Even in negative addiction, there is no proof for the claim that people 'lose control.' Chapter 8 has shown that negatively addicted people use drugs purposefully and adaptively under the circumstances they must confront. Claims that drugs rob people of control camouflage the motivation of drug warriors to deny people the prerogative to use drugs that might augment their personal powers as against societal control.

A further indication of drug warriors' underlying motivation to subdue personal autonomy is that they typically treat resisters and addicts in ways that crush their personal power. Methods include compulsory 'treatment' in which people are kept under the control of institutions for indefinite periods, and only released when they comply, or pretend to comply, with institutional demands. Drug warriors also favour large-scale imposition of the Alcoholics Anonymous philosophy, which requires repeated public affirmations of inability to control one's drug and alcohol use and the public affirmation that one's personal control has been given over to a 'higher power.'

To me, the strongest proof of the importance of the power issue to drug warriors comes from the statements of drug warriors about themselves. Many supporters of the War on Drugs have told me privately that they feel themselves incapable of controlling their impulses if illicit drugs were to become freely available. Drug warriors genuinely fear their own individual autonomy as well as that of the resisters. Thus, the drug warriors' 'War' does not really seem to be 'on Drugs.' Rather, it is a war on the private, non-institutionalized use of those drugs that can give individuals, including themselves, dangerous, uncontrollable power against the institutions of societal control.

## Power Needs of Resisters

Like drug warriors, resisters are intensely concerned with issues of power and social control. In contrast to drug warriors, resisters are dominated by the need for personal autonomy and by fear of societal control. The rhetoric of the resisters celebrates, and typically overstates the virtues of drugs in personal development and growth. The rhetoric of the 1960s proclaimed that psychedelic drugs could create new undreamed of individual powers (see Heinlein 1961; Leary 1968). Naturally, resisters often deny in themselves the need for the security that societal control offers.

The resisters' political stance stresses the need for absolute freedom of people to control their own bodies and minds, and to behave freely if their actions do not harm others. However, this position reveals a blind spot. Such doctrinaire libertarianism long ago proved unworkable in the complexity of the modern world. For example, health and safety standards prevent people from purchasing many food additives, medical products, automobile components, toys, fabrics, paints, and so on (Grabowski and Vernon 1978). Fisheries are periodically closed because of small changes in the contaminant level of fish. In most cases, consumption is prevented purely on the basis of the potential toxicity to the primary consumer. Most resisters (apart from the most extreme libertarians) mount little objection to public health and safety regulations and may, in fact, support them. I submit that their passionate defence of the right to use drugs is, to an extent, a symbolic affirmation of a long-lost ideal of complete personal freedom, rather than a logically consistent position. Drugs can symbolize the appeal of individual autonomy in a way that food additives and paints cannot, because the effects of psycho-active drugs are immediate and dramatic. Drugs may also be uniquely well suited to serve as a symbol because they can enable people to take their fantasies a little more seriously, at least for a time.

The resisters' opposition to the War on Drugs does not really grow from a positive disposition towards drugs so much as an overriding concern with personal autonomy. Far from condoning drug use in general, resisters are often appalled by the use of drugs in mental hospitals and in military applications. These are identified as exploitative and degrading to individuals. Resisters are concerned with putting the power to control drugs in the hands of individuals rather than social institutions.

If they accept the concept of 'treatment' at all, resisters hope to treat addicts by empowering them to the degree that excessive drug use is no longer needed, and to make prescribed drugs easily available to those who cannot function without them. Again, the underlying concern seems to be with enhancing individual power. Resisters are unduly casual about drug use that is visibly unhealthful. Some of the more zealous members of the movement for the legalization of marijuana that I met at a recent conference seemed to be in a perpetual drug haze and often showed signs of chronic lung congestion. Their colleagues in the movement to legalize marijuana, who personally used the drug in a more careful way, did not seem overly concerned about this chronic impairment as long as the movement was not embarrassed by it. There is a tacit recognition among resisters that individual power necessarily includes the power to harm oneself, and that this price must be paid by those who do not use the freedom wisely. Even normal forms of social control seem out of place in this context.

The underlying conflict between personal autonomy and societal control can be expressed through many other contemporary issues in addition to drugs. For example, the same conflict also appears to underlie arguments over pornography, homosexuality, gun control, euthanasia, capital punishment, abortion, and so on. However, the War on Drugs appears to be overshadowing these other social issues, as if it were becoming the paramount symbol of the control issue.

## Ending the War

Clearly, the War on Drugs cannot be ended in a day, for it has spanned two centuries and its underlying assumptions are deeply etched in the public mind. But I believe that its demise can be hastened by paying attention to the motives that have sustained it. These motives are powerful, but they can be satisfied peacefully.

### OVERCOMING THE TEMPTATION TO BLAME

Since violence and other social problems cannot be quelled by blaming, it is necessary to unearth the real causes of the horrors that wrack society, and find a remedy. This analysis requires a meticulous, open-minded study of modern society, and the application of the sort of pragmatic remedies suggested in chapter 9. Weighing against patient analysis and measured response there always lurks the strong temptation to lapse into blaming. Blaming does not solve problems, but instead provides instant drama and moral excitement. It is a difficult addiction to give up.

Replacing blaming is still more difficult because there is a form of it that is more seductive than the more familiar kinds already described. Educated people who scorn persecution of minority groups often assert that the cause of perennial violence is 'just human nature.'

On the surface, blaming 'human nature' appears to be more humane than blaming a group of people, but in the long run it is not. Whereas this variant of blaming cannot directly justify physical persecution of a group of people, it insidiously distracts from the kind of patient analysis that is needed, by resignedly attributing the blame to human nature. Human nature is given to us as it is, with little room for modification. Therefore, blaming it engenders helplessness: if people were not persecuting one group they would be persecuting another, so why struggle against a War on Drugs, a purge of Jews, or any other persecution? Moreover, blaming human nature can be used as an indirect justification for violence. It only makes sense to strike first in a world that is populated by instinctive killers. When society is stressed, this seemingly humane form of blaming easily gives way to active persecution.

Blaming human nature is an ancient habit. It is at the core of the Judeo-Christian tradition, dramatized in the story of original sin, the fall of Adam and Eve in the Garden of Eden, and the indelible stain that resulted. The curse of Adam is reborn in each of us, condemns us to wickedness, and can be borne only through divine forgiveness. A more contemporary rationale for blaming 'human nature' can be stated in evolutionary terms, starting with the doctrine of 'survival of the fittest' and 'nature red in tooth and claw.' The adherents of a biological philosophy once called 'social Darwinism,' and, in its modern form called 'sociobiology,' often claim that ruthless selfishness is the essential evolved characteristic of *Homo sapiens* (see Dawkins 1976).

However great their convictions, proponents of original sin and social Darwinism have not proved their point. Neither belief in God nor the theory of evolution forces the conclusion that the human species has evolved a selfish and murderous nature. Many theists reject the doctrine of original sin, even though it is fixed in the doctrine of most Christian denominations. Darwin himself believed that conscience and the moral sense were among the most conspicuous traits of the human species and that human morality evolved inevitably because of the coexistence of strong social instincts and intelligence in the human species (Darwin 1871/1981, 70–2). A small group of contemporary evolutionary biologists have explored the evolution of co-operation and restraint in more modern terms and have explicitly rejected the concept that human nature is innately selfish or violent (Allee 1958, Wynne-Edwards 1986; Tolman 1987). However, regardless of the evolved propensities of *Homo sapiens*, modern behavioural science shows that the evolved potentials in a species do not manifest themselves irrepressibly, but depend on particular circumstances for their appearance. In other words, violence is not inevitable, even if the potential for it is inborn. Genetic potential is not destiny.

Thus, the assumption that evolution inevitably maximizes selfishness and violence is only an article of faith, not a necessary deduction from the theory of evolution. Blaming human nature is no more logical or scientific than blaming groups of Jews or 'drug lords.' Blaming of any sort is a simplistic way of understanding that needs to be replaced with real analysis to end the War on Drugs.

## BALANCING POWER NEEDS

When the underlying conflict between needs for societal control and personal power is exposed, the outcome of the War on Drugs can be foreseen. Ultimately, accommodation is the only possible outcome because both the need for societal control and the need for personal power are inalienable characteristics of civilized people. Civilization requires careful balancing of the powers of the individual and of various levels of government. A major step towards ending the War on Drugs is recognizing that the real needs that animate both sides must be met and seeking ways to reconcile them.

To preserve the benefits of both societal control and personal power, there must be some gravitation of the control of currently illicit drugs to individuals. This step seems inevitable in many localities for marijuana, which millions of people have shown they enjoy and can use with minimal problems. Correspondingly, drugs that are socially abhorrent in a particular locality can legitimately be restricted in the public interest, to the degree that restriction is possible without introducing war measures that do more harm than good. The transition to a more balanced policy should be gradual. It would seem unwise to make too many new drugs publicly available in a short time, because time is required for society to adapt to new ways of thinking. Most importantly, it must be recognized that the underlying conflict between advocates of societal control and of personal power is simplistic. The libertarian image and the authoritarian urge are both impoverished visions of perfection. Effective control rests at many levels of organization *between* the individual and the nation. The power to restrict drug use is better vested in local communities, rather than in either individuals or nations.

The War on Drugs may best be understood as a panicky reaction to the sudden appearance of a huge new psycho-active pharmacopoeia. The obvious futility of the present frantic clash of competing power needs may instigate a more balanced approach to the domestication of drugs.

## RE-EDUCATING 'SOLDIERS'

In most wars, active combatants are enlisted and their enthusiasm kindled by simplistic slogans that obscure motives that are the war's real driving force. Ending wars requires drawing the combatants' thinking back to more normal, complex forms. This transition has been difficult after conventional wars and it must be anticipated that it will be difficult after the War on Drugs. Like highly trained soldiers, enforcement agents with whom I have spoken appear to firmly believe the simplistic slogans. They see themselves as protecting their country against an impending epidemic of drug addiction or against pharmaceutical subversion by insidious foreign powers. When confronted with the fact that their efforts have no measurable effect, they express faith that the situation would be far worse if not for them and express the need to keep up the fight because there are no alternatives to the familiar war measures. When confronted with the violence they sometimes inflict, they justify themselves by asserting that their victims are not really human: 'they're scum,' 'they can't feel pain,' and so forth. (These are quotes from Canadian police officers.)

In their work, these men are often exposed to great hardships, dangers, and challenges to their personal integrity, but they are sheltered from the emotional stress of acknowledging the underlying motives of the War on Drugs. For the war to end they must be asked to understand social problems in a more complex, emotionally taxing way.

On the other side of the War on Drugs, some resisters reveal something like a 'soldier' mentality as well. Some users believe that personal happiness can be attained directly through the use of illicit drugs and that their own drug use makes them true defenders of freedom. Soldier-like, these drug users and traffickers often endure great hardships, risk prison and sometimes their lives, and sometimes hold to an admirable code of honour (as in the case of youthful marijuana users who have gone to jail rather than betray the friends who supplied their drugs). As in the case of the enforcement officers, resisters' colleagues are not over-eager to remind them that most people acquire no lasting happiness from drugs, that the liberty they hold sacred is an illusion in modern society, and that their steadfastness may have a psychological origin in their needs and conflicts.

The slogans on both sides are deceiving – both the fear of an apocalyptic epidemic of addiction and the hope of a drug-inspired renaissance of freedom are baseless. Drugs are powerful, but not nearly so powerful as either side proclaims. But, as in wars through the centuries, the deceptions are sufficient to their task. The armies bravely recite the simple slogans that actually commit them to the service of deeper and more complex needs. Ending the War on Drugs requires acknowledging the fact that, like soldiers, large groups of people have been indoctrinated with a black-and-white outlook that makes it impossible for them to function in the real world of greys. It will require diligent efforts to re-educate these people, but it is an unavoidable task.

## THE ROLE OF NEUTRALS: REFUSING COMPLICITY

Drug warriors and resisters can only fight their War on Drugs to the degree that they engage the sympathy and support of the much larger group in society that is not obsessed with drugs. Neutrals pay the bills for the drug war with their taxes and support it with their votes and in more direct ways that will be illustrated below. The power to end the War on Drugs lies with the majority of society that has no great psychological stake in it.

It is difficult for neutrals to reject the War on Drugs, however, for they are flattered, deceived, and deliberately frightened by those drug warriors and resisters who seek their co-operation. At this time in history, the drug warriors are obviously more persuasive, and the task of neutrals is to avoid complicity with them. In the 1960s, the situation was different, and the resisters seemed able to convince many otherwise neutral people that policemen were pigs and that marijuana and LSD could lead humanity to an 'Age of Aquarius' in which the liberated individuals, happily organized into tribes within technologized nations, would somehow transcend the complex problems of the age. Neutrals must resist the simplistic doctrines of both sides if the war is actually to end.

I will use some of the realities of professional psychology to show the rewards that can come from complicity in the drug war in contemporary society. I have not chosen this example to suggest that psychologists are more inclined to careless complicity than are other people, but because, as a psychologist, I know the possibilities more fully. In psychology, there is money to be made and professional stature to be achieved by complicity in the War on Drugs: for example, by setting up 'treatment' programs (like rigid, bureaucratic methadone clinics) that do not really help the 'clients,' but in fact degrade them and potentially increase their dependence on drugs and other substitute adaptations. This kind of complicity is well paid by the government, which thereby gives itself the appearance of 'doing something about the drug problem.'

Psychologists can also be rewarded by serving as paid professional witnesses in criminal cases. Considerable payments for lost time and for administering standardized tests can be earned by psychologists who testify in drug cases. For example, I have been asked to testify in a child-custody case that a mother with a record of having used heroin is incapable of taking care of her child. Simply mouthing the myths of the War on Drugs can be lucrative for a professional.

Research psychologists can make large amounts of money from drug companies by doing research to demonstrate that new drugs do not produce withdrawal symptoms in laboratory rats and then publishing articles arguing that the new drug is 'non-addictive.' To do such research necessitates repressing one's awareness that (1) withdrawal symptoms have no strong relationship to addiction and (2) although rats do voluntarily consume some addictive drugs under the right conditions, they don't get addicted in any way similar to human 'overwhelming involvement' (see *PM*, chaps 4, 5). This sort of research obscures these crucial facts and enlists impressive scientific technology in tacit support of War on Drugs logic.

Another temptation for research psychologists is to accept research contracts from the government that bring status to them among other researchers and the opportunity to buy expensive equipment and hire research assistants. Some such contracts involve compromising scientific integrity to help the government attain political ends. For example, a contract that has been described to me involves evaluating a prison-based 'treatment' program for drug abuse. Prior research makes it almost certain that the program is not benefiting the prisoners. However, the terms of the research contract make it impossible to obtain information that would demonstrate that the program was unsuccessful, even though the research project is well funded and gives the outward appearance of being thorough. By participating in a research project that can only obtain positive or inconclusive results, the research psychologists lend the support of social science to the invalid doctrines of the War on Drugs.

It is difficult to resist temptations such as these, especially in the current situation where research that supports the War on Drugs is generously funded, many other research topics are meagrely funded, and research that embarrasses the War on Drugs is not funded at all. However, although the concessions that each professional must make are relatively minor, the reality is that a monstrosity like the War on Drugs has been built out of thousands of slightly selfish compromises. The situation can only improve when people understand how important it is, in the words of Nancy Reagan, to 'just say no' to the War on Drugs.

DECLARING PEACE

The War on Drugs may be in the last frantic buildup before its demise. The scholars whose work is reviewed in this book have shredded its logic and its supposed scientific base. The governments that have promoted the War on Drugs are being forced to acknowledge its costs in money, human suffering, and credibility. Newspaper cartoonists are beginning to expose its absurdities. People in business are beginning to see that it does not increase productivity, but instead erodes the atmosphere of the workplace. Drug warriors eventually weary of new promises, re-worked horror stories, and new beginnings of the old war. Resisters are finding that access to prohibited drugs does not produce happiness or usher in an Age of Aquarius. Like other great persecutions of the past, the War on Drugs will eventually subside.

An 'armistice,' that is, a formal declaration of peace, is far preferable to a long period of winding down, because the war mentality can obscure issues for a long time unless society finds a way to formally reject it. It seems to me that the task of the next few years will be to bring the drug war to a final, visible end and make sure that the public understands why peaceful measures are the order of the day. This is no small chore. It requires the active leadership of politicians and professionals who have the fortitude to reject the false promises of the drug war and work towards more useful goals.

## Conclusions

On a larger record of human history, the War on Drugs is only a small blot. But war and persecution are problems of all times. It is possible to hope that careful study of the War on Drugs might provide an opportunity to learn about the kind of needs and anxieties that provoke wars of persecution and of the ever-freshening potential for peaceful solutions.

There is a darker possibility as well. This book is built on the assumption that reasoned analysis can lead society to reverse a mistaken position and a cruel war. However, I have met many concerned and thoughtful people who deny this possibility. They say, in essence, that the War on Drugs serves too many important functions for it to be stopped by any heightened understanding. In a way, they propose an 'adaptive model' of the War on Drugs. They point to the great authority that the drug war gives to power-hungry officials, the wealth it confers on treatment and administrative bureaucracies, the way it facilitates domination of poor countries by richer ones, and the way it serves the psychological needs identified in this chapter. Beyond all this they point with resignation to the irrepressible centralization of authority everywhere, and suggest that the drug war is just a manifestation of this trend. All these facts, they say, explain the otherwise perplexing failure of society to acknowledge the transparent fabrications and falsehoods of the War on Drugs rhetoric. They doubt if such a serviceable war can be ended.

I cannot know whether these people are correct or not. On bright days I reject their pessimism, but on darker ones, I cannot. On the darkest days, I note that people who advance these views often come from more violent places than Vancouver, British Columbia. These people may simply live closer to the heart of things than I do. I am, after all, exceptionally sheltered by the good fortune of being Canadian.

If the pessimistic views are correct, the sanguine recommendations in the last two chapters of this book are unrealistic. If the War on Drugs is a social tidal wave, then it cannot be quelled by the puny voice of humane analysis. However, it is none the less essential to preserve one's own critical understanding from being swept away in the flood, and to defer the application of this knowledge until later, more reflective times.

# References

Aaron, P., and D. Musto. 1981. 'Temperance and Prohibition in America: A Historical Overview.' In M.H. Moore and D.R. Gerstein, eds, *Alcohol and Public Policy: Beyond the Shadow of Prohibition*. Washington: National Academy Press

Abel, E.L. 1980. *Marihuana: The First Twelve Thousand Years*. New York: Plenum

Abel, E.L., and R.J. Sokol. 1987. 'Incidence of Fetal Alcohol Syndrome and Economic Impact of FAS-related Anomalies,' *Drug and Alcohol Dependence* 19: 51–70

Abelson, H.I., and J.D. Miller. 1985. 'A Decade of Trends in Cocaine Use in the Household Population.' In Kozel and Adams, eds, *Cocaine Use in America*

Acker, D., B.T. Sachs, K.J. Tracey, and W.E. Wise. 1983. 'Abruptio Placentae Associated with Cocaine Use,' *American Journal of Obstetrics and Gynecology* 146: 220–1

Adams, E.H., and J. Durrell. 1984. 'Cocaine: A Growing Public Health Problem.' In Grabowski, ed., *Cocaine: Pharmacology, Effects, and Treatment of Abuse*

Adlaf, E.M., and R.G. Smart. 1982. 'Risk-taking and Drug-use Behaviour: An Examination,' *Drug and Alcohol Dependence* 11: 287–95

Adler, A. 1933/1954. *Social Interest: A Challenge to Mankind*. London: Faber & Faber

Adorno, T.W., E. Frenkel-Brunswik, D.J. Levinson, and R.N. Sanford. 1950. *The Authoritarian Personality*. New York: Harper

Agar, M.H., and R.C. Stephens. 1975. 'The Methadone Street Scene: The Addict's View,' *Psychiatry* 38: 381–87

Albee, G.W. 1986. 'Toward a Just Society: Lessons from Observations in the Primary Prevention of Psychopathology,' *American Psychologist* 41: 891–8

Alcoholics Anonymous. 1987. 'Information on Alcoholics Anonymous.' One-page fact sheet; publication no. 100M4/87(RCH). New York

Alcoholics Anonymous World Services, Inc. 1976. *Alcoholics Anonymous: The Story of How Many Thousands of Men and Women Have Recovered from Alcoholism*. 3d edition. New York

Alexander, B.K. 1978. 'A Critique of "An Evaluation of the California Civil Addicts Program" by W.H. McGlothlin, M.D. Anglin, & B.D. Wilson.' Unpublished paper prepared for the British Columbia Civil Liberties Association, Vancouver

- 1982. 'James M. Barrie and the Expanding Definition of Addiction,' *Journal of Drug Issues* 11: 77–91
- 1985. 'Drug Use, Dependence, and Addiction at a British Columbia University: Good News and Bad News,' *Canadian Journal of Higher Education* 15: 13–29
- 1987. 'The Disease and Adaptive Models of Addiction: A Framework Analysis,' *Journal of Drug Issues* 17: 47–66
- Forthcoming. 'Empirical and Theoretical Bases for an Adaptive Model of Addiction,' *Journal of Drug Issues*

Alexander, B.K., B.L. Beyerstein, P.F. Hadaway, and R.B. Coambs. 1981. 'The Effect of Early and Later Colony Housing on Oral Ingestion of Morphine in Rats,' *Pharmacology, Biochemistry, and Behavior* 15: 571–6

Alexander, B.K., B.L. Beyerstein, and T.M. MacInnes. 1987. 'Methadone Treatment in B.C.: Bad Medicine?' *Canadian Medical Association Journal* 136: 25–8

Alexander, B.K., R.B. Coambs, and P.F. Hadaway. 1978. 'The Effect of Housing and Gender on Morphine Self-administration in Rats,' *Psychopharmacology* 58: 175–9

Alexander, B.K., and G.S. Dibb. 1975. 'Opiate Addicts and Their Parents,' *Family Process* 14: 499–514

Alexander, B.K., M. Driscoll, and J. Gayton. Article in preparation. 'Drug Use among Young Offenders and University Students in British Columbia'

Alexander, B.K., and P.F. Hadaway. 1982. 'Opiate Addiction: The Case for an Adaptive Orientation,' *Psychological Bulletin* 92: 367–81

Alexander, B.K., P.F. Hadaway, and R.B. Coambs. 1988. 'Rat Park Chronicle.' In J.S. Blackwell and P.G. Erickson, eds, *Illicit Drugs in Canada: Risky Business.* Scarborough, Ont.: Nelson Canada

Alexander, B.K., T.M. MacInnes, and B.L. Beyerstein. 1988. 'Methadone and Addict Mortality,' *British Columbia Medical Journal* 30: 160–3

Alexander, B.K., and A.R.F. Schweighofer. 1988. 'Defining "Addiction,"' *Canadian Psychology* 29: 151–62

- Forthcoming. 'Drug Addiction among University Students,' *The Psychology of Addictive Behaviors*

Allee, W.C. 1958. *The Social Life of Animals.* Boston: Beacon Press

Allen, M.E. 1982. 'The "Runner's Calm,"' *Journal of the American Medical Association* 248: 3094

Allen, M.E., and D. Coen. 1987. 'Blockade of Running Induced Mood Changes by Naloxone: Endorphins Implicated,' *Annals of Sports Medicine* 7: 190–5

Alsop, S. 1974. 'The Right to Die with Dignity,' *Good Housekeeping* 69 (August): 130, 132

Altemeyer, B. 1988. 'Marching in Step: A Psychological Analysis of State Terror,' *The Sciences* 28 (2): 30–9

- 1989. 'Right Wing Authoritarianism.' Presented at Psychology Colloquium, Simon Fraser University, Burnaby, BC, 15 November

Altman, L.K. 1986. 'Drug Tests Gain Precision but Can Be Inaccurate,' *New York Times*, 16 September

*Amato v. R.* 1982. *Criminal Reports* (SCC), 3rd ser., vol. 29. Toronto: Carswell

Ambre, J., T.I. Ruo, J. Nelson, and S. Belknapp. 1988. 'Urinary Excretion of
    Cocaine, Benzoylecgonine, and Ecgonine Methyl Ester in Humans,' *Journal of
    Analytical Toxicology* 12: 301–6
American Psychiatric Association. 1980. *Diagnostic and Statistical Manual of Mental
    Disorders.* 3d edition. Washington: American Psychiatric Association
Amnesty International. 1985. *Reports.* London: Amnesty International Publications
– 1987. *Reports.* London: Amnesty International Publications
– 1988. *Reports.* London: Amnesty International Publications
Anderson, J. 1985. 'CAMP Agents out of Hand?' *San Francisco Chronicle*, 20 August
Annis, H.M. 1979. 'Group Treatment of Incarcerated Offenders with Alcohol and Drug
    Problems: A Controlled Evaluation,' *Canadian Journal of Criminology* 21: 3–15
– 1979a. 'Self-report Reliability of Skid-Row Alcoholics,' *British Journal of
    Psychiatry* 134: 459–65
– 1981. 'Treatment in Corrections: Martinson Was Right,' *Canadian Psychology* 22:
    321–6
Annis, H.M., and C. Watson. 1975. 'Drug Use and School Dropout: A Longitudinal
    Study,' *Canadian Counsellor* 9: 155
Ansbacher, H.L., and R.R. Ansbacher. 1956. *The Individual Psychology of Alfred
    Adler: A Systematic Presentation in Selections from His Writings.* New York:
    Harper & Row
Appleby, L. 1985. 'The Big Fix,' *Saturday Night* 100 (11): 13–20
Appleton, P., and A. Sweeny. 1987. 'Canada's Monstrous Drug Problem,' *Globe and
    Mail*, 24 February
Aristotle. Circa 330 BC/1925. *The Nicomachean Ethics.* Translated by D. Ross.
    Oxford: Oxford University Press
Arnao, G. 1988. 'Report 1987 of the International Narcotic Control Board (INCB),'
    *Newsletter of the European Movement for the Normalization of Drug Policy* 1 (3):
    25–8
Aronson, T.A., and T.J. Craig. 1986. 'Cocaine Precipitation of Panic Disorder,'
    *American Journal of Psychiatry* 143: 643–5
Ascher, E., J.C.E. Stauffer, and W.H. Gaasch. 1988. 'Coronary Artery Spasm,
    Cardiac Arrest, Transient Electrocardiographic Q Waves and Stunned Myocardium
    in Cocaine-associated Acute Myocardial Infarction,' *American Journal of
    Cardiology* 61: 939–41
Aston, R. 1984. 'Drug Abuse: Its Relationship to Dental Practice,' *Dental Clinics of
    North America* 28: 595–610
Augustine, St. Circa AD 397/1963. *The Confessions of St. Augustine.* Translated by
    Rex Warner. New York: New American Library
Austin, G. 1978. *Perspectives on the History of Psychoactive Substance Abuse.*
    Washington: National Institute on Drug Abuse
Baekeland, F. 1970. 'Exercise Deprivation: Sleep and Psychological Reactions,'
    *Archives of General Psychiatry* 22: 365–9
Baker, T.B., and S.T. Tiffany. 1985. 'Morphine Tolerance as Habituation,'
    *Psychological Review* 92: 78–108
Bale, R.N., W.W. Van Stone, J.M. Kuldair, T.M.J. Engelsing, R. Elashoff, and V.P.

Zarcone. 1984. 'Three Therapeutic Communities: A Prospective Controlled Study of Narcotic Addiction Treatment: Process and Two Year Follow-up Results,' *Archives of General Psychiatry* 41: 185–91

Ball, J.C., J.W. Shaffer, and D.N. Nurco. 1983. 'The Day-to-Day Criminality of Heroin Addicts in Baltimore – A Study in the Continuity of Offence Rates,' *Drug and Alcohol Dependence* 12: 119–42

*Baltimore Sun*. 1986. 'Family Honor,' 20 August

Barash, P.G. 1977. 'Cocaine in Clinical Medicine.' In R.C. Peterson and R.C. Stillman, eds, *Cocaine: 1977*. NIDA Research Monograph 13. Rockville, MD: National Institute on Drug Abuse

Barnes, D.M. 1988. 'Drugs: Running the Numbers,' *Science* 240: 1729–31

Barnett, G., R. Hawks, and R. Resnick. 1981. 'Cocaine Pharmacokinetics in Humans,' *Journal of Ethnopharmacology* 3: 353–66

Barrett, P.M. 1989. '"Drug Czar" Nominee, Awaiting Confirmation, Quietly Peruses Controversial Ideas on Policies,' *Wall Street Journal*, 1 March

Barrie, J.M. 1892. *My Lady Nicotine*. 4th edition. London: Hodder and Stoughton

– 1928. *Peter Pan, or the Boy Who Would Not Grow Up*. London: Hodder and Stoughton

Barth, C.W. III, M. Bray, and W.C. Roberts. 1986. 'Rupture of the Ascending Aorta during Cocaine Intoxication,' *American Journal of Cardiology* 57: 496

Baselt, R.C. 1982. *Disposition of Toxic Drugs and Chemicals in Man*. 2d edition. Davis, CA: Biomedical Publications

Bates, C.K. 1988. 'Medical Risks of Cocaine Use,' *Western Journal of Medicine* 148: 440–4

Bates, M.E., H.R. White, and E.W. Labouvie. 1985. 'A Longitudinal Study of Sensation Seeking Needs and Drug Use.' Presented at Poster session, APA, Los Angeles, August

Beck, M. 1985. 'Feeding America's Habit,' *Newsweek*, 25 February: 22–3

Becker, H.S. 1963. *Outsiders: Studies in the Sociology of Deviance*. Glencoe, IL: Free Press

Beecher, H.K. 1959. *The Measurement of Subjective Responses: Quantitative Effects of Drugs*. New York: Oxford University Press

Bejerot, N. 1980. 'Addiction to Pleasure: A Biological and Social-psychological Theory of Addiction.' In D.J. Lettieri, M. Sayers, and M.W. Pearson, eds, *Theories on Drug Abuse*. NIDA Research Monograph 30. Rockville, MD: National Institute on Drug Abuse

Bellis, D.J. 1981. *Heroin and Politicians: The Failure of Public Policy to Control Addiction in America*. Westport, CT: Greenwood Press

Bennett, R., R. Batenhorst, D. Graves, T.S. Foster, T. Bauman, W.O. Griffen, and B.D. Wright. 1982. 'Morphine Titration in Postoperative Laparotomy Patients using Patient-controlled Analgesia,' *Current Therapeutic Research* 32: 45–51

Benowitz, N.L. 1988. 'Drug Therapy: Pharmacologic Aspects of Cigarette Smoking and Nicotine Addiction,' *New England Journal of Medicine* 319: 1318–30

Bergin, A.E., and M.J. Lambert. 1978. 'The Evaluation of Therapeutic Outcomes.' In S.L. Garfield and A.E. Bergin, eds, *Handbook of Psychotherapy and Behavioral Change*. 2d edition. New York: Wiley

Berridge, V., and G. Edwards. 1981. *Opium and the People: Opiate Use in Nineteenth Century England*. London: Allan Lane

Beyerstein, B.L. 1987. 'A Report on the Current Status of Mass Urine Screening in the Workplace.' Unpublished report, Department of Psychology, Simon Fraser University, Burnaby, BC

Beyerstein, B.L., and B.K. Alexander. 1985. 'Why Treat Doctors Like Pushers?' *Canadian Medical Association Journal* 132: 337–41

Birkin, A. 1979. *J.M. Barrie and the Lost Boys*. London: Constable

Blackwell, J.S. 1982. 'Drifting, Controlling, and Overcoming: Opiate Users Who Avoid Becoming Chronically Dependent,' *Journal of Drug Issues* 13: 219–35

– 1985. 'Opiate Dependence as a Psychophysical Event: Users' Reports of Subjective Experiences,' *Contemporary Drug Problems* 12: 331–50

– 1987. 'Academic Censorship and the "War on Drugs": The Case of Responsible Drug Use.' Presented at Canadian Law and Society Association Meetings, Hamilton, June

– 1988. 'Canada in a Global Setting: Notes on the International Drug Market.' In J.S. Blackwell and P.G. Erickson, eds, *Illicit Drugs in Canada: A Risky Business*. Scarborough, Ont.: Nelson Canada

Block, W. 1976. *Defending the Undefendable: The Pimp, Prostitute, Scab, Slumlord, Libeler, Moneylender, and Other Scapegoats in the Rogue's Gallery of American Society*. New York: Fleet

Blum, R.H., and Associates. 1969. *Society and Drugs*. San Francisco: Jossey-Bass

Blum, R.H., E. Garfield, J. Johnstone, and J.G. Magistad. 1978. 'Drug Education: Further Results and Recommendations,' *Journal of Drug Issues* 8: 379–426

Bock, W.J. 1980. 'The Definition and Recognition of Biological Adaptation,' *American Zoologist* 20: 217–27

Bohman, M., S. Sigvardsson, and C.R. Cloninger. 1981. 'Maternal Inheritance of Alcohol Abuse: Cross Fostering Analysis of Adopted Women,' *Archives of General Psychiatry* 38: 965–9

Booth, W. 1988. 'War Breaks Out over Drug Research Agency,' *Science* 241: 648–50

Boyd, M. 1986. 'Reagan Proposes New Drug Laws and Orders Tests of U.S. Workers,' *New York Times*, 16 September

Boyd, N. 1983. 'The Supreme Court on Drugs: Masters of Reason in Disarray?' *Canadian Lawyer*, March: 6–10

– 1983a. 'Canadian Punishment of Illegal Drug Use: Theory and Practice,' *Journal of Drug Issues* 13: 445–59

– 1984. 'The Origins of Canadian Narcotics Legislation: The Process of Criminalization in Historical Context,' *Dalhousie Law Journal* 8: 102–36

Bozarth, M.A., and R.A. Wise. 1985. 'Toxicity Associated with Long-term Intravenous Heroin and Cocaine Self-administration in the Rat,' *Journal of the American Medical Association* 254: 81–3

Braucht, G.N., D. Brakarsh, D. Follingstad, and K.L. Berry. 1973. 'Deviant Drug Use in Adolescence: A Review of the Psychosocial Correlates,' *Psychological Bulletin* 79: 92–106

Brecher, E.M. 1972. *Licit and Illicit Drugs*. Boston: Little, Brown

Brecher, J., E. Ipsen, A. Wallace, B. Burgewer, H. Morris, D. Shirley, and
    P. Abramson. 1983. 'Taking Drugs on the Job,' *Newsweek*, 22 August: 52–60
British Columbia Alcohol and Drug Programs. 1986. *Methadone Policy and Procedure*.
    Victoria: Ministry of Health
Browman, C.P. 1981. 'Physical Activity as a Therapy for Psychopathology: A
    Reappraisal,' *Journal of Sportsmedicine* 21: 192–7
Brown, B.S. 1984. 'Treatment of Nonopiate Dependency: Issues and Outcomes.' In
    R.G. Smart, H.D. Cappell, F.B. Glaser, Y. Israel, H. Kalant, R.E. Popham, W.
    Schmidt, and E.M. Sellers, eds, *Recent Advances in Alcohol and Drug Problems*,
    vol. 8. New York: Plenum
Brown, J.A.C. 1963. *Techniques of Persuasion: From Propaganda to Brainwashing*.
    Baltimore: Penguin
Brown, R., and R. Middlefell. 1989. 'Fifty-five Years of Cocaine Dependence,' *British
    Journal of Addiction* 84: 946
Brown, R.R., and J.E. Partington. 1942. 'The Intelligence of the Narcotic Drug
    Addict,' *Journal of General Psychology* 26: 175–9
Browne, A., and D. Finkelhor. 1986. 'Impact of Child Sexual Abuse: A Review of the
    Research,' *Psychological Bulletin* 99: 66–77
Bry, B.H., P. McKeon, and R.J. Pandina. 1982. 'Extent of Drug Use as a
    Function of Number of Risk Factors,' *Journal of Abnormal Psychology* 91:
    273–9
Bureau of Dangerous Drugs. 1984. *Narcotic, Controlled and Restricted Drug Statistics*.
    Ottawa: Department of National Health and Welfare
– 1985. *Narcotic, Controlled and Restricted Drug Statistics*. Ottawa: Department of
    National Health and Welfare
– 1986. *Narcotic, Controlled and Restricted Drug Statistics*. Ottawa: Department of
    National Health and Welfare
Burroughs, W.S. 1959. *Naked Lunch*. New York: Grove Press
Byck, R., ed. 1974. *Cocaine Papers by Sigmund Freud*. New York: Stonehill
– 1987. 'Cocaine Use and Research: Three Histories.' In S. Fisher, A. Raskin, and
    E.H. Uhlenhuth, eds, *Cocaine: Clinical and Biobehavioral Aspects*. New York:
    Oxford University Press
Caffrey, R.J. 1984. 'Counter-attack on Cocaine Trafficking: The Strategy of Drug Law
    Enforcement,' *Bulletin on Narcotics* 36: 57–63
Cahalan, D. 1987. *Understanding America's Drinking Problem*. San Francisco:
    Jossey-Bass
Cameron, S. 1988. 'Evil Empire? Poll Says Americans Don't Think So,' *Globe and
    Mail*, 23 May
Canadian Intramural Recreation Association. 1985. *Student Leadership Development
    Program*. Ottawa: Canadian Intramural Recreation Association
*Canada Legislative Index*. 1987. 'An Act to Amend the Criminal Code, the Food and
    Drugs Act, and the Narcotics Control Act (Bill C-61).' Release no. 43.
    Vancouver: British Columbia Courthouse Library Society
*Canada Statute Citator*. 1986. Aurora, Ont.: Canada Law Book
Caplovitz, D. 1976. *The Working Addict*. White Plains, NY: M.E. Sharpe

Capote, T. 1965. *In Cold Blood*. New York: New American Library

Carnap, R. 1952. 'Empiricism, Semantics, and Ontology.' In L. Linsky, ed., *Semantics and the Philosophy of Language*. Urbana, IL: University of Chicago Press

Cashman, S. 1981. *Prohibition – The Lie of the Land*. New York: Macmillan

Cassell, J. 1976. 'The Contribution of the Social Environment to Host Resistance,' *American Journal of Epidemiology* 104: 107–23

CBC Radio. 1985. 'Sunday Morning,' 17 November

– 1987. 'Sunday Morning,' 27 September

Chaiken, J.M., and M.R. Chaiken. 1982. *Varieties of Criminal Behavior*. Santa Monica: Rand

Chaikin, T., and R. Telander. 1988. 'The Nightmare of Steroids,' *Sports Illustrated* 69 (24 October): 82–102

Chambers, B. 1987. 'National "Battle" on Smoking Launched,' *The Journal* 16 (8): 2

Chaney, E.F., and D.K. Roszell. 1985. 'Coping in Opiate Addicts Maintained on Methadone.' In S. Shiffman and T.A. Wills, eds, *Coping and Substance Use*. Orlando: Academic Press

Chaney, E.F., D.K. Roszell, and C. Cummings. 1982. 'Relapse in Opiate Addicts: A Behavioral Analysis,' *Addictive Behaviors* 7: 291–7

Chase, C. 1981. *The Great American Waistline: Putting It On and Taking It Off*. New York: Coward, McCann, & Geoghegan

Chasnoff, I.J., K.A. Burns, and W.J. Burns. 1987. 'Cocaine Use in Pregnancy: Perinatal Morbidity and Mortality,' *Neurotoxicology and Teratology* 9: 291–3

Chasnoff, I.J., W.J. Burns, S.H. Schnoll, and K.A. Burns. 1985. 'Cocaine Use in Pregnancy,' *New England Journal of Medicine* 313: 666–9

Chasnoff, I.J., G.M. Chisum, and W.E. Kaplan. 1988. 'Maternal Cocaine Use and Genitourinary Tract Malformations,' *Teratology* 37: 201–4

Chasnoff, I.J., D.E. Lewis, and L. Squires. 1987. 'Cocaine Intoxication in a Breast-fed Baby,' *Pediatrics* 80: 838

Chatwin, B. 1987. *The Songlines*. Harmondsworth: Penguin

Chein, I., D.L. Gerard, R.S. Lee, and E. Rosenfeld. 1964. *The Road to H: Narcotics, Delinquency, and Social Policy*. New York: Basic Books

Chesher, G.B. 1987. 'Drug Policy Reform in Australia.' Paper presented at the International Conference on Drug Policy Reform, London, 13–17 July

Chiniquy, C.P.T. 1847. *Manual of the Temperance Society*. Montreal: Lovell & Gibson

Chitwood, D.D. 1985. 'Patterns and Consequences of Cocaine Use.' In Kozel and Adams, eds, *Cocaine Use in America*

Clark, W.B., and D. Cahalan. 1976. 'Change in Problem Drinking over a Four-Year Span,' *Addictive Behaviors* 1: 251–60

Clayton, R.R. 1985. 'Cocaine Use in the United States: In a Blizzard or Just Being Snowed?' In Kozel and Adams, eds, *Cocaine Use in America*

Cocores, J.A., R.K. Davies, P.S. Mueller, and M.S. Gold. 1987. 'Cocaine Abuse and Adult Attention Deficit Disorder,' *Journal of Clinical Psychiatry* 48: 376–7

Cohen, P.D.A. 1987. 'Cocaine Use in Amsterdam in Non Deviant Subcultures.' Presented at the International Council on Alcohol and Addictions Congress, Lausanne, Switzerland, May/June

– 1988. 'The Dutch Experience: The Place of Dutch Drug Policy in a General Framework of Social Administration.' Presented at the International Forum on Antiprohibition of Drugs, Brussels, 29 September–1 October

– Forthcoming. *Cocaine Use in Amsterdam in Non Deviant Subcultures*. Amsterdam: Universiteit van Amsterdam

Cohen, S. 1985. 'Reinforcement and Rapid Delivery Systems: Understanding Adverse Consequences of Cocaine.' In Kozel and Adams, eds, *Cocaine Use in America*

Coleman, V. 1975. *The Medicine Men: Drug Makers, Doctors, & Patients*. London: Temple Smith

Collier, H.O.J. 1963. 'Aspirin,' *Scientific American* 209 (5): 96–108

Collins, J.J., and M. Allison. 1983. 'Legal Coercion and Retention in Drug Abuse Treatment,' *Hospital and Community Psychiatry* 34: 1145–7

Committee of the Health Protection Branch. 1977. 'Trends in Methadone Use in the Treatment of Opiate Dependence in Canada,' *Canadian Journal of Public Health* 68: 111–15

Community Epidemiology Work Group. 1987. *Patterns and Trends of Drugs Abuse in the United States and Europe*. Proceedings, June 1987. Rockville, MD: National Institute on Drug Abuse

– 1988. *Epidemiologic Trends in Drug Abuse*. Proceedings, December 1988. Rockville, MD: National Institute on Drug Abuse

Connaughton, J.F., Jr, D. Reeser, J. Schut, and L.P. Finnegan. 1977. 'Perinatal Addiction: Outcome and Management,' *American Journal of Obstetrics and Gynecology* 129: 679–86

Cook, D.R. 1987. 'Self-identified Addictions and Emotional Disturbances in a Sample of College Students,' *Psychology of Addictive Behaviors* 1: 55–61

Cook, S.J. 1969. 'Canadian Narcotics Legislation 1908–1923: A Conflict Model Interpretation,' *Canadian Review of Sociology and Anthropology* 6: 36–46

Coombs, R.H. 1981. 'Drug Abuse as a Career,' *Journal of Drug Issues* 11: 369–87

Cooper, J.R., F. Altman, B.S. Brown, and D. Czechowicz, eds. 1983. *Research on the Treatment of Narcotic Addiction: State of the Art*. Treatment Research Monograph Series. Rockville, MD: National Institute on Drug Abuse

Co-ordinated Law Enforcement Unit. 1987. *Final Report: Cocaine: Demand Reduction Strategies*. Victoria, BC: Ministry of the Attorney General

Courtwright, D.T. 1982. *Dark Paradise: Opiate Addiction in America before 1940*. Cambridge, MA: Harvard University Press

Courtwright, D.T., H. Joseph, and D. DesJarlais. 1989. *Addicts Who Survived: An Oral History of Narcotic Use in America, 1923–1965*. Knoxville: University of Tennessee Press

Cousineau, D.F., and S.D. Chambers. In preparation. 'Psychotherapy: Effective for What?' Department of Criminology, Simon Fraser University, Burnaby, BC

Cox, S. 1988. 'Caravetta Swings Vote against Meals in School,' *Vancouver Sun*, 11 May

Craig, R.J. 1988. 'Psychological Functioning of Cocaine Free-basing Derivedd from Objective Psychological Tests,' *Journal of Clinical Psychology* 44: 599–606

Critchley, H.O.D., S.M. Woods, A.J. Barson, T. Richardson, and B.A. Lieberman. 1988. 'Fetal Death in Utero and Cocaine Abuse. Case Report,' *British Journal of Obstetrics and Gynecology* 95: 195–6

Crowley, A. 1922/1972. *Diary of a Drug Fiend*. London: Sphere

Cucco, R.A., O.H. Yoo, L. Cregler, and J.C. Chang. 1987. 'Nonfatal Pulmonary Edema after "Freebase" Cocaine Smoking,' *American Review of Respiratory Disease* 136: 179–81

Cummings, C., J.R. Gordon, and G.A. Marlatt. 1980. 'Relapse: Prevention and Prediction.' In W.R. Miller, ed., *The Addictive Behaviors*. Oxford: Pergamon

Dackis, C.A., and M.S. Gold. 1985. 'New Concepts in Cocaine Addiction: The Dopamine Depletion Hypothesis,' *Neuroscience & Biobehavioral Reviews* 9: 469–77

Daher, D.M. 1984. 'Procrastination and University Students: Theories and Programming.' Presented at American Psychological Association Meetings, Toronto, August

Darwin, C. 1871/1981. *The Descent of Man and Selection in Relation to Sex*. Princeton: Princeton University Press

Davis, D., D. Berensen, P. Steinglass, and S. Davis. 1974. 'The Adaptive Consequences of Drinking,' *Psychiatry* 37: 209–25.

Dawkins, R. 1976. *The Selfish Gene*. London: Granada

Devenvi, P., and M.A. McDonough. 1988. 'Cocaine Abuse and Endocarditis,' *Annals of Internal Medicine* 109: 82

Deverell, W. 1979. *Needles*. Toronto: McClelland & Stewart

Dewey, J. 1922. *Human Nature and Conduct*. New York: Modern Library

Deykin, E.Y., J.C. Levy, and V. Wells. 1987. 'Adolescent Depression, Alcohol and Drug Abuse,' *American Journal of Public Health* 77: 178–81

Doberczak, T.M., S. Shanzer, R.T. Senie, and S.R. Kandall. 1988. 'Neonatal Neurologic and Electroencephalographic Effects of Intrauterine Cocaine Exposure,' *Journal of Pediatrics* 113: 354–8

Dole, V.P. 1972. 'Narcotic Addiction, Physical Dependence and Relapse,' *New England Journal of Medicine* 286: 988–92

– 1980, 'Addictive Behavior,' *Scientific American* 234 (6): 138–54

Dole, V.P., and M.E. Nyswander. 1983. 'Behavioral Pharmacology and Treatment of Human Drug Abuse – Methadone Maintenance of Narcotic Addicts.' In J.E. Smith and J.D. Lane, eds, *The Neurobiology of Opiate Reward Processes*. Amsterdam: Elsevier

Donovito, M.T. 1988. 'Cocaine Use during Pregnancy: Adverse Perinatal Outcome,' *American Journal of Obstetrics and Gynecology* 159: 485–6

Dorn, N., C. Jones, and N. South. 1988. 'The Rise and Fall of Family Support Groups,' *Druglink*, January/February: 8–11

Drug Abuse Policy Office (Office of Policy Development, The White House). 1984. *National Strategy for Prevention of Drug Abuse and Drug Trafficking*. Washington: Superintendent of Documents, U.S. Printing Office

Dunbar, J. 1970. *J.M. Barrie: The Man behind the Image*. Boston: Houghton, Mifflin

DuPont, R. 1988. 'Letters to the Editor,' *The Economist* 307: 4–6

DuPont, R.L., Jr. 1984. *Getting Tough on Gateway Drugs: A Guide for the Family*. Washington: American Psychiatric Press

Durkheim, E. 1897/1951. *Suicide: A Study in Sociology*. Translated by J.A. Spaulding and G. Simpson. Glenco, IL: Free Press

Dyer, G. 1985. *War*. Toronto: Stoddard

*Economist*. 1988. Letters to the editor, 30 April

*Edmonton Journal*. 1986. 'Aussie Drug Traffickers Both Hanged at Dawn,' 7 July

Edwards, G., A. Arif, and R. Hodgson. 1982. 'Nomenclature and Classification of Drug- and Alcohol-related Problems: A Shortened Version of a WHO Memorandum,' *British Journal of Addiction* 77: 3–20

Edwards, J., and R.N. Rubin. 1987. 'Aortic Dissection and Cocaine Abuse,' *Annals of Internal Medicine* 107: 779–80

Emrich, H.M., and M.J. Millan. 1982. 'Stress Reactions and Endorphinergic Systems,' *Journal of Psychosomatic Research* 26: 101–14

Engelsman, E. 1987. 'Moralistic versus Pragmatic Drug Control Policy: A Dutch Approach.' Presented at the International Conference on Drug Control Policy Reform, London, 13–17 July

Epp, J. 1986. *Achieving Health for All – A Framework for Health Promotion*. Ottawa: Health and Welfare Canada

Epstein, E.J. 1977. *Agency of Fear: Opiates and Political Power in America*. New York: Putnam

Erickson, D.H. 1984. 'An Evaluation of a Grade Six Drug Education Program.' Unpublished MA thesis, Department of Psychology, Simon Fraser University, Burnaby, BC

Erickson, P.G., E.M. Adlaf, G.F. Murray, and R.G. Smart. 1987. *The Steel Drug: Cocaine in Perspective*. Lexington, MA: D.C. Heath

Erickson, P.G., and B.K. Alexander. 1989. 'Cocaine and Addictive Liability,' *Social Pharmacology* 3: 249–70

Ericson, R.V., P.M. Baranek, and J.B.L. Chan. 1987. *Visualizing Deviance: A Study of News Organization*. Toronto: University of Toronto Press

Erikson, E.H. 1963. *Childhood and Society*. 2d edition. New York: Norton

– 1968. *Identity: Youth and Crisis*. New York: Norton

Factor, S.A., J.R. Sanchez-Ramos, and W.J. Weiner. 1988. 'Cocaine and Tourette's Syndrome,' *Annals of Neurology* 23: 423–4

Falk, J.L. 1983. 'Drug Dependence: Myth or Motive?' *Pharmacology, Biochemistry, and Behavior* 19: 385–91

Fazey, C.S.J. Unpublished. 'The Evaluation of Liverpool Drug Dependency Clinic: The First Two Years, 1985–1987.' Report to the Mersey Regional Health Authority, England

Feasby, W.R. 1953. *Official History of the Canadian Medical Services*, vol. II. Ottawa: Queen's Printer

Feehan, H.F., and A. Mancusi-Ungaro. 1976. 'The Use of Cocaine as a Topical Anesthetic in Nasal Surgery: A Survey Report,' *Plastic and Reconstructive Surgery* 57: 62–5

Ferrier, I. 1985. 'A Victory over Addiction,' *Maclean's*, 15 July: 48–9

Feyerabend, P. 1978. *Against Method: Outlines of an Anarchistic Theory of Knowledge*. London: Verso

Fingarette, H. 1988. *Heavy Drinking: The Myth of Alcoholism as a Disease*. Berkeley: University of California Press

Fingarette, H., and A.F. Hasse. 1979. *Mental Disabilities and Criminal Responsibility.* Berkeley: University of California Press

Fink, L., and M.P. Hyatt. 1978. 'Drug Use and Criminal Behavior,' *Journal of Drug Education* 8: 139–49

Finkle, B.S., and K.L. McCloskey. 1978. 'The Forensic Toxicology of Cocaine (1971–1976),' *Journal of Forensic Sciences* 23: 173–89

Finnigan, L.P., and K. Fehr. 1980. 'The Effects of Opiates, Sedative-Hypnotics, Amphetamines, Cannabis, and Other Psychoactive Drugs on the Fetus and Newborn.' In O.J. Kalant, ed., *Alcohol and Drug Problems in Women.* New York: Plenum

Firth, J. 1988. 'Registrations with Cocaine as the Major Problem Substance, July 1983–December 1987.' Unpublished data, Clinical Institute, Addiction Research Foundation, Toronto

Fischman, M.W. 1984. 'The Behavioral Pharmacology of Cocaine in Humans.' In J. Grabowski, ed., *Cocaine: Pharmacology, Effects, and Treatment of Abuse.* NIDA Research Monograph 50. Rockville, MD: National Institute on Drug Abuse

Fischman, M.W., and C.R. Schuster. 1980. 'Experimental Investigations of the Actions of Cocaine in Humans.' In F.R. Jeri, ed., *Cocaine 1980.* Lima, Peru: Pacific Press

Fischman, M.W., C.R. Schuster, L. Resnekov, J.F.E. Shick, N.A. Krasnegor, W. Fennell, and D.X. Freedman. 1976. 'Cadiovascular and Subjective Effects of Intravenous Cocaine Administration in Humans,' *Archives of General Psychiatry* 33: 983–9

Fiscina, S. 1986. 'Death Associated with Aspirin Overdose,' *Military Medicine* 151: 499

Fitzgerald, K.W. 1983. 'Living with Jellinek's Disease,' *Newsweek,* 17 October: 22

Flower, R.J., S. Moncada, and J.R. Vane. 1985. 'Analgesic-Antipyretics and Anti-inflammatory Agents: Drugs Employed in the Treatment of Gout.' In A.G. Gilman et al., eds, 1985. *Goodman and Gilman's The Pharmacological Basis of Therapeutics*

Folkins, C., and N. Wieselberg-Bell. 1981. A Personality Profile of Ultramarathon Runners: A Little Deviance May Go a Long Way,' *Journal of Sport Behavior* 4: 119–27

Foltz, K., M. Hager, P. King, and N. Joseph. 1984. 'Alcohol on the Rocks,' *Newsweek,* 31 December: 52–4

Foucault, M. 1970. *The Order of Things: An Archaeology of the Human Sciences.* London: Tavistock

– 1979. *Discipline and Punish: The Birth of the Prison.* New York: Vintage Books

Fowler, G. 1930. *The Dawn Patrol.* New York: Grosset & Dunlop

Francis, K.T., and R. Carter. 1982. 'Psychological Characteristics of Joggers,' *Journal of Sportsmedicine* 22: 368–91

Franco, J. 1931. 'The Beaver: A Cure for All Ills,' *The Beaver* (September): 283–4

Franks, L. 1985. 'A New Attack on Alcoholism,' *New York Times Magazine,* 20 October: 47–69

Fraser, A. 1976. 'Drug Addiction in Pregnancy,' *Lancet* 2: 896–9

Frawley, P.J. 1987. 'Neurobehavioral Model of Addiction,' *Journal of Drug Issues* 17: 29–46

Freud, A. 1946. *The Ego and the Mechanisms of Defense*. New York: International Universities Press

Freud, S. 1922/1955. 'Some Neurotic Mechanisms in Jealousy and Paranoia and Homosexuality.' In J. Strachey, ed., *The Complete Psychological Works of S. Freud*, vol. 18

– 1929. *Civilization and Its Discontents*. Chicago: Great Books

– 1884/1974. 'Über Coca.' Translated in R. Byck, ed., *Cocaine Papers by Sigmund Freud*. New York: Stonehill

– 1885/1974. 'Über die Allgemeinwirkung des Cocaïns.' Translated in R. Byck, ed., *Cocaine Papers by Sigmund Freud*. New York: Stonehill

– 1887/1974. 'Beiträge über die Anwendung des Cocaïn. Zweite Serie. I. Bemerkungen über Cocaïnsucht und Cocaïnfurcht mit Beziehung auf einem Vortrag W.A. Hammond's.' Translated in R. Byck, ed., *Cocaine Papers by Sigmund Freud*. New York: Stonehill

– 1920/1979. 'The Psychogenesis of a Case of Homosexuality in a Woman.' In S. Freud, *Case Histories II*. Harmondsworth: Penguin

Friedman, A.S. Unpublished. 'A Follow-up Study of Clients of the Straight, Inc. Program.' Philadelphia Psychiatric Center, Philadelphia

Fussell, P. 1989. 'The Real War 1939–1945,' *The Atlantic* (August), 264 (2): 32–48

Garriott, J.C., W.Q. Sturner, and M.F. Mason. 1973. 'Toxicologic Findings in Six Fatalities Involving Methadone,' *Clinical Toxicology* 6: 163–73

Gawin, F.H., D. Allen, and B. Humblestone. 1989. 'Outpatient Treatment of "Crack" Cocaine Smoking with Flupenthixol Deconate,' *Archives of General Psychiatry* 46: 322–5

Gawin, F.H., and H.D. Kleber. 1985. 'Cocaine Use in a Treatment Population: Patterns and Diagnostic Distinctions.' In Kozel and Adams, eds, *Cocaine Use in America*

– 1986. 'Abstinence Symptomatology and Psychiatric Diagnosis in Cocaine Abusers,' *Archives of General Psychiatry* 43: 107–13

Genet, J. 1943/1963. *Our Lady of the Flowers*. New York: Grove Press

Gergen, K. 1985. 'The Social Constructionist Movement in Modern Psychology,' *American Psychologist* 40: 266–75

– 1987. 'Warranting the New Paradigm: A Response to Harré,' *New Ideas in Psychology* 5: 19–24

Gervais, C.H. 1980. *The Rumrunners: A Prohibition Scrapbook*. Thornhill, Ont.: Firefly Books

Getto, C.J., D.T. Fullerton, and I.H. Carlson. 1984. 'Plasma Immunoreactive Beta-endorphin Response to Glucose Ingestion in Human Obesity,' *Appetite* 5: 329–35

Ghent, W.R. 1986. 'Heroin: Panacea or Plague,' *Queen's Quarterly* 93: 808–20

Gibbon, E. 1788/1952. *Decline and Fall of the Roman Empire*. Chicago: W. Benton

Gibbons, M. 1974. 'Walkabout: Searching for the Right Passage from Childhood and School.' *Phi Delta Kappan* 55: 596–602

Giffen, P.J., and S. Lambert. 1988. 'What Happened on the Way to Law Reform?' In J.S. Blackwell and P.G. Erickson, eds, *Illicit Drugs in Canada: A Risky Business*. Scarborough, Ont.: Nelson Canada

Gifford-Jones, W. 1986. 'The Doctor Game: Even a Small Dose of Cocaine Can
    Trigger a Heart Attack,' *Globe and Mail*, 30 December
–  1987. 'Heroin Fights for Acceptance,' *Province*, 9 March
    Gilbert, R. 1986. 'Unprofessional Conduct,' *The Journal* 16 (1): 8
–  1987. 'Replying to Critics,' *The Journal* 16 (6): 12
–  1988. 'Caffeine: Cardiovascular Effects,' *The Journal* 17 (5): 12
Gilliland, K., and D. Andress. 1981. 'Ad lib Caffeine Consumption, Symptoms of
    Caffeinism, and Academic Performance,' *American Journal of Psychiatry* 138:
    512–14
Gilman, A.G., L.S. Goodman, T.W. Rall, and F. Murad, eds. 1985. *Goodman and
    Gilman's The Pharmacological Basis of Therapeutics*. 7th edition. New York:
    Macmillan
Girard, R. 1977. *Violence and the Sacred*. Baltimore: John Hopkins University Press
Girodo, M. 1984. 'Entry and Re-entry Strain in Undercover Agents.' In V.L. Allen and
    E. van de Vliet, eds, *Role Transitions*. New York: Plenum
Glaser, F.B. 1974. 'Psychologic vs. Pharmacologic Heroin Dependence,'
    *New England Journal of Medicine* 290: 231
Glaser, F.B., and A.C. Ogborne. 1982. 'Does AA Really Work?' *British Journal of
    Addiction* 77: 123–9
Glasser, W. 1976. *Positive Addiction*. New York: Basic Books
*Globe and Mail*. 1985. 'Ontario Tobacco Growers Faced with Long Row to Hoe,'
    6 August
Golbe, L.I., and M.D. Merkin. 1986. 'Cerebral Infarction in a User of Free-Base
    Cocaine ("Crack"),' *Neurology* 36: 1602–4
Gold, M.S. 1984. *800-COCAINE*. Toronto: Bantam Books
Gold, M.S., and C.A. Dackis. 1984. 'New Insights and Treatments: Opiate Withdrawal
    and Cocaine Addiction,' *Clinical Therapeutics* 7: 6–21
Gold, M.S., and N. Miller. 1987. 'How Effective Is the Disease Model? ("Point-
    Counterpoint"),' *U.S. Journal of Drug and Alcohol Dependence* 12 (11): 7
Gold, M.S., A.L.C. Pottash, I. Extein, and H.D. Kleber. 1980. 'Anti-endorphin
    Effects of Methadone,' *Lancet* 2 (8201): 972–3
Gold, M.S., and W.S. Rea. 1983. 'The Role of Endorphins in Opiate Addiction, Opiate
    Withdrawal and Recovery,' *Psychiatric Clinics of North America* 6: 489–520
Gold, M.S., A.M. Washton, and C.A. Dackis. 1985. 'Cocaine Abuse: Neuro-
    chemistry, Phenomenology, and Treatment.' In Kozel and Adams, eds, *Cocaine Use
    in America*
Goldberg, M.F. 1984. 'Cocaine: The First Local Anesthetic and the "Third Scourge of
    Humanity,"' *Archives of Ophthalmology* 102: 1443–7
Goldman, A. 1981. *Elvis*. New York: McGraw-Hill
Goldman, B. 1987. 'The Prescription Drug Sting,' *Canadian Medical Association
    Journal* 136: 629–38
–  1987a. 'Fighting Back: The Search for a Solution to Prescription Drug Abuse,'
    *Canadian Medical Association Journal* 136: 745–52
–  1987b. 'Confronting the Prescription Drug Addict: Doctors Must Learn to Say No,'
    *Canadian Medical Association Journal* 136: 871–6

Goldstein, A. 1972. Heroin Addiction and the Role of Methadone in Its Treatment,'
Archives of General Psychiatry 26: 291–7
– 1976. 'Opioid Peptides (Endorphins) in Pituitary and Brain,' Science 193: 1081–6
– 1979. 'Heroin Maintenance: A Medical View. A Conversation between a Physician
and a Politician,' Journal of Drug Issues 9: 341–7
Goodwin, D.W. 1979. 'Alcoholism and Heredity: A Review and Hypothesis,' Archives
of General Psychiatry 36: 57–61
– 1985. 'Alcoholism and Genetics: The Sins of the Fathers,' Archives of General
Psychiatry 42: 171–4
Goodwin, D.W., F. Schulsinger, J. Knop, S. Mednick, and S.B. Guze. 1977.
'Alcoholism and Depression in Adopted-out Daughters of Alcoholics,' Archives of
General Psychiatry 34: 751–5
Goodwin, D.W., F. Schulsinger, N. Moller, L. Hermansen, G. Winokur, and S.B.
Guze. 1974. 'Drinking Problems in Adopted and Nonadopted Sons of
Alcoholics,' Archives of General Psychiatry 31: 164–9
Gordon, B.R. 1987. 'Topical Cocaine Nasal Anesthesia,' Archives of Otolaryngology –
Head and Neck Surgery 113: 211
Grabowski, H.G., and J.M. Vernon. 1978. 'Consumers Product Safety Regulation,'
Economics of Life and Safety: American Economic Association 68: 285–9
Grabowski, J., ed. Cocaine: Pharmacology, Effects, and Treatment of Abuse. NIDA
Research Monograph 50. Rockville, MD: National Institute on Drug Abuse
Grabowski, J., and S.I. Dworkin. 1985. 'Cocaine: An Overview of Current Issues,'
International Journal of the Addictions 20: 1065–88
Graham, A. 1986. 'Trickling Down and Out.' In P. Ekins, ed., The Living Economy:
A New Economics in the Making. London: Routledge & Kegan Paul
Gray, J.H. 1972. Booze: The Impact of Whiskey on the Prairie West. Toronto:
Macmillan of Canada
– 1982. Bachannalia Revisited: Western Canada's Boozy Skid to Social Disaster.
Saskatoon: Western Producer Prairie Books
Greden, J.F. 1974. 'Anxiety or Caffeinism: A Diagnostic Dilemma,' American
Journal of Psychiatry 131: 1089–92
Green, M., and R.D. Miller. 1975. 'Cannabis Use in Canada.' In V. Rubin, ed.,
Cannabis and Culture. The Hague: Mouton
Greenberg, J. 1983. 'Natural Highs in Natural Habitats,' Science News 124: 300–1
Grinspoon, L., and J.B. Bakalar. 1976. Cocaine: A Drug and Its Social Evoluion. New
York: Basic Books
Gross, J. 1988. 'Speed's Gain in Use Could Rival Crack, Drug Experts Warn.' New
York Times, 27 November
Gusfield, J.R. 1963. Symbolic Crusade: Status Politics and the American Temperance
Movement. Urbana, IL: University of Illinois Press
Hacking, I. 1983. Representing and Intervening: Introductory Topics in the Philosophy
of Natural Science. Cambridge: Cambridge University Press
Hadaway, P.F., B.K. Alexander, R.B. Coambs, and B.L. Beyerstein. 1979. 'The
Effect of Housing and Gender on Preference for Morphine-Sucrose Solutions in
Rats,' Psychopharmacology 66: 87–91

Hadaway, P.F., and B.L. Beyerstein. 1987. 'Then They Came for the Smokers But I Didn't Speak Up Because I Wasn't a Smoker: Legislation and Tobacco Use,' *Canadian Psychology* 28: 259–65

Haddad, L.M. 1983. 'Cocaine.' In L.M. Haddad and J.F. Winchester, eds, *Clinical Management of Poisoning and Drug Overdose*. Philadelphia: W.B. Saunders

Haines, J.D., and S. Sexter. 1987. 'Acute Myocardial Infarction Associated with Cocaine Abuse,' *Southern Medical Journal* 80: 1326–7

Hallowell, G.A. 1972. *Prohibition in Ontario 1919–1923*. Toronto: Ontario Historical Society

– 1985. 'Prohibition.' In J.H. Marsh, ed., *The Canadian Encyclopedia*, vol. 3. Edmonton: Hurtig

Hanna, J.M., and C.A. Hornick. 1977. 'Use of Coca Leaf in Southern Peru: Adaptation or Addiction,' *Bulletin on Narcotics* 29: 63–74

Hanreich, W. 1984. 'Drug-related Crime and Sentencing Policies From the Perspective of the United Nations Crime Prevention and Criminal Justice Programme,' *Bulletin on Narcotics* 36 (3): 47–76

Hanson, D.J. 1982. 'Alcohol and Drug Education,' *Journal on Alcohol and Drug Education* 2: 1–13

Harber, V.J., and J.R. Sutton. 1984. 'Endorphins and Exercise,' *Sports Medicine* 1: 154–71

Hargreaves, W.A. 1983. 'Methadone Dosage and Duration for Maintenance Treatment.' In J.R. Cooper, F. Altman, B.S. Brown, and D. Czechowicz, eds, *Research on the Treatment of Narcotic Addiction: State of the Art*. Treatment Research Monograph Series. Rockville, MD: National Institute on Drug Abuse

Harris, M. 1974. *Cows, Pigs, Wars, and Witches*. New York: Random House

Hauschildt, E. 1988. 'Prevention Long-term Answer: Enforcement Only Short-term,' *The Journal* 17 (8): 1

Health and Welfare Canada. 1984. *Cancer Pain: A Monograph on the Management of Cancer Pain*. Ottawa: Health and Welfare Canada

Heinlein, R.A. 1961. *Stranger in a Strange Land*. New York: Putnam

Helzer, J.E., L.N. Robins, and D.H. Davis. 1975/76. 'Antecedents of Narcotic Use and Addiction. A Study of 898 Vietnam Veterans,' *Drug and Alcohol Dependence* 1: 183–90

Henderson, I.W.D. 1983. 'Chemical Dependence in Canada: A View from the Hill.' In Committee on Problems of Drug Dependence, Inc., eds, *Problems of Drug Dependence*. NIDA Research Monograph 43. Rockville, MD: National Institute on Drug Abuse

Hendtlass, J. 1987. 'Drug Policy Reform in Australia.' Presented at the International Conference on Drug Policy Reform. London, 13–17 July

Herman, E.S., and N. Chomsky. 1988. *Manufacturing Consent: The Political Economy of the Mass Media*. New York: Pantheon

Herz, A. 1981. 'Role of Endorphins in Addiction,' *Modern Problems in Psychopharmacology* 17: 175–80

Herzberg, J.L., and S.N. Wolkind. 1983. 'Solvent Sniffing in Perspective,' *British Journal of Hospital Medicine* 29: 72 6

Herzlich, B.C., E.L. Arsura, M. Pagala, and D. Grob. 1988. 'Rhabdomyolysis Related to Cocaine Abuse,' *Annals of Internal Medicine* 109: 335–6

Hiebert, A.J. 1969. 'Prohibition in British Columbia.' Unpublished MA thesis, Department of History, Simon Fraser University, Burnaby, BC

Hill, C.S.H. 1987. 'Painful Prescriptions,' *Journal of the American Medical Association* 257: 2081

Hinson, R.E., and C.X. Poulos. 1981. 'Sensitization to the Behavioral Effects of Cocaine: Modification by Pavlovian Conditioning,' *Pharmacology, Biochemistry, and Behavior* 15: 559–62

Hobbes, T. 1651/1962. *Leviathan, or the Matter, Forme, and Power of a Commonwealth Ecclesiasticall and Civil.* New York: Collier

Hochhauser, M. 1980. 'A Chronobiological Control Theory.' In D.J. Lettieri, M. Sayers, and M.W. Pearson, eds, *Theories on Drug Abuse.* NIDA Research Monograph 30. Rockville, MD: National Institute on Drug Abuse

Hodding, G.C., M. Jann, and I.P. Ackerman. 1980. 'Drug Withdrawal Syndromes: A Literature Review,' *Western Journal of Medicine* 133: 383–91

Hodgson, M. 1987. *Indian Communities Develop Futuristic Addictions Treatment and Health Approach.* Edmonton: Nechi Institute on Alcohol and Drug Education

Hodgson, R., and P. Miller. 1982. *Selfwatching: Addictions, Habits, Compulsions: What to Do about Them.* London: Century

Hogarth, D.A., Judge. 1986. *Reasons for Judgment R. v. Gudbrandson.* New Westminster, BC: County Court of New Westminster

Holden, C. 1987. 'Alcoholism and the Medical Cost Crunch,' *Science* 235: 1132–3
– 1988. 'Is Alcoholism Treatment Effective?' *Science* 236: 20–2
– 1988a. 'Supreme Court Denies Plea of Alcoholic Vets,' *Science* 240: 597

Holthuis, G. 1987. 'Institutional Tolerance of Marijuana in Holland: Quasi-legal Soft Drugs Reduce Hard Drug Crime,' *Whole Earth Review*, Spring: 54

Home Office. 1986. *Tackling Drug Misuse: A Summary of the Government's Strategy.* 2d edition. London: Home Office

Honer, W.G., G. Gewirtz, and M. Turey. 1987. 'Psychosis and Violence in Cocaine Smokers,' *Lancet* 2 (8556): 451

Horowitz, G.P., G. Whitney, J.C. Smith, and F.K. Stephan. 1977. 'Morphine Ingestion: Genetic Control in Mice,' *Psychopharmacology* 52: 119–22

Householder, J., R. Hatcher, W. Burns, and I. Chasnoff. 1982. 'Infants Born to Narcotic-addicted Mothers,' *Psychological Bulletin* 92: 453–68

Howard, G.S. 1985. 'The Role of Values in the Science of Psychology,' *American Psychologist* 40: 255–65

Howard, R.E., D.C. Hueter, and G.J. Davis. 1985. 'Acute Myocardial Infarction Following Cocaine Abuse in a Young Woman with Normal Coronary Arteries,' *Journal of the American Medical Association* 254: 95–6

Howlett, T.A., S. Tomlin, L. Ngahfoong, L.H. Rees, B.A. Bullen, G.S. Skriner, and J.W. McArthur. 1984. 'Release of Beta Endorphin and Met-enkephalin during Exercise in Normal Women: Response to Training,' *British Medical Journal* 288: 1950–2

Hughes, J., A. Beaumont, J.A. Fuentes, B. Malfroy, and C. Unsworth. 1980. 'Opioid Peptides: Aspects of Their Origin, Release and Metabolism,' *Journal of Experimental Biology* 89: 239–55

Hughes, R. 1987. *The Fatal Shore: The Epic of Australia's Founding*. New York: Knopf

Hughes, R., and R. Brewin. 1979. *The Tranquilizing of America: Pillpopping and the American Way of Life*. New York: Harcourt, Brace, Jovanovich

Hunt, W.A., L.W. Barnet, and L.G. Branch. 1971. 'Relapse Rates in Addiction Programs,' *Journal of Clinical Psychology* 27: 455–6

Hutchinson, C.C.J. 1985. *Reasons for Judgment Voir Dire R. v. Coupal*. Vancouver: County Court of Vancouver

Huxley, A. 1963. *The Doors of Perception and Heaven and Hell*. New York: Harper

Illich, I. 1973. *Tools for Conviviality*. New York: Harper & Row

– 1981. *Shadow Work*. Boston: M. Boyars

Inciardi, J.A. 1977. *Methadone Diversion: Experiences and Issues*. NIDA Services Research Monograph Series. Rockville, MD: National Institute on Drug Abuse

– 1986. *The War on Drugs: Heroin, Cocaine Crime, and Public Policy*. Palo Alto, CA: Mayfield

– 1987. 'Beyond Cocaine: Basuco, Crack, and Other Coca Products,' *Contemporary Drug Problems* 14: 461–92

Ingold, F.R. 1986. 'Study of Deaths Related to Drug Abuse in France and Europe,' *Bulletin on Narcotics* 38: 81–9

'Inquest on the body of John Dennis Williams.' 1980. Official Court Reports, New Westminster, 4 Sept

Inturrisi, C.E., and K. Verebely. 1972. 'The Levels of Methadone in the Plasma in Methadone Maintenance,' *Chemical Pharmacology and Therapeutics* 13: 633–7

Isaacs, S.O, P. Martin, and J.H. Willoughby. 1987. 'Crack (an extra potent form of cocaine) Abuse: A Problem of the Eighties,' *Oral Surgery, Oral Medicine, Oral Pathology* 63: 12–16

Isikoff, M. 1989. 'Civil Air Patrol Enlists in Drug War,' *Washington Post*, 20 April

– 1989a. 'Bennett Mulls Drug-abuser Boot Camps,' *Washington Post*, 8 May

Isner, J.M., N.A.M. Estes, P.D. Thompson, M.R. Costanzo-Nordin, R. Subramanian, G. Miller, G. Katsas, K. Sweeney, and W.Q. Sturner. 1986. 'Acute Cardiac Events Temporally Related to Cocaine Abuse,' *New England Journal of Medicine*, 315: 1438–43

Istvan, J., and J.D. Matarazzo. 1984. 'Tobacco, Alcohol, and Caffeine Use,' *Psychological Bulletin* 95: 301–26

Itkonen, J., S. Schnoll, and J. Glassroth. 1984. 'Pulmonary Dysfunction in "Freebase" Cocaine Users,' *Archives of Internal Medicine*, 144: 2195–7

Jaffe, J.H. 1980. 'Drug Addiction and Drug Abuse.' In A.G. Gilman, L.S. Goodman, and A. Gilman, eds, *Goodman and Gilman's The Pharmacological Basis of Therapeutics*. 6th edition. New York: Macmillan

– 1985. 'Drug Addiction and Drug Abuse.' In Gilman et al., eds, *Goodman and Gilman's The Pharmacological Basis of Therapeutics*. 7th edition

– 1985a. 'Foreword.' In Kozel and Adams, eds, *Cocaine Use in America*

Jaffe, J.H., R. Petersen, and R. Hodgson. 1980. *Addiction: Issues & Answers*. New York: Harper & Row

Jaffe, J.H., and W.R. Martin. 1980. 'Opioid Analgesics and Antagonists.' In A.G. Gilman, L.S. Goodman, and A. Gilman, eds. *Goodman and Gilman's The Pharmacological Basis of Therapeutics*. 6th edition. New York: Macmillan

– 1985. 'Opioid Analgesics and Antagonists.' In Gilman et al., eds, *Goodman and Gilman's The Pharmacological Basis of Therapeutics*. 7th edition

James, J.C.M., and M.A. McConville. 1986. *Symposium Proceedings: Symposium on Street Youth*. Toronto: Covenant House

James, J.E., and K.P. Stirling. 1983. 'Caffeine: A Survey of Some of the Known or Suspected Deleterious Effects of Habitual Use,' *British Journal of Addiction* 78: 251–8

James, W. 1906/1963. *Pragmatism and Other Essays*. New York: Washington Square Press

Jasinski, D.R., and K.L. Preston. 1986. 'Comparison of Intravenously Administered Methadone, Morphine, and Heroin,' *Drug and Alcohol Dependence* 17: 301–10

Javaid, J.I., M.W. Fischman, C.R. Schuster, H. Dekirmenjian, and J.M. Davis. 1978. 'Cocaine Plasma Concentration: Relation to Physiological and Subjective Effects in Humans,' *Science* 202: 227–8

Jekel, J.F., H. Podlewski, S. Dean-Patterson, D.F. Allen, N. Clarke, and P. Cartwright. 1986. 'Epidemic Free-base Cocaine Abuse,' *Lancet* 1: 459–62

Jellinek, E.M. 1960. *The Disease Concept in Alcoholism*. New Brunswick, NJ: Hill House

Jeri, F.R. 1986. 'Somatic Disorders Associated with the Abuse of Coca Paste and Cocaine Hydrochloride.' In C.D. Kaplan and M. Kooyman, eds, *Proceedings 15th International Institute on the Prevention and Treatment of Drug Dependence*. Rotterdam: Erasmus University

Johanson, C.E. 1984. 'Assessment of the Dependence Potential of Cocaine in Animals.' In J. Grabowski, ed., *Cocaine: Pharmacology, Effects, and Treatment of Abuse*. NIDA Research Monograph 50. Rockville, MD: National Institute on Drug Abuse

Johnson, B.D. 1978. 'Investigating Impact of Methadone Treatment upon the Behaviour of New York City Street Addicts,' *Proceedings of the Section Meetings of the 32nd International Congresss on Alcoholism and Drug Dependence, Warsaw, 1978*. Lausanne, Switzerland: International Council on Alcohol and Addictions

Johnson, H. 1988. 'Illegal Drug Use in Canada,' *Canadian Social Trends*, Winter, 5–8

Johnston, L.D., P.M. O'Malley, and J.G. Bachman. 1986. *Illicit Drug Use, Smoking, and Drinking by America's High School Students, College Students, and Young Adults, National Trends through 1985*. Rockville, MD: National Institute of Mental Health

– 1988. *Illicit Drug Use, Smoking, and Drinking by America's High School Students, College Students, and Young Adults, 1975–1978*. Rockville, MD: National Institute of Mental Health

Joint Advisory Committee on the Treatment Uses of Methadone in the Province of British Columbia. 1985. *AUG 08 '85 10:51 HEALTH(HO)7HFLP*. Internal BC Government document

Jones, D. 1987. 'More Ammunition in Drug War,' *Globe and Mail*, 28 May

Jones, E. 1953. *The Life and Work of Sigmund Freud*. New York: Basic Books

Jones, H., and H. Jones. 1977. *Sensual Drugs*. Cambridge: Cambridge University Press

Jones, J., producer and director. 1987. 'Eight Seconds to Heaven.' Channel 4 (London, Eng.)

Joseph, H., P. Appel, and J. Schmeidler. 1981. *Deaths during and after Discharge from Methadone Maintenance Treatment. Outcome Study Report #18*. New York: New York State Division of Substance Abuse Services

Judson, H.F. 1973. *Heroin Addiction in Britain: What Americans Can Learn from the English Experience*. London: Harcourt, Brace, Jovanovich

Julien, R.M. 1978. *A Primer of Drug Action*. San Francisco: Freeman

– 1981. *A Primer of Drug Action*. 3d edition. San Francisco: Freeman

Kandall, S.R., S. Albin, J. Lowinson, B. Berle, A.I. Eidelman, and L.M. Gartner. 1976. 'Differential Effects of Maternal Heroin and Methadone Use on Birthweight,' *Pediatrics* 58: 581–5

Kandel, D.B., D. Murphy, and D. Karus. 1985. 'Cocaine Use in Young Adulthood: Patterns of Use and Psychosocial Correlates.' In Kozel and Adams, eds, *Cocaine Use in America*

Kaplan, B. 1982. *Drugs Both in Our Society and in Our Prisons*. Address to the Canadian Symposium on Drug Diversion, Ottawa

Kaplan, J. 1983. *The Hardest Drug: Heroin and Public Policy*. Chicago: University of Chicago Press

Kaye, B.R., and M. Fainstat. 1987. 'Cerebral Basculitis Associated with Cocaine Abuse,' *Journal of the American Medical Association* 258: 2104–6

Keen, S. 1986. *Faces of the Enemy: Reflections of the Hostile Imagination*. New York: Harper & Row

Khantzian, E.J. 1974. 'Opiate Addiction: A Critique of Theory and Some Implications for Treatment,' *American Journal of Psychotherapy* 28: 59–70

– 1983. 'An Extreme Case of Cocaine Dependence and Marked Improvement with Methylphenidate Treatment,' *American Journal of Psychiatry* 140: 784–5

– 1985. 'The Self-medication Hypothesis of Addictive Disorders: Focus on Heroin and Cocaine Dependence,' *American Journal of Psychiatry* 142: 1259–64

Khantzian, E.J., F. Gawin, H.D. Kleber, and C.E. Riordan. 1984. 'Methylphenidate (Ritalin) Treatment of Cocaine Dependence – A Preliminary Report,' *Journal of Substance Abuse Treatment* 1: 107–12

Khantzian, E.J., and N.J. Khantzian. 1984. 'Cocaine Addiction: Is There a Psychological Predisposition?' *Psychiatric Annals* 14: 753–9

Khantzian, E.J., J.E. Mack, and A.F. Schatzberg. 1974. 'Heroin Use as an Attempt to Cope: Clinical Observations,' *American Journal of Psychiatry* 131: 160–4

Khavari, K.A., and M.E. Risner. 1973. 'Opiate Dependence Produced by ad libitum Drinking of Morphine in Water, Saline and Sucrose Vehicles,' *Psychopharmacologia* 30: 291–302

Kielholz, P. 1970. 'Present Problems of Drug Dependence in Switzerland,' *Bulletin on Narcotics* 22: 1–6

Kielholz, P., and D. Ladewig. 1977. 'Abuse of Non-narcotic Analgesics.' In W.R. Martin, ed., *Drug Addiction I: Morphine, Sedative/Hypnotic and Alcohol Dependence*. Berlin: Springer-Verlag

King, R. 1972. *The Drug Hang-up: America's Fifty Year Folly*. New York: Norton

Kirsch, S. 1983. *Unemployment: Its Impact on Body and Soul*. Toronto: Canadian Mental Health Association

Kissner, D.G., W.D. Lawrence, J.E. Selis, and A. Flint. 1987. 'Crack Lung: Pulmonary Disease Caused by Cocaine Abuse,' *American Review of Respiratory Disease* 136: 1250–2

Klatt, E.C., S. Montgomery, T. Namiki, and T.T. Noguchi. 1986. 'Misrepresentation of Stimulant Street Drugs: A Decade of Experience in an Analysis Program,' *Journal of Toxicology: Clinical Toxicology* 24: 441–50

Kleinman, J.C., and J.H. Madans. 1985. 'The Effects of Maternal Smoking, Physical Stature, and Educational Attainment on the Incidence of Low Birth Weight,' *American Journal of Obstetrics and Gynecology* 121: 843–55

Klenka, H.M. 1986. 'Babies Born in a District General Hospital to Mothers Taking Heroin,' *British Medical Journal* 293: 745–6

Kline, D. 1985. 'The Anatomy of Addiction,' *Equinox* 4 (23): 77–86

Knightly, P. 1975. *The First Casualty: From the Crimea to Vietnam: The War Correspondent as a Hero, Propagandist, and Mythmaker.* New York: Harcourt, Brace, Jovanovich

Kobler, J. 1973. *Ardent Spirits: The Rise and Fall of Prohibition.* New York: G.P. Putnam's Sons

Koob, G.F., H.T. Le, and I. Creese. 1987. 'The DI Dopamine Receptor Antagonist SCH 23390 Increases Cocaine Self-administration in the Rat,' *Neuroscience Letters* 79: 315–20

Kooyman, M. 1983. 'Development of Treatment Policies for Drug Addicts in the Netherlands.' Presented in Frankfurt am Main (FRG), 8–9 June

Koring, P. 1989. 'Zero Tolerance to Fight Drugs Urged by Jelinek,' *Globe and Mail*, 26 April

Kossowsky, W.A., and A.F. Lyon. 1984. 'Cocaine and Acute Myocardial Infarction: A Probable Connection,' *Chest* 86: 729–31

Kozel, N.J., and E.H. Adams. 1985. 'Cocaine Use in America: Summary of Discussions and Recommendations.' In N.J. Kozel and E.H. Adams, eds, *Cocaine Use in America: Epidemiologic and Clinical Perspectives.* NIDA Research Monograph 61. Rockville, MD: National Institute on Drug Abuse

Krebs, C.J. 1978. *Ecology: The Experimental Analysis of Distribution and Abundance.* New York: Harper & Row

Krupka, L.R., A.M. Vener, C.S. Stewart, and M.M. Zaenglein-serger. 1978. 'Patterns of Aspirin Use among American Youth,' *International Journal of the Addictions* 13: 911–19

Kuhn, T.S. 1970. *The Structure of Scientific Revolutions.* 2d edition, enlarged. Chicago: University of Chicago Press

Kumar, R., and I.P. Stolerman. 1977. 'Experimental and Clinical Aspects of Drug Dependence.' In L.L. Iverson, S.D. Iverson, and S.H. Snyder, eds, *Handbook of Psychopharmacology*, vol. 7. New York: Plenum

Kumar, S. 1988. 'Third World Toils to Feed the West,' *Globe and Mail*, 15 April

Lakatos, I. 1978. *The Methodology of Scientific Research Programmes: Philosophical Papers*, vol. 1. Cambridge: Cambridge University Press

Lalonde, M. 1974. *A New Perspective on the Health of Canadians: A Working Document.* Ottawa: Government of Canada

*Lancet.* 1984. 'Psychotherapy: Effective Treatment or Expensive Placebo?' Unsigned editorial, 1: 83–4

– 1987. 'Screening for Drugs of Abuse.' Unsigned editorial, 1: 365–6

Land, E.H. 1971. 'Addiction as a Necessity and Opportunity,' *Science* 171: 151–3

Leary, T. 1968. *High Priest*. New York: World

Le Dain, G. 1972. *Cannabis: A Report of the Commission of Inquiry into the Non-medical Use of Drugs*. Ottawa: Information Canada

– 1973. *Final Report of the Commission of Inquiry into the Non-medical Use of Drugs*. Ottawa: Information Canada

Leukefeld, C.G., and F.M. Tims, eds. 1988. *Compulsory Treatment of Drug Abuse: Research and Clinical Practice*. NIDA Research Monograph 86. Rockville, MD: National Institute on Drug Abuse

Leuw, E. 1987. 'Official Ideology in International Drug Policies in Relation to Drug Policies in the Netherlands.' Presented at the International Conference on Drug Policy Reform, London, 13–17 July

Leventhal, H., and P.D. Cleary. 1980 'The Smoking Problem: A Review of Research and Theory in Behavorial Risk Modification,' *Psychological Bulletin* 88: 370–405

Leventhal, H., S. Jones, and G. Trembly. 1966. 'Sex Differences in Attitudes and Behavior Changes under Conditions of Fear and Specific Instructions,' *Journal of Experimental Social Psychology* 2: 387–99

Levanthal, H., R.P. Singer, and S. Jones. 1965. 'Effects of Fear and Specificity of Recommendations,' *Journal of Personality and Social Psychology* 2, 20–9

Levanthal, H., and J.C. Watts. 1966. 'Sources of Resistance to Fear Arousing Communications,' *Journal of Personality* 34: 155–75

Levanthal, H., J.C. Watts, and F. Pagano. 1967. 'Effects of Fear and Instructions on How to Cope with Danger,' *Journal of Personality and Social Psychology* 6: 313–21

Levine, H.G. 1978. 'The Discovery of Addiction: Changing Conceptions of Habitual Drunkenness in America,' *Journal of Studies on Alcohol* 39: 143–74

– 1984. 'The Alcohol Problem in America: From Temperance to Alcoholism,' *British Journal of Addiction* 79: 109–19

Levine, S.R., J.M. Washington, M.F. Jefferson, S.N. Kieran, M. Moen, H. Feit, and K.M.A. Welch. 1987. '"Crack" Cocaine-Associated Stroke,' *Neurology* 37: 1849–53

Levine, S.R., J.M. Washington, M. Moen, S.N. Kieran, S. Junger, and K.M.A. Welch. 1987. 'Crack-Associated Stroke,' *Neurology* 37: 1092–3

Lewis, C.T., and C. Short. 1879. *A Latin Dictionary: Founded on Andrews Edition of Freund's Latin Dictionary*. Oxford: Oxford University Press

Liban, C.B., and R.G. Smart. 1982. 'Drinking and Drug Use among Ontario Indian Students,' *Drug and Alcohol Dependence* 9: 161–71

Lichtblau, L., and S.B. Sparber. 1981. 'Opiate Withdrawal in Utero Increases Neonatal Morbidity in the Rat,' *Science* 212: 943–5

Lindesmith, A.R. 1980. 'A General Theory of Addiction to Opiate-Type Drugs.' In D.J. Lettieri, M. Sayers, and M.W. Pearson, eds, *Theories on Drug Abuse*. NIDA Research Monograph 30. Rockville, MD: National Institute on Drug Abuse

Lipski, J., B. Stimmel, and E. Donoso. 1973. 'The Effects of Heroin and Multiple Drug Abuse on the Electrocardiogram,' *American Heart Journal* 86: 663–8

Little, B.B., L.M. Snell, V.R. Klein, and L.C. Gilstrap, III. 1989. 'Cocaine Abuse during Pregnancy: Maternal and Fetal Implications,' *Obstetrics and Gynecology* 73: 157–60

Locke, J. 1690/1959. *An Essay Concerning Human Understanding*. Edited by A.C. Fraser. New York: Dover

Lombard, J., B. Wong, and J.H. Young. 1988. 'Acute Renal Failure due to Rhabdomyolysis Associated with Cocaine Toxicity.' *Western Journal of Medicine* 148: 466–8

London, W.D. 1986. 'Handedness and Alcoholism: A Family History of Left-handedness,' *Alcoholism: Clinical and Experimental Research* 10: 357

Lore, R., and K. Flannelly. 1977. 'Rat Societies,' *Scientific American* 236 (5): 106–16

Low, K. 1978. 'Prevention.' In L.A. Phillips, G.R. Ramsey, L. Blumenthal, and P. Crawshaw, eds, *Core Knowledge in the Drug Field*. Ottawa: Non-medical Use of Drugs Directorate, National Health and Welfare

– 1982. 'Responsible Approaches to Safe Intoxicant Use Needed in Age of Reason,' *Canadian Pharmaceutical Journal* 115: 327–31

Lowenstein, D.H., S.M. Massa, M.C. Rowbotham, S.D. Collins, H.E. McKinney, and R.P. Simon. 1987. 'Acute Neurologic and Psychiatric Complications Associated with Cocaine Abuse,' *American Journal of Medicine* 83: 841–6

Lutz, E.G. 1978. 'Restless Legs, Anxiety, and Caffeinism,' *Journal of Clinical Psychiatry* 39: 693–8

MacDonald, F. 1986. Form letter beginning 'Welcome to the New Methadone Treatment Clinic here at 307 West Broadway ... ,' dated 9 April 1986, with two attached documents entitled Executive Summary and Conditions of the Methadone Treatment Service for Narcotic Dependency (Ministry of Labour and Consumer Services, Alcohol and Drug Programs, Victoria, BC)

MacInnes, T.M. 1988. 'The Effect of Prescribing Methadone on the Opiate User Death Rate.' Unpublished honour's thesis, Department of Psychology, Simon Fraser University, Burnaby, BC

Mackail, D. 1941. *The Story of J.M.B.* London: Peter Davies

MacKenzie, C. 1989. 'Bush to Unveil $7.5 Billion Anti-drug Campaign on National TV,' *Globe and Mail*, 22 August

*Maclean's*. 1985. Cover picture, 17 June

MacLennan, A. 1986. 'Ottawa Charter Provides for Global Alliance in Public Health,' *The Journal* 16 (1): 1

Mahoney, M.J. 1982. 'Psychotherapy and Human Change Processes.' In J. Harvey and M. Parks, eds, *Psychotherapy Research and Behavior Change*. Washington: American Psychological Association

– 1985. 'Cognitive Developmental Life Counseling.' Presented at American Psychological Association Meetings, Los Angeles, August

Malcolm, A.I., and B.E. Malcolm. 1981. 'An Examination of STRAIGHT, incorporated.' Unpublished manuscript, available through Straight, inc.

Malyon, T. 1986. 'Full Tilt towards a No-win "Vietnam" War on Drugs,' *New Statesman*, October: 7–10

Mandenhoff, A., F. Fumeron, M. Appelbaum, and D.L. Margules. 1982. 'Endogenous Opiates and Energy Balance,' *Science* 215: 1536–8

Manschreck, T.C., D.F. Allen, and M. Neville. 1987. 'Freebase Psychosis: Cases from a Bahamian Epidemic of Cocaine Abuse,' *Comprehensive Psychiatry* 28: 555–64

Margules, D.L. 1981. Opioid and Anti-opioid Functions in the Survival and Reproduction of Individuals.' In S.J. Cooper, ed., *Theory in Psychopharmacology*, vol. 1. London: Academic Press

Markoff, R.A., Ryon, P., and T. Young. 1982. 'Endorphins and Mood Changes in Long Distance Running,' *Medicine and Science in Sports and Exercise* 14 (1): 11–15

Marlatt, G.A. 1985. 'Coping and Substance Abuse: Implications for Research, Prevention, and Treatment.' In S. Shiffman and T.A. Wells, eds, *Coping and Substance Use*. Orlando, FL: Academic Press

– 1985a. 'Relapse Prevention: Theoretical Rationale and Overview of the Model.' In G.A. Marlatt and J.R. Gordon, eds, *Relapse Prevention*. New York: Guilford

– 1985b. 'Situational Determinants of Relapse and Skill-training Interventions.' In Marlatt and Gordon, eds, *Relapse Prevention*

Marshall, E. 1988. 'Flying Blind in the War on Drugs,' *Science* 240: 1605–7

– 1988a. 'A War on Drugs with Real Troops,' *Science* 241: 13–15

Martin, J.C. 1982. 'An Overview: Maternal Nicotine and Caffeine Consumption and Offspring Outcome,' *Neurobehavioral Toxicology and Teratology* 4: 421–7

Martin, W.R. 1980. 'Emerging Concepts concerning Drug Abuse.' In D.J. Lettieri, M. Sayers, and M.W. Pearson, eds, *Theories on Drug Abuse*. NIDA Research Monograph 30. Rockville, MD: National Institute on Drug Abuse

Martin. W.R., and H.F. Fraser. 1961. 'A Comparative Study of Physiological and Subjective Effects of Heroin and Morphine Administered Intravenously in Addicts,' *Journal of Pharmacology and Experimental Therapeutics* 133: 388–99

Massam, A. 1985. 'British MPs Order All-out Drug War,' *The Journal* 14 (7): 1

– 1985a. 'Britain Will Freeze Assets of Drug Traffickers,' *The Journal* 14 (12): 2

Maugham, W.S. 1922. *On a Chinese Screen*. London: William Heinemann

May, P.A. 1982. 'Substance Abuse and American Indians. Prevalence and Susceptibility,' *International Journal of the Addictions* 17: 1185–1209

Maynard, A., G. Hardman, and A. Whelan. 1987. 'Data Note – 9. Measuring the Social Costs of Addictive Substances,' *British Journal of Addiction* 82: 701–6

Mayr, E. 1982. *The Growth of Biological Thought: Diversity, Evolution, and Inheritance*. Cambridge, MA: Harvard University Press

McAuliffe, W.E. 1975. 'A Second Look at First Effects: The Subjective Effects of Opiates on Nonaddicts,' *Journal of Drug Issues* 5: 369–99

McCarthy, C. 1989. 'An Empty Plan to Fight Crime,' *Washington Post*, 27 May

McConnell, H. 1985. 'U.S. to Step up Anti-trafficking Efforts,' *The Journal* 14 (8): 1–2

McFadden, J. 1987. 'Guilt Is Soluble in Alcohol: An Ego Analytic View,' *Journal of Drug Issues* 17: 171–86

McGlothlin, W.H., and M.D. Anglin. 1981. 'Long-term Follow-up of Clients of High- and Low-Dose Methadone Programs,' *Archives of General Psychiatry* 38: 1055–63

– 1981a. 'Shutting Off Methadone: Costs and Benefits,' *Archives of General Psychiatry* 38: 885–92

McGlothlin, W.H., M.D. Anglin, and B.D. Wilson. 1977. 'A Follow-up of Admissions to the California Civil Addict Program,' *American Journal of Drug and Alcohol Abuse* 42: 179–99
– 1978. 'Narcotic Addiction and Crime,' *Criminology* 16: 293–315
McGuire, W.J. 1980. 'Communication and Social Influence Processes.' In P. Feldman and J. Orford, eds, *Psychological Problems: The Social Context*. New York: Wiley
McIntyre, G. 1988. 'Students Drop Out to Party,' *Province*, 10 January
McLellan, A.T., L. Luborsky, G.E. Woody, C.P. O'Brien, and R. Kron. 1981. 'Are the "Addiction-Related" Problems of Substance Abusers Really Related?' *The Journal of Nervous and Mental Disease* 169: 232–9
Medical Services Commission of British Columbia. 1985. *Financial Statements*. Victoria: Queen's Printer
Medina-Mora, M.E., and G.G. Zavala. 1988. 'Inhalant Use in Latin America: A Review of Literature,' *Consejo Nacional Contra los Adiciones: Disolventes Inhalables*. Mexico: Centros de Integracion Juvenil
Mello, N.K., and J.H. Mendelson. 1971. 'A Quantitative Analysis of Drinking Patterns in Alcoholics,' *Archives of General Psychiatry* 25: 527–39
– 1972. 'Drinking Patterns during Work Contingent and Noncontingent Alcohol Acquisition,' *Psychosomatic Medicine* 34: 139–64
Mendelson, J.H., and N.K. Mello. 1979. 'Biologic Concomitants of Alcoholism,' *New England Journal of Medicine* 301, 912–21
Merton, R.K. 1957. *Social Theory and Social Structure*. New York: Free Press
– 1975. 'Social Structure and Anomie.' In R.A. Farrell and V.L. Swigert, eds, *Social Deviance*. Philadelphia: Lippincott
Milkman, H., and W. Frosch. 1980. 'Theory of Drug Use.' In D.J. Letteri, M. Sayers, and M.W. Pearson, eds, *Theories on Drug Abuse*. NIDA Research Monograph 30. Rockville, MD: National Institute on Drug Abuse
Miller, A. 1981. *The Drama of the Gifted Child: The Search for the True Self*. New York: Basic Books
Miller, N.S., and M.S. Gold. Forthcoming. 'The Disease and Adaptive Models of Addiction: A Reevaluation,' *Journal of Drug Issues*
Milligan, B.C. 1982. *Milligan's Correlated Criminal Code – Selected Federal Statutes*. Toronto: Butterworths
Mingo, J. 1983. *The Official Couch Potato Handbook: A Guide to Prolonged Television Viewing*. Santa Barbara, CA: Capra
Mitchell, A.A., F.H. Lovejoy, Jr, D. Slone, and S. Shapiro. 1982. 'Acetaminophen and Aspirin. Prescription, Use and Accidental Ingestion among Children,' *American Journal of Diseases of Children* 136: 976–9
Mittleman, R.E., and C.V. Wetli. 1984. 'Death Caused by Recreational Cocaine Use – An Update,' *Journal of the American Medical Association* 252: 1889–93
– 1987. 'Cocaine and Sudden "Natural" Death,' *Journal of Forsenic Sciences* 32: 11–19
Mizrahi, S., D. Laor, and B. Stamler. 1988. 'Intestinal Ischemia Induced by Cocaine Abuse,' *Archives of Surgery* 123: 394

Mody, C.K., H.B. Miller, S.K. McIntyre, S.K. Cobb, and M.A. Goldberg. 1988. 'Neurological Complications of Cocaine Use,' *Neurology* 38: 1189–93

Mohatt, G. 1972. 'The Sacred Water: The Quest for Personal Power through Drinking among the Teton Sioux.' In D.C. McClelland, W.N. Davis, R. Kalin, and E. Wanner, eds, *The Drinking Man*. New York: Free Press

Monge, M.C. 1952. 'The Need for Studying the Problem of Coca Leaf Chewing,' *Bulletin on Narcotics* 4: 13–15

Moore, G.F., J.M. Emanuel, T.P. Ogren, and A.J. Yonkers. 1986. 'Cocaine: Current Clinical Use and Potential Abuse,' *Nebraska Medical Journal* 71: 317–21

Moore, M. 1982. 'Endorphins and Exercise: A Puzzling Relationship,' *The Physician and Sportsmedicine* 10: 111–14

Morales, E. 1987. 'The Politics of Control and Eradication of Coca and Cocaine in Peru.' Unpublished manuscript, City University of New York Graduate School
– 1989. *Cocaine: White Gold Rush in Peru*. Tucson: University of Arizona Press

Morgan, H.W. 1981. *Drugs in America: A Social History, 1800–1980*. Syracuse: Syracuse University Press

Morgan, J.P. 1984. 'Problems of Mass Urine Screening for Misused Drugs,' *Journal of Psychoactive Drugs* 16: 305–17

Morgan, W. 1979. 'Negative Addiction in Runners,' *The Physician and Sportsmedicine* 7: 57–69

Morganthau, T., and M. Miller. 1989. 'The Drug Warrior,' *Newsweek*, 10 April: 20–4

Morton, J. 1974. *In the Sea of Sterile Mountains: The Chinese in British Columbia*. Vancouver: J.J. Douglas

Mowat, F. 1979. *And No Birds Sang*. Toronto: McClelland & Stewart

Mrosovsky, N., and D.F. Sherry. 1980. 'Animal Anorexias,' *Science* 207: 837–42

Mullens, A., and P. Flather. 1986. 'Strict No-smoking Bylaw Kicks in Today,' *Vancouver Sun*, 1 December

Multiple Risk Factor Intervention Group. 1982. 'Multiple Risk Factor Intervention Trial: Risk Factor Changes and Mortality Results,' *Journal of the American Medical Association* 248: 1465–77

Murad, F., and A.G. Gilman. 1985. 'Appendix III: Drug Interactions,' in Gilman et al., eds, *Goodman and Gilman's The Pharmacological Basis of Therapeutics*

Murphy, E. 1922/1973. *The Black Candle*. Toronto: Coles

Murphy, S.B., C. Reinarman, and D. Waldorf. 1989. 'An 11-Year Follow-up of a Network of 27 Cocaine Users.' Presented at the Society for the Study of Social Problems Meetings, New York, August

Murray, G.F. 1988. 'The Road to Regulation: Patent Medicines in Canada in Historical Perspective.' In J.C. Blackwell and P.G. Erickson, eds, *Illicit Drugs in Canada: A Risky Business*. Scarborough, Ont.: Nelson Canada

Murray, R.J., R.J. Albin, W. Mergner, and Q.J. Criner. 1988. 'Diffuse Alveolar Haemorrhage Temporally Related to Cocaine Smoking,' *Chest* 93: 427–8

Murray, R.M. 1973. 'Dependence on Analgesics in Analgesic Nephropathy,' *British Journal of Addiction* 68: 265–72
– 1980. 'Minor Analgesic Abuse: The Slow Recognition of a Public Health Problem,' *British Journal of Addiction* 75: 9–17

Murray, R.M., C.A. Clifford, and H.M.D. Gurling. 1983. 'Twin and Adoption
    Studies: How Good Is the Evidence for a Genetic Role?' In M. Galanter, ed., *Recent
    Developments in Alcoholism*, vol. 1. New York: Plenum
Murray, R.M., G.C. Timbury, and A.L. Linton. 1970. 'Analgesic Abuse in Psychiatric
    Patients,' *Lancet* 1: 1303–5
Musto, D.F. 1973. *The American Disease: Origins of Narcotic Control*. New Haven:
    Yale University Press
Nadelmann, E.A. 1987. 'Cops across Borders: Transnational Crime and International
    Law Enforcement.' Unpublished PhD dissertation, Department of Political Science,
    Harvard University
– 1989. 'Drug Prohibition in the United States: Costs, Consequences, and
    Alternatives,' *Science* 245: 939–47
Nahas, G.G. 1979. *Keep Off the Grass: A Scientific Inquiry into the Biological Effects
    of Marijuana*. Oxford: Pergamon
National Institute on Drug Abuse. 1986. *Data from the Drug Abuse Warning Network:
    Annual Data 1985*. Statistical Series 1, 5. Rockville, MD: National Institute on
    Drug Abuse
– 1988. *Data from the Drug Abuse Warning Network: Annual Data 1987*. Statistical
    Series 1, 7. Rockville, MD: National Institute on Drug Abuse
National Institutes of Health. 1984. 'Analgesic-associated Kidney Disease,' *Journal of
    the American Medical Association* 251: 3123–5
Newcomb, M.D., and P.M. Bentler. 1986. 'Cocaine Use among Young Adults,'
    *Advances in Alcohol and Substance Abuse* 6: 73–96
Newcomb, M.D., and L.L. Harlow. 1986. 'Life Events and Substance Use among
    Adolescents: Mediating Effects of Perceived Loss of Control and Meaningfulness
    in Life,' *Journal of Personality and Social Psychology* 51: 564–77
Newcomb, M.D., E. Maddahian, and P.M. Bentler. 1986. 'Risk Factors for Drug Use
    among Adolescents: Concurrent and Longitudinal Analyses,' *American Journal of
    Public Health* 76: 525–31
Newman, P.C. 1985. *Company of Adventurers*, vol. 1. New York: Wiley
Newman, R.G. 1987. 'Methadone Treatment: Defining and Evaluating Success,' *New
    England Journal of Medicine* 317: 447–50
– 1987a. 'Frustrations among Professionals Working in Drug Treatment Programs,'
    *British Journal of Addiction* 82: 115–17
*Newsweek*. 1982. 'A Tough New Non-smoking Law,' 26 November: 63
– 1989. 'Turf Wars in the Federal Bureaucracy,' 10 April: 24–6
*New York Times*. 1979. 'The Drug That May Have Killed Howard R. Hughes,' 11 July
– 1986. 'U.S. Troops Extending Drug Mission in Bolivia,' 17 September
– 1989. 'A Disaster of Historic Dimension, Still Growing,' 28 March
Nolan, M. 1988. 'Science for Madmen.' Book review of R. Proctor, *Racial Hygiene:
    Medicine under the Nazis* (Harvard University Press), in *New York Times*, 21 August
Noorlander, D. 1987. 'Intentional and Unintentional Effects of the Dutch Methadone
    System.' In C.D. Kaplan and M. Kooyman, eds, *Proceedings 15th International
    Institute on the Prevention and Treatment of Drug Dependence*. Rotterdam: Erasmus
    University

Novick, D.M., I. Khan, and M.J. Kreek. 1986. 'Acquired Immunodeficiency Syndrome and Infection with Hepatitis Viruses in Individuals Abusing Drugs by Injection,' *Bulletin on Narcotics* 38: 15–25

Nurco, D.N., J.C. Ball, J.W. Shaffer, and T.E. Hanlon. 1985. 'The Criminality of Narcotic Addicts,' *Journal of Nervous and Mental Disease* 173: 94–102

Oates, W. 1977. *Confessions of a Workaholic: The Facts about Work Addiction.* New York: World

O'Brien, C.P. 1976. 'Experimental Analysis of Conditioning Factors in Human Narcotic Addiction,' *Pharmacological Reviews* 27: 533–43

Office of the Press Secretary, White House. 1986. 'Remarks by the President and the First Lady in a National Television Address on Drug Abuse and Prevention,' Washington, 14 September

Ogborne, A.C., and F.B. Glaser. 1981. 'Characteristics of Affiliates of Alcoholics Anonymous: A Review of the Literature,' *Journal of Studies on Alcohol* 42: 661–75

O'Hara, J. 1981. 'The Science of Running,' *Maclean's*, 6 April: 36–42

O'Malley, P.M., L.D. Johnston, and J.G. Bachman. 1985. 'Cocaine Use among American Adolescents and Young Adults.' In Kozel and Adams, eds, *Cocaine Use in America*

Orford, J. 1985. *Excessive Appetites: A Psychological View of Addictions.* Chichester, England: Wiley

Ostrowski, J. 1989. *Thinking about Drug Legalization.* Policy Analysis no. 121. Washington: CATO Institute

Oswald, I. 1969. 'Personal View,' *British Medical Journal* 3: 438

*The Oxford English Dictionary.* 1933. Oxford: Oxford University Press

Packer, H.L. 1968. *The Limits of the Criminal Sanction.* Stanford: Stanford University Press

Paly, D., P. Jatlow, C. Van Dyke, F. Cabieses, and R. Byck. 1980. 'Plasma Levels of Cocaine in Native Peruvian Coca Chewers.' In F.R. Jeri, ed., *Cocaine 1980.* Lima, Peru: Pacific Press

Paly, D., P. Jatlow, C. Van Dyke, F.R. Jeri, and R. Byck. 1982. 'Plasma Cocaine Concentrations during Cocaine Paste Smoking,' *Life Sciences* 30: 731–8

Paly, D., C. Van Dyke, P. Jatlow, F.R. Jeri, and R. Byck. 1980. 'Cocaine: Plasma Levels after Cocaine Paste Smoking.' In F.R. Jeri, ed., *Cocaine 1980.* Lima, Peru: Pacific Press

Pannekoek, F. 1979. 'Corruption at Moose,' *The Beaver*, Spring: 4–11

Papasava, M., and G. Singer. 1985. 'Self-administration of Low-Dose Cocaine by Rats at Reduced and Recovered Body Weight,' *Psychopharmacology* 85: 419–25

Parssinen, T.M., and K. Kerner. 1980. 'Development of the Disease Model of Drug Addiction in Britain, 1870–1926,' *Medical History* 24: 275–96

Parton, N. 1985. 'Now Here's a New Incentive against Drinking Driving,' *Vancouver Sun*, 15 July

Pasternack, P.F., S.B. Colvin, and F.G. Bauman. 1985. 'Cocaine-induced Angina Pectoris and Acute Myocardial Infarction in Patients Younger than 40 Years,' *American Journal of Cardiology* 55: 847

Patel, R.C., D. Dutta, and S.A. Schonfield. 1987. 'Free-base Cocaine Use Associated with Bronchiolitis Obliterans Organizing Pneumonia,' *Annals of Internal Medicine* 107: 186–7

Pattison, E.M., M.B. Sobell, and L.C. Sobell. 1977. *Emerging Concepts of Alcohol Dependence*. New York: Springer

Peachy, J., and T. Franklin. 1985. 'Methadone Treatment of Opiate Dependence in Canada,' *British Journal of Addiction* 80: 291–9

Peele, S. 1978. 'Addiction: The Analgesic Experience,' *Human Nature* 1: 61–7

– 1979. 'Redefining Addiction II. The Meaning of Addiction in Our Lives,' *Journal of Psychedelic Drugs* 11: 289–97

– 1981. *How Much Is too Much?* Englewood Cliffs, NJ: Prentice-Hall

– 1985. *The Meaning of Addiction: Compulsive Experience and Its Interpretation*. Lexington, MA: D.C. Heath

– 1986. 'The Implications and Limitations of Genetic Models of Alcoholism and Other Addictions,' *Journal of Studies on Alcohol* 47: 63–73

– 1987. 'A Moral Vision of Addiction: How People's Values Determine Whether They Become and Remain Addicts,' *Journal of Drug Issues* 17: 187–215

Peele, S., and A. Brodsky. 1975. *Love and Addiction*. Scarborough, Ont.: New American Library of Canada

Pellegrini-Quarantotti, B., E. Paglietti, A. Bonanni, M. Petta, and G.L. Gessa. 1979. 'Naloxone Shortens Ejaculation Latency in Male Rats,' *Experimentia* 35: 524–5

Perino, L.E., G.H. Warren, and J.S. Levine. 1987. 'Cocaine-induced Hepatotoxicity in Humans.' *Gastroenterology* 93: 176–80

Pfohl, S.J. 1985. *Images of Deviance and Social Control: A Sociological History*. Glencoe, IL: Free Press

Phillips, K. 1988. 'Headache Sufferers Risk Addictions,' *The Journal* 17 (5): 2

Plato. Circa 375 BC/1955. *The Republic*. Translated by Desmond Lee. Harmondsworth: Penguin

– Circa 390 BC/1956. *Protagoras and Meno*. Translated by W.K.C. Guthrie. Harmondsworth: Penguin

Platt, J.J., A.R. Hoffman, and R.K. Ebert. 1976. 'Recent Trends in the Demography of Heroin Addiction among Youthful Offenders,' *International Journal of the Addictions* 11, 221–36

Pohl, R., R. Balon, and V.K. Yergani. 1987. 'More on Cocaine and Panic Disorder,' *American Journal of Psychiatry* 144: 1363

Poirier, P. 1986. 'Proposed Bill Would Allow Seizure of Accused's Assets,' *Globe and Mail*, 30 May

Pollin, W. 1985. 'The Danger of Cocaine,' *Journal of the American Medical Association* 254: 98

Pomerleau, O.F., and C.S. Pomerleau. 1987. 'A Biobehavioral View of Substance Abuse and Addiction,' *Journal of Drug Issues* 17: 111–31

Post, R.M., J. Kotin, and F.K. Goodwin. 1974. 'The Effects of Cocaine on Depressed Patients,' *American Journal of Psychiatry* 131: 511–17

Price, L. 1986. 'Being Tested for Drugs: A Victim's View.' Presentation at the National Organization for the Reform of Marijuana Laws Conference, Portland, Oregon, June

Province of British Columbia, Ministry of Health, Alcohol and Drug Commission. No date. *Fact Sheet: Narcotic Analgesics*

Quayle, D. 1983. 'American Productivity: The Devastating Effect of Alcoholism and Drug Abuse,' *American Psychologist* 38: 454–8

*R. v. Coupal*. 1987. *Canadian Criminal Cases* (BCCA). 3d ser., vol. 31: Aurora, Ont.: Canada Law Book

*R. v. Gudbrandson*. 1987. Vancouver Court of Appeals, Registry no. CA005837

Ramer, C.M., and A. Lodge. 1975. 'Neonatal Addiction: A Two-Year Study. Part I. Clinical and Developmental Characteristics of Infants of Mothers on Methadone Maintenance,' *Addictive Dieseases* 2: 227–34

Rappaport, J. 1976. *Community Psychology: Values, Research and Action*. New York: Holt, Rinehart, and Winston

Rawson, R.S., J.L. Obert, M.J. McCann, and A.J. Mann. 1986. 'Cocaine Treatment Outcome: Cocaine Use following Inpatient, Outpatient, and no Treatment.' NIDA Research Monograph 67, Rockville, MD: National Institute on Drug Abuse

Reagh, J. 1988. 'The Effects of Opiate Use during Pregnancy on Fetal Development: A Review of the Literature.' Unpublished paper, Department of Psychology, Simon Fraser University, Burnaby, BC

Rebhun, J. 1988. 'Association of Asthma and Freebase Smoking,' *Annals of Allergy* 60: 339–42

Rech, R.H., and K.F. Moore. 1971. *An Introduction to Psychopharmacology*. New York: Raven Press

Reich, W.P., W.J. Filstead, and F. Slaymaker. 1984. 'Validity of the DSM-III Alcoholism Diagnosis: Inadequacy of the Medical Model.' Presented at American Psychological Association Meetings, Toronto, August

Reinarman, C., and H.G. Levine. Forthcoming. 'The Crack Attack: Politics and Media in America's Latest Drug Scare.' In J. Best, ed., *Images and Issues: Current Perspectives on Social Problems*. New York: Aldine de Gruyer

Resnick, R.B., R.S. Kestenbaum, and L.K. Schwartz. 1977. 'Acute Systemic Effects of Cocaine in Man: A Controlled Study by Intranasal and Intravenous Routes,' *Science* 195: 696–8

*Revised Statutes of Canada*. 1970. Ottawa: Queen's Printer
War Measures Act. Vol. 2, chap. W-2, 7707–10
An Act Respecting the Northwest Territories. Vol. 5, chap. N-22, 5551–78

Ritchie, J.M. 1985. 'The Aliphatic Alcohols.' In Gilman et al., eds, *Goodman and Gilman's The Pharmacological Basis of Therapeutics*

Ritchie, J.M., and N.M. Greene. 1985. 'Local Anesthetics.' In Gilman et al., eds, *Goodman and Gilman's The Pharmacological Basis of Therapeutics*

Robins, L.N., J.E. Helzer, and D.H. Davis. 1975. 'Narcotic Use in Southeast Asia and Afterwards,' *Archives of General Psychiatry* 32: 955–61

Robins, L.N., and G.E. Murphy. 1967. 'Drug Use in a Normal Population of Young Negro Men,' *American Journal of Public Health* 57: 1580–96

Robins, L.N., and T.R. Przybeck. 1985. *Age of Onset of Drug Use as a Factor in Drug Use and Other Disorders*. NIDA Research Monograph 56. Rockville, MD: National Institute on Drug Abuse

Robinson, B.E. 1989. *Work Addiction: Hidden Legacies of Adult Children*. Deerfield Beach, FL: Health Communications

Rodriguez, E., J.C. Cavin, and J.E. West. 1982. 'The Possible Role of Amazonian Psychoactive Plants in the Chemotherapy of Parasitic Worms – A Hypothesis,' *Journal of Ethnopharmacology* 6: 303–9

Rogers, C.R. 1980. *A Way of Being*. Boston: Houghton Mifflin

Rollingher, I.M., A.S. Belzberg, and I.L. Macdonald. 1986. 'Cocaine-induced Myocardial Infarction,' *Canadian Medical Association Journal* 135: 45–6

Rootman, I. 1988. 'Epidemiologic Methods and Indicators.' In J.C. Blackwell and P.G. Erickson, eds, *Illicit Drugs in Canada*. Scarborough, Ont.: Nelson Canada

Rose, N. 1985. *The Psychological Complex: Psychology, Politics and Society in England, 1869–1939*. London: Routledge and Kegan Paul

Rosenbaum, J.F. 1986. 'Cocaine and Panic Disorder,' *American Journal of Psychiatry* 143: 1320

Roskies, E., and R.S. Lazarus. 1979. 'Coping Theory and the Teaching of Coping Skills.' In P.O. Davidson and S.M. Davidson, eds, *Behavorial Medicine: Changing Health and Life Styles*. New York: Bruner/Mazel

Royal Canadian Mounted Police. 1988. *National Drug Intelligence Estimate 1987/ 1988*. Ottawa: Ministry of Supply and Services Canada

Russell, B. 1949. *Authority and the Individual*. Boston: Beacon Press

Russell, J. 1986. *Comments on the Treatment and Management of Methadone Patients in Private Care in B.C.: A Response to the Joint Advisory Committee on the Treatment Uses of Methadone*. Vancouver: British Columbia Civil Liberties Association

Ruter, C.F. 1987. 'Law Enforcement and Drug Policy Control in the Netherlands.' Presented at the International Conference on Drug Policy Reform, London, 13–17 July

Ryan, L., S. Ehrlich, and L. Finnegan. 1987. 'Cocaine Abuse in Pregnancy: Effect on the Fetus and Newborn,' *Neurotoxicology and Teratology* 9: 295–9

Sachs, M.L., and D. Pargman. 1979. 'Running Addiction: A Depth Interview Examination,' *Journal of Sports Behavior* 2: 143–55

– 1983. 'Running Addiction.' In M.L. Sachs and G.W. Buffone, eds, *Running as Therapy: An Integrated Approach*. Lincoln: University of Nebraska Press

Salzman, G.A., F. Khan, and C. Emory. 1987. 'Pneumomediastinum after Cocaine Smoking,' *Southern Medical Journal* 80: 1427–9

Sandler, D.P., J.C. Smith, C.R. Weinberg, V.M. Buckalew, Jr, V.W. Dennis, W.B. Blythe, and W.P. Burgess. 1989. 'Analgesic Abuse and Chronic Renal Disease,' *New England Journal of Medicine* 320: 1238–43

Sandwijk, P., I. Westerterp, and S. Musterd. Forthcoming. 'The Use of Legal and Illegal Drugs in Amsterdam: Report of a Survey among the Population of 12 Years and Older.' University of Amsterdam report (available only in Dutch)

Sapira, J.D. 1968. 'The Narcotic Addict as a Medical Patient,' *American Journal of Medicine* 45: 555–88

Sartre, J.-P. 1938/1964. *Nausea*. New York: New Directions

– 1948/1976. *Anti-Semite and Jew*. New York: Schocken

Schachne, J.S., B.H. Roberts, and P.D. Thompson. 1984. 'Coronary-Artery Spasm and Myocardial Infarction Associated with Cocaine Use,' *New England Journal of Medicine* 310: 1665–6

Schacter, S. 1982. 'Recidivism and Self-cure of Smoking and Obesity.' *American Psychologist* 37: 436–44

Schaps, E., S. Churgin, C. Palley, B. Takata, and A.Y. Cohen. 1980. 'Primary Prevention Research: A Preliminary Review of Program Outcome Studies,' *International Journal of the Addictions* 15: 756–76

Schenk, S., G. Lacelle, K. Gorman, and Z. Amit. 1987. 'Cocaine Self-administration in Rats Influenced by Environmental Conditions: Implications for the Etiology of Drug Abuse,' *Neuroscience Letters* 81: 227–31

*Schneider v. The Queen.* 1982. *Canadian Criminal Cases* (SCC) 2nd ser., vol. 68. Aurora, Ont.: Canada Law Book

Schnoll, S.H., J. Karrigan, S.B. Kitchen, A. Daghestani, and T. Hansen. 1985. 'Characteristics of Cocaine Abusers Presenting for Treatment.' In Kozel and Adams, eds, *Cocaine Use in America*

Schön, D.A. 1983. *The Reflective Practitioner: How Professionals Think in Action.* New York: Basic Books

Schuckit, M.A. 1980. 'A Theory of Alcohol and Drug Abuse: A Genetic Approach.' In D.J. Lettieri, M. Sayers, and M.W. Pearson, eds, *Theories on Drug Abuse.* NIDA Research Monograph 30. Rockville, MD: National Institute on Drug Abuse

– 1984. 'Differences in Plasma Cortisol after Ethanol in Relatives of Alcoholics and Controls,' *Journal of Clinical Psychiatry* 45: 374–9

– 1987. 'Biological Vulnerability to Alcoholism,' *Journal of Consulting and Clinical Psychology* 55: 3, 301–9

Schwartz, J.E. 1984. 'Chronic Aspirin Intoxication: A Case Report and Literature Review,' *Arizona Medicine* 41: 799–802

Schweighofer, A.R.F. 1988. 'Temperance in Canada,' *Canadian Journal of Law and Society* 3: 175–93

Searles, J.S. 1988. 'The Role of Genetics in the Pathogenesis of Alcoholism,' *Journal of Abnormal Psychology* 97: 153–67

Sears, V. 1986. 'PM Promises Tough New Measures in War on Drug Abuse "Epidemic,"' *Toronto Star*, 15 September

Sells, S.B., and D.D. Simpson. 1980. 'The Case for Drug Abuse Treatment Effectiveness, Based on the DARP Research Program,' *British Journal of Addiction* 75: 117–31

Selye, H. 1976. *The Stress of Life.* Revised edition. New York: McGraw-Hill

Senay, E.C. 1985. 'Clinical Experience with T's and B's,' *Drug and Alcohol Dependence* 14: 305–12

Shaw, G., and K. Baldrey. 1986. 'Methadone Plan Worries Ex-addict,' *Vancouver Sun*, 24 January

Siegel, R.K. 1980. 'Long-term Effects of Recreational Cocaine Use: A Four Year Study.' In F.R. Jeri, ed., *Cocaine 1980.* Lima, Peru: Pacific Press

– 1980a. 'Cocaine Substitutes,' *New England Journal of Medicine* 302: 817

– 1982. 'Cocaine Smoking,' *Journal of Psychoactive Drugs* 14: 271–359

- 1985. 'New Patterns of Cocaine Use: Changing Doses and Routes.' In Kozel and Adams, eds, *Cocaine Use in America*
- 1985a. 'Cocaine and the Privileged Class: A Review of Historical and Contemporary Images,' *Advances in Alcohol and Substance Abuse* 4: 37–49
Siegel, S. 'The Effects of Opiates on Addicts.' Unpublished manuscript, Department of Psychology, McMaster University
Siegel, S., R. Hinson, M.D. Krank, and J. McCully. 1982. 'Heroin "Overdose" Death: Contribution of Drug Associated Environmental Cues,' *Science* 216: 436–7
Siegel, S., M.D. Krank, and R.E. Hinson. 1987. 'Anticipation of Pharmacological and Nonpharmacological Events: Classical Conditioning and Addictive Behavior,' *Journal of Drug Issues* 17: 83–110
Silver, G., and M. Aldrich. 1979. *The Dope Chronicles: 1850–1950.* New York: Harper and Row
Simpson, D.D. 1986. '12-Year Follow-up Outcomes of Opioid Addicts Treated in Therapeutic Communities.' In G. DeLeon and J.T. Ziegenfuss, Jr, eds, *Therapeutic Communities for Addicts: Readings in Theory, Research, & Practice.* Springfield, IL: Thomas
Simpson, D.D., and S.B. Sells. 1982. 'Effectiveness of Treatment for Drug Abuse: An Overview of the DARP Research Program,' *Advances in Alcohol and Substance Abuse,* 2: 7–29
Skirrow, J. 1985. *Primary Prevention: A New Approach to Adolescents and Alcohol.* Edmonton: Alberta Alcohol and Drug Abuse Commission
Skolnik, J.H. 1984. 'The Limits of Narcotics Law Enforcement,' *Journal of Psychoactive Drugs* 16: 119–27
Slater, P. 1980. *Wealth Addiction.* New York: Dutton
Smart, R. 1979. 'Drinking Problems among Employed, Unemployed and Shift Workers,' *Journal of Occupational Medicine* 21: 731–6
Smart, R.G. 1983. *Forbidden Highs: The Nature, Treatment and Prevention of Illicit Drug Abuse.* Toronto: Addiction Research Foundation
- 1986. 'Solvent Use in North America: Aspects of Epidemiology, Prevention, and Treatment,' *Journal of Psychoactive Drugs* 18: 87–96
- 1988. '"Crack" Cocaine Abuse in Canada: A New Epidemic?' *American Journal of Epidemiology* 127: 1315–17
- 1989. 'Is the Postwar Drinking Binge Ending? Cross-National Trends in Per Capita Alcohol Consumption,' *British Journal of Addiction* 84: 743–8
Smart, R.G., and E.M. Adlaf. 1984. *Alcohol and Drug Use among Ontario Adults in 1984 and Changes since 1982.* Toronto: Addiction Research Foundation
- 1986. 'THC Consumption among Students: Its Estimation and Log-normality,' *British Journal of Addiction* 81: 59–63
- 1987. *Alcohol and Other Drug Use among Ontario Students in 1987, and Trends since 1977.* Toronto: Addiction Research Foundation
- 1988. 'Alcohol, Cannabis, Cocaine, and Other Substance Use among Ontario Adults, 1977–1987,' *Canadian Journal of Public Health* 79: 206–7
  - 1989. 'The Ontario Student Drug Use Survey: Trends between 1977–1989.' Toronto: Addiction Research Foundation

Smart, R.G., and L. Anglin. 1987. 'Do We Know the Lethal Dose of Cocaine?' *Journal of Forensic Sciences* 32 (2): 303–12

Smart, R.G., and A.C. Ogborne. 1986. *Northern Spirits: Drinking in Canada Then and Now.* Toronto: Addiction Research Foundation

Smith, D.E., and G.R. Gay, eds. 1972. *It's So Good Don't Even Try It Once: Heroin in Perspective.* Englewood Cliffs, NJ: Prentice-Hall

Snyder, S.H. 1977. 'Opiate Receptors and Internal Opiates,' *Scientific American* 236 (3): 44–56

Solomon, R.R. 1988. 'The Noble Pursuit of Evil: Arrest, Search, and Seizure in Canadian Drug Law.' In J.C. Blackwell and P.G. Erickson, eds, *Illicit Drugs in Canada: A Risky Business.* Scarborough, Ont.: Nelson Canada

– 1988a. 'Canada's Federal Drug Legislation.' In J.C. Blackwell and P.G. Erickson, eds, *Illicit Drugs in Canada: A Risky Business.* Scarborough, Ont.: Nelson Canada

Solomon, R.R., and M. Green. 1982. 'The First Century: The History of Non-medical Opiate Use and Control Policies in Canada, 1870–1970,' *University of Western Ontario Law Review* 20: 307–36

Solomon, R.R., E. Single, and P.G. Erickson. 1988. 'Legal Considerations in Canadian Cannabis Policy.' In J.C. Blackwell and P.G. Erickson, eds, *Illicit Drug Use in Canada: A Risky Business.* Scarborough, Ont.: Nelson Canada

Solzhenitsyn, A.I. 1985. *The Gulag Archipelago 1918–1936.* New York: Harper & Row

Sonnedecker, G. 1962. 'Emergence of the Concept of Opiate Addiction,' *Journal Mondial de Pharmacie* 5: 275–90

– 1963. 'Emergence of the Concept of Opiate Addiction,' *Journal Mondial de Pharmacie* 6: 27–34

Sours, J.A. 1983. 'Case Reports of Anorexia Nervosa and Caffeinism,' *American Journal of Psychiatry* 140: 235–6

Sowell, T. 1987. *Comparison versus Guilt and Other Essays.* New York: William Morrow

Spanos, N.P. 1978. 'Witchcraft in Histories of Psychiatry: A Critical Analysis and an Alternative Conceptualization,' *Psychological Bulletin* 85: 417–39

Spear, H.B., and M.M. Glatt. 1971. 'The Influence of Canadian Addicts on Heroin Addiction in the United Kingdom,' *British Journal of Addiction* 66: 141–9

Spence, R.E. 1919. *Prohibition in Canada.* Toronto: The Ontario Branch of the Dominion Alliance

Spotts, J.V., and F.C. Shontz. 1982. 'Ego Development, Dragon Fights, and Chronic Drug Abusers,' *International Journal of the Addictions* 17: 945–76

– 1984. 'Drug-Induced Ego States. I. Cocaine: Phenomenology and Implications,' *International Journal of the Addictions* 19: 119–51

Spurgeon, P., and D. Black. 1987. 'The British System: Views from the Inside.' Presentation at the Institute on Drugs, Crime, and Justice, London, 3–19 July

Staats, G. 1978. 'An Empirical Assessment of Controls Affecting Marijauna Usage,' *British Journal of Addiction* 73: 391–8

Stanton, M.D., T.C. Todd, and Associates. 1982. *The Family Therapy of Drug Abuse and Addiction*. New York: Guilford

Starr, P. 1982. *The Social Transformation of American Medicine: The Rise of a Sovereign Profession and the Making of a Vast Industry*. New York: Basic Books

Statistics Canada. 1988. *Canadian Crime Statistics*. Ottawa: Ministry of Supply and Services Canada

Statute Revision Commission. 1978. *Consolidated Regulations of Canada*. Ottawa

Sternberg, R.G., M.D. Winniford, L.D. Hillis, G.P. Dowling, and L.M. Buja. 1989. 'Simultaneous Acute Thrombosis of Two Major Coronary Arteries Following Intravenous Cocaine Use,' *Archives of Pathology Laboratory Medicine* 113: 521–4

Stevenson, G.H. 1956. 'Drug Addiction in British Columbia: A Research Report.' Unpublished manuscript, University of British Columbia

Stiles, W.B., D.A. Shapiro, and R. Elliot. 1986. 'Are All Psychotherapies Equivalent?' *American Psychologist* 41: 165–80

Stimmel, B., and K. Adamsons. 1976. 'Narcotic Dependency in Pregnancy: Methadone Maintenance Compared to Use of Street Drugs,' *Journal of the American Medical Association* 235: 1121–4

Stimson, G.V., and E. Oppenheimer. 1982. *Heroin Addiction: Treatment and Control in Britain*. London: Tavistock

Stober, M.I. 1985. *Entrapment in Canadian Criminal Law*. Toronto: Carswell

Stoddart, K. 1982. 'The Enforcement of Narcotics Violations in a Canadian City: Heroin Users' Perspectives on the Production of Official Statistics,' *Canadian Journal of Criminology* 24: 425–38

Strange, W.G. 1977. 'Job Loss: A Psychosocial Study of Worker Reactions to a Plant Closing in a Company Town in South Appalachia.' Unpublished PhD dissertation, Department of Psychology, Cornell University

Stroud, C. 1983. *The Blue Wall: Street Cops in Canada*. Toronto: McClelland and Stewart

Symons, D. 1979. *The Evolution of Human Sexuality*. New York: Oxford University Press

Szasz, T. 1975. *Ceremonial Chemistry: The Ritual Persecution of Drugs, Addicts, and Pushers*. Garden City, NJ: Anchor Press

– 1985. *Ceremonial Chemistry: The Ritual Persecution of Drugs, Addicts, and Pushers*. Revised edition. Holmes Beach, FL: Learning Publications

– 1987. 'Justifying Coercion through Religion and Psychiatry,' *Journal of Humanistic Psychology* 27: 158–73

Tarter, R.E., A.I. Alterman, and K.I. Edwards. 1985. 'Vulnerability to Alcoholism in Men: A Behavior-Genetic Perspective,' *Journal of Studies on Alcohol* 46: 329–56

Tarter, R.E., and K.L. Edwards. 1987. 'Vulnerability to Alcohol and Drug Abuse: A Behavior-Genetic View,' *Journal of Drug Issues* 17: 67–81

Tashkin, D.P., M.S. Simmons, A.H. Coulson, V.A. Clark, and H. Gong, Jr. 1987. 'Respiratory Effects of Cocaine "Freebasing" among Habitual Users of Marijuana with or without Tobacco,' *Chest* 92: 638–44

Taylor, R. 1967. 'Determinism.' In P. Edwards, ed., *The Encyclopedia of Philosophy*, vol. 1. New York: Macmillan

Taylor, R.L. 1966. *Vessel of Wrath: The Life and Times of Carry Nation*. New York: New American Library

Tesh, S.N. 1988. *Hidden Arguments: Political Ideology and Disease Prevention Policy*. New Brunswick, NJ: Rutgers University Press

Thompson, J.C. 1988. *How to "Make the Most of You": Evaluation Trends*. Edmonton: Alberta Alcohol and Drug Abuse Commission

Thompson, J.C., J. Skirrow, and C. Nutter. 1987. 'The AADAC Preventive Program for Adolescents: Achieving Behaviour Change.' Joint plenary presentation to the 33d International Institute on the Prevention and Treatment of Alcoholism, and the 16th International Institute on the Prevention and Treatment of Drug Dependence, Lausanne, Switzerland, 31 May–5 June

Thompson, J.H. 1972. 'The Beginning of Our Regeneration: The Great War and Western Canadian Reform Movements.' In R.D. Francis and D.B. Smith, eds, *Readings in Canadian History*. Toronto: Holt, Rinehart and Winston

Thor, D.H. 1972. 'Can Rats Be Addicted to Opiates?' *Psychological Record* 22: 289–303

Thoreau, H.D. 1854–1942. *Walden, or Life in the Woods*. New York: New American Library

Thornhill, R. 1980. 'Rape in Panorpa Scorpionflies and a General Rape Hypothesis,' *Animal Behaviour* 28: 52–9

Thornhill, R., and N.W. Thornhill. 1983. 'Human Rape: An Evolutionary Analysis,' *Ethology and Sociobiology* 4: 137–74

Thornton, E.M. 1986. *The Freudian Fallacy*. Revised edition. London: Paladin

Tillich, P. 1952. *The Courage to Be*. Glasgow: Collins

*Time*. 1988. 'Thinking the Unthinkable,' 30 May: 14–20

Timmer, S.G., J. Veroff, and M.E. Colton. 1985. 'Life Stress, Helplessness, and the Use of Alcohol and Drugs to Cope: An Analysis of National Survey Data.' In S. Shiffman and T.A. Wells, eds, *Coping and Substance Use*. Orlando, FL: Academic Press

Tolman, C.W. 1987. 'What's so Critical about "Kritische Psychologie"?' Presented at Canadian Psychological Association Meetings, Vancouver, June

Trebach, A.S. 1982. *The Heroin Solution*. New Haven: Yale University Press

– 1983. 'The Lesson of Ayatollah Khalkhali,' *Journal of Drug Issues* 13: 379–400

– 1984. 'Peace without Surrender in the Perpetual Drug War,' *Justice Quarterly* 1: 125–44

– 1987. *The Great Drug War: And Radical Proposals That Could Make America Safe Again*. New York: Macmillan

– 1989. 'When Will We Learn the Lesson of Ayatollah Khalkhali?' *The Drug Policy Letter* 1 (3): 1–3

Troyer, R.J., and G.E. Markle. 1984. 'Coffee Drinking: An Emerging Social Problem?' *Social Problems* 31: 403–16

Trulson, M.E., and M.J. Ulissey. 1987. 'Chronic Cocaine Administration Decreases Dopamine Synthesis Rate and Increases [3H] Spiroperidol Binding in Rat Brain,' *Brain Research Bulletin* 19: 35–8

Tuchman, A.J., M. Daras, P. Zalzal, and J. Mangiardi. 1987. 'Intracranial Hemorrhage after Cocaine Abuse,' *Journal of the American Medical Association* 257: 1175

Tucker, M.B. 1985. 'Coping and Drug Use among Heroin-addicted Women and Men.' In S.
    Shiffman and T.A. Wills, eds, *Coping and Substance Use*. Orlando, FL: Academic Press
Turner, T.B., V.L. Bennett, and H. Hernandez. 1981. 'The Beneficial Side of Moderate
    Alcohol Use,' *Johns Hopkins Medical Journal* 148: 53–63
Tuttle, C.B. 1985. 'Drug Management of Pain in Cancer Patients,' *Canadian Medical
    Association Journal* 132: 121–33
Twycross, R.G. 1974. 'Clinical Experience with Diamorphine in Advanced Malignant
    Disease,' *International Journal of Clinical Pharmacology, Therapy, and Toxicology* 9:
    184–98
United Nations Department of International Economic and Social Affairs. 1988. *1985/
    86 Statistical Yearbook*. New York: United Nations
U.S. Bureau of the Census. 1975. *Historical Statistics of the United States, Colonial
    Times to 1970, Part 1*. Washington: U.S. Department of Commerce
– 1983. *Statistical Abstract of the United States. 104th Edition*. Washington: U.S.
    Department of Commerce
– 1988. *Statistical Abstract of the United States*. Washington: U.S. Department of
    Commerce
Vaillant, G.E. 1977. *Adaptation to Life*. Boston: Little, Brown
– 1983. *The Natural History of Alcoholism: Causes, Patterns, and Paths to Recovery*.
    Cambridge, MA: Harvard University Press
Vancouver *Province*. 1979. 'Blind Man Has "Good Chance" of Seeing Children,' 29
    November
*Vancouver Sun*. 1977. 'City Officers Guilty of Beating Mountie,' and 'Innocent
    Couple Manhandled,' 14 July
– 1983. 'Ski Association Feels Heat: Anti-tobacco Coalition Adds Fuel to Fire,' 23
    November
– 1985. 'Narco-Terrorism,' 9 December
– 1986. 'Victoria Clamps Down on Control of Methadone,' 8 January
– 1986a. 'RCMP Drug Plot Called Scandalous,' 3 July
– 1987. 'Federal Court to Hear,' 24 April
van de Wijngaart, G.F. 1985. 'Drug Policy in the Netherlands.' Presented at Simon
    Fraser University, Burnaby, BC, August
van de Wijngaart, G.F., and H. Vendelbosch. 1987. 'The Normalization of Cannabis
    Use.' Presented at the 16th International Institute on the Prevention and Treatment of
    Drug Dependence, Lausanne, Switzerland, June
Van Dyke, C., P.G. Barash, P. Jatlow, and R. Byck. 1976. 'Cocaine Plasma
    Concentrations after Intranasal Application in Man,' *Science* 191: 859–61
Van Dyke, C., and R. Byck. 1982. 'Cocaine,' *Scientific American* 246 (3): 128–41
Van Dyck, C., J. Ungerer, J. Jatlow, P. Barash, and R. Byck. 1982. 'Intranasal Cocaine:
    Dose Relationships of Psychological Effects and Plasma Levels,' *International
    Journal of Psychiatry in Medicine* 12: 1–13
Van Santen, G. 1987. 'Methadone Prescribing in Amsterdam.' Presented at the
    International Conference on Drug Policy Reform, London, 13–17 July
*Victoria Colonist*. 1922. 'Spy Evidence,' 20 October
Vlasov. A. 1987. 'Drug Wars,' *Druglink: Journal on Drug Misuse in Britain* 2 (3): 8–10

Waldorf, D. 1983. 'Natural Recovery from Opiate Addiction: Some Social-psychological Processes of Untreated Recovery,' *Journal of Drug Issues* 13: 237–80

Waldorf, D., S.B. Murphy, C. Reinarman, and B. Joyce. 1977. *Doing Coke: An Ethnography of Cocaine Users and Sellers*. Washington: Drug Abuse Council

Waldorf, D., M. Orlick, and C. Reinarman. 1974. *Morphine Maintenance*. Washington: Drug Abuse Council

Walker, H. 1986. 'Drunk Drivers Hazardous Sober Too,' *The Journal* 15 (3): 2

Wallace, G.B. 'The Rehabilitation of the Drug Addict,' *Journal of Educational Sociology* 4: 347–57

Wallach, R.C., E. Jerez, and G. Blinick. 1975. 'Comparison of Pregnancies and Births during Methadone Detoxification and Maintenance,' *Pediatric Annals* 4: 398–407

Wang, T., F. Hadidi, F. Triana, and M. Bargout. 1988. 'Morning Report at Christ Hospital: Myocardial Infarction Associated with the Use of Cocaine,' *American Journal of Medical Sciences* 295: 569–70

Ward, D. 1988. 'Kelleher Favors U.S. Get-tough Drug Policy,' *Vancouver Sun*, 3 May

Washton, A.M., M.S. Gold, and A.C. Pottash. 1986. 'Crack,' *Journal of the American Medical Association* 256: 711

Watkins, L.K., and D.J. Mayer. 1982. 'Organization of Endogenous Opiate and Nonopiate Pain Control Systems,' *Science* 216: 1185–92

Way, E.L. 1983. 'Some Thoughts about Opiopeptins, Peptides with Opiate-like Activity,' *Drug and Alcohol Dependence* 11: 23–31

Webster, N. 1828/1970. *An American Dictionary of the English Language*. New York: Johnson Reprint

Weeks, J.R., and R.J. Collins. 1968. 'Patterns of Intravenous Self-injection by Morphine-addicted Rats.' In A.H. Wikler, ed., *The Addictive States*. Baltimore, MD: Williams and Wilkins

Weil, A. 1972. *The Natural Mind. A New Way of Looking at Drugs and the Higher Consciousness*. Boston: Houghton Mifflin

Weiss, R.D., D.S. Tilles, P.D. Goldenheim, and S.M. Mirin. 1987. 'Decreased Single Breath Carbon Monoxide Diffusing Capacity in Cocaine Freebase Smokers,' *Drug and Alcohol Dependence* 19: 271–6

Wenger, J., and S. Einstein. 1970. 'The Use and Misuse of Aspirin: A Contemporary Problem,' *International Journal of the Addictions* 5: 757–75

Westermeyer, J. 1982. *Poppies, Pipes, and People: Opium and Its Use in Laos*. Berkeley: University of California Press

Wetli, C.V., and D.A. Fishbain. 1985. 'Cocaine-induced Psychosis and Sudden Death in Recreational Cocaine Users,' *Journal of Forensic Sciences* 30: 873–80

Wetli, C.V., and R.K. Wright. 1979. 'Death Caused by Recreational Cocaine Use,' *Journal of the American Medical Association* 241: 2519–22

White, H.R. 1988. 'Longitudinal Patterns of Cocaine Use among Adolescents,' *American Journal of Drug and Alcohol Abuse* 14: 1–15

White, M., and M. Tran. 1987. 'Contra Links with Drugs under Spotlight,' *Guardian* 1 July: 5

Wiener, M.D., and C.E. Putnam. 1987. 'Pain in the Chest of a User of Cocaine,' *Journal of the American Medical Association* 258: 2087–8

Wikler, A. 1971. 'Some Implications of Conditioning Theory for Problems of Drug Abuse,' *Behavioral Science* 16: 92–7
– 1980. 'A Theory of Opioid Dependence.' In D.J. Lettieri, M. Sayers, and M.W. Pearson, eds, *Theories on Drug Abuse*. NIDA Research Monograph 30. Rockville, MD: National Institute on Drug Abuse
Williams, H.R., W. Moy, and W. Johnston. 1970. 'Low and High Methadone Maintenance in Out-patient Treatment of the Heroin Addict,' *International Journal of the Addictions* 5: 637–44
Williamson, R.S. 1983. 'International Illicit Drug Traffic: The United States Response,' *Bulletin on Narcotics* 34 (4): 33–45
Winick, C. 1962. 'Maturing Out of Narcotic Addiction,' *Bulletin on Narcotics* 14 (1): 1–7
Winn, M. 1977. *The Plug-in Drug*. New York: Bantam Books
Wise, R. 1984. 'Neural Mechanisms of the Reinforcing Action of Cocaine.' In Grabowski, ed., *Cocaine: Pharmacology, Effects, and Treatment of Abuse*
– 1988. 'The Neurobiology of Craving: Implications for the Understanding and Treatment of Addiction,' *Journal of Abnormal Psychology* 97: 118–32
Wishnie, H. 1977. *The Impulsive Personality: Understanding People with Destructive Character Disorders*. New York: Plenum
Wisotsky, S. 1983. 'Exposing the War on Cocaine: The Futility and Destructiveness of Prohibition,' *Wisconsin Law Review* 6: 1305–1426
– 1986. *Breaking the Impasse in the War on Drugs*. New York: Greenwood
Wojack, J.C., and E.S. Flamm. 1987. 'Intracranial Hemorrhage and Cocaine Use,' *Stroke* 18: 712–15
Womack, S. 1980. '"I Haven't Stopped Drinking, I Just Changed My Brand,"' *Journal of Drug Issues* 10: 301–10
Wong, L.S., and B.K. Alexander. Forthcoming. 'Causes of Cocaine-related Deaths,' *Journal of Drug Issues*
Woodman, M. 1982. *Addiction to Perfection: The Still Unravished Bride*. Toronto: Inner City
Woods, J.R., M.A. Plessinger, and K.E. Clark. 1987. 'Effect of Cocaine on Intrauterine Blood Flow and Fetal Oxygenation,' *Journal of the American Medical Association* 257: 957–61
Woods, S.E., Jr. 1983. *The Molson Saga: 1763–1983*. Toronto: Doubleday Canada
Woodward, B. 1984. *Wired: The Short Life and Fast Times of John Belushi*. New York: Simon and Schuster
Woody, G.E., L. Luborsky, T. McLellan, C.P. O'Brien, A.T. Beck, J. Blaine, I. Herman, and A. Hole. 1983. 'Psychotherapy for Opiate Addicts: Does It Help?' *Archives of General Psychiatry* 40: 639–45
Woody, G.E., A.T. McLellan, L. Luborsky, and C.P. O'Brien. 1987. 'Twelve Month Follow-up of Psychotherapy for Opiate Dependence,' *American Journal of Psychiatry* 144: 590–6
Wright, A. 1976. *J.M. Barrie*. Edinburgh: Ramsay Head Press
Wurmser, L. 1978. *The Hidden Dimension: Psychodynamics in Compulsive Drug Use*. New York: Jason Aronson

Wynne-Edwards, V.C. 1986. *Evolution through Group Selection.* Oxford: Blackwell

Yaffe, B. 1986. 'Grit Minister Got "Fair Share" for His Native Newfoundland,' *Globe and Mail*, 20 November

Yeary, J. 1982. 'Incest and Chemical Dependency,' *Journal of Psychoactive Drugs* 14: 133–5

York, P., D. York, and T. Wachtel, 1982. *Toughlove.* New York: Bantam

Zacune, J. 1971. 'A Comparison of Canadian Narcotic Addicts in Great Britain and Canada,' *Bulletin on Narcotics* 23 (4): 41–9

Zeese, K. 1986. 'No More Drug War,' *National Law Journal*, 7 July: 13

– 1987. 'Marijuana Reform in the United States: A Remarkable Success Story.' Presented at the International Conference on Drug Policy Reform, London, 13–17 July

Zinberg, N.E. 1976. 'Observations on the Phenomenology of Consciousness Change,' *Journal of Psychedelic Drugs* 8: 59–76

– 1984. *Drug, Set, and Setting: The Basis for Controlled Intoxicant Use.* New Haven: Yale University Press

Zinberg, N.E., W.M. Harding, and R. Apsler. 1978. 'What Is Drug Abuse?' *Journal of Drug Issues* 8: 9–35

Zinberg, N.E., and D.C. Lewis. 1964. 'Narcotic Usage. I: A Spectrum of a Difficult Medical Problem,' *New England Journal of Medicine* 270: 989–93

Zucker, R.A., and E.S.L. Gomberg. 1986. 'Etiology of Alcoholism Reconsidered: The Case for a Biopsychosocial Process,' *American Psychologist* 41: 783–93

Zuckerman, M., M.S. Buchsbaum, and D.L. Murphy. 1980. 'Sensation Seeking and Its Biological Correlates,' *Psychological Bulletin* 88: 187–214

# Index